T. Nugent

A new Method of learning with Facility the Latin Tongue

Containing the Rules of Genders, Declensions, Preterites, Syntax, Quantity and

Latin Accents - Vol. I

T. Nugent

A new Method of learning with Facility the Latin Tongue
Containing the Rules of Genders, Declensions, Preterites, Syntax, Quantity and Latin Accents - Vol. I

ISBN/EAN: 9783337106768

Printed in Europe, USA, Canada, Australia, Japan

Cover: Foto ©ninafisch / pixelio.de

More available books at **www.hansebooks.com**

A NEW METHOD

Of learning with Facility the

LATIN TONGUE,

Containing the RULES of

GENDERS,	SYNTAX,
DECLENSIONS,	QUANTITY, and
PRETERITES,	LATIN ACCENTS.

Digested in the clearest and concisest Order.

Enlarged with variety of solid remarks, necessary not only for a perfect knowledge of the Latin tongue, but likewise for understanding the best authors: extracted from the ablest writers on this language.

With a Treatise on LATIN POETRY.

TRANSLATED *from the* FRENCH *of the Messieurs* DE PORT ROYAL, *and* IMPROVED,

By T. NUGENT, LL.D.

A NEW EDITION,
Carefully Revised and Corrected.

In TWO VOLUMES.

VOL. I.

LONDON:
Printed for F. WINGRAVE, Successor to
Mr. NOURSE, in the Strand.
MDCCXCI.

The PREFACE,

Shewing the additions that have been made to this work in the second, and in this last edition, extracted from the best modern grammarians.

With general Directions for the conveniency of teachers as well as learners of the Latin tongue.

THIS NEW METHOD having met with a most favourable reception upon its being first published, and moreover having had the good fortune to contribute towards his Majesty's improvement in the Roman language, of all others the most useful: I thought it incumbent upon me to consider, before I gave a second edition of it, whether I might not make some alterations or additions, that would render it more clear and comprehensive than when it was first sent abroad: which I have most carefully endeavoured to perform in this last edition. And, as I am naturally averse from all the little disputes of grammarians, which, as Quintilian excellently observes, serve only to perplex and to weaken the undeſtanding; I have been at the pains of peruſing the beſt authors, both antient and modern, who have wrote concerning this art, the inlet to all others.

Having therefore been informed of the high reputation, which Sanctius acquired in theſe latter times by a treatiſe on this ſubject, greatly eſteemed by the learned, but rare * and difficult to purchaſe; I contrived to get a copy of this treatiſe, which I peruſed with all poſſible attention, and at the ſame time with ſuch ſatisfaction as I want words to expreſs. But before I declare the great value I ſet upon this author; and that what I ſhall ſay concerning him may not be liable to ſuſpicion of partiality; I ſhall give a ſhort idea of his character, and of the reputation he acquired by this performance even in his life time.

Sanctius was a celebrated profeſſor of the univerſity of Salamanca, who attempted to examine after what manner the learned Scaliger had reaſoned upon the Latin tongue in his book intitled, *De cauſis Linguæ Latinæ*; and finding that the above critic had omitted, as he ſays himſelf, whatever relates to ſyntax, our profeſſor luckily undertook this latter province as the moſt neceſſary, in a work intitled likewiſe, *Of the cauſes of the Latin Tongue*. Here he detected an infinite number of errors, which had crept into this art; and he

* The caſe is greatly altered ſince our author wrote this preface, Sanctius's Minerva being now in every body's hands.

explained

explained the chief parts thereof with such judgment and perspicuity as infinitely surpass any thing that had appeared before his time; insomuch that he was admired by the whole kingdom of Spain, and honoured with the splendid titles of *Father of letters*, and *Restorer of the sciences*. His Catholic Majesty having nominated Ferdinand Henriquez, a grandee of Spain, his ambassador to the court of Rome in M.DC.XXV; this nobleman, being a lover of polite literature, carried Sanctius's book along with him: for indeed he had conceived a high esteem of the author, and considered his performance as the glory of the Spanish nation.

Sanctius has dwelt particularly on the structure and connexion of speech, by the Greeks called syntax, which he explains in the clearest manner imaginable, reducing it to its first principles, and to reasons extremely simple and natural; shewing that expressions which seem contrary to rule, and founded on the caprice of language, are easily reduced to the general and ordinary laws of construction, either by supplying some word understood, or by searching into the usage observed by writers of remote antiquity, of whom some vestiges are to be seen in those of later date: and in short by establishing a marvellous analogy and proportion through the whole language.

For it is observable that the parts of speech may be connected together, either by simple construction, when the several terms are all arranged in their natural order, so that you see at a single glance the reason why one governs the other: or by a figurative construction, when departing from that simplicity, we use some particular turns and forms of expression, on account of their being either more nervous, more concise, or more elegant, in which there are several parts of speech not expressed but understood. The business therefore of a person who excels in the art we are speaking of, is to reduce this figurative construction to the laws of the simple, and to shew that these expressions, which seem to have a greater elegance in proportion to their extraordinary boldness, may be defended nevertheless upon the principles of the ordinary and essential construction of the language, provided we are well acquainted with the art of reducing them to those principles.

This is what Sanctius has performed in so masterly a manner, that Scioppius, a person eminent in the same art, to whom the Spanish ambassador upon his arrival at Rome shewed this book, expressed a particular esteem for it as soon as he had perused it: in consequence hereof despising those who chuse to go by other roads because they are more frequented, rather than be conducted by so skilful a guide, he became the humble disciple of Sanctius in an excellent work which he wrote on this same subject; but which is so very scarce, that I should have found a difficulty to get sight of it, had it not been for Messrs DU PUY, who did me the favour

vour to lend it me. Some years after this, Vossius, whose reputation as a polite scholar is well established in the literary world, having had occasion to publish different pieces on the Latin tongue, followed the footsteps of these two writers almost in every part, and indeed he seems only to have transcribed them.

That nothing therefore may be omitted, which can any way contribute to improve and illustrate this art, I have joined these three authors together; and extracting from each what to me appeared most clear and solid, I have annexed it to the rules, giving after the syntax such remarks as are more general and extensive. I have also in compliance with their opinion made some additions and alterations either in the substance or order of the rules: though I have preserved some things, which according to them might be left out, because of their evident connexion with the rest; my intention being to recede as little as possible from the usual forms that obtain in the instruction of youth.

Hence this book has been so improved in these latter editions, that though in substance it be still the same, yet in some respects it may be deemed a new work; because it contains a second performance of quite another kind, which will not perhaps be less serviceable than the former. For whereas it seemed calculated before for boys only, or for such as were desirous of learning the Latin rudiments; I hope now

now it will be of use not only to those who are employed in teaching, but likewise in general to every body that is willing to have a perfect knowledge of this tongue, and to learn it of themselves by such sure and established rules, as may be of further advantage to them in the study of the Greek and of every other language.

Were my share in this work greater than it is, I should never have passed this judgment on it, for fear of being justly charged with vanity and presumption. But as I present the public with nothing but my labour, without any invention of my own; I should doubtless do injustice to the reputation and merit of those three celebrated writers, could I imagine that a faithful extract of their sentiments would not be of service to the lovers of polite learning. For I advance nothing at all of my own head, nor do I affirm any thing but what is corroborated by their authority; though I do not always quote them, but only on such points as seem most important, in order to avoid being tedious.

It has been my particular care not to insert any thing in this work, that was not demonstrated in the writings of those three excellent grammarians by clear and indubitable authorities; and that did not appear to me most necessary and conducive to the practice of the language, and to understand the purest authors; so that I have often reduced within the compass of a few lines what others have swelled into many

many pages. It has been also my attention to avoid some observations that seemed to me of little utility, remembering this excellent saying of Quintilian: * *it becomes an able grammarian to know, that there are some things not worth his knowledge.*

But I flatter my self that the solid and judicious remarks of those authors, which I have illustrated here by examples, and confirmed by authorities from the antients, will sufficiently demonstrate with what reason the same Quintilian said: † *that they are very much mistaken, who make a jest of grammar, as a mean and contemptible art: since in respect to eloquence, it is the same as the foundation in regard to a building; unless this be deeply laid, the whole superstructure must tumble down.* This art, he goes on, *is necessary to children, agreeable to those advanced in years, and serves for an amusement to retired persons, who apply themselves to polite literature. And it may be said that of all arts it has this particular advantage, to be possessed of more real and solid value, than of glitter and outward shew.* For which reason he adds, what I hope this work will fully evince, *that there are a great many things in grammar, which not only help to form the minds of beginners, but likewise to exercise and to try the capacities of the most learned.*

And indeed we ought to set a very high va-

* Quint. l. 1. c. 8.   † Ib. c. 4.

lue upon an art, which, at the same time that it shews how to distinguish the property and natural force of each part of speech, and the reason of the great variety of expressions, makes us see the various significations of terms, which frequently arise from their different connexion, and directs us to the meaning of several important passages. For even the most trifling things become great, when they can be rendered subservient to those of a higher nature.

I have therefore no manner of doubt but that this book will upon trial appear to be of immense service, towards grounding us so firmly in the principles of the Latin tongue, that when once we have thoroughly comprehended those rules, by which some words are made to govern others (which in the technical term is generally called government) we shall retain them with a particular facility, because they are all natural; we shall also avoid committing some mistakes, into which, men of abilities in other respects have fallen; and without any hesitation we shall make use of some particular phrases which may appear too bold, or even inaccurate, though borrowed from the very best authors, and established on the general use and analogy of the language.

In regard to boys, I have mentioned in the following advertisement, the use they ought to make of the rules; where I have also taken notice of the manner and ease with which they

may

may be made to learn them. And though I have added a great many things in the latter editions, yet the rules will be full as concise, and more clear than before; because some of them are put into better order; and there is a different type for the annotations and additional remarks, which are not designed for young beginners, but for those who have the care of their instruction, to the end that they may inculcate occasionally and *viva voce* whatever they think best suited to their capacity and age.

It will be adviseable to put into their hands as soon as possible the fables of Phædrus, which will please them greatly, and notwithstanding the seeming unimportance of the subject, are full of wit and spirit. It will be very proper also for them to read the three comedies of Terence, which, as well as Phædrus, have been lately translated into French, and rendered as pure in respect to morality as to language.

Here I think it will not be amiss to take notice, that there are three things to which in my opinion it is owing, that children, or even those of a more advanced age, after having spent many years in learning Latin, have nevertheless but a slender and incompetent knowledge of this tongue, particularly in regard to writing, which ought to be the principal fruit of their studies.

The first is, that they oftentimes content themselves with not committing any error against the rules of grammar, which, as Quintilian observeth, is a very great abuse; because, as he says,
there

there is a vast difference betwixt speaking according to the rules of grammar, and according to the purity of the language: *Aliud est grammaticè, aliud Latinè loqui.* We ought indeed to follow those rules; but afterwards we should proceed to the knowledge of things, to which that of words is only an introduction. We should begin with laying the foundation before we can build a house; but if we only lay the foundation, the house will never be finished. The human body must be supported by the bones of which it is composed; but a person that has nothing but bones, is a skeleton, and not a man.

The second mistake some are guilty of, is that to remedy the abovementioned evil, they apply a cure as bad as the disease. For in order to enable boys to write not only according to the rules of grammar, but to the purity of style, it has been the practice to make them read books of phraseologies and idioms, and to accustom them to make use of such as are the most elegant, that is such as appear the farthest fetched and most uncommon. Hence to express the meaning of the verb *to love*, they will be sure not to say *amare*, but *amore prosequi, benevolentiâ complecti*; whereas the plain verb has frequently more strength and beauty than any circumlocution whatever.

Thus they form a style intirely variegated with those elegancies and studied turns of expression, which may impose upon superficial

cial perſons, but muſt appear ridiculous to thoſe who are thoroughly acquainted with the language, for when they talk Latin it is all bombaſt, that is, an unnatural and affected ſtyle.

And this corrupt ſtyle we not only obſerve in young people, but likewiſe in perſons of riper years, who betray it even in their public ſpeeches, becauſe they had imbibed it in the courſe of their ſtudies. Not but that we are allowed to make uſe of thoſe phraſes, which are indeed the great ornament of language; but we ought to know when, and where, and in what manner we ſhould apply them: which is not to be learnt by thoſe rhapſodies of confuſed and detached expreſſions, but by a diligent and conſtant reading of the moſt celebrated authors.

For as in order to be a complete architect, it is not ſufficient to poſſeſs a great number of ſtones well hewn and poliſhed, and which have even made part of ſome magnificent and regular ſtructure; but we are alſo carefully to conſider the whole edifice, to the end that we may obſerve the order, the connexion, and relation which the ſtones ought to have in conſtituting one whole: ſo to form a ſpeech according to rules, it is not ſufficient to have a great ſtock of phraſes, extracted from the beſt writers; but we ſhould view their works together and intire, in order inſenſibly to accuſtom ourſelves to that judicious elegance, which they ſo admirably obſerve in the choice, the dreſs, and arrangement of their expreſſions,

in

in order to form the whole structure and symmetry of speech. Thus we shall learn of the Romans themselves to speak their language, conversing constantly with them in their works, wherein they speak to us even after they are dead. Otherwise our phrases heaped one upon another will no more form a real Latin composition, than a confused mass of stones will constitute a house.

The third mistake frequently committed by those who want to learn Latin, is their not making a proper choice of such authors as have wrote with the greatest purity, but indifferently reading the first that comes into their head, and most generally pitching upon the worst: by which means they form an irregular and unequal style, composed of variety of patched phrases very ill put together, and founded rather on their own caprice and whim, than on the rules and authority of the best masters of the language.

In order therefore to make this choice of authors, I should think that those on whom we ought to ground our knowledge of the Latin tongue in its greatest purity, I mean not only to understand it, but to speak and write it, are Terence, Cicero, Cæsar, Virgil, and Horace, whose Latin, exclusive of a few poetic expressions in the two latter, may be perfectly reconciled. For if we read Virgil with attention, we shall find that several of his phrases which are looked upon as extraordinary and uncommon,

mon, have nevertheless been used by Cicero and Terence, as *cujum pecus*, by the former; and *da Tityre nobis*, instead of *dic*, by the latter. Hence he was called even by St. Austin, *Egregius loquutor:* and Horace, particularly in his satires and epistles, writes in the strictest purity of the language, his verses being rather prose than metre, as he says himself.

All the rest, among whom Quintus Curtius, Sallust, and Livy deserve the preference, ought to be read with attention in their proper order, and may be of great service towards forming the mind and judgment, but not the style; except a few elegant and sprightly phrases, the selecting of which is so much the more difficult, as it supposeth a perfect knowledge of the real purity of the language, which we should have learnt of the first mentioned writers.

But what generally is most prejudicial to those who are desirous of having a thorough knowledge of the Latin tongue, is their not sufficiently valuing, nor reading Cicero, an author to whom no other Pagan writer can be compared, either as to language, or sentiment; on which very account he was called the ROMAN PLATO by Quintilian, and held in very high esteem by the most eminent writers of the church. For he has wrote with such dignity and spirit on all sorts of subjects, on eloquence, on ethics, and the different sorts of philosophy; on public and private business in the great number of letters he left behind him; on the manner of pleading and speaking wisely and eloquently on all sorts of subjects; that he alone is equivalent to many authors, and ought to be the constant entertainment of those who intend to devote their days to polite literature. Therefore it was justly observed by Quintilian, that whoever is fond of Cicero's works, may be said already to have made a great progress: * *Ille se profecisse sciat, cui Cicero valde placebit.*

But I should carry this digression too far, since it would form the subject of a whole book, were I to enter minutely into whatever relates to the proper manner of instructing youth. I hope nevertheless that what I have here hinted, will have its use, in pointing out the object we ought to aim at in this NEW METHOD, which is to lead our pupils gradually, by means of a solid and exact knowledge of grammar, to understand the best authors; so that by a judicious and well chosen imitation, they may form to themselves a polite style, and rise at length to a noble and manly eloquence, the great end of grammatical institution.

For which reason it hath been my endeavour not only in the SYNTAX, and in the REMARKS that come after it, to omit nothing that might be conducive to this purpose: but moreover it will appear that I have thrown into the other parts of this work, whatever might be of most use and advantage in regard to the analogy and per-

* Lib. 18. cap. 1.

fect

fect knowledge of this language; wherein I have chiefly followed Vossius, as the most accurate writer on this subject. It is true that as I undertook in this last edition to verify passages and to consult the originals, I found myself now and then under a necessity of differing from his opinion, having met with authorities in very good writers contrary to what he has laid down.

To the remarks I have subjoined some other OBSERVATIONS on the Roman names, on their figures or arithmetical characters, and on the manner of computing time and sesterces, because these are things useful and necessary, and may be easily explained to boys, as occasion offers.

After these select observations, I have added in this last edition a TREATISE ON LETTERS, which may serve as a ground-work to account for a great many things in the language, and especially in what relates to QUANTITY, which I have afterwards explained more exactly than in the preceding editions. In the same treatise I have also shewn the antient pronunciation of the Latin tongue, and that which we ought still to observe in the Greek. Whence we learn the etymology of several terms, and the reason of a great many changes which happen in the dialects, and in words communicated from one language to another.

In this last edition I have also added a treatise on the LATIN ACCENTS, where I demonstrate in a few words the fundamental reason of the rules

of

of pronunciation, and of the differences observed therein by the antients, besides those subsisting to this very day. The whole concludes with a new treatise on LATIN POETRY, where I reduce the most agreeable sorts of verse to three; shewing their feet, their figures, and their several beauties, in the clearest order.

In short I have omitted nothing that I thought might be of use towards easing the master or advancing the scholar; and I hope that the reader will of himself perceive, that this work, though still of no great bulk, if we consider the great variety of matter, comprehends nevertheless almost every thing that can be desired in a book, which is to serve not only as a foundation and beginning, but moreover as a general guide to all the rest. Nay I presume to flatter myself that its utility will soon be discovered, if in using it, we take care, as already hath been observed, to make our pupils join the practice and use of authors to the rules, and not to detain them so long in these first principles, as to prevent their aspiring to the highest attainments. For doubtless it would be equally a mistake, either if we wanted intirely to dispense with the rules and maxims of grammar, or if we never chose to go any farther than these institutions. * *Non obstant hæ disciplinæ per illas euntibus, sed circa illas hærentibus.*

But if after all there should be any persons so unconcerned about the ease and im-

---

* Quint. lib. 1. cap. 7.

provement

provement of youth, as not to approve of this manner of inſtructing them by rules drawn up in their mother tongue: I beg they will conſider that I am not the only one who finds fault with the cuſtom of making them learn the rules of Latin, in a language to which they are as yet ſtrangers; or who ſhould be glad to ground them as much in their own, as in a foreign tongue. In confirmation of what I have been ſaying, I ſhall only add here a letter of Monſr. DES MARETS to Monſr. HALE, the King's profeſſor, whereby it will appear that the moſt converſant in polite literature at this time, are of the ſame opinion with me: and that this NEW METHOD met with their approbation at its firſt appearance, though it was far from being ſo finiſhed a work as the late editions have made it.

EX LIBRO PRIMO

EPISTOLARUM PHILOLOGICARUM

ROLANDI MARESII.

EPISTOLA XVI.

*ROL. MARES. PETRO HALÆO, POETÆ
& Interpreti Regio, S.*

MAGNA vis est profectò consuetudinis, quæ facit, ut ritus quoquo modo inducti, manifestum licèt vitium & incommodum habeant, antiquitate tamen defendantur. Quod mihi in mentem venit, dum meo judicio non satis expeditam, quæ ab aliquot sæculis ubique viget, linguam Latinam docendi rationem apud me reputo. Grammatica enim, ut nihil de illius obscuritate & prolixitate dicam, non uniuscujusque nationis vernaculo sermone, sed ipso Latino conscripta, nunc est in usu: quasi jam pueri id sciant, quod discere in animo habent. Quæ methodus, licèt experientiâ teste, usus valdè incommodi; imò, si verum dicere licet, planè inepta sit, mordicus tamen retinetur. Paucos quidem ante annos quædam grammatica idiomate Gallico
edita

edita est; quæ mihi cum hoc nomine, tum quòd vulgari brevior multò est & facilior, mirum in modum probatur: quam memini, cùm ante aliquot menses apud me domi esses, tibi ostendisse, & aliqua in eam rem tecum disseruisse: quorum ut tibi memoriam refricem, visum est hæc ad te perscribere, ut pro autoritate, quâ in academiâ polles, quàm primùm huic malo mederi coneris; & si minùs in præsens, saltem cùm ejus supremum Magistratum, qui tibi aliquando ex merito continget, consecutus fueris, veterem consuetudinem aboleas, hacce novâ substitutâ, quam esse commodissimam, rem modò attentiùs consideres, haud dubiè fateberis. Grammatica enim, quæ nunc omnibus in scholis docetur, ab homine quidem docto conscripta, nimiùm tamen est prolixa; quam videlicet pueri vix quatuor annis addiscant: plerisque verò in locis obscura & intricata: cujus autor, cùm nihil omissum vellet, multa non necessaria intulit; cùm tamen pleraque usui relinquenda essent. Verissimè enim à Ramo proditum est, grammaticæ pauca præcepta, usum verò in autoribus legendis multum esse debere; sed majus incommodum in eo est, quòd Latino sermone scripta est. Ille quidem grammaticus, ut suas præceptiones cum omnibus gentibus communicaret, non aliâ linguâ scribere debuit: sed mirum mihi profectò videri solet, nemini in mentem venisse, ut eas in suam transfunderet, quò à popularibus nullo negotio intelligerentur: donec tandem unus apud nos extitit (si modò unus, nam plures audio operam contulisse) qui id nostris hominibus præstaret; mihi quidem ignotus, suum enim nomen suppressit, sive quòd esset ab omni ostentatione alienus, & minime ambitiosus, sive quòd ex hujusmodi scripto tanquam humili laudem capere aspernaretur, vir, ut quidem videtur,

detur, majorum capax. Quæ modeſtia vulgus ſcriptorum ambitionis condemnat, qui ferè in id ſolum ſcribere videntur, ut nomen ſuum poſteritati commendent, & ſæpiſſimè etiam in muſtaceo laureolam quærunt. Quàm verò longum ſit iter hactenus tritum, quàm pueris inamœnum manifeſtò videmus: quorum plerique viâ tam difficili à ſtudiis abſterrentur, cùm tenera ætas potiùs omnibus illecebris ad litteras allicienda eſſet. Verùm ſicut grammatica Græca Latino idiomate concepta in uſu eſt, nimirum iis uſui futura, qui in Latina lingua profectum fecerunt, & ejus jam uſum aliquem habent: ſimiliter Latina noto ſermone ſcribi deberet. Quod ſi fiat, non nimium temporis ſit compendium, cujus magna ſit jactura in diſcendis verſibus Latinis obſcuris magnopere & perplexis. Sed præter id lucrum, quod ut rei pretioſiſſimæ magni faciendum eſt, alia etiam utilitas hinc emergeret, linguæ ſcilicet noſtræ exactior notitia, quam eâdem viâ conſequeremur: cujus nobis turpior eſt ignorantia quàm Latinæ, licèt ob ſolœciſmum in alia admiſſum non perinde, ut in hac pueri ferulis objurgentur. Quamvis enim noſtram linguam omnes planè noſſe videamur; tamen quid peculiare, nec cum aliis commune, quid elegans habeat plerique ignoramus. Romani verò etiam ſuam in ſcholis diſcebant, nec ſolùm Μῆνιν ἄειδε Θεά, ſed etiam *Arma virumque cano*, illis prælegebatur. Cæterùm cùm pueros in gymnaſiis tot annos detineri conſidero; in quæ, tanquam in aliquod piſtrinum detruduntur & compinguntur, & ex quibus etiam pro illo ſtudio & amoris ardore, ſine quo in vita nihil quidquam egregium neminem unquam aſſecuturum Cicero ait, litterarum odium plerumque domum referunt; facere non poſſum, quin illius temporis diſpendium conquerar, quo illi memoria tum maximè tenaci, fimul Græcam linguam tam necessariam, & alia quæ mox adultis ediscenda sunt, etiam edoceri possent. Sed de his hactenus. Nec verò me fugit, quòd hæc epistola sit de rebus etiamsi necessariis, ut ait Quintilianus, procul tamen ab ostentatione positis, ut operum fastigia spectantur, latent fundamenta. Sed quæ primo aspectu vilia & abjecta erunt, ea diligentius inspicienti maximè utilia esse videbuntur. Vale.

ADVERTISEMENT

Concerning the Rules of this NEW METHOD.

IT has been long observed by several, that the usual manner of learning Latin is very difficult and obscure, and that it is pity but young beginners had a more agreeable introduction to the knowledge of this useful tongue.

This hath excited the labours of sundry persons, who while they proposed one general end, have pursued nevertheless very different means. Some considering that Despauter's verses were oftentimes too obscure, have attempted to write others more perspicuous and elegant.

Others reflecting on the trouble that boys take to commit such a number of verses to memory, in a language they do not understand, have thrown the rules into prose. Others still consulting brevity, and unwilling to load either the memory or the understanding of young beginners, have reduced all those rules to simple tables.

If I may be permitted to speak my opinion concerning these different plans, I should think that the authors of the first had reason to find fault with Despauter's verses for their obscurity in several places; but that they ought to have gone a step further, and entered into the views of those we mentioned next, who saw plainly into the absurdity of laying down Latin rules to learn Latin. For who is it that would pretend to draw up a Hebrew grammar in Hebrew verse, or a Greek grammar in Greek verse, or a grammar in Italian verse to learn Italian? To propose
the

the first institutions of a language, in the very terms of that language, which of course are unknown to beginners, is supposing them to be already masters of what they are about to learn, and to have attained the object which they have only begun to pursue.

Since even common sense tells us that we ought ever to commence with things the most easy, and that what we know already should serve as a guide to what we know not; it is certainly the right way to make use of our mother tongue, as a means to introduce us to foreign and unknown languages. If this be true in regard to persons of maturity and judgment, so far that there is no man of sense whatever but would think we jested with him, were we to propose a grammar in Greek verse for him to learn Greek; how much stronger is the argument in relation to boys, to whom even the clearest things appear obscure, through immaturity of years, and weakness of judgment?

As to what concerns the third method, which consists in exhibiting simple tables, I am not ignorant that this way is very striking at first, because it seems as if nothing more was requisite than the eye, to become master of the rules in a minute, and that they might be learnt almost at a single glance. But this apparent facility is generally owing, if I am not mistaken, to this, that upon seeing in those tables an abstract or general idea of things which we know already, we imagine it will be as easy for others to learn by this means what they are ignorant of, as it is for us to recollect what we have once learned.

But it is beyond all doubt that though tables are concise, yet they are also obscure, and therefore cannot be proper for beginners: because a learner stands as much in need of perspicuity to help his understanding, as of brevity to assist his memory. Hence those tables seldom serve for any useful purpose, except it be to represent at a single view, what we have been learning for some time. As indeed I have myself for this same purpose, comprised in two separate tables, whatever

hath

hath been mentioned at large in respect to the nouns, pronouns, and verbs, in the rudiments annexed to the Abridgment of this New Method.

But even if tables could be of service to persons of riper years towards initiating them in the Latin tongue, still it is great odds but they would be useless to young beginners. For the imagination must be greatly on the stretch to imprint them in the memory, a thing generally beyond the reach of boys, who are incapable of giving close application to an object of itself extremely ungrateful, and whose imagination besides is generally as weak as their judgment. The memory may be said to be the only faculty that is strong and active in that age; and therefore it is here we must lay the principal groundwork of our instructions.

For which reason, having considered all this with great impartiality, I thought it would be proper for youth to be taught the rules of Latin in their mother tongue, and obliged to learn them by heart. But I was afterwards made sensible of another inconveniency; which is, that understanding the rules with such ease, by being naturally acquainted with their own language, they used to take the liberty of changing the arrangement of words, mistaking a masculine for a feminine, or one preterite for another; and thus satisfied with repeating nearly the sense of their rules, they imagined themselves masters thereof upon a single reading.

Therefore still abiding by that principle of common sense, that youth should be taught the rules of Latin in their maternal language, the only one they are acquainted with; just as in common use the precepts of the Greek and Hebrew tongues are delivered in Latin, because it is supposed to be known to the persons who want to learn Greek and Hebrew: I have been induced further to think that while I assisted their understandings by rendering things clear and intelligible; at the same time it was incumbent upon me to fix their memories, by throwing these rules into verse, to the end they may not have it in their power any longer to alter the words, being tied down to a

certain

certain number of syllables of which those verses are composed, and to the jingle of rhime, which renders them at the same time more easy and agreeable.

True it is that at first I thought this would be almost impossible, for I was desirous that notwithstanding this constraint of verse the rules should be almost as concise, as clear, and as intelligible as if they had been in prose. Nevertheless, use hath made the thing less difficult: and though I may have not succeeded according to the plan I proposed to myself, yet my endeavours have not been wanting.

There is no need, I think, to beg the favour of the reader, not to look for elegance in the versification of this work. I flatter myself that they who understand French poetry, will be so good as to excuse me for not exactly following the rule of masculine and feminine verse, with the exactness of rhime, and some other things observed by those who have the knack of versifying. For my only aim was to be as concise and clear as possible, and on this account to avoid all circumlocution, the necessary concomitant of verse. And it is particularly on such occasions that a regard should be paid to this saying of an excellent poet.

Ornari res ipsa negat, contenta doceri.

I have conformed to Despauter's order as nearly as possible, without even altering his expressions, except to substitute others that to me appeared more clear and intelligible. Nor have I omitted any one word in the rules, but such as being unusual or entirely Greek, seemed remote from the analogy of the Latin, and of course such as ought to be reserved for the use of authors, and for a greater maturity of judgment: at the same time I have added others, of which Despauter had taken no notice in his verses.

Abundance of unnecessary matter hath been left out in the rules of heteroclites, which are apt to create the greatest difficulty to young beginners: for I was satisfied

fied with inserting whatever appeared most difficult, in the annotations or remarks; because it is a constant maxim, that we should not perplex the minds of young people, with such a multitude of particular rules, often either erroneous or insignificant; but make them pass as quick as possible through the most general notices, and then set them upon the practical part or the use of authors, where they will with pleasure become acquainted with the remainder, which they could not have otherwise learnt without confusion and dislike. For as the rules are an introduction to practice, so practice confirms these rules, and clears up every seeming obscurity.

But though I have omitted nothing that seemed to me of any use, and even in several rules I have taken notice of some words which perhaps may not appear altogether so necessary, chusing rather to trespass this way than the other; still it it manifest how much shorter these rules are than those of Despauter, since the French verses have only eight syllables, whereas Despauter's in general have fifteen, sixteen, or seventeen, and boys will sooner learn eight or ten of these than two of his. Besides it is of no sort of use to know Despauter's verses, unless you understand the comment, which is frequently more obscure than the text; whereas these short rules appear so clear, that there are very few lads, but may comprehend their meaning, either of themselves, or with the least instruction viva voce.

For what swells in some sort the size of this book, is the translation of the examples, which I have inserted throughout, and particularly all the simple verbs in capitals, with their compounds also translated, which I have marked in the different preterites; besides several annotations and considerable remarks. This I have done not only to consult the conveniency of young beginners, but moreover of those concerned in their instruction, to the end that they may have no further occasion to look out for examples and illustrations of these rules, in any other book whatsoever.

Upon

Upon the whole I have taken pains that this work should have every thing that could contribute to ease and perspicuity. To each rule I have prefixed a cypher, with a title signifying what it contains, that the subject matter may be seen at once, and found with less difficulty. The large rules I have divided into two parts, to prevent their being tiresome: and I have accented the Latin words, in order to accustom young people betimes to the right pronunciation. The terminations, as VEO, BO, LO, and the like, are printed in capitals, the Latin words in a different type from the rest, and the annotations in a still smaller letter, that every thing may appear most clear and distinct, and whatever is disproportioned to weak capacities be overlooked. Therefore it is sufficient at first for boys to get their rules by heart, and afterwards they may learn the most familiar examples with the signification thereof in their mother tongue; and in short they may be occasionally instructed in such parts of the annotations or remarks, as are most necessary and best adapted to their tender capacities, so that their instruction shall increase in proportion as they advance in maturity and judgment.

As for the rest, these short institutions will be of service not only to young beginners, but likewise to persons of riper years, who may be desirous of learning Latin, but are frequently discouraged by the obscurity and difficulty of Despauter's rules. Here they will find a most easy introduction; for not to mention what I have observed within my own experience, by which I have been chiefly directed in this New Method, I may take upon me to affirm, after having made a trial with a few boys of but indifferent parts and memory, that in less than six months all Despauter may be learnt by means of these short rules; though generally speaking, boys can hardly go through that author in three years, without a great deal of labour and dislike; which oftentimes makes them detest, during their younger days, the Latin tongue, together with their Latin master.

What

What remains now would be for me to mention the utility, which I as well as several others have experienced, of that maxim of Ramus; few precepts, and a great deal of practice: and therefore that as soon as boys begin to have a smattering of these rules, it would be proper to lead them into the practice, by putting into their hands a few select dialogues, or some of the purest and clearest writers, such as Cæsar's commentaries, and making them translate into their mother tongue part of Cicero's easiest epistles, in order to learn both languages at the same time, reserving to compose in Latin, till they are more advanced, this being without doubt the most arduous part of grammatical learning.

But this is not a proper place to treat of such a subject, which would require a whole dissertation; besides it may be liable to variety of opinions. As for what regards the present institutions, I believe there are very few but will agree with me, that a great deal of time might be saved by making use of this NEW METHOD: and I flatter myself that young beginners at least will be obliged to me for endeavouring to rescue them from the trouble and anxiety of learning Despauter, for attempting to dispel the obscurity of the present forms of teaching, and for enabling them to gather flowers on a spot hitherto overrun with thorns.

The Translator's

PREFACE.

THE following work completes the translation of the grammatical pieces of Messieurs de Port Royal, in which I engaged some years ago, beginning with the *Greek Method*, and concluding now with the *Latin*, a performance of equal reputation and use with the other. The favourable reception the public vouchsafed to give to this undertaking, was an encouragement to proceed; and I am pleased to think that the success has been such as answered my expectation. Though I must own that this success was not so greatly to be wondered at, when there were such heavy complaints here in England, against the obscurities, defects, superfluities, and errors, that render the common method of teaching, an insuperable impediment to the progress of education. These in part some gentlemen have lately endeavoured to remove, by introductions of various names and titles; but their labours seem to be calculated only for boys, and not to take in a more comprehensive scheme of grammatical learning. The performances of Messieurs de Port Royal seem therefore to be the only attempt that has answered this double view, of initiating young pupils, and

grounding

grounding those of riper judgment. In the present translation, I have endeavoured to exhibit a faithful copy of the original; only that the rules are not drawn up in verse, for the reason observed in the preface to the Greek grammar; that this work is not calculated so much for tender capacities, as for persons more advanced, and who are desirous of having a critical and complete knowledge of the Roman language. As for the scheme of drawing up such instructions in one's mother tongue, the reasons for it are so strongly enforced in the learned author's preface, that it would be superfluous to add any thing further upon this head; except that he seems to have been the first who broke the ice, and his example has been since followed by a multitude of learned men both in England and abroad. The order of the original has been uniformly observed throughout; but for the greater distinction the work has been divided into books, a division arising from the nature of the subject, pursuant to the method observed in the Greek grammar. The quotations from the classics have been verified and corrected in a vast number of places, and recourse had to the originals where there was any suspicion of the passages being corrupt or imperfect. So far I thought proper to advertise the reader concerning the present undertaking; but as the author out of his great modesty chose to conceal himself under the general name of the Society of Port Royal, I shall therefore subjoin this short character of him in honour to his memory.

Claude Lancelot was born at Paris in 1613, and brought up from the age of twelve in the seminary of St. Nicholas du Chardonnet,

where

PREFACE. xxxiii.

where he entered himself in the year 1627. After having finished his studies, he retired to Port Royal, and was employed in the education of youth. This province he executed with all the care and application possible; and became so expert in the art of teaching, as to draw up those excellent methods of learning the Latin, Greek, Italian, and Spanish tongues, generally called the Port Royal Grammars: performances equally recommendable for order and ease, as for a profound knowledge of the principles and analysis of the grammar of those languages. He is also said to have wrote the general and rational grammar, which we lately rendered into English; and to be the author of the *Jardin des racines Grecques*, of which we have likewise given a translation under the name of the *Greek Primitives*. Thence ascending to higher studies, he applied himself with great assiduity in the edition of the famous bible de Vitris, to which he added some chronological dissertations in the folio edition, that were much esteemed abroad, as well as the tables of the quarto edition, which have been inserted at the end of Royaumont's discourses on the bible. He likewise wrote a Dissertation on the half Sextary of wine and pound of bread, of which mention is made in the rule of St. Benedict; whereby he shews how much he had studied the matter of weights and measures of the antients. By these works he acquired a high reputation among the learned. He is also reported to have left a treatise on the rule of St. Benedict, esteemed a master-piece. His merit recommended him to the princess of Conti to take care of the education of the young princes; in which honourable employment he continued in some measure against his inclination till the death of that princess. This event taking place, the marquis of Louvois would fain commit the care of his children to him, with offers of a very confiderable gratification; but he chofe to retire to the abby of St. Cyran, to execute a defign he had long before conceived of entering into a monaftic life. After giving all his fubftance to the poor, he betook himfelf to this retreat, where he continued fome years; and at length died at the abby of Quimperlé in Britany, the 15th of April, 1695, in his eightieth year, of a cold that fell upon his breaft, attended with a fever and fpitting of blood. He was naturally of a mild temper, of remarkable fimplicity, fincere in his religion, conftant in ftudy, fond of retreat, a contemner of glory, fond of peace, and an enemy to all animofities and difputes.

CONTENTS.
VOL. I.

THE PREFACE, with general directions for the conveniency of teachers as well as learners of the Latin tongue. Pag. III
Rolandi Marsii Epistola. xx
ADVERTISEMENT to the reader concerning the rules of this NEW METHOD. XXIV
The Translator's PREFACE. XXXI

BOOK I. OF GENDERS. 1

RULE I. Of nouns which agree with either sex. 3
Whence the necessity arises of being acquainted with the genders. 5
RULE II. Of adjectives. *Ibid.*
Of adjectives taken substantively, or which stand by themselves in discourse. 6
RULE III. That the gender of the termination is frequently changed into that of the signification, or vice versâ. 7
RULE IV. Of *As* with its compounds and derivatives. 11
RULE V. Of the names of winds, rivers, and mountains. 12
List of the names of rivers and mountains. 13
RULE VI. Of the names of towns, provinces, ships, and islands. 14
List of the names of towns. 15
Whence comes it that these general words, *urbs, civitas, terra,* are feminine? 18
Of the names of trees, and why *arbor* is feminine. *Ibid.*
RULE VII. Of the names of trees. 19
Of the names of fruits. 21
RULE VIII. Of indeclinable nouns, 22
RULE IX. Of plural nouns. 23
RULE X. Of nouns singular in A and E. 24
Of nouns in I. 26
RULE XI. Of nouns in O. *Ibid.*
RULE XII. Of nouns in M, C, L, T. 29
RULE XIII. Of nouns in N. 30

CONTENTS.

RULE XIV. Nouns in AR or in UR. 31
RULE XV. Of nouns in ER. 32
Of the nouns in IR. 33
RULE XVI. Of the nouns in OR. 34
Of the nouns in UR. *Ibid.*
RULE XVII. Of the nouns in AS. 35
RULE XVIII. Of the nouns in ES. 36
Of the gender of *dies.* 38
RULE XIX. Of the nouns in IS. *Ibid.*
RULE XX. Of the nouns in IS that are of the doubtful gender. 39
List of the nouns in IS. 40
RULE XXI. Of the nouns in OS. 42
RULE XXII. Of the nouns in US of the second or fourth declension. 43
List of Latin nouns in US. 45
Of the Greek nouns in US. 46
RULE XXIII. Of the nouns in US which are of the third declension. 48
RULE XXIV. Of *laus* and *fraus*, and of nouns ending in S, with another consonant. 49
RULE XXV. Exception to the preceding rule. 50
RULE XXVI. Of nouns in X. 51
List of nouns in X. 54
RULE XXVII. Of epicene nouns. 55
Epicenes excepted from the rules of the termination. 56

BOOK II. OF THE DECLENSION OF NOUNS. 59

RULE I. Of compound nouns. 60
RULE II. Of nouns compounded of two nouns joined together. *Ibid.*
The first declension. 62
RULE III. Of the dative and ablative plural of the first declension. 64
The second declension. 65
Of the Greek terminations. *Ibid.*
RULE IV. Of the genitive singular of the second declension. 66
RULE V. Of the vocative singular. 68
For the plural. 69
RULE VI. Of the dative and ablative plural. *Ibid.*
The third declension. 70
RULE VII. The genitive of nouns in A and E. 71
RULE VIII. Of the nouns in O. *Ibid.*
RULE IX. Of the nouns in C and D. 72
RULE X. Of the nouns in L. *Ibid.*

CONTENTS. xxxvii

RULE XI. Of the nouns in N. 73
RULE XII. Of the nouns in R. 74
RULE XIII. Of the nouns in BER. 75
RULE XIV. Of the adjectives in CER. Ibid.
RULE XV. Of the nouns in TER. Ibid.
RULE XVI. Of *iter, cor*, and *Jupiter*. 76
RULE XVII. Of the nouns in UR. 77
RULE XVIII. Of the nouns in AS. Ibid.
RULE XIX. Of the nouns in ES. 78
RULE XX. Of those which make ETIS. Ibid.
RULE XXI. Of the other nouns in ES. 79
RULE XXII. Of the nouns in IS. 80
RULE XXIII. Exceptions to the preceding rule. 81
RULE XXIV. Of nouns in OS. 82
RULE XXV. Of the nouns in US which make the genitive in ERIS. 83
RULE XXVI. Of those which make URIS, UIS, UDIS, AUDIS, and ODIS. 84
RULE XXVII. Of those which make UTIS and UNTIS. 86
RULE XXVIII. Of nouns in BS and in PS. Ibid.
RULE XXIX. Of the nouns in NS and in RS. 87
RULE XXX. Of the participle *iens, euntis*, with its compounds. 88
RULE XXXII. Of *caput* and its compounds. Ibid.
RULE XXXIII. Of the nouns in X. 89
RULE XXXIV. Exception to the preceding rule. 90
RULE XXXV. General for the accusatives. 91
RULE XXXVI. Of the accusatives in IM. Ibid.
RULE XXXVII. The accusative in EM or in IM. 92
RULE XXXVIII. General for the ablative. 93
Of some adjectives that have been doubted of, and which follow nevertheless the general rule. Ibid.
Of *Par* and its compounds. Ibid.
Of the adjectives in IX, fem. and neuter. 94
Of the names of countries in AS. Ibid.
EXCEPTIONS to the rule of the ablative, relating to substantives. Ibid.
RULE XXXIX. Exception 1. of nouns that make I in the ablative. Ibid.
Of the analogy of the terminations included in this rule. 96
Of the proper names in AL or in E. Ibid.
Poetical licence in regard to other nouns. Ibid.
RULE XL. Exception 2. of substantives that have E or I in the ablative. Ibid.

c 3 RULE

CONTENTS.

RULE XLI. Of some nouns which do not entirely conform to the analogy of the preceding rule. 97

RULE XLII. Third exception. Of other substantives whose ablative is in E or in I. 98

A list of nouns substantives that form the ablative in I or in E.

That the dative and the ablative were always alike; and that the Greeks have an ablative. 100

EXCEPTIONS to the rule of ablatives in regard to the adjectives. 101

RULE XLIII. First exception. Of adjectives that have only the ablative in E. Ibid.

For the adjectives in NS. 102

RULE XLIV. Second exception. Of those adjectives which have the ablative only in I. Ibid.

To distinguish the ablative according as the noun is taken either adjectively or substantively. 103

Of the plural of the third declension. 104

RULE XLV. Of the plural of nouns neuter. Ibid.

RULE XLVI. General rule for the genitive plural. 106

EXCEPTIONS to the rule of the genitive. 107

RULE XLVII. Exception 1. Of comparatives and others which make UM. Ibid.

RULE XLVIII. Exception 2. Of nouns of more than one syllable in AS, ES, IS, and NS, which have ïUM in the genitive. 109

Of the nouns in AS and in NS. 110

RULE XLIX. Exception 3. Of monosyllables that make ïUM. 111

Greek monosyllables, LINX. 112

Of *lar, mus, crux,* and some others. 113

Of those monosyllables that make UM. Ibid.

Monosyllables unusual in the genitive plural. Ibid.

RULE L. Exception 4. Of some other nouns that make ïUM. 114

A great many more nouns heretofore made ïUM. 115

What nouns most frequently admit of this syncope. Ibid.

What nouns seldom admit of this syncope. 116

Of the epenthesis. Ibid.

Of the accusative plural. Ibid.

In what manner the antients judged of their language. Ibid.

RULE LI. Of nouns that have no singular, and of the names of festivals in ïA. 117

Of the names of festivals in ïA. 118

RULE LII. Of the dative plural; and of some particular cases borrowed from the Greeks. Ibid.

CON-

CONTENTS. xxxix

Considerable Observations on the Greek nouns of this declension. 119
Of the genitive in OS. *Ibid.*
The genitive of proper names in ES. 120
The accusative in A. 121
The accusative of nouns in IS and in YS. *Ibid.*
The accusative in O and UN or UM. 122
The accusative in YS. *Ibid.*
Of the vocative. *Ibid.*
Of the genitive plural. *Ibid.*
Of the dative plural. *Ibid.*
The fourth declension. 123
Rule LIII. Of the dative plural in UBUS. *Ibid.*
The fifth declension. 124
That the Æolians dropped the I subscribed in all the datives, and that in this they were followed by the Latins. 125
Some cases unusual in this declension. *Ibid.*

BOOK III. THE HETEROCLITES. 126

Of nouns irregular in their gender. 127
Rule I. Of those that are masculine in the singular and neuter in the plural. *Ibid.*
Rule II. Of those that are masculine in the singular, and in the plural are masculine and neuter. *Ibid.*
Rule III. Of nouns that are feminine in the singular and neuter in the plural. 128
Of the word *Pergamus*. *Ibid.*
Rule IV. Of those that are neuter in the singular, and masculine in the plural. 129
Of the word *Argos*. 130
Rule V. Of nouns that are neuter in the singular, and masculine or neuter in the plural. *Ibid.*
Rule VI. Of nouns that are neuter in the singular, and feminine in the plural. 131
Of nouns irregular in their declension. 132
Rule VII. Of *jugerum* which is of the second in the singular, and of the third in the plural. *Ibid.*
Rule VIII. Of *vas*, which is of the third in the singular, and of the second in the plural. *Ibid.*
Rule IX. Of *domus* which follows the second and fourth. 133
Rule X. Of *vis* and *bos*, which are irregular in some cases. *Ibid.*
Of defective nouns, or irregulars that want something. 134
Of those that have no plural. *Ibid.*

CONTENTS.

Of nouns that have no singular. 135
Rule XI. General for nouns that have no singular at all, or but very seldom. Ibid.
The first list. Of nouns that admit of different terminations in the nominative. 136
Of US and UM. 143
The second list. Of nouns that follow different declensions, whether in one or in different numbers. 147
Whether there are any nouns of the first and fifth declension. 149
Of those which change declension in different numbers. Ibid.
The third list. Of those nouns which by grammarians are said to want the plural in sense. Ibid.
The fourth list. Of those nouns which, as grammarians say, are not used in the plural, though we sometimes meet with examples to the contrary. 150
The fifth list. Of those nouns which grammarians mention as wanting the singular, though we sometimes meet with instances to the contrary in authors. 155
On indeclinable nouns. 164
The sixth list. Of nouns that have not all their cases. 165

BOOK IV. OF THE CONJUGATIONS OF VERBS. 171

General rules. Rule I. Of the compounded verbs. 173
Rule II. Of Verbs that redouble their first syllable in the preterite. Ibid.
Rule III. Of those which having changed the A into I, take an E in the supine. 176
Rule IV. Of those that have no preterite. 177
Rule V. Of the syncope. Ibid.
The first conjugation. Rule VI. General for verbs of the first conjugation. 178
Rule VII. Of the verbs *do* and *sto* with their compounds. 180
Rule VIII. Of *lavo*, *poto*, and *juvo*. 182
Rule IX. Of those which make üi and ITUM. 183
Rule X. Of *plico* and its compounds. 184
Rule XI. Of those which make UI and CTUM. 186
The second conjugation. Rule XII. General for the verbs of the second conjugation. 187
Rule XIII. Exception for the supine. 189
Rule XIV. Of the verbs neuter that have no supine. 191
Rule XV. Of the compounds of *oleo*. 194
Rule XVI. Of *arceo* and *taceo* with their compounds. 196
Rule XVII. Of the verbs in VEO. Ibid.

CONTENTS.

RULE XVIII. Of *forbeo* and its compounds. 198
RULE XIX. Of some other verbs that make UI and TUM. 199
RULE XX. Of verbs that make DI and SUM. 290
RULE XXI. Of other verbs which form DI, SUM, with a reduplication in the preterite. 201
RULE XXII. Of verbs that make SI, SUM. 202
RULE XXIII. Of those which make SI, TUM. 203
RULE XXIV. Of those which make XI, and CTUM. 204
RULE XXV. Of those which make SI or XI, without a supine. 205
The third conjugation. RULE XXVI. Of the verbs in CIO. 206
RULE XXVII. Of *fodio* and *fugio*. 209
RULE XXVIII. Of the verbs in PIO. Ibid.
RULE XXIX. Of the verbs in RIO and TIO. 211
RULE XXX. Of the verbs in UO. 213
RULE XXXI. Of the verbs in UO that have no supine. 216
RULE XXXII. Of the verbs in BO. 217
RULE XXXIII. Of the verbs in CO. 220
RULE XXXIV. Of the verbs in SCO. 223
RULE XXXV. Of inceptive verbs. 226
RULE XXXVI. Of the verbs in DO. 227
RULE XXXVII. Of the verbs in DO that have a reduplication. 229
RULE XXXVIII. Of the compounds of *do* and *fido*. 231
RULE XXXIX. Of the verbs in NDO which lose N. 233
RULE XL. Of the verbs that make SI, SUM. 234
RULE XLI. Of *cado*, *cædo* and *cedo*, with their compounds. 237
On the preterites of some verbs in DO. 240
RULE XLII. of the verbs in GO. Ibid.
RULE XLIII. Of those verbs which drop their N in the supine. 243
RULE XLIV. Of the verbs which make IGI or EGI, and ACTUM. 244
RULE XLV. Of *pungo* and of *lego* with its compounds. 247
RULE XLVI. Of *mergo*, *spargo* and *tergo*. 249
RULE XLVII. Of those verbs which either have no supine, or no preterite. 250
RULE XLVIII. Of the verbs in HO, and of *meio*. Ibid.
RULE XLIX. Of the verbs in LO. 252
RULE L. The second part of the verbs in LO. 254
RULE LI. Of the verbs in MO. 256
RULE LII. Of the verbs in NO. 258

CONTENTS.

Rule LIII. The second part of the verbs in NO. 261
Rule LIV. Of the verbs in PO and QUO. 263
Rule LV. Of the verbs in RO. 265
Rule LVI. Of *fero* and its compounds. 271
Rule LVII. Of the verbs in SO. 272
Rule LVIII. Of verbs in TO. 274
Rule LIX. The second part of the verbs in TO. 277
Rule LX. Of the verbs in VO. 280
Rule LXI. of the verbs in XO. 281
The fourth conjugation. Rule LXII. General for the verbs of the fourth conjugation. 282
Rule LXIII. Of those words that have no supine. 285
Rule LXIV. Of *singultio, sepelio, veneo* and *venio*. Ibid.
Rule LXV. Of *sancio, vincio* and *amicio*. 287
Rule LXVI. Of the verbs which make SI, SUM; and of those which make SI, TUM. Ibid.
Rule LXVII. Of *haurio, sepio* and *sa'io*. 288
Rule LXVIII. of the compounds of Pa'rio. 290
Rule LXIX. Of the verbs of desire, called Desideratives. 291
Of the verbs deponents. Rule LXX. What a verb deponent is. 293
Rule LXXI. General for the preterite of the deponents. Ibid.
Rule LXXII. Of the verbs in EOR. 296
Rule LXXIII. Of the verbs in OR. 297
Rule LXXIV. Of the verbs in SCOR. 300
Rule LXXV. Of the verbs in IOR. 301
Rule LXXVI. Of deponents that have no preterite. 303
Rule LXXVII. Of the verbs called neuter passive. 304
Rule LXXVIII. Of neuters which seem to have a passive signification. 305
Rule LXXIX. Of impersonals. 307
Rule LXXX. Of the imperatives of *dico, duco, facio* and *fero*. 308
Observations on the different conjugations, and on the derivative and compound verbs. 309
On derivative verbs. 310
On compound verbs. 312
A Method of finding out the present by the preterite. 314
Art. I. The most natural analogy of forming the preterite. Ibid.
Art. II. Four general irregularities and three particular changes in for verbs. 315
Art. III. Of the first general irregularity. 316
List of preterites that come from verbs in *vo*, or *veo*. 317

CONTENTS.

Of preterites which come from verbs of other terminations, and are more irregular. *Ibid.*
ART. IV. Of the second general irregularity. 318
ART. V. Of the third general irregularity. 319
List of the preterites in *si* or *xi*, by the addition of an *s* after the characteristic of the present. 320
List of the preterites in *si*, or *ssi*. 321
Some preterites in *xi* that are still more irregular, having neither *c* nor *g* in the present. 322
ART. VI. Of the fourth general irregularity. 323
List of the preterites which retain the characteristic of the present. 324
ADVERTISEMENT concerning the method of finding out the present by means of the supine. And the chief advantage that may be derived from the above lists of preterites. 325
OBSERVATIONS on the figure of metaplasm, as far as it relates to etymology or analogy. 327

CONTENTS.

VOL. II.

BOOK V. SYNTAX.

GENERAL diſtribution of the whole ſyntax 1
The rules of ſyntax. RULE I. Of the adjective and ſubſtantive. 3
RULE II. Of the relative and antecedent. 4
The following caſe underſtood. *Ibid.*
The preceding caſe underſtood. 5
The preceding and the following caſe both underſtood. *Ibid.*
The relative betwixt two nouns of different genders. 6
The relative agreeing with a gender or number underſtood. *Ibid.*
Of thoſe nouns which are called relatives of quantity or quality. 7
RULE III. Of the caſe which the verb requires before it. *Ibid.*
Of the infinitive. 8
Obſervations in regard to the next rule. 9
RULE IV. Of the difference of genders and perſons. *Ibid.*
Whether the feminine ought to be preferred to the neuter. 11
Of the reaſon of theſe governments, with ſome particular remarks on the conſtruction of inanimate things. *Ibid.*
Whether we ought always to name ourſelves the firſt in Latin, and in what manner we ought to do it in French. 12
RULE V. Of verbs that have the ſame caſe after as before them. *Ibid.*
RULE VI. Of two ſubſtantives of the ſame or of different ſenſe. 14
Government of the genitive. 15
'That the ſame noun agreeing with the poſſeſſive, governs alſo a genitive. 17
All verbal nouns heretofore governed the caſe of their verb. 18

RULE

CONTENTS. xlv

RULE VII. Of some particles that require a genitive. 18
RULE VIII. Of nouns of property, blame, or praise. 19
RULE IX. Of nouns adjectives derived from verbs. 20
Difference between the participle and the verbal noun. 21
Cause of the government of these verbal nouns. *Ibid.*
Of the active verbals in BUNDUS. *Ibid.*
RULE X. Of affective verbs. *Ibid.*
RULE XI. Of *sum, refert,* and *interest.* 23
RULE XII. Natural signification of the dative. 25
Some extraordinary constructions with the dative. 28
RULE XIII. Of verbs which take two datives. 29
RULE XIV. Of the accusative which the verb governs after it. *Ibid.*
RULE XV. Of verbs that govern the person in the accusative. 31
RULE XVI. Of five verbs that take the person in the accusative, and the thing in the genitive. 32
RULE XVII. Of verbs of remembering and forgetting. 33
RULE XVIII. Of two verbs coming together. 34
RULE XIX. Of prepositions which govern the accusative. 35
RULE XX. Of prepositions which govern the ablative. 38
RULE XXI. Of prepositions which govern the accusative and the ablative. 40
That almost every government may be resolved by the prepositions. 42
RULE XXII. Of verbs compounded with a preposition. 43
RULE XXIII. Of verbs that govern the accusative with *ad.* *Ibid.*
RULE XXIV. Of verbs which take two accusatives, or that have different governments. *Ibid.*
RULE XXV. Of the four questions of place. 46
The question UBI. 48
The question UNDE. 49
The question QUA. *Ibid.*
The question QUÒ. *Ibid.*
Particular observations on the question UBI. 50
Of nouns of the first declension in E. 51
Concerning apposition. *Ibid.*
Concerning nouns of the third declension. 52
Observations on compound nouns. *Ibid.*
RULE XXVI. Of the questions of time, measure, and distance. 53
RULE XXVII. Of the comparative and of partitives. 55
Of the comparative. *Ibid.*
Difficulties in regard to the comparative. 57

CONTENTS.

Of *prior* and *primus*. 58
Of *plus*. Ibid.
Of the partitive in general. 59
Of the superlative in general. Ibid.
Difficulties in regard to the superlative. 60
RULE XXVIII. Of the verbs and nouns which govern an ablative; or a genitive, the ablative being understood. 61
Plenty or want. 62
Some other adjectives. 63
Of the noun OPUS. 64
RULE XXIX. Of nouns of price, and verbs of valuing. 65
RULE XXX. Of verbs passive, and others which require the ablative with the preposition *A* or *Ab*. 66
That the verb passive properly speaking governs nothing of itself. 67
Of the verbs called neuter passives, *veneo*, *vapulo*, &c. 68
RULE XXXI. Of the matter of which any thing is composed. 69
RULE XXXII. Of those nouns that are put in the ablative with a preposition. Ibid.
RULE XXXIII. Of particular verbs that govern the ablative, some of which have likewise the accusative. 70
RULE XXXIV. Of the ablative absolute. 72
RULE XXXV. Of some particles which govern different cases. 73
RULE XXXVI. Of the reciprocal pronouns *sui* and *suus*. 75

BOOK VI. PARTICULAR REMARKS on all the parts of speech. 79

SECT. I. REMARKS ON THE NOUNS.

CHAP. I. Of nouns common, doubtful and epicenes. Ibid.
I. Of common nouns. Ibid.
II. Nouns common in their signification only. 80
III. Nouns common that are put in both genders. 81
IV. Of doubtful nouns. Ibid.
V. Of epicenes. 82
CHAP. II. Remarks on some particular cases. 83
I. Of the vocative. Ibid.
II. Of the dative and the ablative. Ibid.
CHAP. III. Remarks on numeral nouns. 84
I. Of *ambo* and *duo*. Ibid.
II. Of the other numeral nouns. 85
CHAP. IV. Of the motion, or variation of adjectives. 86
I. Of the variation according to the genders. Ibid.

II. Of

CONTENTS. XLVII

II. Of the comparison of nouns — 87
III. Of defectives, or those which are deprived of some degree of comparison. — 88
IV. Superlatives that are compared. — Ibid.
V. Adjectives that are not compared. — Ibid.
List of nouns that are compared, though they have a vowel before US. — 89
CHAP. V. Of diminutives. — Ibid.

SECT. II. REMARKS ON THE PRONOUNS.

CHAP. I. Of the number of pronouns, with the signification and declension of some in particular. — 90
I. The nature of a pronoun. — Ibid.
II. Difference in the signification of pronouns. — Ibid.
III. Concerning the cases, and the declension of pronouns. — 92
IV. Of the nature of the relative. — Ibid.
V. Of *qui* or *quis*. — Ibid.
VI. Of *meus* and *suus*. — 94
VII. Pronouns in C, or those compounded of *en* and *ecce*. — 95
CHAP. II. Remarks on the construction of pronouns. — 96
I. Of the construction of *ipse*. — Ibid.
II. Of the construction of *idem*. — Ibid.
III. Of the construction of the possessives *meus, tuus, &c.* and of the genitives *mei, tui, &c.* — 97

SECT. III. REMARKS ON THE VERBS.

CHAP. I. Of the nature and signification of verbs — 98
I. List of verbs absolute and active. — 99
II. List of verbs active which are taken in an absolute sense. — 100
III. List of verbs passive taken actively. — 101
IV. List of deponents, which are taken passively. — 102
V. List of deponents that are terminated in O and in OR. — 104
CHAP. II. Of the difference of tense and moods. — 106
I. Of tenses. — Ibid.
II. Of moods. — Ibid.
III. Of the subjunctive. — 107
IV. That we may oftentimes put the indicative or the subjunctive indifferently one for the other. — 108
V. Of the imperative. — 109
VI. Of the infinitive. — Ibid.
VII. Of FORE. — 111
VIII.

CONTENTS.

VIII. Manner of expressing the future of the infinitive in the other verbs. 112
IX. Another manner of supplying the future of the infinitive, especially when the verbs have no supine. 113
X. That the infinitive hath frequently the force of a noun substantive. *Ibid.*

CHAP. III. Of irregular verbs. 115
I. Of SUM and its compounds. *Ibid.*
II. Of *edo, queo,* and *fio.* 116
III. Of *fero,* and *eo,* with their compounds. 117
IV. Of *volo,* and its compounds. 118

CHAP. IV. Of defective verbs. *Ibid.*
I. Of *odi, memini,* and others which are thought to have only the preterite, and the tenses depending thereon. 119
II. Of *fari,* and other defective verbs of the same signification. 120
III. Of *faxo, ausim, forem,* and *quæso.* 121

CHAP. V. Of verbs called impersonal, and of their nature. 122
I. What is meant by a verb impersonal, and that in reality there is no other but the infinitive. *Ibid.*
II. That the verbs called impersonals are not deprived of all the persons we imagine, even in the most elegant language. 124

SECT. IV. REMARKS ON THE GERUNDS, SUPINES, AND PARTICIPLES.

CHAP. I. Remarks on the gerunds. 125
I. What the antient and modern grammarians thought of Gerunds. *Ibid.*
II. That the gerunds are nouns substantives, and what is the real cause of their government. 126
III. Whether the gerunds are taken actively or passively. 128

CHAP. II. Remarks on the supines. 129
I. That the supines are likewise nouns substantives. *Ibid.*
II. Whether the supines are active or passive, and what time is expressed by their circumlocution in *ire* or *iri.* 131
III. What case the accusative of the supines governeth, what this accusative itself is governed by, and of some expressions of this sort difficult to account for. 132
IV. Of the supines in U, what they are governed by, and how they may be rendered by the infinitive, by the gerund, or by the verbal nouns in *io.* 133

CHAP. III. Remarks on the participles. 134
I. Diffe-

CONTENTS.

I. Difference between a participle and a noun adjective. 134
II. Whether every participle may exprefs every difference of time: and firſt of the participle in NS. *Ibid.*
II. Of the participle in US. 135
III. Of the participle in DUS. 137
IV. Of the participle in RUS. *Ibid.*
V. Signification of the participle in verbs common and deponents. 138
Deponents whoſe participle in US is ſometimes taken paſſively. *Ibid.*
VI. Some particular remarks on the participle in DUS. 140
VII. Of the participle of the verbs called imperſonals. 141
Nouns or participles in US, whoſe verbs are either rare or unuſual. *Ibid.*
VIII. Of *cœnatus, pranſus,* and *potus.* 142
IX. Whether *adventus* may be ſometimes alſo an adjective. 144

SECT. V. REMARKS ON THE INDECLINABLE PARTICLES.

CHAP. I. Remarks on the adverbs. *Ibid.*
I. That the adverbs admit of compariſon; but not of number. *Ibid.*
II. That what is taken for an adverb is frequently another part of ſpeech. *Ibid.*
III. That *quod* is never any thing elſe but a pronoun relative. 146
IV. Whether *quod* may be put like the Greek Ὅτι, after the verbs. 148
V. Remarkable ſignifications of ſome adverbs, where the origin of ſeveral words is pointed out. *Ibid.*
CHAP. II. Remarks on the prepoſitions. 152
CHAP. III. Remarks on the conjunctions. 153
I. That the conjunctions have not always the ſame thing before as after them. *Ibid.*
II. Which conjunctions require rather the indicative, and which the ſubjunctive? *Ibid.*
III. Of negative conjunctions. 155
IV. Some other remarks concerning particular conjunctions. *Ibid.*

SECT. VI. REMARKS ON SOME PARTICULAR TURNS OF EXPRESSION.

CHAP. I. Of *vereor ut,* and *vereor ne.* 159
I. *Vereor ut.* 161
II. *Vereor ne.* 162

CONTENTS.

III. *Vereor ut ne,* or *vereor ut non.*   162
IV. *Vereor ne non.*   164
V. *Non vereor ut,* or *non vereor ne non.*   Ibid.
VI. *Non vereor ne,* or *non vereor ut ne.*   165
CHAP. II. Of this other phrase, *haud scio an, &c.*   Ibid.

BOOK VII. OF FIGURATIVE SYNTAX.

What is meant by figures in syntax, of their use, and that they may be all reduced to four.   167
CHAP. I. Of the first figure called *ellipsis.*   168
I. Verb understood.   Ibid.
II. The nominative understood before the verb.   169
III. The accusative understood after the verb.   Ibid.
IV. When the infinitive is alone, the verb that governs it is understood.   170
V. When an adjective is alone, some substantive or other is understood. Of the word *negotium.*   Ibid.
VI. Antecedent with the relative understood.   172
VII. What is to be understood when the genitive comes after an adjective, or after a verb.   Ibid.
VIII. What we are to understand, when the accusative is by itself.   173
IX. What we are to understand, when the ablative is by itself.   Ibid.
X. Two other very remarkable ellipses; one where we are to understand the nominative of the verb, and the other, where we must supply the verb by the context.   174
XI. Of other more remarkable particles that are understood.   175
XII. First list. Of several nouns understood in Latin authors.   176
XIII. Second list. Of several verbs understood.   181
XIV. Third list. Of prepositions that are to be understood.   Ibid.
CHAP. II. Of the second sort of ellipsis, called ZEUGMA.   183
I. A word understood as it was expressed before.   Ibid.
II. A word understood otherwise than it was expressed before.   Ibid.
III. A word understood in the enumeration of parts.   Ibid.
IV. Elegance to be observed in regard to the Zeugma.   184
CHAP. III. Of the second figure called PLEONASM.   Ibid.
CHAP. IV. Of the third figure called SYLLEPSIS.   185
I. The simple syllepsis.   Ibid.
II. The relative syllepsis.   186
CHAP. V. That the syllepsis is frequently joined with another figure, and of some difficult passages which ought to be referred thereto.   188

I. The

CONTENTS.

I. The syllepsis with a zeugma. 188
II. With an entire ellipsis. 189
III. With an hyperbaton. 190
CHAP. VI. Of the fourth figure called HYPERBATON. *Ibid.*

CHAP. VII. Of HELLENISM or Greek phrase. 192
I. Hellenism by ATTRACTION. *Ibid.*
II. Hellenism of the preposition KATA. 193
III. Hellenism of the preposition EK. 194
IV. Other more particular expressions, which depend on the figure of hellenism. *Ibid.*
CHAP. VII. Of antiptosis and enallage. 195
I. Whether we ought to join antiptosis and enallage to the foregoing figures, and what the grammarians understand by these two words. *Ibid.*
II. Examples of the antiptosis taken particularly from Despauter. *Ibid.*
III. Other examples taken from those who wrote upon Despauter. 197
IV. Examples of the enallage. 198
List of verbs of different governments. 200

BOOK VIII. PARTICULAR OBSERVATIONS.

On the Roman names. On their figures or arithmetical characters. On their manner of counting the sesterces. And on the division of time. Useful for the understanding of authors. 226

CHAP. I. Of the names of the antient Romans. Taken from VAL. MAXIMUS, SIGONIUS, LIPSIUS, and other authors. *Ibid.*
I. Of the proper name, PRÆNOMEN. *Ibid.*
II. Of the general name, NOMEN GENTIS. 228
III. Of the particular surname, COGNOMEN and AGNOMEN. *Ibid.*
IV. OBSERVATIONS on the names of slaves, freedmen, women, and adoptive children. 229
And first of slaves and freedmen. *Ibid.*
2. Of women. *Ibid.*
3. Of adoptive children. *Ibid.*
V. Other observations on changing the order of those names. 230
1. The *cognomen* before the *nomen*. *Ibid.*
2. The *cognomen* become *nomen*. *Ibid.*
3. The *prænomen* become *nomen*. *Ibid.*
4. The *prænomen* put in the second place. *Ibid.*
5. The

CONTENTS.

5. The *prænomen* or proper name put laſt under the emperors. 231
6. Exception to this rule of taking the laſt name under the emperors. 232
7. Other names changed as well as the latter. *Ibid.*

CHAP. II. Of figures, or arithmetical characters among the Romans. 233
I. In what manner the Romans marked their numbers. *Ibid.*
II. Proper obſervations in order to underſtand theſe figures thoroughly. *Ibid.*
III. What this manner of reckoning has been owing to, and whence theſe figures have been taken. 234
IV. Whether there are other methods to mark the Roman cypher than the preceding. 235

CHAP. III. Of the Roman feſterces. *Ibid.*
II. Reaſon of theſe expreſſions, and that *mille* ſtrictly ſpeaking is always an adjective. 236
III. Other remarkable expreſſions in regard to the ſame ſubject. 238

CHAP. IV. Of the diviſion of time according to the antients. 239
I. Of days. *Ibid.*
II. Of hours. *Ibid.*
III. Of the watches of the night. 240
IV. Of weeks. *Ibid.*
V. Of months. *Ibid.*
VI. The antient manner of reckoning the days of the month. 241
VII. Of the year. 242
VIII. Of the ſpaces of time compoſed of ſeveral years. And firſt of Olympiads and luſtres. 243
2. Of the indiction and the golden number. *Ibid.*
3. Of the ſolar cycle, and the dominical letters. 244
4. The Julian period, the ſabbatic years, a jubilee, an age. 245
5. Of Epochas, and the word ÆRÆ. *Ibid.*

BOOK IX. OF LETTERS,

And the orthography and pronunciation of the antients. Wherein is ſhewn the antient manner of pronouncing the Latin tongue, and occaſion is taken to point out alſo the right manner of pronouncing the Greek. Extracted from the beſt treatiſes both of ancient and modern writers on this ſubject. 246

CONTENTS.

CHAP. I. Of the number, order, and division of letters. 247
CHAP. II. Of vowels in general, as long or short. 248
CHAP. III. Of vowels in particular. And particularly of those that are called open. 250
I. Of A. *Ibid.*
II. Of E. *Ibid.*
III. Of I. 253
CHAP. IV. Of the three last vowels which are called shut. 254
I. Of O. *Ibid.*
II. Of U. 255
III. Of Y. 258
CHAP. V. Of diphthongs. 259
I. Of the diphthongs Æ and AI. *Ibid.*
II. Of the diphthongs AU and EU. *Ibid.*
III. Of the diphthong EI. 260
IV. Of the diphthongs OE and OI. 261
CHAP. VI. Of the nature of I and V consonants. Whether there are any triphthongs or other diptongs among the Latins, than those above explained. 262
I. Whether the I and V were consonants among the antients. *Ibid.*
II. Whether there are any triphthongs. 263
III. Whether the I may sometimes pass for a double consonant. 265
CHAP. VII. Of liquids. 266
CHAP. VIII. Of the mute consonants, and first of those of the first order, P, B, F, V. 267
I. Of B and P. 268
II. Of the F and the V consonant. *Ibid.*
III. Relation between the V and the *digamma*. 269
IV. Other relation between V and B. *Ibid.*
V. Relation of B to F, and to Φ. 270
VI. Other relations of B or P to M, and of P to F or PH. *Ibid.*
CHAP. IX. Of the second class of mutes, C, Q, G, J. *Ibid.*
I. Relation between C and Q. 271
II. Whether Q ought to pass for a double letter. 272
III. Of the U which always accompanies the Q. 273
IV. Relation between C and G. *Ibid.*
V. Relation between G and J consonant. 274
VI. Whether the antients pronounced Gn in the manner the French do at present. *Ibid.*
VII. That there is still a middle sound between G and N, which is neither intirely one nor the other, and has given the

CONTENTS.

the Greeks occasion to change N into Γ before γ, κ, χ, or ξ. 274
CHAP. X. Of the third class of mutes, which are D and T. 275
CHAP. XI. Of the hissing letters. 276
I. Of the letter S. Ibid.
II. Of the double letters. 277
CHAP. XII. Of the aspiration H. 279
I. Of H before vowels. Ibid.
II. Of H after consonants. 280
III. Of the pronunciation of CH. 281
IV. Of the Pronunciation of Ph. Ibid.
V. Of TH and RH. Ibid.
VI. From whence the Latins borrowed this aspiration H. 282
VII. Of some relations between the H and the Æolic digamma, which at length was change into V consonant, and into β. Ibid.
Table of the manner of writing of the antients. 284
CHAP. XIII. Of the genuine orthography to be observed at present. 285
List of some particular words, whose orthography may be depended upon. Ibid.
CHAP. XIV. Of some other remarks on orthography. 289
I. Of words that ought to begin with capitals. Ibid.
II. Of those words which the Romans expressed by a few letters only. Ibid.
III. Of the right manner of putting syllables together. 290
Exception to this rule. Ibid.
IV. Of some other particular marks. 291
CHAP. XV. Of punctuation. Ibid.
I. Of three sorts of distinctions. Ibid.
II. Of the comma. 292
III. Of the colon, or two points. 293
IV. Of the full point or period. Ibid.
V. Of the semicolon, or point and comma. 294
VI. Of the points of interrogation and admiration. Ibid.

BOOK X. OF PROSODY.

SECT. I. Of the quantity of syllables. 295
RULES of the quantity of syllables. 296
RULE I. Every syllable formed by contraction is long. Ibid.
RULE II. Of diphthongs. 297
RULE III. Of a vowel before another vowel. Ibid.
OF GREEK WORDS. 299

CONTENTS.

Of those which are written with long or short vowels.	299
Of those which are variously writ.	Ibid.
Of three common vowels.	Ibid.
Of words that have a diphthong in Greek.	300
Cause of the deviation in Greek words from the foregoing rules.	Ibid.
RULE IV. Of a vowel long by position.	301
RULE V. Of a mute and liquid.	Ibid.
Whether I be sometimes a double letter, and V sometimes a liquid.	303
OF DERIVATIVE WORDS.	Ibid.
Exceptions to the preceding rule.	304
OF COMPOUND WORDS.	Ibid.
RULE VI. Of divers compounding particles.	305
RULE VII. Of the other prepositions.	306
RULE VIII. Of words compounded without a preposition.	307
OF PRETERITES AND SUPINES.	309
RULE IX. Of preterites of two syllables.	Ibid.
RULE X. Of preterites with a reduplication.	Ibid.
RULE XI. Of supines of two syllables.	310
Of the supine *statum*.	311
Of *citum* and *scitum*.	Ibid.
RULE XII. Of the supines of polysyllables.	312
OF THE INCREASE OF VERBS.	Ibid.
RULE XIII. The nature of the increase of verbs.	Ibid.
RULE XIV. Of the increase in A.	313
RULE XV. Of the increase in E.	Ibid.
RULE XVI. Of the increase in I.	315
RULE XVII. Of the increase in O.	316
RULE XVIII. Of the increase in U	317
OF THE INCREASE OF NOUNS.	Ibid.
RULE XIX. What is meant by the increase of nouns.	Ibid.
Of the first declension.	Ibid.
RULE XX. Increase of the second declension.	318
INCREASE OF THE THIRD DECLENSION.	Ibid.
RULE XXI. Of the increase of nouns in L.	Ibid.
RULE XXII. Increase of nouns in N and O.	319
RULE XXIII Of the increase ARIS.	320
RULE XXIV. Of the increase ERIS.	Ibid.
RULE XXV. Of the increase of nouns in OR.	Ibid.
RULE XXVI. Increase of nouns in UR.	321
RULE XXVII. Of the increase of nouns in AS.	Ibid.
RULE XXVIII. Of the increase ATIS.	322
RULE XXIX. Of the increase of nouns in ES.	Ibid.
RULE XXX. Of the increase of nouns in IS.	323
RULE XXXI. Of the increase of nouns in OS.	Ibid.

CONTENTS.

Rule XXXII. Of the increase of nouns in US. 323
Rule XXXIII. The increase of nouns ending in S with another consonant. 324
Rule XXXIV. Of the noun *caput* and its compounds. 325
Rule XXXV. Of the nouns in X which form their genitive in GIS. Ibid.
Rule XXXVI. Of the increase of nouns in AX. Ibid.
Rule XXXVII. Of the increase of nouns in EX. 326
Rule XXXVIII. Of the increase of nouns in IX. Ibid.
Rule XXXIX. Of the increase OCIS. Ibid.
Rule XL. Of the increase UCIS. 327
Of the increase of other declensions. Ibid.
Rule XLI. Of the increase of the plural. Ibid.
Of the last Syllable. 328
Rule XLII. A final. Ibid.
Of the vocative ending in A. 329
Of some adverbs in A. Ibid.
Of the nouns in *ginta*. 330
Rule XLIII. E final. Ibid.
Rule XLIV. I final. 332
Rule XLV. O final. 334
Rule XLVI. U final. 335
Rule XLVII. B and C final. 336
Rule XLVIII. D and L final. 337
Of words ending in M. Ibid.
Rule XLIX. N final. 338
Rule L. R. final. Ibid.
Rule LI. AS final. 340
Rule LII. ES final. Ibid.
Rule LIII. IS final. 342
Of the termination RIS in the subjunctive. 343
Rule LIV. OS final. 344
Rule LV. US final. Ibid.
Rule LVI. T. final. 345
Rule LVII. Of the last syllable of the verse. 346
Observations on divers syllables whose quantity is disputed. 347
List of words whose quantity is disputed. Ibid.

Sect. II. Of Accents,

And the proper manner of pronouncing Latin. 354

Chap. I. 1. Of the nature of accents, and how many sorts there are. Ibid.
II. Rules of accents and of Latin words. 355
For monosyllables. Ibid.

CONTENTS.

For diſſyllables and polyſyllables. 355
II. Reaſons for the above rules. Ibid.
IV. Some exceptions to theſe rules of accents. 356
CHAP. II. Particular obſervations on the practice of the antients. 357
I. In what place the accents ought to be marked in books. Ibid.
II. In what manner we ought to mark the accent on words compounded of an enclitic. 358
III. That neither *que* nor *ne* are always enclitics. Ibid.
IV. That the accent ought to be marked, whenever there is a neceſſity for diſtinguiſhing one word from another. Ibid.
V. Whether we ought to accent the laſt ſyllable, on account of this diſtinction. 359
VI. In what manner we ought to place the accent in verſe. 360
CHAP. III. I. Of the accents of words which the Latins have borrowed of other languages, and particularly thoſe of Greek words. Ibid.
II. Of the accents of Hebrew words. 361
CHAP. IV. Further obſervations on the pronunciation of the antients. 362
I. That they diſtinguiſhed between accent and quantity, and made ſeveral differences even in quantity. Ibid.
II. Difficult paſſages of the antients, which may be ſolved by thoſe principles. 364
III. Whether from the difference they made in the pronunciation of ſhort and long vowels, we may conclude that U was ſounded like the French diphthong OU in long ſyllables only. 365

SECT. III. OF LATIN POETRY,

And the different ſpecies of metre; as alſo of the feet, the figures, and beauties to be obſerved in verſifying; and of the manner of intermixing them in divers ſorts of compoſition. Divided in the cleareſt order and method. 367
CHAP. I. Of feet. Ibid.
I. Of the nature of feet in verſe. Ibid.
II. Of feet of two ſyllables. Ibid.
III. Of feet of three ſyllables. Ibid.
RULE of the ſix neceſſary feet. 370
IV. Of compound feet. Ibid.
A Regular table of all the feet. 372
CHAP. II. Of verſe in general. 373
I. Of the cæſura and its different ſpecies. Ibid.

CONTENTS.

II. In what place the cæsura is most graceful; and of the beauty it gives to verse. 374

III. That the cæsura has the power of lengthening short syllables. *Ibid.*

IV. Of the final cadence called DEPOSITIO, and of the four names it gives to verse. 375

CHAP. III. Of the measure or manner of scanning verse, and of the figures used therein. 376

I. Of ecthlipsis. *Ibid.*

II. Of synalæpha. 377

III. Directions in regard to the use of those two figures, Ecthlipsis and synalæpha. *Ibid.*

IV. The synalæpha omitted. 379

V. Of the contraction of syllables, which includes the SYNÆRESIS and the SYNECPHONESIS. 380

VI. Of DIÆRESIS. 382

VII. Of SYSTOLE and DIASTOLE. *Ibid.*

VIII. Of the caution with which we ought to make use of those licences. 383

CHAP. IV. Of the chief species of verse. And first of Hexameters, and such as are relative thereto. 384

I. Of Hexameter verse. *Ibid.*

II. Whether an Hexameter verse may sometimes end with a Dactyl. 386

III. Division of Hexameters into Heroic and Satyric, and cautions to be observed in order to render them elegant. *Ibid.*

IV. Of neglected Hexameters. Excellence of those of Horace. 389

V. Of Pentameter verse. 390

VI. Observations for making elegant Pentameters. *Ibid.*

VII. Six lesser verses which make part of an Hexameter. And 1. Of three which form the beginning. 391

VIII. Of the other three lesser verses, which form the end of an Hexameter. 392

CHAP. V. Of Iambic verses, and first of the different species of Iambics, according to the different feet of which they are composed. *Ibid.*

II. Of a Scazon or Claudicant Iambic. 394

III. Of Iambics according to the number of their feet. *Ibid.*

1. Of Dimeters, or four feet. 395
2. Of Trimeters, or Iambics of six feet. *Ibid.*
3. Of Tetrameters, or Iambics of eight feet. *Ibid.*

IV. Of Iambics either defective or redundant, whereto we must refer those which are commonly called TROCHAICS. 396

CONTENTS.

1. Of Imperfect Dimeters. 397
2. Of Imperfect Trimeters. Ibid.
3. Of Imperfect Tetrameters. 398

CHAP. VI. Of Lyric verses, and those any way relative to Lyrics. Ibid.
I. Of four sorts of Choriambics. Ibid.
II. Of verses of eleven syllables, Sapphic, Phaleucian, and Alcaic. 399
  1. Of Phaleucian verse. Ibid.
  2. Of Sapphic verse. 400
  3. Of Alcaic verse. 401
  4. Of the lesser Alcaic. Ibid.
III. Of Anapæstic verse. Ibid.
IV. Of Archilochian verse, and others less frequently used. 402

CHAP. VII. Of compositions in verse, and the mixture of different sorts of metre. 403
I. Compositions of one sort of metre only. Ibid.
II. Compositions of different metre, and their division into stanzas, called STROPHES. Ibid.
III. Compositions of two sorts of metre. And first of those in which the stanza has but two verses, and which are called δίκωλον δίςροφον. 404
IV. Compositions of two sorts of metre in stanzas of four verses. Which are called δίκωλον τέτράςροφον. 406
V. Compositions of three sorts of metre in stanzas of three verses. Which are called τρίκωλον τρίςροφον. Ibid.

The First Table. Of different species of verse reduced to three. 408

Examples of the different species of verse contained in the foregoing table according to the correspondent figures. 409.

The Second Table. Of the mixture of Latin verse in compositions, with the figures referring to the precedent table, to point out the examples. 410

BOOKS *printed for* F. WINGRAVE, *Succeſſor to the late* Mr. NOURSE, *in the Strand.*

THE Primitives of the Greek Tongue, containing a complete Collection of all the Roots or Primitive Words, together with the moſt conſiderable Derivatives of the Greek Languages. New Edition, 8vo. 6s.

A New Method of Learning with Facility the Greek Tongue. The Third Edition, 8vo. 7s. 6d.

An Abridgment of the ſame, 12mo. 3s.

A New Method of Learning the Italian Tongue, 8vo. 4s. 6d.

A General and Rational Grammar, containing the Fundamental Principles of the Art of Speaking, 12mo. 2s.

N. B. The above five articles are tranſlated from the French of Meſſieurs de Port-Royal, by Dr. Nugent.

The WORKS of JAMES HARRIS, Eſq.—Containing,

Vol. I. Three Treatiſes: The firſt concerning Art: The ſecond concerning Muſic, Painting, and Poetry: The third concerning Happineſs.

Vol. II. Hermes; or, A Philoſophical Inquiry concerning Univerſal Grammar.

Vol. III. Philoſophical Arrangements, containing a Variety of Speculations, logical, phyſical, ethical, and metaphyſical, derived from the Principles of the Greek Philoſophers, and illuſtrated by Examples from the greateſt Writers both antient and modern.

Vol. IV. and V. Philological Inquiries: In Three Parts.— Containing,

1. The Riſe and different Species of Criticiſm and Critics.

2. An Illuſtration of Critical Doctrines and Principles, as they appear in diſtinguiſhed Authors, as well antient as modern.

3. An Eſſay on the Taſte and Literature of the middle Ages.

To which are added, four Appendixes.—Firſt, An Account of the Arabic Manuſcripts belonging to the Eſcurial Library in Spain. Second, Concerning the Manuſcripts of Livy, in the ſame Library.—Third, Concerning the Manuſcripts of Cebes, in the Library of the King of France.—Fourth, Some Account of Literature in Ruſſia, and of its Progreſs towards being civilized.

In 5 vols. 8vo. The 4th Edition, illuſtrated with Plates, and a Head of the Author by Bartolozzi, 1l. 10s.

A NEW METHOD

Of LEARNING with EASE the

LATIN TONGUE.

BOOK I.

OF GENDERS.

THE Latins have three different genders for their nouns, the Masculine, the Feminine, and the Neuter, which for brevity sake, are marked by the pronoun *hic, hæc, hoc.* Yet we must observe, that as the first origin of genders was owing to the distinction of the two sexes, there are properly speaking only two genders, the *Masculine* and the *Feminine*; and hence it is that no more are admitted in the oriental tongues, and in the vulgar languages of the West.

But because the Greeks, and after their example the Latins, happened to meet with several nouns, which they knew not how to refer to either of those two genders, they have given them the name of *Neuters*, that is, properly speaking, they are of *neither gender*, neither masculine nor feminine.

These genders are known either by the *Signification*, of which some general rules may be given; or by the *Termination*, which includes the particular rules.

The termination ought to be considered in regard to the *Declension*, which has oftentimes the power of changing the gender in the same termination, as we shall demonstrate in a great many rules.

But because there are some nouns which have several of these genders together, the Grammarians have added two more to those three: the COMMON, as *hic et hæc adolescens*, a young man and a young woman: and the DOUBTFUL, as *hic aut hoc vulgus*, the common people.

There is this difference between these two sorts of genders, that the common has two genders, by reason of the signification of the noun; which as it includes the two sexes, is the cause of its being al-

VOL. I.   B   ways

ways put in the masculine, when it is applied to man; and in the feminine, when applied to woman. Hence it is, that the Common has, for the two genders of which it is composed, only the masculine and the feminine.

And the Doubtful has several genders, only because the practice was doubtful in the beginning; for some gave one gender to a noun, and others another; just as we see several nouns in French, whose gender has either changed, as *Eveché*, feminine in Ronsard, and now masculine; or is still doubtful, as *Theriaque, absinthe,* which are sometimes masculine, and sometimes feminine. Thus, some said, for example, *hic finis*; and others *hæc finis*; for which reason we are at liberty to put the same noun in which gender we please.

From hence it follows 1. that a noun of the doubtful gender may be either masculine or feminine, as *hic aut hæc finis*: either masculine or neuter, as *hic aut hoc vulgus*: either feminine or neuter, as *hæc aut hoc Prænefte*, the name of a town: and in fine may be of all the three genders, masculine, feminine, or neuter, as *penus, pecus,* and others.

2. It follows, that when you have put one of these nouns in one gender at the beginning of a discourse, you may put it in the other gender in the sequel, according to the observation made by Vivés, though this is not always to be imitated, as we shall observe in another place.

But there are some nouns which participate of the common and of the doubtful: of the common, inasmuch as their different genders suit them, because of their different significations; as *ftirps*, which is either masculine or feminine, to signify a root, and always feminine to signify descent or extraction: and of the doubtful, inasmuch as custom alone has given rise to these different genders, even in different significations. And there are instances of the same nature in French, as *Periode*, which is masculine when it signifies the highest pitch to which a thing can arrive; and feminine when it is taken for a part of discourse, the sense of which is quite complete.

There are also some nouns common to the two sexes, with respect to the signification, but not to the construction: Thus *homo*, signifies indeed *a man and a woman*, but we are not permitted to say *mala homo*, a bad woman. We shall give a list of them in the remarks which follow the syntax.

And as for the gender which the grammarians call *Omne,* we shall take notice of it in the annotation to the second rule.

THE

THE RULES of GENDERS.

RULE I.
Of Nouns which agree with either sex.

1. *The names of men are masculine.*
2. *The names of women are feminine.*
3. *When a noun agrees with both, its gender then is* common, *4, not doubtful.*

EXAMPLES.

1. NOUNS which agree with man only are of the masculine gender. Of these there are two sorts; some of which agree with each man in particular, and are called proper names; as *Petrus*, Peter; *Plato*, Plato. *Hic Dinácium*, Plaut. Dinace, the name of a man. Others, which agree with man in general, and are called appellatives; as *vir magnus*, a great man. *Primi senatóres*, the principal senators. *Rex fortíssimus*, a very brave king. *Hic ádvena*, a stranger. *Hic áffecla*, an attendant, and several others of the like nature.

It is the same in regard to the names of angels, as *Michaël, Gábriël:* of devils, as *Lúcifer:* of false deities, as *Júpiter, Mars*; *Mammóna* or *Mammónas*, the god of riches; because we always represent them to ourselves under a human form.

2. Nouns which agree with woman only, are of the feminine gender, whether they be proper names; as *María sanctíssima*, the most holy Mary; *Sancta Eustóchium*, Saint Eustochia: or whether they be appellatives; as *múlier púdica*, a chaste woman; *mater óptima*, a very good mother. The same may be said of the names of Goddesses, as *Pallas, Juno, Venus*, &c.

3. But nouns agreeing with man and woman both together, are of the common gender; as *hic & hæc conjux*,

jux, the husband or wife. *Parens sanctus*, the holy father. *Parens sancta*, the holy mother. *Civis bonus*, a good citizen of the male sex. *Civis bona*, a good citizen of the female sex.

4. We say that these nouns are not doubtful, because there is a wide difference between the common and doubtful genders, as we have already observed p. 2.

ANNOTATION.

Mammona or *Mamona*, or else *Mammonas*, or *Mamonas*, with one or two M. which Despauter puts in the neuter gender, and Beza has translated in the feminine, *veram Mammonam*, St. Luke, chap. xvi. ought rather to be in the masculine, as it is in the Syriac language, in which CHRIST spoke. Hence St. Ambrose calls him *Mammonam improbum*, and others do the same. The Greek termination *as*, is likewise in favour of this gender. As in St. Chrysostom, Καὶ ὁ μὲν τὸν μαμμωνᾶν ἡγεῖται Κύριον, ὁ δὲ τὴν κοιλίαν Θεόν. *Some make a god of their riches, and others of their belly.* And this termination is also used by Tertullian. *Quis magis serviet Mammonæ, quàm quem Mammonas redimit?* The signification likewise favours it, because it frequently signifies the same thing among the Hebrews, as πλοῦτος among the Greeks, *the god of riches*; which does not hinder it's being taken likewise for *gain*, and for *avarice*, as St. Austin and Clement of Alexandria observe: or for *riches*, according to St. Jerome.

Some have thought that the names of goddesses were also used in the masculine gender, because as on the one hand Virgil says *Magna Pales*, to signify the goddess of shepherds, on the other we meet with, *hic Pales*, in Varro and other writers, as Servius has observed 3. Georg.; And *Venus* is also to be found in the masculine gender. Besides *Deus* itself is taken for a goddess in Virgil, Lucan, and Claudian.

As for *Pales*, Arnobius *lib*. 3. *contra Gent*. shews there was a god of that name, different from the goddess, whom he also calls, *Ministrum & villicum Jovis*. And Varro must have meant this god, to which Servius did not sufficiently attend.

With regard to *Venus*, we may say with Macrobius, that she was considered as of two sexes; and hence it is that she was painted as a man dressed in woman's apparel, with a bearded chin; which is the reason of Aristophanes's calling her Ἀφρόδιτον instead of Ἀφροδίτην.

And if Virgil and others have also included her under the word *Deus*, doubtless they have done it in imitation of the Greeks, who make Θεός of the common gender. Πρῶτον μὲν Θεοῖς εὔχομαι πᾶσι ͗ κỳ πάσαις. Demosth. pro corona; *Primùm quidem deos deásque omnes precor*.

Of the names of Animals.

The names of brutes and animals follow the same distinction of masculine and feminine, as those of the human species, in regard to the two sexes, when they exactly agree either with the male or female; as *hic aries*, a ram, *hic taurus*, a bull; *hæc ovis*, a sheep; *hæc vacca*, a cow. And in like manner when there are two distinct nouns derived from the same root, as *lupus, lupa; equus, equa; leo, leæna.*

But if there be only one noun for the male and female, then it is either of the common gender, as *hic & hæc canis*, a dog or a bitch; *hic & hæc bos*, an ox or a cow: or else under one gender, which is generally that of the termination, it comprehends both kinds; as *hæc vulpes*, a fox; *hæc aquila*, an eagle: Whether we speak of the male or of the female, yet without determining them.

And it is the latter which the Greeks call ἐπίκοινα, that is, which have something *above* the *common* nouns; because they agree with both kinds as well as these, and moreover they comprehend them under a single gender.

But as all this is subject to a great many exceptions, and besides it is a thing of little or no necessity to beginners (from whence Quintilian takes occasion to blame the exactness of those masters, who oblige children to too scrupulous a knowledge of these nouns) we shall reserve them for a separate rule at the end of the genders, and we shall likewise speak particularly of them in the first chapter of the remarks which follow the syntax.

Whence the necessity arises of being acquainted with the genders.

Now the necessity of being acquainted with the genders arises from this only, that the adjectives have frequently different terminations, one for one gender, and another for another. For if all the adjectives had only one termination in each case, the knowledge of the genders would be of no manner of use, because this termination would agree with all the genders: for which reason we must take notice of the different sorts of adjectives.

RULE II.
Of Adjectives.

Adjectives admit of three genders, the difference of which is known by the change of their termination.

EXAMPLES.

Under the word adjective, we comprehend the noun, the pronoun, and the participle.

Now, there are three sorts of adjectives; some that have only one termination, which is joined to all genders, as *hic* & *hæc* & *hoc felix*, happy. *Hic* & *hæc* & *hoc amans*, loving. Though even these change their termination as well in the accusative singular, as in the nomina-

nominative and accusative plural, thus *felicem* or *felices*, for the masculine and feminine: *felix* & *felicia* for the neuter.

Others have two terminations: the first for the masculine and feminine, and the second for the neuter; as *hic* & *hæc omnis*, & *hoc omne*, all. Or the first for the masculine, and the second for the feminine and neuter, as *hic victor*; *hæc* & *hoc victrix*, victorious.

Others in fine have three terminations for the three genders; as *bonus*, good, for the masculine; *bona*, good, for the feminine; and *bonum*, good, for the neuter. *Niger, nigra, nigrum*, black. *Uber, úbera, úberum*, fruitful. *Ille, illa, illud*, he, she, it, &c.

ANNOTATION.

Grammarians call the gender of adjectives, *omne*, the whole. But not to mention that they ought rather to have called it *commune omnibus*, as Quintilian expresses himself: Sanctius, and after him Vossius have sufficiently proved, that strictly speaking, adjectives have no genders, but only an aptitude, and sometimes different terminations, to join in construction with different genders. And the reason is because an adjective cannot stand by itself in discourse, just as an accident cannot subsist without a substance: so that when I say, *bonus, bona*, good, &c. this expresses as yet no meaning, and of course does not properly specify any gender, but only shews that we ought to give this adjective one of these two terminations, according to the gender of the noun to which it may be joined; *bonus rex*, a good king; *bona regina*, a good queen, &c.

Of adjectives taken substantively, or which stand by themselves in discourse.

This does not hinder an adjective from being oftentimes found alone in discourse; but then it is either because custom has made a substantive of the adjective, as *patria*, country, which was once the adjective of *terra*; or what is indeed more usual, the substantive is understood, and thus as the adjective supposeth and is relative to that substantive, consequently it assumes its gender.

This remark is of great importance for regulating a considerable number of nouns by this single maxim. For it is by this that we know for example that the following are

MASCULINE.

Annuláris, auriculáris; index; *sup. Digitus.*
Mortális, *Homo*. Maiális, nefrens; *Porcus.*
Maxilláris, *Dens.* Moláris, *Dens* or *lapis.*
Mártius, Aprílis, Quintílis, Septémber, &c. *Mensis.*
Oriens, óccidens, *sup. Sol.*
Prófluens, cónfluens, torrens; *Amnis* or *flúvius.*

FEMININE.

OF GENDERS.

FEMININE.
A'rida, cóntinens, erémus ; *Terra.* Frígida ; *Aqua.*
Bipénnis ; *secúris.* Bidens ; *secúris,* or *ovis.*
Curúlis ; *sella.* Cónsonans *or* vocális ; *Líttera.*
Dipthóngus ; *syllaba.* Prægnans ; *Múlier.*
Tertiána, quartána ; *febris.*

NEUTER.
Altum or *profúndum,* sup. *Mare.*
Præsens, sup. *Tempus.*
Suburbánum ; *Rus* or *prædium,* &c.

In like manner as often as the adjective is in the neuter gender, and there is no particular substantive expressed or understood, we should refer it to *Negotium,* thing or affair: as, *Triste lupus stábulis,* that is, *Negótium triste,* it is a vexatious thing. Thus when we say, *Accidens, Antecedens, Cónsequens,* &c. we are always to understand *negótium,* which is a word of as extensive a signification as that of *Res* itself, by which the grammarians explain all those neuter words, seeking for another turn of expression in the feminine. But of this we shall take farther notice in the syntax and in the remarks on the figure of ellipsis.

We must now come to another maxim which is not less general than the foregoing for the knowledge of genders.

RULE III.

That the gender of the termination is frequently changed into that of the signification, or vice versâ.

1. *The common word oftentimes regulates the gender of those nouns which it includes.*
2. *Or else the signification gives way to the termination.*

EXAMPLES.

1. The common and general word frequently regulates the gender of all the other nouns comprehended under it. This will manifestly appear in the four following rules, of which this ought to be considered as the basis. Besides, there are a great many other nouns which ought to be referred to this rule. For

It is by this rule that pieces of poetry are oftentimes in the feminine, by understanding *fábula* or *poésis.* *In Eunúchum suam.* Ter. in his comedy of the Eunuch. It is true these nouns are sometimes put in the masculine gender, by giving the name of the principal character to the piece ; thus Suetonius says *Ajácem suum,* his Ajax. And Juvenal, *necdum finitus Oréstes,* Orestes is not yet finished. Just as the French say, *le Cid, le Cinna,* &c.

It is by the same rule that the names of letters are sometimes feminine, by referring them to *littera*; *A longa, E brevis*; A long, E short, &c. though it is more usual to put them in the neuter gender, as we shall hereafter more particularly observe in the rule of indeclinable nouns.

It is also by this same rule that the names of precious stones are sometimes masculine, when they refer to *lapillus*; and sometimes feminine, when they refer to *gemma*; as *hic achátes*, an agate. *Hæc sapphirus*, a saphir, &c. See the annotation on the rule of the nouns in *us*.

The names of specific numbers terminated in *io* are masculine, because they suppose *Númerus*; as *hic únio*, a unite; *hic térnio*, the number three; *hic sénio*, the sixth point.

ANNOTATION.

In a word, whenever you are in any doubt concerning the gender of a noun, the most general rule that can be given, is to consider the nature of the thing it signifies, and under what general word it may be comprized. This holds good even in French, for if we say, for instance, *la Seine*, we understand, *la riviere, Sequana*: and if we say, *le Rhone*, we understand, *le fleuve, Rhodanus*.

By the same principle we must regulate the gender of diminutives, which they generally borrow of their primitive.

Insomuch that we may often draw an inference from the gender of the diminutive to the gender of the primitive with which we are not so well acquainted, as Quintilian has observed. For instance, we may judge that *ensis* is of the masculine gender, because from thence is formed *ensículus*; and in like manner *funis*, because it forms *funículus*; it being very probable that if *funis* or *ensis* had been of the feminine gender, they would rather have said *funícula*, and *ensícula*, which I believe are not to be found in any writer, though Priscian wanted to establish the last without any authority.

This rule, indeed, is not infallible, yet it may be of great service; and we must particularly observe that those who reject it in conjunction with L. Valla, frequently mistake that for a diminutive which is not so; or even are oftentimes deceived by deriving from one word, what comes rather from another. See Vossius 2. *de Anal. cap.* 29. and Sanctius 1. *de causis ling. Lat. cap.* 10.

2. Now tho' the common word, or the general signification, usually regulates the gender of those nouns which

OF GENDERS.

which are comprehended under it; yet it sometimes quits its gender to assume that of the termination. This we shall shew in the following rules, as also in these nouns.

O'peræ, árum, always feminine, though it signifies workmen, artists, people daily hired, and at our disposal and command. *O'peræ Clodiánæ*, Cic. Clodius's attendants.

Custódiæ, guards or soldiers. *Vigíliæ*, *Excúbiæ*, centinels, always feminine. *Ad continéndas custódias meas*, Trajan. ad Plin. epist. 233. to watch and guard the prisoners.

Mancípium, always neuter, though it is said of a man, or woman.

Scortum, a whore, a courtesan: *Prostíbulum*, a prostitute: always neuter.

ANNOTATION.

The reason of this is because these words always retain something of their proper and natural signification. For in regard to the first, they seem originally to signify not so much the man as the employment, the action or circumstances of the man, for which reason they could not retain the gender of the termination.

Not but we sometimes observe that these very nouns follow the gender of the person. For as the French say *Un trompette*; to express a man; and not *une trompette*; *un garde*, to signify a soldier, and not *une garde*, which signifies a nurse: Thus we find that the Latins put *optio* in the masculine, when it is taken for an officer or agent appointed by the captain, according to Festus; or for a body of reserve, according to Varro; or for the master of the arsenal, in the civil law; or for a goal keeper, in S. Ambrose: and in the like manner the Greeks have their κουροπαλάτης of the masculine. But instead of this noun we find in the civil law and elsewhere, *curam palatii*, which Vossius thinks ought to be always taken in the feminine, though it is understood of the person that has the care.

With respect to the other nouns abovementioned, it is very certain that *Scortum*, properly speaking signifies no more than a skin, which is the reason that Tertull. in his book *de Pall.* speaking of the lion's skin with which Hercules was clad, calls it *Scortum Herculis*, so that this name must have been given to a harlot only out of derision and in a metaphorical sense. The same may be said of *Prostibulum*, which properly signifies the place before the door, *quasi* PRO sive ANTE STABULUM, which was one of the most usual places where this sort of women used to expose themselves.

Hereby

Hereby we see that the appellative nouns, that is, which agree only with man or woman in general, do not always vary the gender of their termination. Hence even in Greek we say τὸ γυναικίδιον, *muliercula*, τὸ ἀδελφάσιον, *sorercula*, τὸ κόριον, κορίδιον, κορίσκιον, & κοράσιον, *puella*, and others of the like nature; and in the same manner in Latin, *meum suavium, meum corculum*, Plaut. But if these become proper names, then they change their gender; and we must say, *mea suavium*, which is the same as γλυκήριον, since Terence has *mea Glycerium*.

If it should be objected here, that the names of goddesses sometimes happen to be in the masculine; you may see what answer we have given in the annotation to the first rule.

It is the same thing in regard to the names of men, which becoming proper, constantly follow the gender of their signification. Hence if we were speaking of *Majoregius*, whose parents gave him the name of *Maria* in honour of the virgin, there is no manner of doubt but we should say *Doctam & facundum Mariam*, as Vossius very justly observes. And it is a great mistake in Priscian, lib. xii. to say that the names of men or women in *um* were of the neuter gender: for the contrary appears in *mea Glycerium*, which I just now quoted from Terence: besides, *Dinacium & Pegnium*, names of men in Plautus are always masculine; and there is a much greater number of names of women than men of this termination, in the same author and others, which are always feminine. Hence we find in the fathers: *Eustochium, Sophronium, Melanium, Albinum*, and the like names of women. For want of rightly considering this, several passages have been corrupted.

It seems that S. Augustin has made use of *Albinus*, to express Albina daughter-in-law of Melania the grandmother, widow of her only son, and mother of young Melania married to Plinian. For he not only hath *ad Albinum, Pinianum, & Melanium*; in the title of the 227th letter which is written to them: but moreover in the book concerning the grace of Jesus Christ and original sin which he addresses to them, he says, *Dilecti Deo, Albine, Piniane, & Melania*, where he mentions Albina first, as the mother, and makes the reference to the masculine, because of Pinian, as to the noblest gender. And in like manner in this very place he employs the word *fratres*, though there are two women; as in the city of God he calls a brother and sister, *ambos fratres*.

But we are furnished from ancient inscriptions with several other examples of the names of men being given to women, as *Ramus Ursula*: and of the names of women being given to men, as *Vectius Elpis, Laufeius Apotheca*, &c. And to consider the thing exactly, all the names of men in A, as *Sylla, Perpenna, Lecca, Catilina*, are nouns feminine by their termination, as Sanctius observes after Quintilian, and also Varro in the 8th of LL. which are become masculine, only by being attributed to particular men. Just as the names of women become properly feminine, when they are given to women; nothing more exactly determining the gender, than the

OF GENDERS.

the distinction of the two sexes. Wherefore in these there is strictly speaking no figure, and there is no occasion to have recourse to the common word in the following rules.

RULE IV.

Of *As* with its compounds and derivatives.

1. As, Assis, *is of the masculine gender.*
2. *And so are all its compounds and derivatives.*
3. *Except* U'ncia.

EXAMPLES.

1. The noun *As, ássis,* with all its compounds and derivatives, is of the masculine gender. This word signifies an ancient coin, which may be valued at three farthings English money. It is also taken for a pound of twelve ounces, and for every thing consisting of twelve equal parts.

2. Its compounds are, such as *decússis,* a coin of ten *asses, Centússis,* a coin of one hundred *asses,* and the like.

Its derivatives or parts are such, as *Semíssis,* half an *as: Quincunx,* five ounces; *Sextans,* the sixth part of an *as,* &c.

3. We must except *U'ncia,* an ounce, which is always of the feminine gender.

ANNOTATION.

The reason why *As* and all its compounds and derivatives are of the masculine gender, must be taken from the common and general noun, considering them as a kind of coin that refer to *Numus.* For though the word was so called *quasi æs,* according to the testimony of Varro, because in early times it was no more than a bit of brass which was paid in weight; yet it was even then called *Numus,* a word derived from νόμος, *lex*; because money was introduced by law, in order to be the tie as it were and common measure of traffic.

But *úncia* continued in the feminine, because it is derived *ab una* (sup. *parte*) *quasi unica.* So that

12   NEW METHOD.   Book I.

12.	Ounces made the *As*, called also *Libra*.	The whole, to be divided by twelve.
11.	The *Deunx*, so called because *deest uncia*.	Eleven twelfths.
10.	*Decunx*, as much as to say *decem unciæ*, or *dextans*, because *deest sextans*.	Ten twelfths, or Five sixths.
9.	*Dodrans*, for *dedrans*, because *deest quadrans*.	Nine twelfths, or three fourths.
8.	*Bes* or *Bessis* for *Des*, because *triens deest*, according to Varro.	Eight twelfths, or two thirds.
7.	*Septunx*, as if it were *septem unciæ*.	Seven twelfths.
6.	*Semissis*, as if it were *Semiassis*.	Half a pound, or one half.
5.	*Quincunx*, as if it were *quinque unciæ*.	Five twelfths.
4.	*Triens*, that is, the third part of the *As*.	One third.
3.	*Quadrans*, that is, the fourth part of the *As*.	One fourth.
2.	*Sextans*, that is, the sixth part.	One sixth.
1½	*Sescunx*, that is, *sesquiuncia*, an ounce and a half.	One eighth.
1.	*Uncia* (quasi unica) an ounce.	One twelfth.

Which agree with the pound or the whole in this proportion.

Rule V.

Of the names of winds, rivers, and mountains.

1. *The names of winds are always masculine.*
2. *As are frequently those of rivers,*
3. *And mountains.*

Examples.

1. The names of winds are always of the masculine gender, as *Eurus*, the East wind; *Zéphyrus*, the West wind; *Auster*, the South wind; *Bóreas* or *A'quilo*, the North wind; *Etésiæ*, the West winds that constantly blow at a certain season of the year.

2. The names of rivers and mountains are also frequently masculine. Of rivers, as *hic Euphrátes*, *hic Tigris*, the Euphrates, and the Tigris, rivers of Armenia: *Hic Ganges*, the Ganges, a river of India: *Hic Matróna*, the Marne: *Hic Séquana*, the Seine.

3. Those

3. Those of mounts or mountains, *hic Eryx*, a mountain in Sicily: *Hic Othryx*, mount Othryx: *Hic Ossa*, Ovid. mount Ossa.

ANNOTATION.

The reason of this rule is likewise taken from the common and general nouns, and it always holds good in the names of winds, whether in Greek, or in Latin, because they refer to ἄνεμος, or *ventus*, wind.

Nor does it make against the rule, that *Lailaps* is feminine: because this noun which is entirely Greek, does not denote a particular wind, but signifies a whirlwind or tempest.

But it is observable in regard to the names of winds, that some of them are substantives, as *Auster*, *Boreas*, &c. and others adjectives, as *Africus*, *Subsolanus*, and perhaps *Iapyx*, which has been used for *Iapygius*, from the word *Iapygia*, which signified the province of Apulia, from whence this wind blowed towards Greece.

In like manner also *Tropæi*, in Greek τροπαῖοι. *Videmus*, says Pliny, *è terra consurgere ventos, qui quidem, cum è mari redeunt Tropæi vocantur; si pergunt, Apogæi*. Whereas Aristotle calls them τροπαῖαι, from the singular τροπαία, which we find in Plut. in Otho. Where it is obvious that in the masculine is understood ἄνεμος, and in the feminine πνοή.

Thus *Etesiæ* & *Ornithiæ* are always masculine when taken substantively, because in Greek they are of the first declension of simples, which are all masculine: hence it is that Pliny uses *Etesias* in the singular, and not *Etesia*. For the same reason Cicero always uses the masculine gender; *Navigatio quæ incurrebat in ipsos Etesias*. In like manner Aristotle, οἱ ἐτήσιαι.

But if they are taken adjectively, then we may say οἱ ἐτήσιαι, sup. ἄνεμοι: & αἱ ἐτήσιαι, sup. πνοαί, as in Apollon. ἐτήσιαι αὖραι. In like manner in Lucretius;

—— *Etesia flabra Aquilonum.*

With regard to the names of rivers and mountains, the rule cannot be general, for which reason we said frequently, because these nouns follow the rule of the termination as much as that of the signification, as may be seen in the following list.

List of the names of rivers and mountains.

Names of rivers.

ALLIA, a river in Italy, is always feminine, according to the termination: Lucan.
Et damneta diu Romanis Allia fastis.
And Vossius thinks it would be a solecism to say, *damnatus Allia*.

Thus *Durantia, Garumna, Matrona, Mosella*, and others, are feminine in Ausonius: and Vossius says they ought always to be so in prose; tho' in verse Tibullus says, *Magnusque Garumna*. And Claudian, *Formosus Duria*. And Ausonius himself, *Celebrande Mosella*.

ACHERON or ACHERONS; which Nonnius calls doubtful, is always masculine, when it signifies a river, Virg.

——— *Acheronte refuso:*

And feminine when it is taken for a part or quarter of hell. *Nulla Acherontis rons.* Plaut. as we still say, *Acheronte,* or *Acheronti aliquid fieri;* to signify in hell.

JADER, neuter. *Tepidum Jader.* Lucan.

NAR. *Lacus Velinus in Nar defluit,* Cic. whereas Tacitus taking it in the masculine, says *Narem,* and so do a great many others. For which reason Cluverius in his division of ancient Italy thinks that this passage of Cicero is corrupted. But Vossius defends it by the authority of almost all manuscript and printed copies, and says that the authority of Cicero is preferable to that of Tacitus and all the rest. And as to Virgil, when he says:

——— *audiit amnis*
Sulphureâ Nar albus aquâ;

it is evident that *albus* may be referred to *amnis,* which goes before; or if it refers to *Nar,* this must be done by a syllepsis, apprehending it under the general word *river.*

XANTHUS. There is no manner of doubt, but it is always masculine, when taken for the river of Troy, or even for that of Lycia, which falling down from mount Cadmus watered a city of the same name. So that when Virg. in *Culice* says

Alma Chimæreo Xanthus perfusa liquore; it is more likely, that he meant this city which is mentioned by all ancient geographers and historians, Herodotus, Dion, Pliny, Strabo, Ptolemæus, and others, than as some commentators pretend, that this is the name of the river, which he took in the feminine.

Names of Mountains.

These likewise most commonly follow the gender of the termination. For if OSSA is masculine in Ovid, it is feminine in Lucan. And if OETA is masculine in Seneca, it is feminine in Ovid an *Claud. and both are feminine in Statius.

OTHRYX is masculine in Lucan and in Statius, and feminine in Greek. τῆς ὀφρύος ὄρος, Strabo.

ÆTHNA is always feminine.
And so is IDA in Virg.

Most of the others follow the gender of the termination, according to our third rule.

RULE VI.
Of the names of towns, provinces, ships, and islands.

The names of towns, provinces, ships, and islands, are generally of the feminine gender.

EXAMPLES.

This rule includes four sorts of nouns, which are generally feminine, because of the common and general word, to which they refer.

1. The names of towns, referring them to *urbs,* are feminine, as *Lutétia,* Paris; *Neápolis,* Naples; *hæc Coríntbus,* Corinth.

2. The names of provinces, referring them to *régio,* or *província,* or even *terra,* are feminine, as *Gállia,* Gaul or France; *Ægýptus fertilíssima,* Egypt the most fruitful.

3. The names of ships, referring them to their common word *navis,* are feminine, as *Centaúrus magna,* Virg. the great ship called Centaur. *Hæc Argo,* the first ship, according to the accounts of the poets, in which Jason sailed to Colchos for the golden fleece.

4. The

OF GENDERS.

4. The names of islands, following their common name *Insula*, are feminine, as *Hæc Delos*, the isle of Delos; *hæc Cyprus*, the isle of Cyprus.

ANNOTATION.

So true is it that the common and general word regulates the gender of all these sorts of nouns, that it is even a mistake to make the rule absolute, and to pretend, as most of the grammarians do, that these nouns, some few excepted, are of themselves feminine. This may be easily seen only by reading the lists here subjoined.

List of the names of towns.

Of those which end in vowels.

In A, as *Roma, Ardea, Larissa*; they are feminine, by the rule of the termination. See lower down rule 10.

And in like manner *Italia, Gallia, Judæa,* which have moreover this particular, that of their own nature they are properly adjectives. For which reason Cæsar says, *ex usu terræ Galliæ*; and Livy, *extra terram Italiam*; and Plautus, *Arabia terra*: and hence *Judæus* is used also in the masculine, as we say *Judæa* (sup. *terra*) in the feminine.

Nouns of the first declension in E, are also feminine, by the same rule, as *hæc Mitylene, es; Helice, es.*

In Æ diphthong are also feminine, by the 9th rule, as *Athenæ, Mycenæ.*

In A plural, are neuter, by the same rule, as *Bactra, Ecbatana.*

In A or in E singular of the third declension, are neuter by the 10th rule, as *Zeugma, Reate, Præneste. Altum Præneste,* Virg. *Frigidum Præneste,* Horat. And when we find in Virg. *Præneste sub ipsa,* this is only a syllepsis, referring it to *urbs,* as Saturninus and Vossius pretend. Or rather it is because formerly they used *hæc Prænestis,* and *hoc Præneste,* pursuant to the observation of Servius. But we also meet with Πραίνεςος, *Prænestus,* in Stephan. τὸ Πραίνεςον, *Prænestum,* in Ptolemy.

In I or in Y in the singular, are neuter, as *Moly,* by the 8th rule, because they are indeclinable, as *Illiturgi, Aixi, Æpy.*

In the plural they are masculine, by the 9th rule, as *Delphi, Parisii, Philippi.*

In O, they are masculine, by the 11th rule, as *hic Sulmo,* Ovid's country; *hic Narbo,* Narbonne. *Est in eadem provincia Narbo Marcius,* Cic. Hence we must refer to the figure of syllepsis that expression of Martial, *pulcherrima Narbo*; as also that of Catullus, *Venusta Sirmio.*

We see by this why Hippo is sometimes masculine because of the termination, and sometimes feminine because of the common word, and by a figure. *Vaga Hippo,* Silius Ital. *Hippo Regius,* Solin. *Dilutus,* Plin. ἐντάυϑα οἱ δύο Ἱππῶνες, ὁ μὲν πλησίον Ἰτύκης, ὁ δὲ ἀπωτέρω πρὸς τῇ Τριτῇ μᾶλλον ἄμφω βασίλεια (sup. ἄςη) Strabo lib. xvii. *Duo hic Hippones, alter Uticæ proximus, alter remotior, & Trito propinquior, ambæ regiæ,* (sup. *urbes.*)

Of those which end in consonants.

Of these there are five sorts according to the final consonants L, M, N, R, S, to which we might join T.

In L, they are neuter, according to the termination, as HISPAL. *Celebre Oceano Hispal,* Silius. Though this noun is formed by syncope from Hispalis, which we read in Pliny, and which by its termination is feminine.

SUTHUL. *Ad oppidam Suthul pervenit* Sal. He does not say *Sutulum,* as without doubt he would have said, if what Priscian advances had been true, viz. that this and other like Carthaginian nouns could not be neuter, because those people, as well as the Hebrews from whom they were descended, had no neuter gender. Nor is it true that Sallust took it for an indeclinable, since after that he says, *relicto Sutbulo.*

In UM or in *n* short are neuter, as *Lugdunum*. Hence it is by a figure that Sidon. Apoll. said *Lugdunúmque tuam*, referring it to *urbs*. And in vain, says Vossius, have some endeavoured to infer from thence that *Lugdunus* might be said as well as *Lugdunum*.

True it is that there are some others, which have two terminations, as *Epidaurus* and *Epidaurum*, the former masc. in Hom.

——— Αμπελόεντ' Ἐπίδαυρον.
——— *Vitibus consitum Epidaurum.*
And feminine in Strabo. ἡ Ἐπίδαυρος. The other is neuter, *Epidaurum celebre*, Plin.

Ilios, & *Ilion* ——— *Ceciditque superbum.*
Ilium ——Virg.—— *Ilios diijecta.* Ovid.

Saguntus & *Saguntum*, the latter always neuter, and the former always feminine.

Thus *Colchos*, which some moderns make use of, ought according to Vossius to be always feminine, like *Ilios*, *Saguntos*, and others. But this word was always taken by the ancients for the people. *Colchus an Assyrius*, Hor. *Auratus aries Colchorum.* Cic. *Cum Colchos peterent.* Mela. ἢ τοὺς Κόλκους αἶδως, Strabo, *Cum Colchos nosset.* Hence Pontanus was doubly mistaken in saying, *Ditatum vellere Colchos.* In the first place a word which signifies the people only, he mistook for the town or country: secondly he put this word in the neuter gender without any authority, when he ought rather to have put it in the feminine, according to the analogy of the other nouns of the same termination. But *Colchis, idis*, is the proper name of the country. And if any one should chuse to make use of the other noun, it should be at least in the plural number and in the masculine gender, according to the remark we shall make in the ninth rule.

In ΩΝ, they vary among the Greeks. For as we find, ἡ Βαβυλὼν, ἡ Λακεδαίμων, ἡ Καλχηδών; so we meet in Strabo with, ὁ Μαραθών, ὁ Μιδεών, ὁ Σούκρων. But in Latin, most writers put them in the feminine because of the common word. *Dorica Ancon*, Juv. *Regia Pleuron*, Silius. *Alta Croton.* Id.

In R, Vossius looks upon them as neuter; since there are names of this gender in this termination. Thus

Tuder, *Tudi*, a city of Umbria, is neuter, *Summum Tuder*, Silius.

Gadir, is neuter, *Tartessum His-paniae civitatem, quam nunc Tyrii mutato nomine Gadir habent*, Sal. For if he had not taken it in the neuter gender, he would have said *Gadirem*. And yet Avienus has made it feminine. *Gadir inserta columnis*, which he refers to *urbs*.

Tibur, *Tivoli*, always neuter, *Hinc Tibur Cabille tuum.* Sil.
——— *Tibúrque tuum.* Virg.

But as the nouns in UR are not so far neuter, but there are some of them masculine; so *Anxur* is either neuter or masculine, and never feminine. *Ad Anxur oppugnandum*, Liv. *Impositum saxis candentibus Anxur*, Hor.

Candidus Anxur aquis, Mart.

Of those in S.

Agragas is a city which the Latins called *Agrigentum*, according to Pliny. This noun is fem. in Strabo. Ακράγας δὲ ἰόντων οὖσα, according to the common word. In other writers it is masc. as in Laert. in the life of Empedocles, τὸν μέγαν Ἀκράγαντα, and in Virg.

Arduus inde Agragas ostentat maxima longè

Mœnia ——— Æn. 3.

Which Servius explaining says, *Mons est muro cinctus, in cujus summa parte oppidum est.* In which he is censured by Vossius, who says that there is no mention made of this mountain by the ancients, Ptolemy, Strabo, and others. But laying Servius aside, Virgil surely was not so unacquainted with geography, and especially with that of a neighbouring country, as to represent *Agragas* in so high a situation, if it did not stand upon a mountain. Besides we learn from Polybius book ix. that this city was seated on the top of a mount or a rock: κεῖται γὰρ τὸ τεῖχος ἐπὶ πέτρας ἀκροτόμου ἢ περιῤῥῶγος; that it was as strong by its situation, as by its fortifications, and that towards the south there was a river of the same name. And therefore *Agragas* must have remained masc. either because it comprehends not only the town, but the whole mountain, or because it likewise signifies the river, from which the town itself derived its name, according to Thucydides, book vi. Or in fine because nouns in AS which make the genitive in *antis*, are masculine, as we shall shew hereafter. And Vossius himself admits of these two last reasons.

By

OF GENDERS.

By the same analogy, we find in Strabo, ὁ Δωρίς, a city of Doris, ὁ Τάρας, Tarentum; and hence Lucan says lib. v.

Antiquusque Taras. ————

ARGOS is neuter by its termination, because in Greek it is of the first declension of contracts, in which all the nouns in ος are neuter, as τὸ τεῖχος. *Aptum equis Argos,* Hor.

US or OS of the third declension of simples in Greek, cannot be easily known by the termination, because it varies, for as we say, ὁ λόγος, *sermo,* so we say also, ἡ ὁδός, *via;* and as we say, *hic fructus,* fruit, we likewise say *hæc manus,* a hand. The surest way therefore is to put them then in the feminine, unless you have some authority to the contrary; because the termination does not oppose it, and they are favoured by the signification.

Thus we say ἡ Νίνος, *Ninus,* Nineve: ἡ Τύρος, *Tyrus,* Tyre; ἡ Ἔφεσος, *Ephesus;* ἡ Μίλητος, *Miletus;* ἡ Ῥόδος, *Rhodus,* Rhodes; and a great many others.

But we meet with Σηςος masculine in Steph. and in Eustath. and on the contrary we find it feminine in Ovid.

Vel tua me Sestos, vel te mea sumat Abydos.

This poet seems also to have made Lesbos masculine.

Et Methymnæi potiuntur littore Lesbi. xi. Met. f. 1.

Which is confirmed by Despauter, though he reads *Metylinæi.* It is true that Aldus and some others read *Metymnææ,* but the ancients read it in the masc.

Some have pretended also to say that this noun is neuter, and that it comes from *Lesbon,* but without authority.

As for *Abydus,* we meet with it in Strabo, and in Dionysius.

Σηςος ὑπὸ καὶ Ἀβυδος ἐναντίον ὅρμον ἔθεντο.

Sestus ubi & Abydus ex adverso stationem posuere.

Others have pretended to say, that *Abydon* is also used in the neuter, because Virgil has,

———— *Ostriferi fauces tentantur Abydi.*

For otherwise, as they will have it, he would have said, *Ostriferæ.* But if we say *Abydon,* it is a city of Italy, as Euthathius and Stephanus observe, and not the town opposite to *Sestus;* and therefore Virgil must either have neglected this difference, or have made it masculine because of the termination in *us,* though Val. Flaccus put it in the feminine.

Cœperat à gemina discedere Sestos Abyde.

We meet with Ἀλίαρτος, *Haliartus,* masc. in Hom. but in Strabo, it is masc. and fem.

Μύρσινος is fem. in Hom. πύργος, masc.

Πληθος is masculine and feminine in Strabo.

CORINTHUS is always fem. in Latin and even in Greek, τὴν Κόρινθον, says Strabo: except perhaps its appearing masculine in this passage of Homer

———— Ἄφνειον τε Κόρινθον.

———— *Opulentamque Corinthum.*

But in Latin we never meet with it in this gender; though Scioppius pretends otherwise. For in Velleius Paterculus lib. i. where he says, *Corinthum qui antea fuerat Ephyre,* we ought to read *quæ* in the feminine, as Vossius proves from all the ancient copies, and best printed editions.

And with regard to the passage of Propertius,

Nec miser æra paro, clade, Corinthe, tua; it is obvious that *miser* relates to the poet himself, *Ego miser,* and not to the city.

CORIOLAUS is perhaps masculine in Florus lib. i. *Coriolaus victus adeo gloriæ fuit,* &c. according to the reading in the first edition of it, and in the ancient manuscripts, as Vinetus and Vossius inform us. Hence Beroaldus is found fault with for making his correction, *Coriolaos victos adeo gloriæ fuisse.*

PONTUS is always masculine according to the termination, not only when it signifies the sea, but likewise the kingdom of Pontus. *Ex eodem Ponto Medea profugisse dicitur.* Cic. and the same among the Greeks, Strabo, Stephanus, Ptolemy, &c.

Those in *us* coming from ους ῦς, by contraction, are also masculine, as *Daphnus,* Steph. *Pessinus, untis,* Cic. *Pessinuntem ipsum vastaris,* de Arusp. resp. And the same of *Amathus, Trapezus, Opus, Hydrus, Phlius,* and others. It is true Ovid says in the fem.

———— *gravidamque Amathunta metallis;* but he could never have said it without referring it to *urbs,* because these nouns come from the Greek termination ους, masc. the feminine of which would be in Α: ουσα.

For this reason Cerasus, a city of Pontus, is also masculine by its termination, Κερασῦς, for Κερασόεις. And this city is so called, according to Vossius, from the number of cherry trees with which it abounds; and not the cherry trees from the town, as St. Jerome writing to Eustochia, and several others imagined, because we find that Lucullus having defeated Mithridates, was the first who transplanted cherry trees from that province into Italy. But not to mention its being very certain, that the word cherries was known long enough before, as appears from Theophrastus, and from what even Athenæus mentions of Diphilus who lived a little after the reign of Alexander; we find by a great many other examples that places are oftener denominated from the natural products of the earth, than these from the buildings or towns erected on the spot. Thus Σελινῦς, so called because of the parsley that grew there; Ραμνῦς, because of the brambles, &c.

So that if Ραμνῦς comes from Ραμνόεις, it must needs be masculine. And if Mela puts it in the feminine, *Rhamnus parva, illustris tamen*, this must be a figure, or perhaps the passage is corrupted.

YS is feminine in the names of towns, as also in other nouns of the like termination, as *Chelys*, *Chlamys*, &c. For which reason *Gortys*, Γόρτυς, is feminine in Homer.

T, *Nepet* (a town of Tuscany, now called *Nepi*) is neuter, either because of the termination T, or because it is only a syncope for *Nepete*, instead of which we meet also with *Nepe* in Velleius, and in the ancient itinerary; as also with Νέπιτα in Ptolemy, and with Νέπιτα in Strabo.

Whence comes it that these general words, urbs, civitas, terra, *are feminine.*

The above is what I had to offer most worthy of notice concerning these nouns. But if I should be further asked why these general words, such as *urbs, civitas, terra*, have followed the feminine gender and termination, it is plain they have been considered as good mothers in respect to their inhabitants: hence it is that they were usually represented in the figure of women, as appears from the book of the Roman provinces. Thus Jerusalem is called the *daughter of Sion* in the holy scripture; and Tertullian calls Utica the sister of Carthage: *sic & in proximo soror civitas vestiebat*, lib. de pall. for *vestiebat se*.

It is for this same reason that TELLUS, which signifies either the globe of the earth, or its respective parts, has been also considered as a noun feminine. The Romans and even the Greeks made a goddess of it, and we find that in Livy lib. 8. it is called *Alma mater*.

Of the names of trees, and why arbor *is feminine.*

And this same reason holds good in regard to the names of trees comprized in the following rule. For tho' the termination OR or OS be masculine among the Latins, yet they have made *arbor* or *arbos* feminine, having considered it as a mother, either because of its fruit, as we see in Ovid.

Pomáque læsissent matrem, nisi subdita ramo
    Longa laboranti furca tulisset opem. De Nuce.

Or because of its branches, as we read in Virgil,

Hic plantas tenero abscindens de corpore matrum
Depostuit sulcis. 2. Georg.

OF GENDERS.

Or because of the little shoots at the feet of it, as in the same poet.

——— *Parnassia laurus*
Parva sub ingenti matris se subjicit umbra. Ibid.

In which respect the Latins act more reasonably than the Greeks, who have made their τὸ δἰνδρος or δἰνδρον neuter, but these have been obliged to depart from this gender, in order to give to most species of trees a termination that either was or might be feminine, as well as that of the Latins. But in French, as the word *arbre* is masculine, almost all its species have followed the gender.

RULE VII.

Of the names of trees.

1. *The names of trees are feminine.*
2. *But those in* STER *are masculine;*
3. *As also* spinus *and* dumus.
4. *We say* hic *and sometimes* hæc rubus.
5. Robur *and* acer *are neuter.*
6. *As also those in* UM, *with* siler, *and* suber.

EXAMPLES.

1. The names of trees are feminine in Latin, for the reason above hinted at; as *pinus alta*, a tall pine-tree. *Quercus magna*, a large oak. *Ulmus annósa*, an old elm-tree. *Infáusta cupréssus*, an unlucky cypress-tree. *Plátanus Cæsariána*, Mart. Cæsar's plane tree. *Hæc pomus*, or *malus* an apple-tree. (But *malus* signifying the mast of a ship is masculine) *hæc pirus*, a pear-tree.

2. Those in STER are masculine, as *Oleáster*, a wild olive-tree; *pináster*, a wild pine-tree; *piráster*, a wild pear-tree.

3. These two are also masculine; *hic spinus*, Serv. a sloe-tree; *hic dumus*, Ovid, a bush.

4. *Rubus* is doubtful, but better in the masculine. *Asper rubus*, Virg. a rough ramble. *Rubus contórta*, Prud. a crooked thorn.

5. These are neuter, *hoc robur, rŏboris*, heart of oak; it is also taken for strength and courage: *hoc acer, ăceris*, a maple-tree: *siler molle*, Virg. the soft osier: *suber silvéstre*, the wild cork-tree.

6. And

6. And in like manner all those in *um*. *Hoc buxum*, box wood: *hoc ebenum*, ebony: *hoc balsamum*, balm: *ligustrum*, privet.

ANNOTATION.

As a great many names of trees were masculine among the Greeks, the same sometimes also happens among the Latins, whether the latter have done it to imitate the former, or whether they have had a regard to the termination.

Thus Ennius has *rectosque cupressos*: Pliny, *folia eorum*, speaking of plane trees. Priscian says the same of the latter, and also of *populus*. And Catullus chose rather to say *ulmus maritus* than *marita*, which we meet with in Pliny and in Colum. This Vossius does not think so natural, because the word *husband* seems to be reserved for the masculine. But it is a noun adjective, for in Colum. we meet with *Olivetum maritum*; and in Livy with *domos maritas vagari*, and in Ovid, with *castæ maritæ, stultæ maritæ*, speaking of married women.

In the vulgate we read, *quasi libanus non incisus*; though Pindar and Euripides read, ἡ λίβανος. It seems also that the Latins have avoided making use of this word. Virgil calls it *thuream virgam*: Colum. *thuream plantam*: Pliny, *arborem thuriferam*, as H. Stephen observes in his Thesaurus, on the word λίβανος. But *thus* which he says he never found to signify a tree, occurs frequently in Pliny; *lignum thuris, virgas thuris*; and very often *thuris arbor*, to remove all ambiguity, though we do not find of what gender the ancients made it in this sense; so that Despauter has no foundation for putting it among the names of trees of the neuter gender, which Verepeus would not do, no more than Vossius.

Spinus is masculine according to Priscian, and there is no doubt but he found it so among the ancients; but because he gives no authority for it, Vossius thinks he has reason to suspend his assent. And yet besides the authority of this learned grammarian Servius on this passage of the 4th Georg.

——— *& spinos jam pruna ferentes*,

says, *prunorum arbor spinus vocatur generis Masculini; nam sentes has spinas dicimus*. And accordingly Despauter ranks it among the masculine nouns, which we have followed.

Rubus is feminine in Seneca, Colum. and Prud. though in every other writer it is rather masculine; wherefore we have marked it as doubtful, whereas Despauter makes it only masculine.

Suber which Despauter makes doubtful, is only neuter: *excepto subere quod sic etiam juvatur*, Plin. What deceived him, is a passage of the same author, where he read *serotino autem germine malus* (sup. *germinat,*) *tardissimus suber*. But it is obvious that the right reading is *tardissimo*, as he said before *serotino*; this is confirmed by the best copies, though Robert Stephen was also mistaken in his Thesaurus, having marked *suber* of all the three genders

OF GENDERS.

genders without any authority. And this mistake of the gender has crept into the other editions of this book, even after the correction of the above passage of Pliny. It has also stole its way into the several editions of his large dictionary, and from thence into a great many others; wherein Verepeus was also mistaken.

Oleaster is marked as masculine both by the ancient and modern grammarians, and not without reason: for Virgil says *Oleaster plurimus*, 2 Georg. *Sacer Oleaster*, 12. Æneid. where Servius particularly observes that we should say, *hic Oleaster*. Vossius indeed in order to defend Gaza who made it feminine in Theophrastus, avails himself of the following passage of Cicero's 3. book against Verres, where Manutius and Robert Stephen read in the feminine, *hominem suspendi jussit in oleastro quadam:* pretending that Lambinus is the only one who reads *in oleastro quodam* in the masculine, but, he adds, *invitis libris.* And yet he should have taken notice that the excellent edition of Gruterus reads it in the masculine, and assures us that this is the reading of all the ancient copies. And we find that in this, as almost in every thing else, it has been followed by the Elzevir edition. This seems to be confirmed by reason; because as Priscian observes, all nouns in *er* of the second declension are masculine without exception.

Hereby we may judge of all other similar nouns in STER, being the termination of wild trees, which we have generally observed to be masculine, as Verepeus, Alvarez, and the ablest grammarians have done.

The termination TUM denotes the ground planted with particular trees, as *Quercetum*, a grove of oaks; *salictum*, a grove of willows; *arbustum*, a copse or grove of trees.

But in barren trees, the termination UM is generally taken for the wood and the materials, as *ebenum*, ebony, *cinnamomum*, cinnamon; *buxum*, box wood; yet it is also taken for the tree, as Servius observes, notwithstanding Priscian affirms the contrary. But the following passage of Ovid *lib.* 4. *de arte* is decisive.

Nec densum foliis buxum, fragilesque myricæ,
Nec tenues cytisi, cultaque pinus abest.

You may see also several names of plants and shrubs taken from the Greek, lower down in the rule of the nouns in US.

Of the names of fruits.

In regard to the names of *fruits*, which the ancient grammarians thought generally to be neuter, we shall take notice of them here, only because this is an error which has been long ago detected.

It is true that when the tree terminates in US, the fruit is oftentimes in UM, and of the neuter gender, as *pomus*, an apple-tree; *pomum*, an apple: *pyrus*, a pear-tree; *pyrum*, a pear: *arbutus*, a wild strawberry-tree; *arbutum*, its fruit, &c. But this is by reason of its termination, not of its signification, since *Castanea*, *nux*, *dactylus*,

dactylus, and others, follow their termination, which Diomedes and Priscian do not seem to have sufficiently considered.

Rule VIII.
Of indeclinable nouns.

Indeclinable nouns are neuter,
Such as manna, gummi, fas, *and the like.*

Examples.

Indeclinable nouns are always of the neuter gender, as *hoc manna,* manna; *hoc pondo,* a pound, or weight.

Hoc fas, a thing lawful: *nefas,* a thing unlawful, a crime.

Hoc moly, a kind of herb: *gummi,* gum: *sinapi,* mustard: and all other nouns in I or Y, which are always neuter, and indeclinable.

Mille unum, one thousand: though in the plural it is declined, *Millia, ium.*

Hoc cornu, a horn: *veru,* a spit: though in the plural they are likewise declined, *córnua, uum, ibus,* and the like.

Melos suavíssimum, most sweet melody: *Chaos antíquum,* the ancient Chaos.

Hoc frit, the little grain at the top of the ear of corn; *hoc Git,* a small seed.

The infinitives of verbs are likewise considered as indeclinable nouns, and consequently are neuter: *scire tuum,* thy knowledge; *velle tuum,* thy will.

In short all words that are taken in a material sense, and as indeclinable, are of the neuter gender: *Triste vale,* Ovid, a sad adieu: *rex derivátum à rego;* the word *rex* is derived from *rego.*

For this same reason the names of letters are also neuter: *illud* A, *illud* B: that A, that B; though we likewise find them in the feminine, when they refer to the common word *líttera,* as has been seen above.

ANNOTATION.

To this rule we may also refer *Cherubim* and *Seraphim,* which in the scripture and in Saint Chrysostom are of the neuter gender (though in the plural) because they are indeclinable, τὰ χιρυβὶμ: unless we should say perhaps that the word *animalia* was then supposed,

OF GENDERS.

supposed, because they were represented under the figure of animals. But generally speaking these nouns are rather masculine, as being the names of angels, which are referred to the rules of proper names, according as we have already shewn. This is the opinion of S. Jerom upon Ezechiel, c. 10. *Et quanquam* says he, *plerique τὰ χερουβὶμ neutro genere, numeroque plurali diei putent: nos scire debemus singulari numero esse* CHERUB *generis masculini, & plurali ejusdem generis* CHERUBIM, which he repeats again, upon the 28th chapter of the same prophet.

But *pondo*, though placed in this list by grammarians, is not of the number. For whereas they looked upon it as an odd kind of a noun, or an indeclinable adjective, as well in the singular as in the plural; it is really an ablative of the second declension, like *mundo*, and serves for the same use as if it were *pondere*; as *aurea corona libræ pondo*, a golden crown of a pound weight. Which they added, because among the ancients the name of a pound and that of its parts were equivocal, signifying sometimes the weight, and sometimes the measure.

It is also to be observed that we say, *hæc gummis*, *hæc sinapis*, which are declined according to the gender of their termination.

From *Melos* seems to come the ablative *melo*,

Fitque repercusso dulcior aura melo.

in the poem on the resurrection attributed to Lactantius. But this is because they used to say *melus*, from whence also came the accusative *melum* in Pacu. according to Non.

In like manner we find the ablative *Chao* in Virgil, Ovid, and Lactantius.

RULE IX.

Of plural nouns.

1. I *plural is masculine.*
2. A; 3. and E *are neuter*; Æ *is feminine.*

EXAMPLES.

1. Nouns in I that have only the plural number, are of the masculine gender, like *dómini*; as *hi Parísii, Parisiórum*, the city of Paris: *hi cancélli, órum*, lattices, balisters, bounds.

2. Those in A are neuter, like *templa*; as *arma impia*, impious arms: *castra, órum*, a camp: *ília, órum*, the flank, the small guts: *Bactra, órum*, the name of a town.

3. And in like manner the Greek nouns in E: *cete grándia*, large whales: *Amœ'na Tempe*, pleasant fields in Thessaly.

4. Those

4. Those in Æ diphthong are feminine, like *musæ*; as *doctæ Athénæ*, the learned city of Athens: *ténebræ densæ*, thick darkness.

ANNOTATION.

Pandectæ is generally feminine. See the remarks upon the figure of ellipsis, list 1.

Cete and *Tempe* come from the Greek contraction, κήτεα, η, τίμπεα, η: so that it is not at all surprizing they should be of the plural number and of the neuter gender. We find that Cicero preferring the Greek word, says, *Reatini me ad sua τίμπη duxerunt*. Whereas Solinus has *cava tempea*.

You are to observe that we also say *cetus*, in the plural *ceti*; hence Pliny has *cetos* in the accusative plural.

Whether there are any proper names in the plural.

After the example of Despauter, we place here this rule of the plural nouns, because of the great number of names of cities which it includes. And yet we must observe with Sanctius, that strictly speaking, there are no proper names in the plural. For *Athenæ*, for instance, were different spots of ground planted with olive trees, *multæ Athenaïdes* five *oliveta*, says he, of which afterwards a town was formed.

So when we say *Parisii*, and the like, we denote as well the people as the town, which afterwards took the name of its inhabitants; just as we say CIVITAS, *quasi* CIVIUM UNITAS. For the word *civitas* in its ancient signification stood rather for a whole nation than for a city: which is proper to take notice of for the better understanding of the ancients, particularly Cæsar in his wars of Gaul. And as to the name of people given to capital cities, we find by the learned remarks of monsieur Sanson, the king's geographer, on his map of Cæsar, that this did not happen till very late, and perhaps after the reign of Constantine: those towns having till then always retained either the name which they had received from their conquerors the Romans, and which was no other than that of the country softened by a Latin termination; or that which flattery had invented under Augustus in honour of the Cæsars, as of *Juliomagus*, *Cæsaromagus*, *Augustodunum*, *Augusta Veromanduorum*, and the like.

RULE X.
Of nouns singular in A and E.

1. *In the first declension nouns in* A *or* E *are feminine.*
2. *Cométa* and *Planéta* *are masculine.*
3. *Pascha is always neuter.*
4. *As are likewise* A *and* E *of the third declension.*

EXAM-

OF GENDERS.

EXAMPLES.

1. Nouns in A or E of the first declension are of the feminine gender: *Hæc ara*, this altar: *fama multa*, great fame: *hæc Allia*, a river of Italy: *hæc músice, músices*, music: *hæc epitome, es*, an abridgment.

2. These two are of the masculine gender, *dirus cométa*, a fatal comet: *pulcher planéta*, a beautiful planet.

3. *Pascha* is neuter. *Pascha próximum*, next Easter; and is either of the first or third declension: *Pascha, æ:* and *Pascha, átis*.

4. Nouns in A or E of the third declension are also neuter: *hoc diadéma, ătis*, a diadem: *ænigma, ătis*, a riddle: *mare sollicitum*, a tempestuous sea.

ANNOTATION.

Adria, which Despauter marks here as a masculine, is indeed of this gender, when taken for the Adriatic gulf, referring then to *sinus*; but it is feminine, when taken for the town which gave name to this gulf; and therefore it always follows the rule of the signification, and of the common and general word.

Pascha is masculine in the Hebrew and Chaldaic tongues, because as we have already observed, these have no neuter. And yet the Greeks have made it neuter; because they considered it as indeclinable: τὸ πάσχα & τῦ πάσχα, in the Septuagint, ἐν τῷ πάσχα, in S. John, Chap. ii. The Latins have followed them in the gender though they make this noun of the first or third declension: of the first, as in Tertull. *Quis solemnibus Paschæ. In Pascha jejunare:* in Ausonius,——*solemnia Paschæ:* in St. Ambrose, *de mysterio Paschæ*, and so almost all the ancients.

And yet it seems to be more commonly used now in the third: which probably is owing to this, that deriving it from πάσχω *patior*, they thought they were to decline it like the other Greek nouns in *ma* derived of verbs, as *ænigma, atis*; *dogma, atis*, &c. However as this is not originally a Greek but Hebrew noun, as St. Jerome observes, the ancients seem to have declined it right: though Tertullian, St. Ambrose, and Lactantius derive it also from πάσχω. See Vossius *de Anal. lib.* i. *cap.* 20.

It is the same with *manna*, taken for bread sent from heaven, which being masculine in Hebrew is neuter in Greek and Latin, because it has continued indeclinable in both these languages. Therefore it is a mistake to say, *cælestem mannam* instead of *cæleste manna*. And in this signification we refer it to the above-mentioned rule of indeclinables p. 22. But we also use *manna, æ* of the first declension, and consequently feminine, which then signifies the crumbs of frankincense or manna used in physic. *Micas (thuris) concussu elisas mannam vocamus*, Plin.

Mam-

Mammena, which Despauter makes neuter, is masculine. See above, p. 4.

Dama, panthera, and *talpa,* shall be included in the rule of the epicenes.

As to *Cometa* and *Planeta,* they are always masculine, because as they come from the Greek nouns in της of the first declension, which includes none but masculines, they have preserved their gender. It is for this reason that they are likewise changed into *tes,* or *ta. Cometes,* or *cometa; planetes,* or *planeta;* and that the first termination occurs more frequently among the ancients; which happens also in a great many others.

And yet we must not think that this rule is general, as Priscian after Varro has observed. For of ὁ κοχλίας they have made *hæc cochlea;* of ὁ χάρτης, *hæc charta;* of ὁ μαρσαρίτης, *hæc margarita;* of ὁ μετρητής, *hæc metreta.* Concerning which we are to take notice of a mistake in Constantin's lexicon, and in some others who write ἡ μετρητή, and were undoubtedly led into this mistake by Pollux; which H. Stephen condemns in his Thesaurus.

But there are a great many more of these nouns in της, that have changed their gender with their termination; and perhaps these two have retained it only because they are generally referred to ἀρχή, though Tacitus has put them in apposition with *sidus. Inter quæ & sidus Cometes effulsit, de quo vulgi opinio est, tanquam mutationem Regis portendat,* An. 14. And Cicero has joined it with *stella: Tum facibus visis cælestibus, tum stellis iis, quas Græci cometas, nostri Crinitas vocant, quæ nuper bello Octaviano, magnarum fuerunt calamitatum prænunciæ.* 2. de Nat. which made a great many imagine that *cometa* might be feminine; whereas both *quæ* and *quas* refer only to *stellæ.*

Of nouns in I.

We take no notice here of nouns in I, because we have already made appear in the 8th rule, that they are neuter and indeclinable; we shall therefore proceed to those in O.

RULE XI.

Of nouns in O.

1. *Nouns in* O, 2. *including* Harpăgo, *are masculine.*
3. *But all others in* DO *and* GO, *of more than two syllables, are feminine.*
4. *To these we must join* Caro, Grando.
5. *As also nouns in* IO *coming either from a verb or a noun.*
6. *Except numeral nouns, and* 7. Pugio.

Ex-

OF GENDERS.

EXAMPLES.

1. Nouns in O are of the masculine gender, as *his sermo, ónis,* speech, or discourse: *hic mucro, ónis,* the sharp point of any thing: *hic scipio,* a walking staff: *hic titio ónis,* a firebrand quenched: *hic ligo, ónis,* a spade: *hic cardo, inis,* a hinge: *hic ordo, inis,* order.

2. And in like manner, *hic harpăgo, ónis,* a grappling hook.

3. But the other nouns in DO, or GO, that have more than two syllables, are feminine, as *hæc arúndo, inis,* a reed: *hæc dulcédo,* sweetness: *hæc formido,* fear: *hæc imágo,* an image: *hæc fuligo,* soot.

4. These two are also feminine; *hæc caro, carnis,* meat, flesh: *hæc grando, grándinis,* hail.

5. Nouns in IO, derived from a noun or from a verb, are also feminine: *hæc pórtio* (from *pars*) a part or portion: *hæc tálio* (from *talis*) like for like, or a requital of an injury: *hæc cóncio,* (from *cieo*) an assembly, an harangue: *hæc contágio* (from *tago* for *tango*) contagion: *hæc óptio,* (from *opto*) choice: *hæc allúvio* (from *álluo,* formerly in the preterit *álluvi*) an inundation of water: *hæc dítio, ónis,* (from *dis, ditis*) power, authority, place of jurisdiction: *hæc relígio, ónis,* (from *ligo* religion, scruple of conscience: *hæc rebéllio, ónis,* (from *bellum*) rebellion, revolt: *hæc légio,* a legion.

And especially those which are formed of the supine: *hæc léctio,* (from *lectum*) lesson, reading: *hæc orátio,* (from *orátum*) oration, discourse: and of the like an infinite number.

6. Of these feminines in IO, derived from verbs or nouns, we must except in the first place numeral nouns, as *hic únio, ónis,* the number one, or a pearl called an union, and an onion or scallion; for then it constantly comes from *unus*; but it is not found in Latin authors to signify union: *hic duérnio,* the number two: *hic térnio,* the number three: *quatérnio,* the number four: *quinquénnio,* the number five, &c.
which

which agrees with the general analogy of the common word abovementioned rule 3.

Secondly *hic púgio, ónis*, (from *pugnus* or *pugno*) a poniard.

ANNOTATION.

Echo, which some grammarians place under this rule, is feminine, because it follows the general word *vox*, or rather because it retains the gender of its first signification; Echo, according to Ovid, being a woman who was changed into sound.

Arrhabo is feminine in Varro; but Cato, Plautus, and Gellius make it masculine, as well as the Greeks ὁ ἀῤῥαβών.

Albedo and *Nigredo*, as well as *gratitudo* and *ingratitudo*, are not Latin, though Sulpicius Severus has made use of the former, and Lipsius of the latter. See Vossius *de vitiis sermonis*. Instead thereof we may use *albor*, Plaut. Varr. *Nigror*, Cic. *Nigrities* and *nigritudo*, Pliny. For the other two we use circumlocutions, *gratus animus*; *ingrati animi crimen*, Cic. &c.

Cupido is sometimes masculine in the writings of the poets, *capta cupidine falso*, Hor. *contracto cupidine*, Idem, but never in prose, except it be to signify the god Cupid.

Margo is feminine in one single passage of Juvenal. *Plena jam margine libri*, Sat. 1. But every where else it is masculine, as in Varro, *Lapidei margines fluvii*; in Ovid, *Gramineus margo fontis*, Met. 3. In Pliny and in others the same. It is true, according to Charis. lib. i. that Macer and Rabinus had also used it in the feminine, but in this they are not to be imitated: for which reason we must refer it to the general rule.

Perduellio is feminine according to Vossius, and masc. according to other grammarians. Perhaps it might be feminine, when it denotes the action, that is the crime of rebellion, and masculine when it signifies the criminal, and the person who commits such an action; for it signifies both. *Talio* is masculine in Tertullian, but Gellius makes it feminine, and that is the safest.

Unio by some writers is taken in the feminine, to signify union; but it is not found to bear that sense in Latin authors. Wherefore when Tertullian says, *Reges qui singulares in unione imperii præsunt*, (lib. i. adv. Marcion. cap. 4.) the word *unio* does not there denote *societatem* but *unitatem*, μονάδα. Where we cannot see of what gender it ought to be in this sense, because there is no adjective.

Scioppius excepts likewise some feminines in *io*, *Ternio*, *quaternio*, and *senio*. But these are adjectives, and suppose *numerus*, when they are in the masculine, as *senio*, which was particularly taken for the fice cast of the dice. Whereas we frequently see at the ends of books published even by printers extremely well skilled in the language, as Robert Stephen, Aldus Manutius, Ascensius, and others, that mentioning the number of printed sheets, they say *sunt omnes terniones*, or *quaterniones*, &c. where they

they understand *scheda, charta, litteræ,* &c. or some other like feminine.

RULE XII.

Of nouns in M, C, L, T.

1. M, C, L, T, *are neuter.*
2. Sal *is masculine or neuter;* 3. Sol *is masculine.*

EXAMPLES.

1. Nouns ending in M have always *um:* these are of the second declension and of the neuter gender, as *hoc templum, templi,* a temple: *aurum fulvum,* yellow gold: *pulchrum Lugdunum,* the fair city of Lyons: *hoc Illyricum,* the province of Illyricum; *hoc ligustrum,* privet; *hoc pomum,* an apple: *hoc mancipium,* a slave.

Those in C, L, or T, are of the third declension, but also of the neuter gender; as *hoc halec, halécis,* a herring, brine: *lac novum,* new milk: *ánimal fortíssimum,* a very strong animal: *mel purum,* pure honey: *caput nítidum,* a clean head.

2. SAL, salt, the sea, wisdom, jests, railleries, is doubtful, but more often masculine. *Sal siccus & acer,* Plin. a dry and sharp salt: *sal coctum,* Colum. baked salt: *sales A'ttici,* Cic. Attic jests.

3. SOL is masculine; *sol ígneus,* a fiery sun.

ANNOTATION.

Among the nouns in UM I do not include the proper names of men or women, which by the general rule always follow the gender of their signification; and this is extremely clear.

Hereto we must refer the Greek nouns in ON of the second declension, which the Latins change into UM, as *hoc gymnasion,* or *gymnasium,* a place of exercise.

Those in ON of the third are comprised under the next rule.

Sal is generally masculine; and sometimes neuter, but then it is only in the singular, and to signify salt. *Sal coctum & modicè infractum,* Colum. In this signification it occurs also in the plural: *si quis sales emerit,* in the civil law. But in the other signification, it is frequently used in both numbers. *Dicendi sales facetiæque,* Cic. *Docti sales,* Claud. *Nullam artem esse salis,* Cic.

Halecem, in Martial, comes from *Halex,* feminine. But *halec* is always neuter; and in the passage of Pliny quoted by Calepin, *halec imperfecta;* the best editions have, *Alex imperfecta, nec colata fex.*

Lac is a word shortened, instead of *lacte*, for which reason they used also to write *lact*. They likewise said *lactis* in the feminine, as in the old glosses we find *lactem* for γάλα, and in Plaut. *in Bacch.*

Nouns in D which are generally placed here, are either adjectives, or pronouns, as *id, aliud, illud, quid, quod,* &c. and therefore should by no means be referred to this rule.

RULE XIII.
Of nouns in N.

1. *Nouns in* N *are masculine,* 2. *except* Sindon, *and* Icon, *which are feminine.*
3. *Those in* MEN *are neuter;*
4. *As also* Gluten, Unguen, Inguen.

EXAMPLES.

1. Nouns of the third declension ending in N, are generally masculine, let them be of whatever termination.

In AN. *Hic Pæan, ánis,* Virg. a song of joy, a hymn in honour of Apollo.

In EN. *Hic pecten, péctinis,* a comb, the stick or quill wherewith they play upon an instrument, a wool card, the slay of a weaver's loom, a rake, all shell fish striated like a cockle. *Hic ren,* in the plur. *renes,* the kidnies or reins: *hic splen, enis,* or *lien, liénis,* the spleen.

In IN. *Hic delphin, ínis,* a dolphin.

In ON. *Hic canon, ŏnis,* a rule, a canon of the sacred councils: *Hic agon, ónis,* a combat.

2. These two are feminine: *hæc sindon,* very fine linnen: *hæc icon,* an image or statue.

3. Those in MEN are neuter: *Lumen jucúndum,* agreeable light: *flumen rápidum,* a rapid river: *hoc flamen, ĭnis,* a blast or puff of wind.

4. To which you may add the following: *Hoc gluten, ĭnis,* glue, paste: *hoc unguen,* ointment: *hoc inguen,* the privy parts.

ANNOTATION.

Nouns in *on* of the second declension are more frequently terminated in *um,* and we have included them in the preceding rule.

Flamen signifying a pagan priest, is masculine by the rule of the names of men.

Hymen

Hymen is also masculine, either because strictly speaking it signifies the god of marriage, or because the names of the gods taken even for the thing over which they preside, always preserve their gender, as *Jupiter* for the air; *Mars* for war, and *Hymen* for marriage, nuptial songs, the membranes that invelop the *fœtus*, and every thin skin, as that which invelops the eye, &c. or because it is an entire Greek word, and has retained its gender, ὁ ὑμὴν, ἐνος.

Icon is also Greek, and seldom occurs in Latin : it is always feminine, though we find in Dion. ὁ εἰκὼν τῦ Πομπηίῦ, lib. xliii. *sub finem*.

Python, for the serpent that was slain by Apollo, is always masculine.

  Cæruleus tali prostratus Apolline Python.

But when Tibullus says :

  Delos ubi nunc, Phœbe, tua est ? ubi Delphica Python ?

There he does not take *Python* for the serpent, nor even for a woman possessed with a prophesying spirit, as Calepin explains it, but for the town itself. This appears plainly by his joining *Delos tua* with *Delphica Python*, as two synonymous things. Accordingly Eustath. informs us that the town, formerly called *Delphi*, was afterwards named Πυθὼ or Πυθὼν ; though it be true that it was so called because of the serpent, under whose figure Apollo received public adoration. Vossius.

Rule XIV.

Nouns in AR or in UR.

1. *Nouns in* AR, 2. *And* UR *are neuter.*
3. *Except* furfur, fúrfuris, *which is masculine.*

Examples.

1. Nouns in AR are of the neuter gender ; as *láquear*, or *lacúnar áureum*, a golden cieling : *jubar*, a sun beam : *calcar argénteum*, a silver spur : *hoc bácchar*, the herb lady glove.

2. Nouns in UR are also neuter : *murmur raucum*, a hollow noise : *ebur venále*, ivory to be sold : *guttur siccum*, a dry throat.

3. The following is masculine : *hic furfur, fúrfuris*, Plin. bran.

Annotation.

Jubar was formerly masculine, for Ennius in Priscian says *albus jubar*, to signify the moon ; but succeeding authors have always made it neuter, as Hor. Ovid, Statius, Pliny, &c.

              Despauter

Despauter says that *lucar*, taken for a bird, is feminine. But it appears by Festus, Charisius, and by the glosses of S. Cyril, that *lucar* never signified any thing more than the money that served to defray the expence of the public games, and to reward the actors. And according to Isidorus this word comes from *lucus*; because the money accruing from the public woods, in the neighbourhood of cities, was assigned to that use. And it is in this sense that even Tertullian has taken it, when speaking of S. John the Baptist, he says: *contumeliosa cæde truncatur, in puellæ salticæ* (for *saltatricis*) *lucar*; lib. Scorpiaces, adversus Gnost. where it is plain he makes it neuter.

Bacchar likewise is always neuter, *bacchar rusticum*, Plin. But we likewise say *baccharis* in the feminine; which led the same Despauter into a mistake. *Baccharis vocatur nardum rusticum*, Plin.

Guttur was formerly masculine, hence we meet with *gutturem* more than once in Plautus.

We meet with *murmur* of the masculine in Varro; *verus murmur* according to Nonnius.

Turtur, see the last rule of genders, which is that of epicene nouns.

RULE XV.
Of nouns in ER.

1. *Nouns in* ER *are masculine.* 2. *Except* linter, *which is feminine.* 3. *And* iter, cadáver, spinter, uber, ver, *which are neuter.* 4. *And the names of plants or fruits which are also neuter;* 5. *But* tuber *is of all genders.*

EXAMPLES.

1. Nouns in ER are of the masculine gender. *Ager almus*, a fruitful soil: *imber frigidus*, a cold shower: *aër salúbris*, wholesome air: *hic cancer*, a crab, a shanker: *hic vomer, eris*, a plowshare.

2. *Linter, lintris*, a little boat, is of the feminine.

3. There are five of the neuter: *iter altum*, the high way: *cadáver infórme*, a filthy carcass: *hoc spinter*, a buckle or clasp: *uber beátum*, happy nipple or teat: *ver amænum*, pleasant spring.

4. The names of plants and fruits are also neuter: *piper crudum*, raw pepper: *siser*, the skirret root: *cicer*, vetches: *laver*, a kind of herb, some call it water parsley: *laser*, benzoin: *suber*, cork.

5. TUBER is used in all genders, but in different senses. For signifying a bump and a swelling, or a bunch

bunch as in a camel's back, it is neuter, from whence comes *Tuberculum*: and even when it is taken for truffles, a kind of mushroom. But when it signifies a kind of tree, it is feminine by the general rule: and signifying the fruit of this tree, which according to Pliny bears more resemblance to a small grain than to a fruit, it is masculine: *oblatos tuberes servari jussit.* Suet.

ANNOTATION.

We find in Martial, *Et vernæ tuberes*; which made a great many believe that *tuber*, for the fruit, was also feminine, without considering, that this is only an apposition, just as this author says, *vernas equites, verna liber*, &c.

Cucumer does not occur in the ancients, but *cucumis, cucumeris*. See the rule in IS.

Verber is not in use, says Vossius; but only the genitive *verberis*, and the ablative *verbere*. We meet indeed with the plural, and by its termination we plainly see that it is neuter; *lenta verbera pati*, Virg. to bear the gentle lash.

Linter is masculine in this single passage of Tibullus, · *Exiguus pullâ per vada linter aquâ*. lib. ii. Eleg. 5. Which he did perhaps for the harmony and beauty of his verse; for it would have had too many A's, if he had wrote *exigua*.

We meet with *laver* of the feminine in Plin. *laver cocta*, sup. *herba*. And in the same author we find *tres siseres*, where it does not appear whether he took it as masculine or feminine.

Cancer, which Despauter, after Priscian, puts in the neuter and in the third declension, when it signifies a *canker*, or spreading sore, is always masculine, and of the third declension, even in this sense, in Latin authors. *Eadem vulnera putrida cancrosque purgabit, sanosque faciet*. Cato de R. R. True it is that in some ecclesiastic authors we find it in the neuter: *sermones eorum ut cancer & pestem fugiendo vitatote*, S. Cypr. but this is not to be imitated. For as to the passage of Ovid, which has led a great many into an error,

Utque malum latè solet immedicabile cancer
Serpere, & illæsas vitiatis addere partes. 2 Met. f. 12.

it is plain that *immedicabile* refers to *malum* and not to *cancer*.

Of the nouns in IR.

With regard to the nouns in IR, *bir*, the hollow of the hand; and *abadir*, the stone which Saturn devoured for one of his children, are indeclinable, according to Priscian, and therefore are neuter, by rule 8.

The others, as *vir, levir*, &c. relate to the general rule of the names of men; wherefore without losing time about this termination, we proceed to that in OR.

Rule XVI.
Of the nouns in OR.

1. *Nouns in* OR *are masculine.*
2. *Except* arbor, *feminine.* 3. *And* cor, ador, marmor, æquor, *neuter.*

Examples.

1. Nouns in OR are of the masculine gender, *amor divinus,* the love of god: *dolor acérbus,* a bitter pain: *hic decor, óris,* grace, beauty, decorum.

2. *Arbor* is feminine: *arbor mala,* a bad tree; because trees are like mothers that bear fruit and branches. See p. 18.

3. These four are of the neuter gender: *cor lapideum,* a heart of stone: *ador, adóris,* fine corn: *marmor antiquum,* ancient marble: *æquor túmidum,* the swelling sea.

Annotation.

A great many nouns in OR were formerly attributed to the female sex, of which we have *uxor* still remaining. Thus we find in Ulpian, *mulier defensor:* in Ovid,

Sponsor conjugii stat dea picta sui.

Whence there is reason to doubt whether these nouns might not have been formerly of the common gender, though this may still be referred to an apposition.

Some nouns in OR were formerly of the neuter gender, as in Plautus, *nec calor nec frigus métuo.* Hence it is that some having changed termination, have still retained their gender, as *jecinor,* from whence by syncope they have made *jecor* and afterwards *jecur, jecoris,* neuter.

In like manner the comparatives in *or* stood for all genders, according to Priscian. *Bellum Punicum posterior.* Cassius Hem. *apud eund.*

Likewise *decor* in Ausonius, for *decus.*

Dum decor egregiæ commeminit patriæ.

This made Vossius in his Etym. believe that *ador, oris,* the penultimate short, as it is in Ausonius, was only an old word for *adus,* neuter, like *decus;* whereas *ador, adóris,* long, as Priscian quotes it from Gannius, is masculine, in the same manner as *decor, decoris:* And yet Horace has also made use of *ador* in the neuter.

Paleâ porrectus in hornâ —— esset ador loliumque. lib. ii, sat. 6.

Of the nouns in UR.

The nouns in UR have gone before with those in AR, because they agree in gender. So that for the nouns in R there are two terminations, which are generally of the masculine, ER and OR; and

OF GENDERS.

and two of the neuter, AR and UR. The termination in IR, embraces both genders, but it follows to the general rules.

Rule XVII.
Of the nouns in AS.

1. AS *in the first declension is of the masculine gender*.
2. *In the third it is of the feminine*.
3. *But* Vas, vasis, *is neuter*.
4. *And* As *making* antis *is masculine*.

Examples.

1. Nouns in AS of the first declension, are of the masculine gender, as *hic tiáras, æ*, a tiara, or turbant: *hic phárias, æ*, a kind of serpent: *hic astérias, æ*, a stone of the fashion of a star. But as these are Greek nouns, they are often changed into the Latin termination in *a*, and then they are feminine: *hæc tiára, æ*, &c.

2. Nouns in AS of the third declension are feminine: *æstas formósa*, a fine summer: *lampas noctúrna*, a night lamp: *pietás antíqua*, ancient piety.

3. *Vas, vasis*, a vessel, is neuter.

4. Nouns in AS that make ANTIS in the genitive, are masculine. *Hic ádamas, ántis*, a diamond: *hic gigas, ántis*, a giant: *hic élephas, ántis*, an elephant.

Annotation.

As, assis, with all its compounds is masculine. See the 4th rule. We likewise say; *hic mas, maris*, the male in all kinds of creatures: but this is by the general rule of the distinction of the two sexes.

Artócreas, & *Erysípelas* are neuter, because they retain the gender they have in Greek, being of the fifth declension of contracted nouns. The former we find in Persius, and the latter in Celsus.

Nonius pretends that *ætas* was formerly of the neuter gender, and endeavours to prove it by this verse from Plautus.

———— *Fuit hoc ætate exercitus.* In Trinum. a. iv. sc. 3.
But the best editions read *hac ætate* in the feminine. Which makes it doubtful whether Plautus did not write *hoc ætatis*, meaning *ætate tam præcipiti & effœta*: just as in Amphit. he uses *hoc noctis*, for *hac nocte*, or *nocte intempestâ*. And this is the opinion of Douza; hence it is to be observed by the way, that we are not always to be determined by the authority of Nonius, and that according

cording to Vossius, the copies he made use of, were in all probability very faulty and imperfect.

RULE XVIII.
Of the nouns in ES.

1. *Nouns in* ES *are feminine.*
2. Dies *is doubtful.* 3. Æs *is neuter.*
4. Poples, limes, stipes, paries, pes, fomes, palmes, trames, gurges, cespes, termes, *are masculine.*
5. *Of the masculine gender are also such Greek nouns as come from those in* ης, *as* magnes, tapes, lebes, *and* sorites.

EXAMPLES.

1. Nouns terminating in ES are of the feminine gender. *Rupes immóta,* an unshaken rock: *merces tuta,* a sure reward: *fides sancta,* holy faith: *hæc ales, ïtis,* a bird.

2. *Dies* is doubtful, but oftener feminine in the singular: *dies sacra,* a holy day: *longa dies,* a great many days, a long time. In the plural it is rather masculine: *prætériti dies,* past days. These compounds are rather masculine: *meridies,* noon: *sesquidies,* a day and a half, &c.

3. *Æs, æris,* brass, copper, is of the neuter gender.

4. There are eleven of the masculine gender: *poples,* the ham of one's leg behind the knee: *limes,* a bound or limit: *stipes,* a log fast in the ground, a stake, a stump of a tree: *páries,* a wall: *fomes,* fuel: *pes,* the foot: *palmes,* the shoot or young branch of a vine: *trames,* a path: *gurges,* a gulf: *termes,* a bough or twig of a tree: *cespes,* a turf.

5. Those derived from the Greek nouns in ης, are also masculine, whether they be of the third declension, as *magnes, ẽtis,* a loadstone: *tapes, ẽtis,* tapestry: *lebes, ẽtis,* a cauldron: *acínaces, is, Medus acinaces,* Hor. a Persian scymitar.

Or

Or whether they be of the first, as *hic cometes, æ,* a comet: *hic sorites,* a sort of argument: *hic pyrites, æ,* a fire-stone, and like the names of precious stones: *hic absinthites, æ,* worm-wood wine : *hic aromatites, æ,* hippocrafs, or wine brewed with spices, and the like.

ANNOTATION.

Aromatites likewise signifies a precious stone, so called because of its agreeable smell. Pliny makes it feminine, *Aromatites & ipsa in Arabia traditur gigni,* referring without doubt to *gemma,* according to the opinion above given, rule 3; and for the same reason we shall find a great many more of these names of precious stones that are of the feminine gender in the same author.

But the other Greek nouns which come from those in *is* are neuter, because they preserve the gender of the Greek; as *nepenthes, is,* a kind of herb: *hoc hippomanes,* a piece of flesh on the forehead of a colt newly foaled, which the mare presently bites off; a kind of poison used in philtres.

Grammarians are at a loss to determine the gender of *Merges*. Despauter, and after him Alvarez, make it masculine. And yet Priscian does not except it from the feminines; in which he has been followed not only by Verepeus and Vossius, but moreover by all the dictionaries which put it down in the feminine. Thus we find in Pliny, *inter duas mergites spica distringitur :* where *merges* is not taken for the ears of corn, but for the iron hitchel or ripple with which they cut it; according to the explication of Calepin, who reads *inter duos* in the masculine. But the ancient editions of Pliny, and the great Thesaurus of the Latin tongue read it in the feminine. Others pretend that this passage is corrupted, and that we ought to read, *iterum è defectâ spica.* Be that as it may, we have followed the most general opinion, leaving it in the feminine.

Despauter places here among the number of masculines in ES, *verres,* a boar pig; *aries,* a ram ; but it is obvious that these must be masculine by the general rule of the two sexes; nor are we to mind the latter's being sometimes taken for a military engine or instrument, since it was but the same word, as we still call it the *ram,* a name owing either to the obstinacy with which it battered the walls, or to its having horns of iron like a ram's head.

In this number he likewise places *ames,* a small stay, or fork, to stay up nets in fowling ; and *tudes,* a hammer. To these others join *trudes,* an instrument to thrust down things with; but it is without authority. For which reason Vossius thinks it is better to forbear joining them with an adjective that determines either gender.

Vepres is not used in the nominative singular: hence we have referred it to the rule of the nouns in IS, as coming rather from *vepris,* according to the opinion of Vossius.

Of the gender of Dies.

Dies, says Asconius, *feminino genere tempus, & ideo diminutivè diecula dicitur breve tempus & mora: dies horarum duodecim generis masculini est, unde hodie dicimus, quasi hoc die.* lib. ii. contra Verr. This distinction, taken from so learned a man, ought not to be intirely rejected, especially since it is agreeable to the opinion of all the ancient grammarians. And yet some authors have neglected it, taking *dies* in the feminine, even to express a determinate day, as *Jamque dies infanda aderat*, Virg. *Nomina se facturum quâ ego vellem die*, Cic. that he would settle his accounts whatever day I pleased. *Quod antiquior dies in tuis literis adscripta fuisset quàm in Cæsaris*, Cic. *Nos in Formiano esse volumus, usque ad Prid. Non. Maias. Eò si ante eam diem non veneris, Romæ te fortasse videbo*, Cic. ad Att. *Eâdem die germinat quâ injectum est*, Plin. *Posterâ die itaque cùm ad statutam horam omnes convenissent*, Justin. lib. vi. &c.

But in the plural this noun is generally masculine, though in Cicero we meet with, *O reliquas omnes dies noctesque eas, quibus*, &c. pro Cn. Planco.

Rule XIX.

Of the nouns in IS.

1. *Nouns in* IS *are feminine*.
2. *Those in* NIS *are masculine*.
3. *As are also* Colis, caulis, collis, axis, orbis, callis, follis, fustis, lapis, vepris, sentis, messis, torris.
4. *To these join* Cúcumis, pollis, sanguis, vectis, fascis, pulvis, unguis, cassis, postis, ensis, aquális.

Examples.

1. Nouns in IS are of the feminine gender, *vestis áurea*, a golden garment: *pellis árida*, a dry skin: *hæc vólucris*, a bird: *hæc cassis, cássidis*, a helmet: *tyránnis, ĭdis*, tyranny, and the like Greek nouns: *hæc scobis, is*, saw-dust, pin-dust.

2. But the other nouns ending in NIS are masculine: *panis Angélicus*, the bread of Angels: *crinis solútus*, dishevelled

OF GENDERS.

dishevelled hair: *hic amnis*, a river: *hic ignis*, fire: *hic cinis*, ashes: *hic funis*, a rope.

3. There are twenty-four more, that are also of the masculine gender: *hic colis* or *caulis*, the stalk or stem of an herb, any kind of pot-herbs, especially coleworts: *collis apértus*, Virg. an open hill: *hic axis*, an axle-tree: *hic orbis*, a circle, the world: *callis*, a path: *calle angústo*, through a narrow path: *follis ventósus*, a windy pair of bellows: *fustis recísus*, a club or staff cut off: *lapis pretiósus*, a precious stone: *hic vepris*, or rather *hi vepres*, briars, brambles: *sentis*, a bramble or thorn; it is more common in the plural, *sentes densi*, thick brambles: *mensis novus*, a new month: *torris ambústus*, a firebrand burnt out.

4. *Hic cúcumis, is* or *ĕris*, rather than *cúcumer*, a cucumber: *hic pollis, póllinis*, fine flour: *hic sanguis, sánguinis*, blood: *vectis ǽreus*, a brazen bar: *fascis injústus*, too heavy a burden: *pulvis multus*, a great deal of dust: *unguis adúncus*, a crooked nail: *hic cassis, hujus cassis*, a net; but *cassis, ĭdis*, a helmet, is feminine. See above. *Postis ferrátus*, an iron door post: *ensis distríctus*, a drawn sword: *hic aquális*, an ewer.

ANNOTATION.

The nouns in YS are also feminine, as *hæc chelys, yos*, a lute or harp: *hæc chlamys, ydis*, a cloak, a soldier's coat. But they may be referred to this rule of the feminines in *is*, since we pronounce *y* like an *i*. But if it were pronounced, as it ought to be, like an *u*, we should refer them to the rule of the Greek nouns in US, which we shall give hereafter.

RULE XX.

Of the nouns in IS that are of the doubtful gender.

The doubtful nouns in IS *are* finis, scrobis, torquis, *and* clunis.

EXAMPLES.

The following four nouns are of the doubtful gender, that is, they are either masculine or feminine;

fines

fines Latini, the boundaries of Latium: *quæ finis ſtandi*, Virg. how long ſhall I wait?

Hic aut hæc ſcrobis, Colum. a ditch: *torquis decórus*, Statius, a handſome collar: *torquis áurea*, Varro, a golden collar.

Hic clunis, Mart. *hæc clunis*, Horat. a buttock, or haunch.

ANNOTATION.

In the rule we have taken notice of no more than theſe four nouns of the doubtful gender. There are others which have ſometimes admitted of a variation in their gender, but are not ſo much to be imitated. This we ſhall ſhew in the following liſt, which ſhall likewiſe include whatever is obſervable in regard to the preceding rule for the better underſtanding of authors, placing the words according to their alphabetical order.

Liſt of the nouns in IS.

AMNIS was formerly of the feminine gender according to Priſcian and Nonius.

Neque mihi ulla obſiſtet amnis, Plaut. And Varro, *ubi confluit altera amnis*. Now it is always maſculine, as are all thoſe which terminate in NIS, according to the obſervation of Caper and Quint.

ANNALIS is an adjective. It is conſidered as maſc. becauſe it ſuppoſes *liber*.

BIPENNIS is alſo an adjective. And if we conſider it as feminine contrary to the nature of nouns in NIS, this is becauſe we ſuppoſe *ſecuris*.

—— *alta bipennis*, Virg.

CALLIS is feminine in Livy, *per devias calles*, as Nonius reads it. Who adds that it frequently occurred in this gender.

CANALIS was formerly to be met with in the maſculine, according to the obſervation of Nonius. But as the ſame Nonius ſays, and after him Iſidorus, it is better in the feminine. For which reaſon we find that Varro often makes uſe of it in this gender. And in the deſcription of Ætna we read:

Quòd ſi diverſas emittat terra canales.

Hence the diminutive is *canalicula* in Lucius, according to Nonius, and in Gellius.

CASSIS to ſignify a hunter's net, is not perhaps to be found in the ſingular but only in the plural, *Caſſes*.

CINIS was formerly feminine; *Cinere multa*, Lucr. *Acerba cinis*, Catullus. And Nonius mentions that Cæſar and Calvus uſed it in the ſame gender.

CLUNIS was very doubtful among the ancients. Soſipater and Priſcian ſhew that ſome made it maſculine, and others feminine. Feſtus as well as Flaccus, always put it in the maſculine. Servius pretends the ſame thing, becauſe of the termination NIS, and condemns Horace for ſaying, *pulchræ clunes*, maintaining that Juvenal did better by putting it in the maſculine. On the contrary Voſſius ſays that it is preſumption in him to cenſure Horace, ſince Acro his ancient commentator, approves of the two genders, as does alſo Nonius.

CORBIS is alſo maſculine according to Priſcian, but it is more generally feminine. *Mſſoria corbe contexit*, Cic. Wherefore Caper ſpeaking of the doubtful nouns, inſiſts upon our ſaying *corbes bæ*, in the fem. and not *corbes bi*.

CRINIS is alſo maſc. *Crines flavos*, Virg. Formerly it was fem. *Cenſeo capiundas crines tibi.* Plaut. apud Non.

FINIS is doubtful, as may be ſeen in Priſcian and in Non. And Virg. as we have above obſerved, uſed it indifferently. Even Cicero puts it in the fem: *Quæ finis funeſtæ familiæ.* It ſeems alſo in Nonius, that Varro, Caſſius, Cælius, Accius,

Accius, Lucretius, and Sisenna, all chose to have it in the fem. But some on the contrary have thought the gender so very extraordinary, that Cominian has presumed to charge Virgil with a solecism for saying

Hæc finis Priamatorum:

And Probus thinks that he receded from the rules of grammar (according to which all the nouns in NIS should be masc.) only for the greater ornament of verse. And Verepeus also insists that this noun is more common in the masc. But Pierius takes notice that in the ancient manuscripts of Virg. and Livy which he saw, it happens also to be fem. in other passages besides those where we find it of this gender.

FUNIS seems to have been fem. in Lucr.

Aurea de cœlo demisit funis in arva.

as Nonius and Gellius give it. Others say, that we should read, *Aureus funis,* &c. And Quintilian affirms that we cannot doubt of this noun's being masc. since its diminutive is *funiculus.*

LAPIS was used in the fem. by Enn. *subblatæ lapides,* as may be seen in Non. This he did perhaps in imitation of the Greeks, who say ὁ & ἡ λίθος.

NATALIS is always masc. in Virg. and others, though it refers to *dies,* which is doubtful.

POLLIS seldom occurs but in the old glosses; wherefore its gender is very uncertain. Probus and Cæsar said, *hoc pollen, pollinis,* as may be seen in Prisc. On the contrary according to the same author, Sosipater Charisius said, *hæc pollen, pollinis;* though the article is not to be found in Charisius. For this reason one would imagine that we ought rather to follow Vossius, who makes it masc. as well as Despauter and Verepeus. For as from *sanguen, sanguinis,* they have by syncope formed *sanguis* masc. it is probable that of *pollen, inis,* they have formed *pollis* masc. And this is the remark made by Phocas. But this nominative is scarce to be met with except among the grammarians. Nevertheless we find *pollinem* in Cato and in Pliny, which shews that it is not always neuter.

PULVIS is generally masculine as in Cic. when he says *eruditum pulverem,* speaking of the mathematics. And yet it is fem. in Enn. *vasta pulvis,* and in Propert. *pulvis Etrusca.*

RETIS was formerly said in the masc. as well as *rete* in the neuter, which is proved by Charisius, because as from *retis* comes *reticulus,* so from *rete* comes *reticulum.* Thus we read *retem* in the accusative in Plaut. and in Varro.

SCROBIS, which is also to be met with in the nominative in Capella and in Columella, was doubtful like *scrobs.* Phocas mentions *hæc scrobis,* fem. and Probus, *hic scrobis,* masc. Plautus has *sexagenos scrobes* in the masc. which is authorized by Cicero, as Servius observes 2 Georg. adding that the authority of Lucan and Gracchus who used it in the fem. ought not to be of so great a weight. But besides these Ovid has in the fem.

—— *Egesta scrobibus tellure duabus.*

Pliny likewise uses it in this gender, and Colum. in both.

But *scobs,* according to Priscian, or *scobis,* is only fem. in his opinion, as also in that of Phocas; and it is a mistake in Calepin and in the great Thesaurus, to say that it is masc. according to the latter, since according to the general rules, from which he does not except it, it is fem. whether we say *scobes* or *scobis.* And we see it in Pliny and in Colum. in the same gender. *Elimatam scobem coquere.* Plin. *Eburnea scobis.* Colum. *Abiegnâ scobe.* Ib.

SEMIS ought to be observed here among the rest. For *semissis* half an *As* is included in the rule of *As* p. 11. But *semis* which we meet with in Varro, Festus, and Hor. properly speaking comes from ἥμισυς, changing the Greek aspiration into S, and then it signifies the moiety of any thing. This noun is either indeclinable, and consequently neuter, *unum semis,* Erasm. *duos & semis cubitos habeat.* Exod. xx. or it takes its cases from *semissis,* and of course is masc. *Cubitum ac semissem habeat,* Ibid. &c.

SENTIS which we likewise find in the singular in Colum. *nos sentem canis appellamus,* is always masc. according to Phocas. Thus Virg. has *densi sentes,* and Colum. also uses it in the masc. So that it is without foundation put by Mantuanus in the fem. and by Caucius made to pass for doubtful; tho' the great Latin Thesaurus quotes from Virgil *Aspræ sentes,* where he would have had more reason to put *aspri,* for the verse being

Impro-

Improvisum aspris veluti qui sentibus anguem
Pressit humi nitens,————*Æn.* ii.
no inference can be drawn from thence in regard to the gender: and every where else both in Virg. and in others it is masc.

SOTULARIS is placed among the masculines by Despauter, but without foundation. His mistake was owing to a corrupt passage of St. Jerom, where he read, *hic sotularis quem,* &c. lib. i. adverf. Jovin. whereas the right reading is, *Et hic soccus quem cernitis,* &c.

TORQUIS is marked as masc. in Priscian, but Nonius, as well as Probus, shew that it is doubtful, Cicero makes it masc. *T. Manlius qui Galli torque detracto nomen invenerat.* In the same manner Ovid, Statius, and Pliny: but we find *torquis unca* in Propertius, eleg. xi. and Varro has in more places than one *Torques aureæ.*

VEPRIS is obsolete in the singular: for which reason there are some who think that *vepres* was formerly used, and others *veper,* as Caper in his treatise of orthography: But if it came from *vepres,* there is some appearance that it ought to increase in the genitive, according to the principal analogy of the masculines and commons of this termination, as we shall see in the declensions. And the same may be said if it came from *veper,* according to the general rule of the nouns in ER. For which reason I chose to put it among the nouns in IS; which Vossius also thinks more reasonable.

This noun occurs in the accusative singular in Colum. who makes it masculine. *Hunc veprem manifestum est interemi non posse.* It is often in the same gender, though in the plural, in Virg. —*& sparsi rorabant sanguine vepres.* And it is better to use it thus, notwithstanding Lucretius's saying *vepres auctas,* in the fem. which Caper does not approve of. Thus Charisius and Diomedes place this noun among the masculines most used in the plural. It is true that Prisc. ranks them among the fem. which form their diminutive of the same gender as themselves, such as *veprecula;* but this has not been followed.

VOMIS, *eris,* is masc. because it is the same as *Vomer,* rule 15.

RULE XXI.

Of the nouns in OS.

1. *Nouns in* OS *are masculine;*
2. *Except* Cos, *and* Dos, *which are feminine;*
3. *And* Epos, *with* Os, oris, *or* ossis, *which are neuter.*

EXAMPLES.

1. Nouns in OS are of the masculine gender. *Flos purpureus,* a purple flower: *ros gratissimus,* most agreeable dew: *mos perversus,* a perverse custom.

2. These two are feminine, *Cos,* a whetstone: *dos,* a portion, or dowry, a property, an advantage.

3. These three are neuter. *Hoc epos,* an heroic poem: *hoc os, oris,* the mouth, the countenance: *hoc os, ossis,* a bone.

OF GENDERS,

ANNOTATION.

It is observable that the nouns in OS which occur more usually in OR, follow the gender they have in their first termination, as *hic bonos, hæc arbos*, and the like.

A great many nouns which are now in US, were formerly also in OS; as *scorpios, avos, flavos*, &c. And on the contrary there are a great many now in OS or OR, whose ending was formerly in US; as *colus*, from whence came *colos*, and afterwards *color*; *dolus* for *dolos* or *dolor*, &c. which is owing to the affinity that subsists between these vowels O and U and the consonants R and S, as we shall hereafter shew in the treatise of letters.

The Greek nouns in OS are frequently feminine. For though the Latins generally change them into US (as we shall in the next rule) or even sometimes into ER; yet there are a great many which retain OS; as *arctos, diametros* in Vitruvius, Macrobius, and Colum. rather than *diametrus* or *diameter*: And these nouns retain the gender of their original tongue. Hence it is a matter of surprize that most dictionaries, and even that of Stephens, as well as the great Thesaurus, which have been revised five or six times, have all of them *diameter* in the masc. contrary to what we find in Archimedes, Euclid, and others; and contrary to the analogy of both languages, according to which we are to understand γραμμὴ or *linea*.

Eos is always feminine, whether it be taken for the morning, or the goddess of the morning.

Proxima victricem cum Romam inspexerit Eos. Ovid.

Epos is neuter, because it is of the first of contracted nouns in Greek. *Forte epos*, Hor. an heroic and warlike poem. Diomedes uses it in the same gender, which we ought to follow in regard to all the nouns in OS of the same declension in Greek. But *epodos* or *epodus* is masculine, being taken for a kind of odes, like the epodes of Horace, coming from ἐπὶ, *super*, and ᾠδὴ, *canticum*.

Exos, compos, impos, are adjectives, and do not come under this Rule.

RULE XXII.

Of the nouns in US of the second or fourth declension.

1. *Nouns in* US *of the second or fourth declension are generally masculine.*
2. *But those derived from the Greek are frequently feminine.*
3. *Of which gender are also in the best Latin authors the following twelve,* alvus, colus, acus, manus, idus, tribus, pórticus, ficus, humus, vannus, cárbasus, *and* domus.
4. Specus,

4. Specus, penus, groſſus, faſélus, *are doubtful.*
5. Virus, *and* pélagus *are neuter.*
6. *But* vulgus *is neuter or maſculine.*

EXAMPLES.

1. Nouns in US of the ſecond and fourth declenſion, are maſculine, *hic óculus, óculi,* the eye: *hic ventus, i,* the wind: *hic fructus, ûs,* fruit: *hic acus, aci,* a kind of fiſh.

But it is otherwiſe with nouns in US derived from Greek words in OS, becauſe they retain the gender they had in Greek. Thus there are ſome of them maſculine which conform to the general rule, as *hic paradíſus, i,* paradiſe, a garden: *hic tomus, i,* a tome, or part of a thing: *hic hyacínthus, i,* a flower called the hyacinth.

2. But moſt of theſe being of the fem. in Greek, retain the ſame gender in Latin. *Hæc Abýſſus,* an abyſs: *hæc papýrus,* paper: *hæc cryſtállus,* cryſtal: *hæc ſýnodus,* a ſynod: *hæc méthodus,* a method: *hæc éxodus,* a going out: *hæc períodus,* a period: *hæc dipthóngus,* a diphthong: *hæc erémus,* a wilderneſs: *hæc átomus,* Cic. an atom.

3. There are twelve more which in the beſt Latin authors are always feminine: *alvus cæca,* a dark belly: *colus ebúrnea,* an ivory diſtaff: *hæc acus, ûs,* chaff, a needle: *manus déxtera,* the right hand: *idus Maiæ,* the ides of May (it is of the plural; *idus, iduum, idibus,*) *Tribus ínfima,* the loweſt tribe, family, or race: *porticus ampla,* a large gallery, or portico: *hæc ficus, ûs,* or *ficus, i,* a fig or a fig-tree. But *hic ficus,* is taken for a ſort of ulcer, and then it is found only in the ſecond declenſion: *humus ſicca,* dry ground: *vannus rúſtica,* a country van, or fan to winnow corn with: *hæc carbáſus,* fine linen, a ſail: *domus ampla,* a large houſe.

4. There are four either maſculine or feminine: *ſpecus denſus,* a dark cave: *ſpecus última,* the furtheſt part of the cavern: *penus ánnuus,* Plaut. yearly proviſion: *magna penus,* ſtore of proviſion.

Hic or *hæc grossus*, a green fig: *hic* or *hæc phasêlus*, a kind of boat; but it is better in the masculine.

5. There are two of the neuter gender: *virus mortiferum*, mortal poison: *pelagus Carpáthium*, Hor. the Carpathian sea.

6. And one which is sometimes masculine, and more frequently neuter: *vulgus diligéntior*, the more diligent vulgar; *vulgus incérium*, Virg. the inconstant vulgar.

ANNOTATION.

We endeavour always to ground our rules upon such authority as is the safest to imitate; as to particular remarks, we throw them into the annotations, and into the lists thereon depending.

List of Latin nouns in US.

Acus, *aci*, is masculine, and signifies a kind of fish, which the Greeks call Βελόνη. *Acus, us*, is feminine and signifies a needle, or a bodkin: *acus, aceris*, is neuter, and is taken for chaff, in which signification it occurs also in the feminine. *Acus resecta & separatæ*, Colum.

Alvus is masculine in old authors, as in Accius and several others according to Priscian; which Erasmus made no scruple to imitate. However the most approved authors make it of the fem.

Carbasus is never masculine according to Caper in his treatise *de verbis dubiis*. And yet neither Phocas, Probus, nor Priscian have ever excepted it from the rule of masculines, which has been the reason that a great many take it for doubtful. But it is generally feminine, as Alvarez and Vossius observe. *Carbasus intenta theatris*, Lucr. *Carbasus alba*, Propert. &c. In the plural we say *carbasa*. See the Heteroclites, rule 3.

Colus is generally feminine. *Quando ad me venis cum tua & colu & lana*, Cic. in Nonius. And yet we find it masc. in Catullus, *Colum amictum lana retinebat*, and in Propertius
—— *Lydo pensa diurna colo.*

Crocus is feminine in Apul. *Crocus vino diluta*. We find *crocum rubentem*, in Virg. *Crocos tenues*, in Ovid. *Spirantes*, in Juvenal; where we cannot tell whether it is feminine or masculine. But we say likewise *crocum*, neuter. Diom. Serv. Sallust.

Faselus or Phaselus, a little ship, a galliot, or pinnace, is masc. according to Nonius, Catullus, Cicero, Columella, and others. But Ovid has made it feminine.
—— *Vos estis fractæ tellus non dura faselo.*
Martial and Statius have used it in the same gender, for which reason we have left it doubtful. But *faselus* or *phaselus* signifying a kind of pulse, will hardly, I think, be found of any other than of the masc. gender in good authors.

Ficus is very doubtful among grammarians, both as to gender and declension. Varro in the 8th de L.L. n. 48. speaking of some of the names of trees, says it is false that *ficus* is of the fourth declension, and he thinks it right to say *hi & hæ fici* in the plural, and not *ficus* like *manus*: whereby he gives it two genders in this sense, and but one declension. Sanctius mentions it only as of the feminine, whether in the second or fourth declension, whether it be taken for a fig or a figtree, or for a kind of ulcer. Others distinguish it according to the signification: as Scioppius who insists upon its being always masc. when it signifies the fig-tree, and fem. when it signifies a fig or an ulcer, which derived this name only from the resemblance it has to a fig. But he gives no authority.

Others add the declension: some, as Despauter, pretending that as *ficus* is only masc. and of the second declension, when it signifies an ulcer; that it is masc. and fem. when it signifies

nifies a fig or a fig-tree; so that it is always of the second declenſion if it be maſc. even in this laſt ſenſe; and of the fourth, if it be feminine.

Others, as Voſſius 1. Anal. cap. xiv. that as it is maſc. when it ſignifies an ulcer, and fem. when it ſignifies a fig; it is indifferently of the ſecond and fourth, in both ſignifications. Which opinion Priſcian favours in his ſixth book, where he ſays that *Etiam hic ficus, vitium corporis, quartæ eſt.* But in this he is cenſured by L. Valla and by Ramus, becauſe he produces no authority for it.

Others that being in like manner maſc. when it ſignifies an ulcer, and fem. when it ſignifies a fig or a fig-tree, it is only of the ſecond declenſion in the firſt ſenſe, and of the ſecond and fourth in the other. This is the opinion of Ramus, Alvarez, Behourt, and of Voſſius alſo in his ſmaller grammar, which I have embraced as much the ſafeſt, being ſupported by the following authorities. *Fici quarum radices longiſſimæ,* Plin. *Uxorem ſuam ſuſpendiſſe ficu.* Cic. 2 Orat. *Fici ſemen naturale intus eſt in ea fico quam edimus,* Varro.

Dicemus ficus quas ſcimus in arbore naſci,
Dicemus ficos Cæciliane tuos. Mart.

It is true that Probus quoting this diſtich puts *ficos* in the firſt verſe, and *ficus* in the ſecond; which might ſerve to confirm the opinion of Priſcian above given; or induce us to believe that the ancients took it to be of two declenſions in both ſenſes. But the paſſages produced from Plihy, from Macrobius, and Lucilius, to prove that this noun is alſo maſc. even when it ſignifies the fruit, appear to be corrupted, and have no great weight, as may be ſeen in Voſſius and in Ramus, Schol. Gramm. 12. And the opinion of L. Valla, who imagines that being of the fourth, and ſignifying a fig, it is alſo maſc. is univerſally rejected.

FIMUS is generally maſc. but in Appul. we find it fem. *Liquidâ fimo ſtrictim egeſtâ.*

GROSSUS is maſc. in Celſus, *groſſi aquâ decocti;* and fem. in Pliny, *Crudæ groſſi.*

INTUBUS, which the grammarians make doubtful, is always maſc. in claſſic authors, *Intubus erraticus,* Pliny.

PAMPINUS, according to Servius, Probus, and Caper, is doubtful; and Varro frequently makes it fem. yet in the pureſt writers of the Latin tongue, it is always maſc. *Omnis fœcundus pampinus.* Colum. *Pampini triti & impoſiti.* Pliny.

SOCRUS was formerly uſed for *ſocer,* as we ſee in Nonius; ſo that this noun was of the common gender, as well as *nepos.*

SEXUS was formerly neuter according to Priſcian; *Virile ſexus nunquam ullum habui.* Plaut. in Rud. where others read *ſecus.* For according to Varro, they formerly uſed to put *ſecus* for *ſexus.* And this word is ſtill to be met with in Salluſt according to Non. in Auſonius according to Scaliger, and in others. *Liberorum capitum virile ſecus ad decem millia capta,* in the Dutch edition of Livy, l. xxvi. c. 37.

SPECUS and PENUS are to be found of all genders. We have mentioned them here only as maſc. and fem. becauſe when they are made neuter, they ſhould be referred to the third declenſion, and to the following rule, though they are ſeldom uſed then but in the three like caſes, viz. the Nominative, the Accuſative and the Vocative, as *ſpecus horrendum,* Virg. *Portare penus,* Hor. And in the plural alſo, *penora,* in Feſtus. But in the fourth declenſion they are oftener fem. than maſc.

Of the Greek nouns in US.

The Greek words, as we have often obſerved, depend on an exact knowledge of the tongue from which they are derived. And yet to omit nothing that may be of uſe, I ſhall give here an explication of thoſe which relate to this rule, where there is any reaſon to doubt, and where the Latins have not always followed the Greeks.

Of the names of plants and shrubs.

BIBLUS or BYBLUS is always fem. whether it be taken for the little tree which was also called *papyrus*, or for the small bark of this very tree, of which they made paper.

CYTISUS in Latin as well as in Greek is masc. Αἲξ τὸν κύτισον δίωκει. *Capra Cytisum sequitur.* Theocr. *Cytisus utilissimus.* Colum.

COSTUS is masc. in Greek, and always fem. in Latin.
—— *Eoáque costus,* Lucan.

HYACINTHUS is doubtful in Greek, but oftener feminine. Nevertheless Virgil has: *Ferrugineos hyacinthos,* and in most Latin authors it is generally masc.

HYSSOPUS is fem. But we say, *hoc* HYSSOPUM, as in Greek they likewise say ἡ ὕσσωπος & τὸ ὕσσωπον.

In the same manner we say, *hic* NARDUS and *hoc* NARDUM, and a great many others, of which we shall take particular notice in a list at the end of the heteroclites.

We say also, *hæc* PAPYRUS, and *hoc* PAPYRUM: but the former is doubtful in Greek, though it is always fem. in Latin.

Of the names of precious stones.

BERYLLUS is masc. *Berylli raro alibi reperti.* Plin.

CHRYSOLITHUS, fem. *Chrysolithon duodecim pondo à se visam.* Plin. And yet Prudentius has made it masc.
Ingens Chrysolithus nativo interlitus auro.

CHRYSOPRASIUS, fem. *Chrysoprasius, porri succum & ipsa referens,* Plin.

CHRYSTALLUS always fem. in Latin:
Crystallúsque tuas ornet aquosa manus. Propert.
though in Greek to signify ice, it is masc. τὸν κρύσταλλον τὸν Κελτικὸν, Lucian. *Glaciem Celticam.*

OPALUS, masc. *veri Opali fulgor,* Plin.
SAPPHYRUS, fem. *Cæruleæ Sapphyri.* Id.

SMARAGDUS, masc. *Smaragdi Scythici.* Id.

TOPASIUS generally fem. *Color fumidæ Topazii.* Plin.

In like manner the rest, which may be learnt by practice. But the reason of this difference of gender, which has been already hinted at p. 8. it that also in Greek, to which these nouns refer, being of the common gender; so in Latin they refer sometimes to *lapis* or *lapillus* masc. and sometimes to *Gemma,* fem.

Of other Greek nouns in US.

ANTIDOTUS is fem. *Hujus regis antidotus celebratissima quæ Mithridatios vocatur,* Gell. But we say likewise ANTIDOTUM, neuter.

ATOMUS is generally fem. in Cic. But Seneca and Lactantius make it masc.

BALANUS a kind of mast or acorn from oak, beech, &c. a date, a suppository, is always fem. in Greek; and Horace has used it in this gender: *Pressa tuis Balanus capillis.* And yet in Pliny we read *Sardianos balanos.* So that this noun seems to be common in Latin, unless there be some mistake in the passage of Pliny.

BARBYTUS, a stringed *instrument of music,* is doubtful. Horace makes it masculine, *barbite primum modulate civi.* Ovid puts it in the feminine.
Non facit ad lacrymas barbitos ulla meas.

COLOSSUS is always masculine.
Quæ super imposito melis geminata colosso. Statius.

as Scaliger and Vossius read it, instead of *gemmata* which is in some editions.

CORYMBUS, always masculine. *Purpureo surgit glomerata corymbo,* Colum. For which reason in Cornelius Severus we must read,
Ut crebro introrsus, spatioque vacante corymbus.
according to the observation of Scaliger, whereas others read, *spatio vacuata corymbus.*

ISTHMUS is masculine
—— *pervius isthmus erat.* Ovid.
Apuleius is the only writer perhaps that has made it fem. *Isthmus Ephyræa,* that is, *Corinthiaca,* because Corinth was formerly called *Ephyra,* according to the testimony of Pliny, Pausanias, and others. But here Apuleius may be justified, for as much he did not understand barely the streight of Peloponnesus, but the whole circumjacent country. Just as he says also in the fem. *Hymetton Atticam,* & *Tænaron Laconicam.* Which cannot be defended but

but by saying that then *Hymettus* is taken not only for the famous mountain in the neighbourhood of. Athens, but for the whole country; and in like manner that *Tænaros* is put not only for the cape of the southern point of the Peloponnesus, but for the whole circumjacent country, or at least for the town of the same name that was built there. For it is certain that both those nouns taken for the mountains are always of the masculine gender.

PHARUS is masc. among the Greeks, and always fem. among the Latins. *Pharus æmula lunæ*, apud Parin. wherefore in Suetonius in *Claud.* we must read, *Supposuit altissimam turrim in exemplum Alexandrinæ Phari*, according to the best editions, and according to the observation of Beroaldus followed by Vossius, and not *Alexandrini*, as some would have it.

This shews how little dependance is to be made on the correction of Pamelius in the following passage of Tertull. at the end of the book de Pænit. *De istis duobus humanæ salutis quasi pharis*; since in this very sense we ought rather to read *duabus* than *duobus*, because *pharus* refers to *turris*. But the genuine reading of this passage is, *duabus quasi plancis*, as monsf. Rigault observes.

There are a great many other Greek nouns, which are always used in the fem. But the bare rule of the common and general noun, to which they refer, is sufficient to determine them.

Thus we say, HÆC ABYSSUS, for properly it is the same as saying, *fundo carens*, understanding the substantive in question, as *aqua*, *vorago*, &c. But this noun does not occur in Latin, except in ecclesiastical writers.

We say HÆC ATOMUS, sup. οὐσία.

HÆC EREMUS, sup. γῆ or χώρα, *terra*, or *regio*, and in like manner the rest.

RULE XXIII.

Of the nouns in US which are of the third declension.

1. *Nouns in* US *of the third declension are neuter.*
2. *But those in* US, *making* UTIS, UNTIS, *or* UDIS, *in the genitive, are feminine.*
3. *To which we may add* Tellus, uris.
4. *But nouns in* Pus *making* Odis *in the genitive are masculine.*

EXAMPLES.

1. Nouns in US of the third declension are of the neuter gender. *Hoc munus, ĕris*, a gift, an employment: *hoc tempus, ŏris*, time: *hoc latus, ĕris*, the side: *hoc acus, ĕris*, chaff.

2. Those which make UDIS, UTIS, or UNTIS, in the genitive, are feminine: *hæc virtus, virtūtis*, virtue: *hæc salus, ūtis*, safety, health: *hæc palus, ūdis*, a morass: *hæc servitus, ūtis*, servitude: *hæc juventus, ūtis*, youth, *hæc subscus, ūdis*, a fastening of boards or timber together, called by the joiners a swallow, or dove tail: *hæc senectus, ūtis*, old age: *hæc incus, ūdis*, an anvil: *hæc hydrus, ūntis*, the name of a river: *hæc Pessinus, ūntis*, the name of a city.

3. Hæc

OF GENDERS.

3. *Hæc tellus, tellúris*, the earth, is also feminine.

4. Nouns in PUS which make *odis* in the genitive, that is, the compounds of *pes, pedis*, or rather of πὲς, ποδὸς, the foot, are masculine like the word of which they are compounded. *Hic tripus, tripodis; hic pólypus, ŏdis*, a fish with a great many feet; *hic chýtrŭpus, ŏdis*, a pot having feet, also a trivet; *hic apus, ápodis*, one that has no feet.

ANNOTATION.

Nevertheless *Lagópus* is feminine, whether it be taken for the herb hare's foot, or for the bird called the white partridge, thus conforming to the common and general word, *avis* or *herba*.

We read in Pliny, *Plurimùm volant, quæ apodes appellantur.* Which does not prove that *apus* is also feminine; for it is plain that the nominative of *volant* is *volucres* understood, to which *quæ* refers as to its antecedent.

RULE XXIV.

Of *Laus* and *Fraus*, and of nouns ending in S, with another consonant.

1. *Nouns ending in S, with another consonant, are feminine.*
2. *Of which gender are also* Laus *and* Fraus.

EXAMPLES.

1. Nouns ending in S, joined to another consonant, are feminine, *urbs opulénta*, a rich city: *puls nívea*, white pap or panado: *hyems ignáva*, the lazy winter, which makes us lazy: *hæc fórceps, ĭpis*, a pair of tongs, or scissars: *hæc frons, frondis*, the leaf of a tree: *hæc frons, frontis*, the forehead: *hæc lens, lentis*, a kind of pulse called lentiles: *hæc stirps sancta*, a holy race: *hæc scobs*, saw-dust, pin-dust. See *scobis* above.

2. These two are also feminine, *laus vera*, true praise: *fraus iniqua*, unjust fraud.

ANNOTATION.

We must not be surprised that these nouns are of the feminine gender, since they come from those in ES or in IS. For even according to Varro, there were no nouns ending in two consonants. Hence they said *plebes* for *plebs*; *artis* for *ars*; *mentis* for *mens*; *frondes* for *frons*; a leaf, &c. Where we see that they always

ways lost the consonant before their termination, when there was still another that preceded it, and they resume it in the genitive only, because it is quite natural to them.

RULE XXV.
Exception to the preceding rule.

1. Dens, chalybs, mons, hydrops, rudens, fons, *and* pons, *are masculine.*
2. *But* scrobs, adeps, *and* stirps, *are doubtful.*

EXAMPLES.

1. The following nouns are excepted from the general rule. Seven of them are masculine, *hic dens*, a tooth; and in like manner all its compounds, *bidens*, an instrument with two teeth: *tridens*, a trident, &c.

Hic hydrops, Hor. the dropsy: *chalybs vulníficus*, the steel that woundeth: *mons incúltus*, a desert mountain: *rudens exténtus*, a cable rope extended: *fons limpidíssimus*, a very clear fountain: *pons sublícius*, a wooden bridge.

2. These three are doubtful; *scrobs*, a ditch; *scrobes ampli*, wide ditches; *scrobs exigua*, Lucan, a little ditch: *lupínus adeps*, Pliny, the fat of a wolf; *hæc adeps*, Colum: *hic aut hæc stirps*, the root or stock of a tree.

ANNOTATION.

Quadrans is included in the rule of *As*, p. 11, and *serpens* in that of the epicenes, p. 58.

Dens is feminine in Apuleius, *dentes splendidas*, in which he is not to be imitated. For it is observable that this author has the particularity of frequently affecting words that were grown obsolete, and as frequently of inventing new ones.

Chalybs is masculine, because it takes its name from the people who dug it out of the earth. *At Chalybes nudi ferrum, &c.* Virg.

Forceps, according to Priscian, is doubtful, but we meet with it only in the feminine.

Seps, for a kind of insect is masculine, wherein it follows the noblest gender; but for a hedge it is feminine, instead of which we meet also with *sepes* in Virg. and elsewhere, and therefore it follows the general rule.

Rudens occurs in the feminine in Plautus, *quam trahis rudentem complico*. But Catullus, Virgil, and others use it in the masculine. Which is owing doubtless to their referring it to *funis* as

OF GENDERS.

to the general word; though the ancients by making it feminine, followed rather the analogy of the termination.

Scrobs is doubtful, but more frequently masculine according to Servius. See here above *scrobis*, p. 41.

Stirps, signifying lineage or extraction, is feminine by the preceding rule; but signifying the root or stem of a tree, it is masculine or feminine. *Lentoque in stirpe moratus*, Virg. The reason of this is perhaps its having been heretofore doubtful in the former signification. *Qui stirpem occidit meum*, Pacuv. But we do not meet with this in pure authors.

RULE XXVI.
Of nouns in X.

1. *Nouns in X are feminine.*
2. *Except* calix, calyx, fornix, spadix, varix, urpix, grex, *which are masculine.*
3. *Except also dissyllables in* AX *or* EX, *which are likewise masculine.*
4. *But* fornex, carex, *and* forfex, *are feminine.*
5. Tradux *and* filex, *are doubtful.*
6. Cortex, pumex, imbrex, *and* calx, *are also doubtful; but oftener masculine.*
7. Sandix, *and* onyx, *are doubtful, but oftener feminine.*

EXAMPLES.

1. Nouns in X are generally feminine, whatever termination they receive.

Whether they be monosyllables, as *fax funésta*, a fatal torch: *pax diutúrna*, a lasting peace: *fax subálba*, whitish dregs: *nex injústa*, unjust death: *pix atra*, black pitch: *hæc vox, vocis*, the voice: *hæc crux, crucis*, a cross: *hæc lux, lucis*, the light: *hæc Styx, Stygis*, the river Styx in hell, a poisonous fountain: *hæc falx, falcis*, an hook, bill, or scythe: *lanx, lancis*, a great broad plate, a scale or bason of the balance: *arx, arcis*, a citadel, &c.

Or whether they have two or more syllables; as *hæc similax*, or *smilax, ăcis*, Pliny, a yew tree, also a kind of herb: *hæc supéllex, supelléctilis*, goods or houshold

houshold stuff: *hæc appéndix, ícis,* an appendage or appendix.

Hæc bombyx, y'cis, silk; for as to the worm, it is masculine: *hæc cervix,* the hinder part of the neck: *chænix,* a kind of measure.

Cicátrix advérsa, Cic. wounds received in the fore part of the body, by facing the enemy. *Avérsa* on the contrary was wounds received behind, upon turning one's back to the enemy.

Hæc lodix, a sheet, blanket, or coverlet: *hæc tomix,* a cord, or rope: *hæc vibix, ícis,* a wheal on the flesh after whipping: *viviradix,* Cic. a quickset.

Hæc phalanx, ángis, a Macedonian battalion: *hæc meninx, ingis,* a thin membrane which incloseth the brain.

2. We must except some that are masculine.

In the first place, those mentioned in the rule: *hic calix, ícis,* a cup or chalice: also *calyx, ycis,* the cup, or bud of a flower: *spadix,* of a bay colour, or light red; tho' properly speaking this is an adjective: *varix,* a crooked vein swelling with melancholy, especially in the legs: *hic urpix, ícis,* Cato, or *hirpix* and *herpix,* Fest. an instrument of husbandry like an harrow: *hic grex, gregis,* a flock, an herd.

3. In the second place, words of two syllables in AX and in EX.

In AX, as *hic abax,* a cupboard: *thorax,* the inward part of the breast, a stomacher, a breast-plate: *storax* or *styrax,* a kind of incense or perfume, Virg. Plin. Dioscor. Signifying a tree, it is feminine by the general rule: *hic mystax,* the mustaches.

In EX, *hic apex,* properly a little woollen tuft, or tassel, on the top of the flamen's or high priest's cap, hence it is taken for the cap itself, for the top of the head, for the top of any thing; for the mark or accent over letters, also a letter or mandate; *caudex,* a stock, or trunk, or stem of a tree, a table-book: *exlex,* lawless, always masculine; as also *index,* a discoverer, a shewer, the index, or table of a book, the forefinger: *latex,* all manner of liquor or juice: *murex,* a shell-

shell-fish of whose liquor purple colour is made: *pollex*, the thumb: *pulex*, a flea: *cimex*, a bug: *culex*, a gnat: *sorex*, a rat: *ramex*, a pectoral vein, burstenness, a rupture: *rumex*, the herb called sorrel, *fæcundus rumex*, Virg. in Moreto: *frutex*, a shrub: *hic obex*, all kind of obstruction, a bolt, a bar: *vertex* or *vortex*, a whirlwind, a whirlpool, colic or the belly-ach, the top or crown of the head, the head itself, and thence the top of any thing.

4. But out of this second branch of dissyllables in AX and in EX we must except,

4. First of all, these which are feminine; *hæc fornax*, a furnace: *hæc forfex*, the same as *forceps*, a pair of scissars or sheers, a pair of pincers: *hæc carex*, Virg. sedge, sheer grass.

5. Secondly, these which are doubtful; *hic tradux*, Varr. *hæc tradux*, Colum. a branch or twig of a vine carried along from tree to tree: *hic aut hæc silex*, a flint.

6. Thirdly, these which are also doubtful, but oftener masculine in prose. *Cortex*, the bark of a tree: *pumex*, a pumice stone: *imbrex*, the gutter tile, or roof tile: *hic calx*, the heel, a kick: but when it signifies lime, it is feminine.

7. Fourthly, these which though doubtful, are oftener feminine; *sandix*, a kind of red or purple colour: *onyx*, signifying a precious stone is feminine, because it refers to *gemma*, *vera onyx*, Plin. but taken for a kind of marble or alabaster, or for the boxes made of that material, it is masculine: *parvus onyx*, Hor. a small box of onyx.

ANNOTATION.

Besides the masculines excepted in the rule, one might also add *hallux*, which is made a masculine, because it is the same as *hallus*, which we find in Festus, signifying the great toe, which he derives from ἅλλομαι, *salio*, because, he says, it generally climbs over the next toe to it. But this word is very rare; besides it is rather an adjective than a substantive, and always supposes *digitus*.

We do not here except *Arctophylax*, the guardian of the bear, which by its signification is masculine, though it be taken for the constellation near the greater bear.

Nor do we make mention of the compounds of *uncia*, as *quincunx*, and others, because they are included in the rule of *As* and its parts. p. 11.

Those of animals or insects shall be included in the following rule, after we have given a list of the words belonging to this, and taken notice of what is most worthy of observation in the ancients concerning this subject.

List of nouns in X.

ATRIPLEX, an herb called orage or orach, is feminine in the poet Macer, according to the general rule. *Atriplicem tritam cum nitro, melle & aceto, Dicunt appositam calidam, sedare podagram.* And yet Pliny makes it neuter: *Atriplex & sylvestre est & sativum.* Doubtless he was determined by the old neuter, *atriplexum*, which according to Festus, was current among the ancients. And it seems it is best to use it in this gender.

CALX, signifying the heel, or end of a thing, is doubtful. *Nunc video calcem ad quem decursum est*, Tusc. 1. *sumus ab ipsa calce revocati*, de Repub. 3. as quoted by Seneca, lib. 19. epist. 119. *Ferrata calce fatigat*, Virg. 11. Æn. as we find it in Charis. and Non. and in the old manuscripts, whereas the modern copies have *ferrato* in the masc. *Candidum ad calcem*, Varr. *Potius quàm unum calcem triverit*, Plaut. in Pænul. act. 4. sc. 2. where it seems to stand for a chess-man or table-man according to Vossius. *Calces rigidi*, Pers. *incussæ*, Sil.

CAUDEX or CODEX were indifferently used one for the other, in the same manner as *caurus* and *corus*, *plaustrum* and *plostrum*. But now we generally take *caudex* for the stock or trunk of a tree, and *codex* for a book.

CORTEX is doubtful according to Nonius, *supremus cortex*, Varr. *corporeus*, id. *raptus*, Virg. Æn. 7. *deceptus, direptus, discussus, cavatus, sectus, scissus*. Ovid. *lentus, rugosus, siccus*, Id. *cortex amara*, Ovid. *corporea*, Varr. *musco circundat amara* ──── *corticis*, Virg. ecl. 6. as Quintius Pierius reads it, as also Servius, who adds notwithstanding that it is better to follow the masculine gender. But we find it feminine in Pliny, in Valerius Maximus, and others.

OBEX is generally masc. yet Pliny makes it fem. *nullæ obices*, and in Virg. l. 10. *Ecce maris magnâ claudit nos obice pontus.* Which even Servius acknowledges, though in most books we find it *magno.* And he affirms moreover that Capero proves it was customary to say *hic & hæc obex, quod hodie*, he adds, *de usu recessit.* Which makes Pierius say: *usque' adeo vates, summus loquendi scribendique artifex, sub ferulam, si Deo placet, revocatur à Grammaticis, qui nolunt ampliùs hic & hæc obex dici, ut veteribus dicere concessum est.* This shews that it was no mistake to put it in the fem. as we still find it in Sidonius, though we more rarely meet with it in this gender.

SILEX, according to Vossius in his grammar, is of the number of those which are masculine in prose, and fem. in verse: and Verepeus makes the same distinction. Yet Nonius, as Vossius himself confesses in his first book of analogy, says it was received by every body in the fem. Though he shews us also two passages where Lucretius has made it masculine, and where Statius has used it in the same manner. For which reason Alvarez places it among those which are used alike in both genders: and this we have followed.

THOMIX is fem. by the general rule, though Hermol. Barbarus writes *thomen:* but the Greek has Θῶμιξ, τὴν Θῶμιγγα συνάγει, says Pausan. Lucil. has made use of *thomices* in the plur. and Pallad. of *thomicibus:* which shews that it does not come from *thomice, es*, of the first declension, as most dictionaries, and even Calepin pretend.

VARIX is masc. according to Phocas. This Despauter, R. Stephen, and Calepin confirm by the authority of Horace: *varice succiso;* which is not to be found. But if it be masc. more

more than once in Celsus, it is fem. in Seneca and Quintilian. However, the masc. is most used.

VIBIX. We write it thus *vibix* according to Vossius and Scioppius, including it under the general rule, though most authors write *vibex*; but this is repugnant to the analogy of the genitive, which is long, *vibicis*, like *radicis*, &c. For those in *ex* make *icis* short.

LUX is always masc. in Plautus; *luce claro diripimus aurum*. In Aulul. And in his *Cistel. Cum primo luce cras*. To which we may refer the following passage of Terence in Adelph. *Cras cum prima lucu* for *luce*; since Donatus explaining it says: *veteres masculino genere lucem dicebant*. And Nonius observes that Cicero made use of it in this same gender, de Offic. l. 3: *et cùm prior ire luce claro non queo*: which is not to be found. Vossius says that a passage of the 2d book resembles it: *luce clare in foro saltet*: nor is this to be found any more than the other. So that in all probability both authors meant this other passage of the third book of offices, in which we read: *luce palam in foro saltet*, where *luce* is taken for *die*.

CRUX was also formerly masc. according to the same Nonius; but we do not use it any longer in this gender.

SANDYX or SANDIX, notwithstanding the authority of all the dictionaries, as well that of Pajot, of Stephens and others, who make it only masc. is generally feminine; *pingentes sandice sublita*, Plin. And in like manner in Greek; καιόμενον δὲ ψιμμύθιον, εἰς τὴν καλυμένην σάνδικα μεταβάλλων, Galen. *Adusta cerussa, in sandicem quam vocant, transit*. Not that we would affirm with Alvarez that this noun is always fem. For we find in Gratius who lived under the reign of Augustus; *Interdum Libyco fucantur sandice pinnæ*, according to the constant reading in Aldus, and in all the best editions. But Despauter has committed a still greater mistake in placing this noun among the masculines.

RULE XXVII.

Of epicene nouns.

1. *The epicenes follow the gender of the termination.*
2. *Thus the following are masculine;* phœnix, glis, turtur, bombyx, oryx, vultur, vermis, piscis, lepus, salar, delphis, mugil, *and* mus.
3. *These are feminine,* álcyon, halex, lagópus, aédon.
4. Limax *and* cenchris *are doubtful.*
5. Anguis *and* Palúmbes *are oftener masculine.*
6. *But* serpens, talpa, grus, perdix, lynx, *and* dama, *are oftener feminine.*

EXAMPLES.

Epicene nouns are those which under one and the same gender include both male and female. These nouns generally follow the gender of their termination, so that this

this idea alone is sufficient in the beginning, without confounding children any farther about it.

Thus we see that the following are masculine; *hic vespertílio, ónis*, a bat: *hic scórpio, ónis*, a scorpion: *hic áttagen*, a delicious bird of Asia, like our woodcock or snipe.

Hic élephas, ántis, an elephant: *monóceros*, an unicorn: *camélus*, a camel: *corax*, a raven: *sorex*, a rat, &c.

On the contrary we find that the following are feminine: *hæc áquila*, an eagle: *alcédo*, the king's fisher: *anas*, a duck or drake: *vulpes*, a fox: *cornix*, a crow or rook, and in like manner the rest.

ANNOTATION.

It must not be imagined that we are speaking here of the names of all sorts of animals, but only of the epicenes, of which we may mention two sorts. Some have only one gender, as *hic turtur*, a bird called a turtle: others have two, as *hic aut hæc limax*, a snail: but in such a manner that they indeterminately include under each of these genders, both male and female, in which they properly differ from the common, which includes them separately under different genders.

Thus it is obvious that the epicene is not a distinct gender from the rest; but only a particular application of the other genders: and therefore,

1. That the general rule of these nouns can be no other than that of their termination. But because there are a great many of them excepted, we have divided these exceptions into different branches under the following cyphers which refer to those of the rule: for

2. Some of them are only masculine, contrary to the analogy of their termination.

3. Others are only feminine.

And others are doubtful; but among these,

4. Some are equally used in both genders.

5. Other are oftener in the masculine.

6. And others are oftener in the feminine.

The following is an alphabetical list, not only of those mentioned in the rule, where we inserted only the most necessary to be known, but likewise of the most remarkable among the rest.

Epicenes excepted from the rules of the termination.

ACCIPITER, *an hawk*, is masc. in Ovid. *Accipiter nulli avi satis æquus*, Met. 11. and in Virg. *Accipiter sacer ales*, Æneid. 11. where he follows the noblest gender, and that of the termination. And yet Lucretius joins it with the feminine, according to Nonius, *Accipitres visæ volantes*.

AEDON, *a nightingale*, is feminine in Seneca *in Octavia*.

OF GENDERS.

—— quæ lacrymis nostris questus
Reddet ædon.

ALCYON, a bird called the *king's fisher*, is feminine, contrary to the rule of its termination. *Dilectæ Thetidi alcyones*, Virg. And thus all the Greek writers have used it. For which reason Servius is censured for affirming that *hic & hæc alcyon* was used; what led him into a mistake was that this noun being common in its signification, he thought it also common in its construction, which are two very different things, as we shall shew in our remarks after the syntax.

ALES, *a bird*, is commonly feminine according to the gender of its termination. And yet Virgil has made it masc. *Fulvus ales*, Æn. 12. which ought to be referred to *Masculus*, according to the opinion of Donatus, who thinks the not expressing a female in this passage, to have been a particular design and management of the poet.

ANGUIS, *a serpent, a snake*, though doubtful, is oftener masc. *Lucidus anguis*, Virg. But Val. Max. puts it in both genders in the same chapter, which is the 6th of the 1st book. *Anguem prolapsam prospexit:* and afterwards, *anguis eximiæ magnitudinis visus*. Tacitus makes it fem. *anguem in cubiculo visam*, as well as Plautus, and also Tibullus, Ovid, and Varro, according to Charisius. So that there is very little foundation for believing with Scioppius, that this noun is an epicene purely of the masc. and used in the other gender, because *fœmina* is understood: just as if in all those passages above quoted it was to be understood more of the female than of the male.

BOMBYX, *a silk-worm*, is masc. but as for the silk itself, it is fem. according to the general rule of nouns in X.

BUBO, an *owl*, is masc. by its termination. And yet Virgil has made it fem. But Servius owns, that this was only by referring it to *avis*.

CAMELUS, which Caucius and a great many others take for doubtful, is always masc. in Latin. What led them into this mistake, is its being feminine in Greek, ἡ κάμηλος, *a camel*.

CENCHRIS is doubtful, and differently declined. For *cenchris, hujus cenchris*, is masc. and signifies a kind of serpent. But *cenchris, idis*, is fem. and signifies a kind of speckled hawk.

COCCYX is masc. *a cuckow*.

DAMA, *a buck or doe*, is generally fem. though Virgil has *timidi damæ*. Which Charisius produced as an instance of barbarism, as Pierius observes. And Servius acknowledges that he would have said *timidæ*, if it had not been to avoid making rhyme. See the remarks on the nouns, chap. 1. n. 5.

DELPHIS is masc. as well as *delphin, inis*, a dolphin; the latter following the gender of its termination.

EXOS is judged to be masc. *a kind of fish that has no bones*.

GLIS, *iris*, masc. *a dormouse*.

GRYPS, *yphis*, masc. the same as *gryphus*, a griffon.

GRUS, *uis*, or *gruis, bujus gruis* in Phædrus, a crane, is doubtful. It is masc. in Hor.

Membra gruis sparsi sale multo.

Others make it oftener fem. *Strymoniæ grues*, Virg. Cicero uses it in the same manner, 1. de Nat. Deor.

HALEX, *ecis*, fem. *an herring*, or rather a common name of all small fish; also a salt liquor made of the entrails of fishes, pickle or brine.

LAGOPUS, fem. a dainty bird about the Alps, with rough hairy feet like an hare, called the *white partridge*.

Si meus aurita gaudet lagopode Flaccus.
Mart.

Also the herb *bares-foot*. See Pliny, book 10. c. 48.

LEPUS, *oris*, an *hare*, masc. *auriti lepores*, Virg.

LIMAX, *acis*, doubtful, *a snail*. Vossius derives it from *limus*, mud. Columella makes it masc. *Implicitus conchæ limax*. Pliny makes it fem.

LYNX is doubtful, but oftener fem. It is hardly to be found in the masc. except in this passage of Horace,

Timidos agitare lyncas.

The lynx is a beast of the nature of a wolf, having many spots like a deer, and is very quick sighted, *an ounce*.

—— *Maculosæ tegmine lyncis.*

MEROPS, masc. a small bird that eateth bees, perhaps a woodpecker, or *martinet*, ὁ μέροψ, Arist. Virgil has made use of it in Latin, 4 Georg.

MUGIL, *ilis*, or *mugilis, is*, masc. Plin. *a mullet*.

MUS, *muris*, masc. *a mouse*.

NEFRENS, *a pig just weaned*. This is properly an adjective, and refers to PORCELLUS, *qui needum fabam frangere possit*,

possit, according to Varro, or to *Aries*, according to Festus. Lucius Andron. has even taken it for an infant; which made some grammarians believe it was common. But Vossius affirms it to be found only in the masc. in construction.

NYCTICORAX, *an owl*, is masc. because it is only a word compounded of CORAX, *a raven*, which is also masc. according to the rule of dissyllables in AX.

ORYX or ORIX, *a sort of wild goat*, is masc. in Pliny, in Martial, and in Juvenal.

PALUMBES, *a ring-dove*, or *wood-pigeon*, is more usual in the masc. as Veirepeus, Alvarez, and Vossius observe. And it is thus that Pliny, Lucilius, Pomponius, and Quintilian use it. And even in Plautus, *duæ unum expetitis palumbem*, in Bach. But Virgil has made it fem.

———— *Raucæ tua cura palumbes*. Eclog. 1.

which ought always to be followed, when we mean the female in particular.

PANTHERA, which Despauter puts down as doubtful, is only fem.

Diversum confusa genus panthera camelo. Hor.

This verse is quoted even by Priscian, who does not mark it of any other gender. And Pliny always uses it in the fem. Wherefore this is not perhaps an epicene noun, since it properly denotes only the female, the male of which is *pardus*, according to Pliny, book 1. c. 17. Varro, l. 8. de L. L. observeth that they said *pantheram & merulam*, and not *pantherum & merulum*. But in Greek we say ὁ πάνθηρ to express confusedly the male and female. And of its accusative τὸν πάνθηρα has been formed the fem. *hæc panthera*, as it happens to a great many others, of which we shall make mention in the heteroclites, list 1.

PERDIX, *a partridge*, is common in Greek: but in Latin it is generally fem. Nonius shews that it was also masc. by this word of Varro, *perdicas Bæotios*.

SALAR, *a young salmon*, a kind of trout, is masc.

SERPENS, *a serpent*, is doubtful, because being of its nature an adjective, it refers to *anguis* abovementioned. And yet it is more usual in the fem. either by reason of its termination, or because it refers to *bestia*.

TALPA, *a mole or wart*, generally fem. though Virgil has, *talpæ oculis capti*, by a particular licence, according to Servius, and to remove the cacophony of *talpæ captæ*.

TURTUR, *uris*, is masc. a bird called *a turtle*. *Turtur aureus*, Mart. a yellow turtle. *Castus turtur*, Ovid. a chaste turtle. Servius has taken it for a fem. in this verse of Virgil, ecl. 1.

Nec gemere aëria cessabit turtur ab ulmo.

But he is censured in this by Vossius, who maintains that *aëria* ought to refer to *ulmo* and not to *turtur*; Salmasius and Ascensius are of the same opinion. And yet it might be alledged in defence of Servius, that *aëria* being in the nominative, might have the last syllable long in virtue of the cæsura, and that the poet therefore referred it to *turtur*, as in another passage speaking of the ring-doves he says

———— *aëriæ quo congessere palumbes*.

But we find no other authority for it in the fem. which gives us more reason to doubt.

VERMIS, *a worm*, is masc. *Vermis vivus*, Pliny.

VOLUCRIS, is generally feminine, wherein it follows its termination. Cicero made it masc. in the 2d book *de Divin*. but in verse only, nor is he in this to be imitated. For as this word is by its nature an adjective, it always supposes *avis* fem. and therefore ought to follow its gender. Perhaps Cicero speaking at that time without distinguishing the sex, referred it to the masc. as the most worthy.

VOLVOX, *ocis*, *a worm that feedeth upon vines*, Pliny. It is esteemed masc. by Despauter, and others, but without authority.

VULTUR, *uris*, *a vulture, or gripe*, is masc. *Dirus vultur*, Valer. We say likewise *hic vulturis*, Pliny, and *vulturius*, Enn.

BOOK II.

OF THE
DECLENSION
OF NOUNS.

T HE Latins have five declensions or different ways of declining of nouns, which arise from the difference of their cases. These, for the sake of brevity, Priscian has reduced to the genitive only, wherein he has been followed by the rest of the grammarians.

Nevertheless it is obvious that this distinction ought to be taken from all the cases in general, since the genitive may be like and the declension different; for instance, *frux* formerly made *frugi* in the genitive, from whence came *homo frugi*; *fames* made *fami*; and yet they were not of the second. *Dido*, and other such words have the genitive sometimes in *ûs*, like *fructûs*, and yet they are not of the fourth; and so of the rest.

The genitive is formed of the nominative, and oftentimes receives an increase in the number of its syllables, and all the other cases depend in this respect on the genitive.

In the rules we shall give only so much as is necessary, omitting what has been already sufficiently explained in the rudiments, which we have published with the abridgment of this work.

But as the genders are much more difficult to know than the declensions, because the analogy of the latter is greater, being repeated almost in every case; whereas the genders depend on the nominative only; therefore I have given the article before the nouns in the examples, to the end that this might serve as a repetition or confirmation of the preceding rules, when boys are made to repeat these examples: though, as I have elsewhere observed, it is not my design to have it joined to every case in declining, because this is needless, and only helps to puzzle young beginners.

THE RULES OF DECLENSION.

Rule I.

Of compound nouns.

Compound nouns are declined,
Like the simple of which they are formed.

Examples.

COMPOUND nouns are declined like their simple. *Hic pes, pedis,* the foot; *hæc compes, cómpedis,* a fetter; *bipes, bípedis,* two footed. *Sanus, sani,* sound in mind or body; *insanus, insani,* mad, frantic.

Some are excepted, as *hic sanguis, sanguinis,* blood; *exánguis, hujus exánguis,* and not *exánguinis,* lifeless, pale. As likewise some others which may be learnt by practice.

Rule II.

Of nouns compounded of two nouns joined together.

1. *Two nominatives joined together are both declined.*
2. *But in the word* altéruter *you must never decline* alter.
3. *When any other case than the nominative is joined, it is not declined.*

Examples.

1. There are some nouns compounded of two nominatives, and then they are both declined; thus of the nominative *res* and of *pública,* is formed *respública:* Genit. *reipúblicæ:* Dat. *reipúblicæ:* Accusat. *rempúblicam,* &c. *Jusjurándum,* an oath, compounded of *jus, júris,* and *jurándum, jurándi:* Genit. *jurisjurándi,* &c.

2. In the word *altéruter,* you must always preserve
alter,

OF DECLENSIONS.

alter, as Genit. *alterutríus* ; Dat. *altérutri,* &c. The reason we shall give in the next annotation.

3. There are nouns compounded of a nominative and another case, and then the nominative is declined, while the other case continues unvaried. This appears in nouns compounded of a genitive and of a nominative; as *senatusconsúltum,* a decree of the senate, compounded of the genitive *senátûs,* and of the nominative *consúltum*; in the genitive, *senatusconsúlti,* of the decree of the senate. *Paterfamílias,* the father of the family; Genit. *patrisfamílias,* of the father of the family: Dat. *patrifamílias,* to the father of the family. *Tribúnus-plebis,* the tribune of the people: *tribúni-plebis, tribúno-plebis. Jurisconsúltus, jurisconsúlti, o, um,* &c. a lawyer.

This appears also in nouns compounded of any other case whatsoever, as *jureconsúltus, jureconsúlti, o, um,* Cic. a lawyer: *omnípotens, omnipoténtis, omnipoténti,* almighty: *adeódatus, adeódati, adeódato,* &c. given by God. And in like manner the rest.

ANNOTATION.

This rule concerning the manner of declining compound nouns, is more general than many imagine; but it has not been rightly understood by some grammarians. For it is a certain thing, that if a noun be compounded of two nominatives joined together, they must both be declined as they would be separately provided they can stand separate in a sentence, as *respublica,* instead of which we may say *publica res.*

And therefore we must not except here *puerpera, puerperæ,* a woman that lieth in childbed ; nor *puerpérium, ii,* childbed; because these are no more than simple nouns derived from *puer* and *parío,* and not compounded of two nouns joined together.

Neither must we except *Marspiter,* which, according to Varro, makes *Marspitris,* though it comes from *Mars* and *pater,* because the latter noun does not continue unaltered and intire.

Nor must we except *rosmarinus,* compounded of *ros,* and of the adjective *marinus,* since we say in the Genit. *rorismarini,* Dat *rorimarino,* &c. But if we also find *rosmarini* and *rosmarino,* it is because there is likewise the word *rosmarinum,* which is no longer a compound noun that can be divided, since it would be a solecism to say *marinum ros,* the latter being always masculine, not only to denote the dew, but likewise this flower, as when Horace says

Parvos coronantem marino
Rore Deos, fragilique myrto. l. 3. od. 23.

Hence

Hence when we say *alteruter*, Genit. *alterutrius*, it is not that these nominatives cannot be declined, since we find even in Cicero and in Cato, *alterius utrius*: but it is because at first they said by syncope *alteriu' utrius*, cutting off *s* according to the ancients, as Julius Scaliger observes, and also cutting off the *m* of the accusative; afterwards to soften it they said *alterutrius, alterutri*, which has remained the most usual.

And if we find in some passages of Cicero, Cæsar, and Tacitus, *jusjurandi*, for *jurisjurandi*, either there must be some syncope, or the passages must be corrupted, which is the opinion of Vossius. Nevertheless *olusatrum*, an herb called *loveage*, has not only *olerisatri*, which we meet with in Colum. but likewise *olusatri*. *Radicem habet olusatri*. Plin. lib. 19. cap. 12.

As for *leopardus*, which has also *leopardi* in the genitive, it is a word introduced towards the decline of the Latin Language. The ancients made use of the words *pardus* and *panthera*, or called them *Africanas & Lybicas feras*. Pliny and Solinus express themselves by a periphrasis; *leonum genus ex pardis generatum*. And yet since the word has been introduced, it has been always the practice to say *leopardos*, as may be seen in Lampridius, Capitolinus, and others, and not *leonespardos*.

Now we are to take particular notice that these compound nouns depend in such a manner on the two nouns of which they are formed, that if one of the two be defective in some cases, the compound noun will be defective also. Thus because *jus* but very rarely occurs in the genitive plural, and has no dative nor ablative, *jusjurandum* is deprived of those cases also, and in like manner the rest.

THE FIRST DECLENSION.

THE first declension comprehends four terminations A, AS, E, ES; as *musa, Æneas, Penelope, Anchises*.

Of all these terminations, that in A is the only Latin one, the others are Greek, of which language they retain some properties in several of their cases.

Those in AS drop S in the vocative, as is customary with the Greek nouns. *Hic Æneas, ô Ænea.*

Those in ES do the same, and moreover make the accusative in *n*. *Hic Anchises, ô Anchise, hunc Anchisen*. And the ablative also in E.

——————— *uno comitatus Achate*, Virg.

Those in E are declined quite differently from the rest, retaining, as Probus says, their Greek declension. And therefore without reason some have pretended to say that their dative was in *æ* diphthong, *huic Penelopæ*, like *huic musæ*. Whereto we may add that the ablative of these nouns being in E simple according to Diomedes, lib. 1. and there being no other way of taking this ablative but from the dative, according to Priscian, lib. 7. because (say they)

OF DECLENSIONS. 63

they) the Greeks have no ablative, it follows from thence that the dative and the ablative muſt be both in E ſimple, and that theſe nouns muſt be thus declined:

Nom. Voc. Epitome.   *Genit.* Epitomes.
Dat.   Epitome.   *Accuſ.* Epitomen.
Ablat.   Epitome.   THE PLURAL, as *muſæ, árum,* &c.

But as this was not a Latin manner of declining, Probus and Priſcian do not give it a place in this declenſion. And we find by theſe authors, as well as by Quintilian, and by other ancients, that the Latins generally changed this Greek termination into A, to decline it like *muſa.*

They did the ſame thing very often with the other two terminations in *As* and in *Es*; and hence it is that ſuch a number of theſe nouns admit of two different terminations, as *Anchiſa* and *Anchiſes*; from whence comes in the vocative *Anchiſa,* and *Anchiſe*; and in the ablative alſo *Anchisâ generâte,* Virg. and the like.

There are likewiſe other nouns, which being of two different terminations in Greek, are alſo differently declined in Latin; as ὁ Χρέμης, τῦ Χρέμου, and τῦ Χρέμητος. Hence we find *ó Chremø* and *ó Chremes: ó Lache* and *ó Laches,* in Ter. the former termination being of the firſt, and the latter of the third declenſion. And therefore we ſay in the third *ó Socrates,* yet we meet with *ó Socrate* in Cicero after the manner of the Greeks, who ſay, ὦ Σωκράτη, cutting off the σ.

The Latins have particularly followed the Dorians and the Æolians in their declenſions, as in every thing elſe. And hence it is that the genitive of the firſt declenſion was formerly in AS, *muſas, monetas*; *dux ipſe vias* for *viæ,* Enn. and in Aï, *muſaï, terraï.* Becauſe the Dorians ſaid μέσας for μέσης; and the Æolians adding an s to it, made it μῦσαις, from which the Latins cutting off the S, have taken *muſai* or *muſæ.* The genitive in *As* has likewiſe remained in ſome compound words, as *pater-familias, mater-familias*; which does not hinder them from being alſo declined after the other manner *quidam pater-familiæ,* Livy. *Singulis patribus-familiarum,* Cic. &c. But that in Aï is particular to poets, who make it a diſſyllable, *terraï,* Cic. in Arato, for *terræ*; *aulaï in medio,* Virg. for *aulæ.* Which happens alſo to the maſculines, *Geryonaï,* Lucr. for *Geryonæ,* taking it from *Geryones,* ὁ Γηρυόνης; and then the dative alſo followed this termination; *huic terraï,* according to Quintilian, though Nigidius in Aulus Gellius believes the contrary. And the ſame we may ſay of the nominative plural, of which ſome grammarians have doubted; ſince it is the ſame analogy. For as the Æolians have taken this *aï* only for the *η* or long *α,* even according to Priſcian; ſo the Latins having taken the *aï* in one caſe, have doubtleſs taken it in the others alſo, juſt as they have made them alike in *æ,* whenever they wanted to make uſe of this termination.

The genitive plural in ARUM comes alſo from the Æolians who made it in αων, to which an R has been added. *Muſarum* for μυσάων.

μυσάων. And this genitive also followed the common dialect, *Æneadum* taken from Αἰνεαδῶν, unless we chuse to say that it is then a syncope for *Æneadarum*; as *Dardanidûm* for *Dardanidarum*, from the nominative *Dardanidæ*. But we must still observe that *Dardanidum* without a syncope comes from *Dardanis, idis,* plur. *Dardanides, idum,* and then it is of the fem. in the same manner as *Achæmenidum* comes from *Achæmenis, idis,* plur. *Achæmenides, idum,* fem. Whereas *Achæmenidûm* for *Achæmenidarum* comes from *Achæmenidæ*, masc. and the rest in the same manner.

We say likewise by syncope, *cœlicolûm* for *cœlicolarum: francigenûm* for *francigenarum*. And Silvius observes, that not only the nouns of family, but likewise the compound and derivative nouns, as likewise the names of coins, weights, measure, and number, *bini, quaterni, ducenti,* &c. are more usual in each declension with a syncope than without.

Rule III.

Of the dative and ablative plural of the first declension.

1. *The dative and ablative plural of the first declension are in* IS.
2. *But* filia, mula, duæ, equa, nata, dea, ambæ, *make both those cases in* ABUS.

Examples.

1. The dative and ablative plural of the first declension, are in IS, as *musa,* dative and ablative plural, *musis.*

2. But there are some that make ABUS in the feminine, as *filia,* dative and ablative plural *filiábus,* a daughter: *mula, mulábus,* a she-mule: *duæ, duábus,* two: *equa, equábus,* a mare: *nata, natábus,* a daughter: *dea, deábus,* a goddess: *ambæ, ambábus,* both.

Annotation.

We likewise find *animabus, dominabus, famulabus, servabus, libertabus, asinabus, sociabus*; and some others of the like sort.

But we say sometimes also in the fem. *natis, filiis, equis,* and likewise *animis. Tullius salutem dicit Terentiæ & Tulliolæ, duabus animis suis.* Which may serve to illustrate an important passage of S. Austin in his book on the true religion, chap. 22. which Monf. Arnaud has corrected with the help of the ancient manuscript of S. Germain in the fields. *Ita universitatis hujus conditio atque administratio solis impiis* ANIMIS *damnatisque non placet, sed etiam cum miseria* EARUM *multis vel in terra victricibus, vel in cœlo sine periculo spectantibus placet.*

See

OF DECLENSIONS.

See the preface to the translation of this book published by that gentleman.

THE SECOND DECLENSION.

THE second declension hath two sorts of terminations, one Greek and the other Latin. The Greek are OS, ON, and EUS, of which we shall treat hereafter. The Latin are ER, US, UM.

The two former come from the Greek nouns in OS, as *ager* from ἀγρός; *Cyrus* from Κῦρος. Hence the same noun sometimes admits of two terminations, as *Leander* and *Leandrus* from Λίανδρος. In like manner we say *super* and *superus*, and some others.

The nouns in US have the nominative plural in I; as *hi domini*: formerly it was in *ei*, as *captivei*, in Plautus, and such like.

Those in UM come from the Greek in ON, as *idolum* from εἴδωλον: which shews the great likeness betwixt these two vowels O and U.

Hence it is that in ancient writers we still meet with OM instead of UM, and with OS instead of US. And this has been extended even to those nouns that are of Latin original, as in Plautus.

Nam bona bonis ferri reor æquom maxime.

And in the same author we likewise find in the nominative, *avos, proavos, atavos*; and in the accusative, *avom*, and the like.

To these terminations we may join two more, IR, and UR, unless we chuse to say that they are made by apocope; for which reason they always resume the increase in the genitive. For *vir, viri*, properly speaking, comes from *virus*, which made even *vira* in the feminine; from whence comes *Querquetulanæ viræ* in Festus, just as the Hebrews say אִישׁ *ish* and אִשָּׁה *isha*. And *satur, saturis*, is taken from *saturus*, whose feminine *satura* we still find in Terence.

Of the Greek Terminations.

The Greek nouns preserve here a good part of their declension, as well as in the first. Those in EUS are thus declined.

Nom. Orpheus.   *Vocat.* Orpheu.
Genit. Orphei.   *Dat.* Orpheo.
Accus. Orpheum, or Orpheon, or Orphea.
Ablat. Orpheo.

These nouns in EUS strictly speaking ought to be of the third declension, since they are of the fifth in Greek, for which reason they sometimes retain the genitive of that declension, as in Ovid, *Typhoëos* for *Typhoëi*; and the dative of the same, as in Virgil, *Orphei* for *Orpheo*; Ecl. 4. And they more usually retain also the accusative, *Persea* for *Perseum*. Their vocative is intirely Greek,

Greek, formed merely by throwing away the *σ* of the nominative, as *Orpheu, Theseu.*

The other Greek nouns also frequently preserve their terminations. Hence we find *hic Androgeos, hujus Androgeo* for *Androgei*, after the Attic form.

In foribus le·hum Androgeo.———Virg.

Which does not hinder the other genitive from being also used.

Androgei galeam —— *induitur.* Virg.

The accusative is oftentimes in *on*; as *Catalogon, diphthongon, Delon, Menelaon,* and the like, which are of the third declension in Greek; or as *Athon* from *Athos,* and others which are of the fourth simple.

Athos makes also in the dative *Atho* in Mela, as likewise in the ablative in Cic. *Athoque perfosso,* 2. de Fin. We find also in the accusative *Atho,* according to the Attics, instead of *Athon.* *Ad montem Atho,* Liv. In the same manner *hunc Androgeo,* and the like.

Further, the Latins sometimes rejecting the *s* of the Attic nominative, form thereof a new noun which they decline through all its cases. Thus of *Athos* they make *Atho, Athonis,* from whence comes *Athone* in Cic. in like manner *Androgeo, onis,* &c. And what is more remarkable, is that though they decline a noun after this manner, giving it a form entirely new, and consequently Latin, yet they suffer it to have a Greek termination in the accusative, for they do not say *Androgeon,* which would be the Greek accusative of *Androgeos,* nor *Androgeonem,* which would be the accusative of the Latin word *Androgeo, onis*; but *Androgeona.*

Restituit patriis Androgeona focis. Propert.

The genitive plural is in *ōn,* as in Greek, *Cimmeriōn*; and sometimes it has been permitted to retain the *ω, Cimmeriων.*

Such are the observations we thought it incumbent upon us to make, for the thorough understanding of authors, in favor of those who have not yet acquired a complete knowledge of the Greek tongue, of which we have given a more ample account in the NEW METHOD *of learning that language.*

RULE IV.

Of the genitive singular of the second declension.

1. Dóminus *makes* dómini.
2. *But* unus, álius, quis, totus, uter, neuter, ullus, solus, alter, *make the genitive in* ÏUS.

EXAMPLES.

1. The genitive singular of the second declension is in *i,* as *hic dómini,* the lord; genitive *domini : hic vir, viri,* a man; *puer, púeri,* a boy: *hic liber, libri,* a book : but *liber,* an adjective, makes *liberi,* free.

ANNOTATION.

By these examples we see, that of the nouns in ER, some increase in the genitive, and others do not. Those which have a vowel, or a semi-vowel before ER, generally increase, as *puer, pueri*; *miser, miseri*; *tener, teneri*, as coming from the ancient terminations, *puerus, miserus, tenerus*. Those which have only a mute before the termination, generally speaking, do not increase; as *faber, fabri*; *cancer, cancri*; *liber, libri*, a book; because they do not come from the termination US. But as this rule is subject to a great many exceptions, we have chosen to leave the matter intirely to practice. The exceptions may be marked here.

Asper, adject. (rough) genitive *asperi*. But *Asper*, a proper name, makes *Aspri. Duobus Aspris, Coss.* Liber, adject. or taken for Bacchus, *liberi*. But *liber*, a book, makes *libri*.

Adulter, adulteri; *lacer, laceri*; *prosper, prosperi*; *socer, soceri*; *presbyter, presbyteri*; *gibber*, adject. *gibberi*; *exter*, adject. *exteri*.

Armiger, armigeri; *Lucifer, Luciferi*. And in like manner the other compounds of *gero* and of *fero*.

Dexter makes *dextri* and *dexteri. Dexterâ sacras jaculatus arces.* Hor. And from thence comes also *dexterior*. For it is to be observed that if these nouns increase in the genitive, they increase in the motion or variation of the adjective. Thus because we say *exter, exteri*, we must also say *exter, extera, exterum*. But because we say *niger, nigri*, we must also say *niger, nigra, nigrum*, and not *nigera, nigerum*.

Celtiber, makes *Celtiberi*, the penultimate long. The Greeks say Ἴβηρ, Ἴβηρος, to signify either the Spaniards, or the people of Iberia, towards Colchis. But in Latin *Iber* or *Iberus* is always of the second declension, to signify a native of Spain.

——— *Profugique à gente vetusta*
Gallorum Celtæ, miscentes nomen Iberis. Lucan. lib. 4.

But to denote the Iberians of Asia, we say rather *Iberes* than *Iberi*. At least this is the opinion of Priscian, though Claudian has used it otherwise.——— *Mistis hic Colchus Iberis.*

2. The following nouns are declined like *ille, illa, illud*, and are ranked by some among the pronouns. They make the genitive in IUS, and the dative in I.

Unus, una, unum, one: Gen. *unius*: Dat. *uni*.

A'lius, ália, áliud, another: Gen. *alius*: Dat. *álii*.

Qui, or *quis, quæ, quod*, or *quid*, which: Gen. *cujus*: Dat. *cui*.

Totus, tota, totum, all, whole: Gen. *totius*: Dat. *toti*.

Uter, a, um, which of the two: Gen. *utrius*: Dat. *utri*.

Neuter, tra, um, neither: Gen. *neutrius*: Dat. *neutri*.

Ullus, a, um, any: Gen. *ullius*: Dat. *ulli*.

Thus, *nullus, a, um*, none, nobody. Gen. *nullíus:* Dat. *nulli.*

Solus, sola, solum, alone: Gen. *solíus:* Dat. *soli.*

Alter, áltera, álterum, another: Gen. *altérius:* Dat. *álteri.*

ANNOTATION.

These nouns formerly made their genitive in I or in Æ like the other adjectives; hence we still meet with *neutri generis* in the genitive in Varro and in Probus; *tam nulli consilii*, in Ter. *Aliæ pecudis jecur*, in Cic. *Non res totæ rei necesse est similis sit*, ad Heren. and such like; and then their dative was also in *o*.

Rule V.

Of the vocative singular.

1. *The vocative of nouns in* US *is in* E.
2. *Except* ô Deus.
3. *Proper names in* ïus *make the vocative in* I.
4. *We also say* fili, mi, *and* geni.

Examples.

1. The vocative in every respect resembles the nominative; but nouns in US of the second declension, make the vocative in E, as *dóminus*, Voc. *dómine*, lord: *hic herus, here,* master.

2. *Deus,* is used as well for the vocative as for the nominative. *Te, Deus alme, colam,* Buchan. I will worship thee, O great God!

3. Proper names in ïus, make the vocative in I, as *Virgílius, Virgíli,* Virgil: *Pompéius, Pompéi,* Pompey: *Antónius, Antoni,* Antony.

4. Also *filius,* a son, makes *fili*; *meus,* my, mine, makes *mi*; and *génius,* a good or evil genius, art, genius, makes *geni* in the vocative.

ANNOTATION.

The other nouns in IUS that are not proper names, make their vocative in E, like the rest of the nouns in US: *Tabellarius,* Voc. *Tabellarie,* a messenger: *pius, pie,* pious.

In like manner, epithets, as *Cynthius, Delius, Tyrinthius,* make the vocative in E; as also those of family, *Laërtius, Laërtie*; because of their nature they cannot pass for proper names.

We likewise meet with the following vocatives in US, *fluvius,* a river; *populus,* the people; *chorus,* a choir; *agnus,* a lamb; but these same

same four had better have their vocatives in E. Besides we may say that it is in imitation of the Attics, who do not distinguish the vocative from the nominative. For which reason Virgil in imitation of them has, *Adsis lætitiæ Bacchus dator*, for *Bacche*. And Horace, *sed des veniam bonus oro*, for *bone*. Sanctius also maintains that the real vocative of *Deus*, is no other than *Deë*; and that if we say *Deus*, addressing ourselves to God, 'tis by virtue of this figure. Besides this vocative *Deë* is found in Tertull. and in Prud. as in Greek, ὦ Θεῖ, Matt. 27.

Proper names formerly made the vocative also in E, as *Virgílie*, *Mercúrie*, according to Priscian. But because this final *e* was hardly pronounced at all, and in all probability very much resembled what the French call their *e* feminine; hence it came to be intirely lost. And for this reason it is, says the same Priscian, that the accent of the former vocative has still continued in prose, *Virgíli*, *Mercúri*, &c. though this penultima be short in verse.

FOR THE PLURAL.

We must also observe that here they admit of a syncope in the plural, as in the nominative *Dî* for *Dii*; in the dative *Dîs* for *Diis*.

And this is still more usual in the genitive; *Deûm* for *Deorum*: unless we chuse rather to say that it comes from the Greek Θιῶν. But there are a great many others in which the syncope is obvious: *nummûm* for *nummorum*, *sestertiûm* for *sestertiorum*: *liberûm* for *liberorum*: and in the same manner *duûm virûm*; *trium virûm*; *centum virûm*, which are scarce ever used otherwise.

Nouns neuter rarely admit of this syncope, though in Ennius we find *duellûm* for *duellorum*; that is, *bellorum*.

RULE VI.
Of the dative and ablative plural.

1. *The dative plural is in* IS, *as* dóminus, dóminis.
2. *But* ambo *makes* ambóbus, *and* duo duóbus.

EXAMPLES.

1. The dative plural is in IS. *Dóminus*, the lord; dative plural, *dóminis*: *puer*, a boy, *púeris*: *lignum*; wood, *lignis*.

2. *Ambo* and *duo*, are of the plural number, and form in the dative *ambóbus*, *duóbus*, for the masculine and the neuter; as *ambábus* and *duábus*, for the fem. See RULE III.

The ablative plural generally follows the dative; wherefore as *dóminis* is dative and ablative, so *ambóbus* and the others are datives and ablatives.

THE THIRD DECLENSION.

WE do not intend to give the terminations belonging to this declension, because this does not appear to be of any manner of use. It is sufficient to mention that it includes the terminations of all the rest, besides several peculiar to itself; and if we were to believe Priscian, who distinguishes them even according to the quantity, we should reckon them to be upwards of fourscore.

But it is observable that a great many of these terminations were formed merely by the apocope of the last syllable. Which will help to shew us, that the analogy of the genitive, in this great variety of its terminations, is more regular than we imagine.

For instead of *lac*, for example, they formerly said *lacte*, from whence comes the genitive *lactis*. In the same manner they said *animale*, from whence comes *animalis*; *vectigale, is*; *melle, mellis*; *felle, fellis*, &c.

Most of the nouns in *o* were ended in *on*: for they said *Platon, onis*: *ligon, ligonis*, &c.

The nouns in *s* impure, or *s* and a consonant, were terminated in *es* or in *is*; so that they said *adipes, hujus adipis*; as *plebes, plebis*; *artes, artis*; *trabes, is*; *concordes, hujus concordis*, &c.

They said also *præceps, præcipis*, whence *præcipem* in Plautus: *anceps, ancipis*, and also *præcipes, hujus præcipitis*; *ancipes, ancipitis*, whence the former nominative hath kept the latter genitive.

They said also, *os, oris*, the mouth; and *os, offis*, a bone.

They said *hæc supellectilis, is*; *iter, iteris*; and *itiner, itineris*; *Jovis, hujus Jovis*; *carnis, hujus carnis*; *gliris, hujus gliris*; *hepas, hepatis*; *jecor, jecoris*, &c.

Many nouns in *es* and in *is*, ended in *er*; thus they said *cucumer, eris*; *ciner, eris*; *puber, eris*, &c.

Others ended in *en*, whence they said not only *sanguis, hujus sanguinis*, which has still continued in *exanguis*; but also *sanguen, sanguinis*, like *pollen, pollinis*: so *turben, turbinis*, from whence *turbo* had its genitive.

They said likewise, *hic ducis*, taken from *duco*; *hæc vocis* from *voco*; as *hic regis*, from *rego*; *hic gregis*, from *grego*, for *congrego*: *hic conjugis*, from *jugo*: they said too *hæc nivis, hujus nivis*.

Whence we may remark in general that the genitive of this declension being of its own nature in *is*, it is made by adding *is* to the final consonant of the nominative, and changing sometimes the penultimate *e* into *i* to shorten the quantity; or by leaving *is* in the genitive as in the nominative. Or if the nominative be in *es*, by changing *e* into *i* in the last syllable; in like manner, if it be in *s*, it is changed into *i*, and *s* is added. But it is now time to come to the particular rules; and whatever is most deserving of notice in regard to the Greek words, we shall give at the end of this declension.

OF DECLENSIONS.

RULE VII.
The genitive of the nouns in A and E.
1. *A hath its genitive in* ATIS.
2. *But E makes its genitive in* IS.

EXAMPLES.

1. Nouns ending in A, form the genitive in ATIS, as *hoc ænigma, ænigmatis,* a riddle: *hoc thema, thématis,* a theme, or subject.

2. And those in E form the genitive in IS; as *hoc mantile, mantilis,* a table-cloth, an hand towel: *hoc sedile, sedilis,* a seat or stool.

ANNOTATION.

The analogy of these genitives in *atis,* consists in this, that being incapable of taking simply *is* after the last vowel of the nominative, because it would make an *hiatus* or meeting of vowels, they insert a *t* to avoid this disagreeable sound. *Thema, thema-is, thematis*: just as the French say *a-t-on, a-t-il,* for *a-on, a-il,* &c.

RULE VIII.
Of the nouns in O.
1. *Nouns in* O *make* ONIS.
2. *The same also does* unédo.
3. *Nouns feminine in* DO *and* GO, *make* INIS.
4. *The same genitive is given to the following masculines,* ordo, homo, turbo, cardo, Apóllo, Cupído, margo.
5. Ánio, Nério, *make* ENIS.
6. *And* caro, carnis.

EXAMPLES.

1. Nouns ending in O, make ONIS in the genitive; as *hic mucro, mucrónis,* the point of a sword: *hic sermo, sermónis,* speech, discourse: *Cícero, Cicerónis,* Cicero: *hic hárpago, ónis,* a grappling hook: *hic Mácedo, ónis,* a Macedonian.

2. In like manner, *hæc unédo, ónis,* the fruit of the arbut or strawberry-tree.

F 4   3. The

3. The other feminine nouns in DO and in GO, make the genitive in INIS. *Hæc grando, grándinis,* hail: *hæc cáligo, caliginis,* darkness: *virgo, virginis,* a virgin, a maid.

But the masculines in DO and GO, make ONIS by the general rule, *hic ligo, ligónis,* a spade.

Except the following seven.

4. *Hic ordo, órdinis,* order: *homo, hóminis,* a man or woman: *nemo, néminis,* nobody; it comes from *homo*: *hic turbo, túrbinis,* a whirling, a whirlwind, a top: *hic cardo, cárdinis,* the hinge of a door: *Apollo, Apóllinis,* the god Apollo: *Cupído, Cupídinis,* the god of love: *hic margo, márginis,* the margin of a book, the bank of a river.

5. *A'nio* makes *Aniénis,* the name of a river; *Nério, énis,* the wife of Mars.

6. *Hæc caro,* makes *carnis,* flesh, meat.

ANNOTATION.

There are some Greek nouns, which are proper names of women, that make the genitive in *ois* and in *us*, as *Dido, Didonis, Didois, D.dûs*; *Gorgo,* genitive *Gorgonis, ois,* and *Gorgus,* from Γοργύος, Γοργοῦς; and a great many others of the like sort.

RULE IX.

Of the nouns in C and in D.

Halec *makes* halécis, *and* lac, lactis.
David *makes* Davídis, *and* Bogud, Bógudis.

EXAMPLES.

These here form their genitive in a different manner.

Hoc halec, or *hæc haleç* a herring, also pickle, brine.

David, Davídis, the prophet David: *Bogud,* the name of a man, *Bógudis,* Liv.

RULE X.

Of the nouns in L.

1. *The genitive of nouns in L is made by adding* IS.
2. *But to* mel *and* fel *you must add* LIS.

EXAMPLES.

1. Nouns ending in L form the genitive by adding IS. *Hoc ánimal, animális,* an animal: *hic, aut hoc fal, falis,* falt: *Dániel, Daniélis,* a proper name: *vigil, vígilis,* a watchman, a fentinel: *hic fol, folis,* the fun: *hic conful, cónfulis,* a conful.

2. The following redouble the L: *hoc mel, mellis,* honey: *hoc fel, fellis,* gall.

RULE XI.
Of the nouns in N.

1. *To Nouns ending in* N, IS *is added.*
2. *But neuters in* EN *make* INIS.
3. *As also* pecten *with nouns ending in* CEN, *and* flamen, *though masculine.*
4. *Proper names in* ON *make sometimes* ONTIS.
5. *As does also* horízon.

EXAMPLES.

1. Nouns ending in EN, have IS added to them in the genitive. *Titan, Titánis,* a proper name; it is taken for the fun: *hic, ren, renis,* the kidney or reins: *hic lien, liénis,* the milt or fpleen: *delphin, delphínis,* a dolphin: *hic Orion, onis,* the name of a conftellation: *Memnon, Mémnonis,* the fon of Aurora.

2. Nouns neuter in EN, change E into I, and make INIS. *Hoc flumen, flúminis,* a river: *hoc lumen, lúminis,* light: *hoc nomen, nóminis,* a name: *hoc gluten, glútinis,* glue: *hoc unguen, ínis,* ointment: *hoc flamen, ínis,* a blaft, or puff of wind.

3. The following, though mafculines, make alfo INIS. *Hic pecten, péctinis,* a comb, the ftick or quill wherewith they play upon an inftrument, the ftay of a weaver's loom. Thofe in CEN, that is the compounds of *cano,* to fing, as *tibícen, ínis,* a piper, or player on a flute: *fídicen,* a harper, he that playeth on a ftringed inftrument; and in like manner the reft. To thefe we may add, *hic flamen, ínis,* a heathen prieft.

The other mafculine nouns follow the general rule, as *hic lien, liénis,* the milt or fpleen, &c.

4. Proper

4. Proper names make sometimes ONTIS, as *Pháëthon, Phaëthóntis,* the son of Phœbus: *Xénophon, Xenophóntis,* an Athenian general. And sometimes they follow the general rule, *Jáson, Jásonis.* A great many have both genitives, as *Ctésiphon, Ctesiphóntis,* and *Ctesiphónis.* But the latter comes rather from *Ctésipho;* as *Démipho, Demiphónis;* and such like.

5. *Hic Horízon* makes also *Horizóntis,* the horizon, a circle dividing the half sphere of the firmament, which we see, from the other half which we see not.

RULE XII.
Of the nouns in R.

1. *Nouns in R make their genitive by adding IS, as* fur, furis; honor, honóris.
2. *But* far *makes* farris.
3. *And from* Hepar *comes the genitive* hépatis.

EXAMPLES.

1. Nouns ending in R, form their genitive by adding IS; as *hoc calcar, calcáris,* a spur: *hic aër, aëris,* the air: *hic æther, ætheris,* the pure air, the sky: *hic carcer, cárceris,* a prison: *hoc uber, úberis,* a nipple, a pap or udder: *hic vomer, vómeris,* a plowshare. And in like manner, *uber,* adjective, genitive *úberis,* fat and fertile: *hic honor, honóris,* honour: *hic decor, decóris,* comeliness, beauty: *hic fur, furis,* a thief: *hic furfur fúrfuris,* bran: *hic et hæc martyr, mártyris,* a martyr, a witness.

2. *Hoc far,* all manner of corn, also meal or flower, redoubles the R: genitive *farris.*

3. *Hoc hepar, hépatis,* the liver. Formerly they said *hépatos:* and this noun has no plural.

ANNOTATION.

Lar, a houshold god, makes *Laris,* according to the general rule. But *Lar* taken for the name of a man, makes *Lartis.* It is to be observed however that *Lars* is also used, which we read in Livy and in Ausonius, from whence regularly comes *Lartis,* as from *Mars* comes *Martis;* though we also meet with *Lar* in Priscian and in Cicero.

OF DECLENSIONS.

RULE XIII.
Of the nouns in BER.

1. Céleber, imber, *and* salúber, *make the genitive in* BRIS.
2. *The same do also the months in* BER.

EXAMPLES.

1. These nouns make their genitive in BRIS. *Céleber*, genitive *célebris*, famous, renowned: *hic imber, imbris*, a shower of rain: *salúber, salúbris*, wholesome.

2. *Hic Septémber, Septémbris*, the month of September: *Október, Októbris*, the month of October: *Novémber, Novémbris*, the month of November: *Decémber, Decémbris*, the month of December.

In the same manner *Insuber, Insubris*, the name of a people.

ANNOTATION.

The analogy of these genitives consists in their making a syncope of the penultimate *e*; *salúbris*, for *salúberis*: *Októbris* for *Októberis*, &c. Which is the case also of some of these that follow.

RULE XIV.
Of the adjectives in CER.

The adjectives in CER *make* CRIS. *Thus we say*, acer, acris.

EXAMPLES.

The adjectives in CER make the genitive in CRIS; as *acer*, genitive *acris*, sharp, sour: *álacer, álacris*, brisk, lively: *vólucer, vólucris*, winged, swift.

RULE XV.
Of the nouns in TER.

1. *The Greek nouns in* TER *make* ERIS.
2. *To which we must join* later, láteris.
3. *The Latin nouns in* TER *make* TRIS.
4. *Which are followed by* pater *and* mater.

EXAMPLES.

1. The nouns in TER, if they be of Greek original, follow the general rule by adding IS after R; as *hic crater, cratéris,* a great cup, or bowl: *hic æther, éris,* the pure air, the sky: *hic stater, statéris,* a kind of ancient coin worth two shillings and four-pence: *hic charáĉter, éris,* a mark, character, or sign: *hic panther, ér s,* a panther.

2. *Later,* though a Latin word, also makes *láteris,* a brick or tile.

3. The other Latin nouns in TER, make only TRIS in the genitive by syncope for TERIS; whether they be adjectives, as *campéſter, campéſtris,* of or belonging to the plain fields; *ſilvéſter, ſilvéſtris,* woody, wild, savage: or whether they be substantives, as *hic accipiter, tris,* an hawk: *hic frater, tris,* a brother.

4. These two, though of Greek original, follow the Latins: *hic pater, patris,* a father: *hæc mater, matris,* a mother.

ANNOTATION.

Linter, which Despauter joins to these, is a downright Latin word. It is true Priscian says that the Greeks used the word, ὁ Λίντης; but he says this without any authority. For this noun is not to be met with in Pollux, where he treats of different sorts of boats, nor in any ancient author. And if Priscian found it any where, it must have certainly been in some author of more modern date, who made use of the Latin word, only giving it a Greek termination.

RULE XVI.

Of *iter, cor,* and *Jupiter.*

Iter *makes* itíneris.

Cor, cordis; Jupiter, Jovis.

EXAMPLES.

These form their genitive in a different manner: *hoc iter,* genitive, *itíneris,* a way, a path, a road, a journey: *hoc cor, cordis,* the heart. The compounds of *cor* take an S at the end, as *secors, secórdis,* senseless, regardless. See the rule of nouns in RS lower down. *Júpiter, Jovis,* the heathen god.

ANNO-

OF DECLENSIONS.

ANNOTATION.

We have already taken notice of the cause of this irregularity in these genitives, which is that the Latins heretofore used to say *Jovis*, *hujus Jovis*; *Jupiter*, *hujus Jupiteris*, whence the latter nominative has retained the former genitive. And Probus judiciously observes, that to pretend that *Jovis* is the real genitive of *Jupiter*, is the same as if we were to decline *hic Phœbus, hujus Apollinis*. Now *Jupiter* was only a corrupt word for *Jovis-pater*, just as they said *Marspiter* for *Mars-pater*, and the rest in the same manner.

RULE XVII.
Of the nouns in UR.

Jecur, robur, femur, *and* ebur, *make the genitive in* ORIS.

EXAMPLES.

The following make the genitive in ORIS. *Hoc jecur, jecóris* (and formerly *jecinoris*) the liver: *hoc robur, róboris*, a kind of hard oak, strength: *hoc femur, fémoris*, the thigh: *hoc ebur, éboris*, ivory.

ANNOTATION.

The analogy of this genitive consists in this, that the *u* of the nominative is changed into *o*, these two vowels having a great affinity with each other.

RULE XVIII.
Of the nouns in AS.

1. *Nouns in* AS *have the genitive in* ATIS.
2. *But the feminine Greek nouns in* AS, *as* Pallas, *make* ADIS.
3. *The masculine Greek nouns in* AS, *as* ádamas, *make* ANTIS.
4. As *makes* assis; *and* mas, maris; hoc vas *hath* vasis; *and* hic vas *hath* vadis.

EXAMPLES.

1. The nouns in AS make the genitive in ATIS. *Hæc pietas, pietátis*, piety: *hæc ætas, ætátis*, age: *hæc bónitas, bonitátis*, goodness.

2. The Greek nouns in AS of the feminine gender, make ADIS; as *hæc Pallas, Pálladis*, the goddess Pallas: *hæc lampas, lámpadis*, a lamp.

3. The

3. The Greek nouns in AS of the masculine gender make ANTIS. *Hic gigas, gigántis*, a giant: *hic ádamas, adamántis*, a diamond: *hic Pallas, Pallántis*, the name of a man: *hic élephas, elephántis*, an elephant: so *Agragas*, the name of a city, but of the masculine gender. See the genders, p. 16.

4. These make their genitive in a different manner; *hic as*, genitive *assis*, a pound weight; also a coin of which ten made a denier: *hic mas, maris*, the male in all kinds of creatures: *vas*, when of the neuter gender, makes *vasis*, a vessel: but when masculine, it makes *vadis*, a surety or bail.

ANNOTATION.

The analogy of the genitives in *atis* or *adis* consists in this, that joining *is* to the nominative, its final *s* is changed into *t* or *d* by a relation which the *s* hath in common to both these consonants *d* and *t* in all languages, which will appear further in rule the 21st. 24th. 25th. and others.

RULE XIX.
Of the nouns in ES.

The nouns in ES *change* ES *into* IS; *as* verres, verris; vates, vatis.

EXAMPLES.

The nouns in ES form their genitive, by changing ES into IS; as *hic verres*, genitive *verris*, a boar pig: *vates, vatis*, a poet, a prophet.

In the same manner *Ulýsses, Ulýssis*, the name of a man: *hæc nubes, nubis*, a cloud: *hæc clades, cladis*, a defeat; and the like.

RULE XX.
Of those which make ETIS.

1. *The following have their genitive in* ETIS;
 - *viz.* lócuples, præpes, páries, seges, perpes, tapes, intérpres, teges, teres, magnes, ábies, áries, hebes.
2. *Also* quies; 3. *And a great many Greek words in* ES.

OF DECLENSIONS.

EXAMPLES.

1. The following nouns make their genitive in ETIS. *Lócuples, locuplétis,* rich: *præpes, prǽpetis,* quick, light, lively: *hic páries, pariétis,* a wall: *hæc seges, ségetis,* standing corn: *perpes, pérpetis,* perpetual, intire: *hic tapes, tapétis,* tapestry: *intérpres, intérpretis,* an interpreter: *hæc teges, tégetis,* a mat: *teres, téretis,* taper as a tree or pillar: *hic magnes, magnétis,* a load-stone: *hæc ábies, abíetis,* a fir-tree: *hic áries, aríetis,* a ram, a military engine: *hebes, hébetis,* blunt, dull.

2. *Hæc quies, quiétis,* rest; and in the same manner its compounds, *réquies,* repose: *inquies,* disquiet.

3. Many Greek nouns in ES also make ETIS, as *hic lebes lebétis,* a cauldron: *Dares, Darétis; Chremes, Chremétis,* names of men: *celes, étis,* one that rides on horseback in public sports, also the horse itself: and such like.

ANNOTATION.

Heretofore they used to say also *mansues, mansuetis,* Plaut. and *indiges, indigetis.* In Julius Frontinus, *Romana urbs indiges, terrarumque dea;* and in Livy, *Jovem indigetem appellant,* lib. 1. But now we say *mansuetus,* mild; and as to the other, it is seldom used except in the plural; *indigites,* the tutelar deities.

RULE XXI.
Of the other nouns in ES.

1. Ceres *makes* Céreris.
2. Bes, bessis: *and* æs, æris.
3. *Nouns derived from* sedes *make* IDIS.
4. Pes, heres, merces, præs, *have* EDIS.
5. Pubes, *signifying soft hair, makes* IS; *but signifying of ripe years, it has* ERIS.
6. *The other masculines have* ITIS.

EXAMPLES.

1. *Ceres* the goddess of corn, makes *Céreris.*

2. *Hic bes*, the weight of eight ounces, makes *beſſis*. *Hoc æs, æris*, braſs, copper.

3. Nouns derived from *ſedeo, ſedes*, to ſit down, make IDIS; as *obſes, óbſidis*, an hoſtage: *præſes, præſidis*, a preſident: *reſes, réſidis*, lazy, ſlothful: *deſes, déſidis*, idle, lazy.

4. The following make the genitive in EDIS; *hic pes, pedis*, the foot: in like manner its compounds, *bipes, bípedis*, two footed: *córnipes, cornípedis*, that which hath a horny hoof: *ſónipes*, that which maketh a noiſe with its feet, a courſer, an horſe, or ſteed: *hic heres, héredis*, an heir: *hæc merces, mercédis*, reward: *præs, prædis*, a ſurety in money matters.

5. *Pubes, pubis*, ſoft hair or down. *Pubes, púberis*, adject. of ripe years; from whence comes *pubértas*, ripe age, puberty.

6. The reſt of the maſculines, and even of the commons in ES, not mentioned in the rules, form their genitive in ITIS; as *hic et hæc miles, mílitis*, a ſoldier: *veles, vélitis*, a ſoldier wearing light harneſs: *eques, équitis*, an horſeman: *palmes, pálmitis*, the ſhoot or young branch of a vine: *hic termes, térmitis*, a bough or twig of a tree: *hic fomes, fómitis*, fuel.

ANNOTATION.

From *pubes* comes the compound *impubes* or *impubis*, & *hoc impube*, as *impubes Iülus* : *impube corpus* : in the genitive *impubis* & *impuberis* : accuſative *impubem* & *impuberem*. Their nominative in *er* we find no where but in the writings of grammarians.

Here we may obſerve, that the nouns in ES, which increaſe in the genitive, are generally maſculines. There are only five of them fem. *ſeges, teges, merces, compes* and *quies*; to which may be added *inquies*, a ſubſtantive, and one neuter, *æs, æris*.

RULE XXII.
Of the nouns in IS.

IS *continues in the genitive the ſame as in the nominative.*

EXAMPLES.

Nouns in IS generally ſpeaking have the genitive like

like the nominative; as *hæc claſſis, hujus claſſis,* a fleet: *dulcis, hujus dulcis,* ſweet: *hic caſſis, hujus caſſis,* a hunter's net: *hic cúcumis, hujus cúcumis,* a cucumber.

ANNOTATION.

They uſed heretofore to ſay *cucumer, eris*; and from hence comes ſtill in the plural *cucumeres,* and not *cucumes,* though in the ſingular *cucumis* is more uſual than *cucumer,* whence comes the dative and ablative *cucumi,* and the accuſative *cucumim* in Pliny. See p. 92.

RULE XXIII.
Exception to the preceding rule.

1. Caſſis, lapis, *and* cuſpis, *form the genitive in* DIS.
2. *Theſe are followed by a great many Greek nouns.*
3. Quiris, Samnis, Dis, lis, *and* charis, *make* ITIS.
4. Pulvis, *and* cinis, *have* ERIS, *and* glis *has* gliris.
5. *But* ſanguis, *makes* ſanguinis.

EXAMPLES.

1. Theſe make the genitive in DIS. *Hæc cáſſis, cáſſidis,* an helmet: *hic lapis, ĭdis,* a ſtone: *hæc cuſpis, ĭdis,* the point of a ſpear or other weapon.

2. There are likewiſe a great many feminine Greek nouns, which make IDIS. *Tyránnis, tyránnidis,* tyranny: *pixis, píxidis,* a box: *chlamys, ўdis,* a cloak, a ſoldier's coat: *graphis, ĭdis,* the art of limning, alſo a pencil. And ſuch like.

3. The following make ITIS. *Quiris, Quirítis,* a Roman: *Samnis, Samnítis,* a people of Italy: *Dis Ditis,* the god of riches, a rich man: *hæc lis, lítis,* a ſtrife, a quarrel, a proceſs at law: *cháris, ĭtis,* or rather in the plural *chárites,* the three ſiſters called the graces.

4. Hic pulvis, púlveris, duſt: *hic cinis, cíneris,* aſhes: *glis, gliris,* a dormouſe.

5. *Hic sanguis, sánguinis,* blood; because heretofore they said *sanguen.*

Its compounds follow the general rule. *Exanguis,* genitive *exánguis,* pale, lifeless.

Pollis, or rather *pollen,* also makes *póllinis,* fine flour.

ANNOTATION.

Hereto we may also refer a great number of Greek nouns ending in IN or IS, as *delphis* or *delphin, delphinis: Salamis* or *Salamin, Salaminis: Eleusis* or *in, inis,* &c. There are likewise some Greek nouns which make *entis,* as *Simoïs, Simoëntis,* the name of a river: *Pyroïs, Pyroëntis,* one of the horses of the sun, &c. But as to those we must reserve a further notice of them for the Greek grammar.

RULE XXIV.
Of nouns in OS.

1. *Nouns in* OS *have the genitive in* OTIS.
2. *But* mos, flos, *and* ros, *make* ORIS.
3. Heros, Minos, Tros, *and* thos, *make* OIS.
4. Bos, *has* bovis; custos, custódis.
5. Os, *a bone, has* ossis; *but signifying the mouth it makes* oris.

EXAMPLES.

1. Nouns in OS generally make their genitive in OTIS; as *hæc dos, dotis,* a portion or dowry: *compos, cómpotis,* one that hath obtained his desire or purpose, a partaker: *impos, ímpotis,* unable, void of: *hic nepos nepótis,* a grandson, also a spendthrift: *hic & hæc sacérdos, sacerdótis,* a priest or priestess: *hic monóceros, monocerótis,* an unicorn: and so a great many more Greek nouns.

2. These are excepted which make ORIS. *Hic mos, moris,* manner or custom: *hic flos, floris,* a flower: *hic ros, roris,* dew.

3. These also which make OIS: *hic heros, heróis,* an hero: *Minos, Minóis,* a Cretan king: *Tros, Troïs,* a Trojan: *thos, thoïs,* a sort of wolf.

4. *Hic et hæc bos, bovis,* an ox or cow: *hic et hæc custos, custódis,* a keeper or guardian.

5. The

5. The word *Os* is always neuter; it makes *ossis* when it signifies a bone; *inhumáta ossa*, bones unburied: but it has *oris* when it signifies the mouth or the face; *gravis odor oris*, the disagreeable stink of the mouth or breath: *decor oris*, the beauty of the countenance.

ANNOTATION.

Bos makes *bovis*, because it comes from the Æolic βῶς, βοFὶς, for βοῦς, βοός; this Æolic digamma being little more in value than the V consonant.

RULE XXV.

Of the nouns in US which make the genitive in ERIS.

1. *Nouns in* US *make the genitive in* ERIS.
2. *But the following have* ORIS, *viz.* pecus, tergus, fœnus, lepus, nemus, frigus, penus, pignus, pectus, stercus, decus, dedecus, littus, tempus, *and* corpus.
3. *The comparative in* US *has the same genitive as that in* OR.

EXAMPLES.

1. The greatest part of the nouns in US have the genitive in *ĕris* short. We reckon twenty of them, viz. *hoc acus, aceris*, chaff: *hoc fœdus, fœderis*, covenant, alliance: *hoc funus, funeris*, a funeral: *hoc genus, generis*, kind, race, extraction: *hoc glomus, ĕris*, a bottom of yarn, or clue of thread: *hoc latus, ĕris*, a side, the waist: *hoc munus, ĕris*, a present, or favour: *hoc olus, ĕris*, any garden-herbs for food: *hoc onus, ĕris*, burthen, obligation: *hoc opus, ĕris*, work, labour: *hoc pondus, ĕris*, weight: *hoc rudus, ĕris*, rubbish: *hoc scelus, ĕris*, wickedness: *hoc sidus, ĕris*, a star: *hoc vellus, ĕris*, a fleece of wool: *hæc Venus, ĕris*, the goddess Venus: *vetus, ĕris*, old, antient, it is an adject.: *hoc viscus, ĕris*, a bowel, or intrail: *hoc ulcus, ĕris*, a boil: *hoc vulnus, ĕris*, a wound.

2. There are fifteen which make the genitive in ORIS; *hoc pecus, pecoris*, a flock of sheep, a single sheep: *hoc tergus, ŏris*, the skin or hide of any beast: *hoc fœnus, ŏris*, usury, interest: *hic lepus, ŏris*, an hare:

hare: *hoc nemus, ŏris*, a grove: *hoc frigus, ŏris*, cold: *hoc penus, ŏris*, provisions of all sorts: *hoc pignus, ŏris*, a pledge: *hoc pectus, ŏris*, the breast: *hoc stercus, ŏris*, dung, excrement: *hoc decus, decŏris*, a credit or honour; and so its compound, *dedecus*, shame, disgrace: *hoc littus, ŏris*, the shore: *hoc tempus, ŏris*, time: *hoc corpus, ŏris*, the body.

3. The comparative in US has the same genitive as that in OR; and of course it makes *ŏris*, the penultimate long; as *major, & hoc majus, majôris*, greater: *mêlior, & hoc mêlius, ôris*, better: *pejor, & hoc pejus*, worse.

ANNOTATION.

It is of no manner of use to inquire which should be the general rule of the nouns in US; that is, whether it be those which make *oris*, or those which make *eris*. For as *eris* comes naturally from ER; so *oris* comes as naturally from OR; therefore one is not more natural than the other to the nouns in US. Hence we ought to take that for the general rule, which comprehends most nouns; this is that of *ĕris*, which I have followed; for the comparatives form a rule by themselves, and ought not to be confounded with the rest, because they make *ŏris* long, which is owing to their taking it from their masculine in *or*.

They used formerly to say *fœneris*, and *pigneris*, which shews that *ĕris* is the more general rule. Thence come the verbs *fœnero* or *fœneror*, to lend out at usury: *pignero* and *oppignero*, to pledge: *lepŏris* long, from *lepor* or *lepos*, masc. mirth, wit, complaisance, a good mien.

Decŏris long, comes also from *decor*, masc. It may therefore be observed that all those nouns which make *eris* or *oris*, in the genitive, have their increase short, and are neuter, except *vetus* adject. and *Venus*, fem. by its signification.

From *decus* comes *indecor, ŏris*, unseemly, misbecoming; and from *decor* comes *indecŏrus* the same.

RULE XXVI.

Of those which make URIS, UIS, UDIS, AUDIS, and ODIS.

1. *Monosyllables in* US, *as also* tellus, *make* URIS *in the genitive*.
2. *But* grus, *and* sus, *make* UIS.
3. Palus, incus, *and* subscus, *have* UDIS.
4. Laus, *and* fraus, *make* AUDIS.
5. *And* tripus, ODIS.

EXAM-

OF DECLENSIONS.

EXAMPLES.

1. All the monosyllables in US, make URIS in the genitive. *Hoc thus, thuris,* frankincense, or the tree on which it grows: *hoc rus, ruris,* the country: *hic mus, muris,* a mouse: *plus, pluris,* more: *hoc jus, juris,* broth, pottage, which was measured out to each person; hence it is taken also for justice, equity, and right: *hoc pus, puris,* matter or corruption that cometh out of a sore.

Hæc tellus, tellúris, the earth.

2. These two make UIS, *hæc grus, gruïs,* a crane: *sus, suïs,* a sow.

3. These have UDIS. *Hæc palus, palúdis,* a morass: *hæc incus, incúdis,* an anvil: *hæc subscus, údis,* a fastening of boards or timber together, called by the joiners a swallow or dove-tail. The old word *pecus,* a beast, unusual in the nominative and the vocative, makes *pécudis. Impurissimæ pécudis sordes,* Cic. in Pison. the filth of that nasty beast.

4. These two have AUDIS, *hæc laus, laudis,* praise: *hæc fraus, fraudis,* fraud, deceit.

5. *Hic tripus, trípodis,* a tripod, or three legged stool; in like manner the other compounds of πὺς.

ANNOTATION.

Ligus, liguris, which is joined to these, comes rather from *Ligur, uris*; this appears plainly from the increase of the genitive which is short, whereas all nouns in US have *uris* long.

Charisius places *pécudes* among those nouns that have neither nominative nor vocative. Hence Vossius thinks that they rather said *pécudis, hujus pécudis,* which is the reason even of the second's being short, whereas in *palus, údis,* and others of the same sort, it is long. And when Priscian quotes from Cæsar de Auguriis, a book no longer extant, *si sincera pecus erat*; this is an expression that has not been followed by any one author, and which Cæsar probably used only in giving an extract from some old Roman ceremonial. For which reason it is better to forbear making use of this nominative.

But there is great probability that they said *hoc pécude,* whence comes *hæc pécuda. Cum adhibent in pecuda pastores,* Cic. 4. de Rep. And we find even *hæc pecua, pecuum,* from the nominative *pecu.*

Rule XXVII.
Of those which make UTIS and UNTIS.

1. Intércus, sálus, virtus, juvéntus, senéctus, *and* sérvitus, *have the genitive in* UTIS. *Greek names of towns in* US *make* UNTIS.

Examples.

1. The following make the genitive in UTIS. *Intércus, intércutis,* adject. *Medicaméntum ad aquam intércutem,* Cic. a remedy for the dropsy: *hæc salus, salútis,* safety, health: *hæc virtus, virtútis,* virtue: *hæc juvéntus, juventútis,* youth: *hæc senéctus, senectútis,* old age: *hæc sérvitus, servitútis,* servitude.

Annotation.

The Greek nouns, which are proper names of towns or other places, generally make UNTIS, as *Opus, Opuntis*; *Trapezus, Trapezuntis: Amathus, untis,* &c. See several of them above, p. 17.

Rule XXVIII.
Of nouns in BS and in PS.

1. *Nouns in* BS *have* BIS; *and those in* PS *have* PIS.
2. *But those which have more than one syllable, change* E *into* I.
3. *Auceps however makes* aúcupis; puls, pultis; *and* hyems, hy'emis.

Examples.

1. Nouns in BS, and in PS, form their genitive by putting an I before S, as *Arabs, A'rabis,* an Arabian: *hæc stips, stipis,* a piece of money, the same with the *as: stirps, stirpis,* the root, a stock or race: *plebs, plebis,* the common people: *hæc seps, sepis,* Cic. an hedge: *hic seps, sepis,* a venomous serpent or eft.

2. Those nouns that have more than one syllable, change E into I in the penultimate, as *cælebs, cæ'libis,* and not *cæ'lebis,* a single, or unmarried person: *hæc forceps, ipis,* a pair of tongs, scissars, or pincers: *princeps,*

OF DECLENSIONS.   87

princeps, principis, a prince, the chief: *hic et hæc adeps, ádipis,* fat: *municeps, 'icipis,* one of a town whose inhabitants were free of the city of Rome: *párticeps, ícipis,* partaker: *manceps, máncipis,* a farmer of any part of the public revenue, an undertaker of any public work that giveth security for its performance, he that buyeth the goods of one proscribed, a proprietor who selleth a thing upon warrantry.

3. *Auceps* however makes *áucupis,* a fowler: *hæc puls,* makes *pultis,* a kind of meat used by the ancients, like a pap or panado: *hæc hyems, hy'emis,* the winter.

ANNOTATION.

Gryps has *gryphis,* a gripe or griffon: *Cynips, iphis,* a river of Lybia; and *cinips, ciniphis,* little flies, but cruelly stinging.

Now the analogy of all these genitives is this, that these words are abbreviated, having terminated heretofore in *is* in the nominative, as well as in the genitive, as we have already observed, p. 70.

RULE XXIX.

Of the nouns in NS and in RS.

1. *Nouns in* NS *and in* RS *form the genitive in* TIS, *and drop their own* S.
2. *But* glans, nefrens, lens, libripens, *and* frons, *the leaf of a tree, change* S *into* DIS.
3. *To these we may join the compounds of* cor, *which take an* S *after* OR.

EXAMPLES.

1. Nouns in NS, or in RS, form the genitives by changing S into TIS; as *hic mons, montis,* a mountain: *hæc frons, frontis,* the forehead: *expers, expértis,* void, exempt: *hæc lens, lentis,* a kind of pulse called lentiles.

2. The following change their S into DIS. *Hæc glans, glandis,* a mast of oak or other tree, an acorn; likewise its compound: *juglans, juglándis,* a walnut: *nefrens, nefréndis,* a barrow pig: *hæc lens, lendis,* a nit: *libripens, libripéndis,* a weigher: *hæc frons, frondis,* the leaf of a tree.

G 4   3. The

3. The compounds of *cor, cordis*, the heart, take an S at the latter end, and form their genitive also in DIS. *Concors, concórdis*, of one mind or will: *discors, discórdis*, discordant, jarring: *excors, órdis*, heartless, foolish; *vecors, órdis*, mad, foolish: *socors*, or *secors, órdis*, lazy, idle.

Rule XXX.

Of the participle *iens, euntis*, with its compounds.

1. Iens *makes* EUNTIS, *and is followed by all its compounds.*
2. *Except* ámbiens.

Examples.

1. The participle of the verb *eo*, I go, and those of its compounds, form the genitive in EUNTIS; as *iens, eúntis*, going: *périens, pereúntis*, perishing: *ábiens, abeúntis*, departing: *rédiens, redeúntis*, returning: *ádiens, adeúntis*, going towards another: *éxiens, exeúntis*, going out: *óbiens, obeúntis*, going round.

In like manner *quiens*, makes *queúntis*, able: *néquiens, nequeúntis*, not able; being taken by some for the compounds of *eo*.

2. Nevertheless *ámbiens* makes *ambiéntis*, surrounding, environing.

Rule XXXII.

Of *caput* and its compounds.

Caput *and all its compounds are declined in* ITIS.

Examples.

Caput, of the neuter gender, makes in the genitive, *cápitis*, the head.

In like manner its compounds, as *hoc sínciput, sincípitis*, the fore part of the head: *ócciput, occípitis*, the hinder part of the head.

Also these adjectives, *anceps, ancípitis*, double headed, ambiguous, doubtful: *biceps, bicípitis*, two headed: *triceps, tricípitis*, three headed.

Rule

Rule XXXIII.
Of the nouns in X.

1. *The nouns in* X *change it into* CIS, *as* vervex, vervécis ; halex, halécis.
2. *But* frux, lex, rex, grex, Styx, Phryx, conjux, *change* X *into* GIS.
3. Remex *makes* rémigis.
4. *All other nouns in* EX *of more syllables than one, have the genitive in* ICIS.

Examples.

1. The nouns in X form their genitive by changing X into CIS; as *hæc halex*, or *alex, écis*, an herring, pickle, brine: *hic vervex, vervécis*, a wether sheep: *hæc fæx, fæcis*, dregs: *felix, felicis*, happy: *hæc filix, filicis*, fern, brake: *hæc vibex, vibícis*, a wheal on the flesh after whipping. See the genders, p. 55. *hæc lux, lucis*, light.

2. The following change X into GIS. *Hæc frux, frugis*, corn, the fruits of the earth: *hæc lex, legis*, a law; as also its compound, *exlex, exlégis*, lawless: *hic rex, regis*, a king; *hic grex, gregis*, a flock, an herd: *hæc Styx, Stygis*, a poetical infernal lake: *Phryx, Phrygis*, a Phrygian: *hic et hæc conjux, cónjugis*, a husband or wife.

Annotation.

To these these we may join *harpax, agis*, a kind of amber that draweth leaves and straw after it: *Biturix, igis*, Cæf. a native of Bourges: *Allobrox, ogis*, a Savoyard, or of that neighbourhood: *strix, igis*, a screech-owl, an hag, or hobgoblin: *Iäpyx, igis*, the western wind: *phalanx, angis*, a kind of Macedonian battalion: *syrinx, gis*, a flute, a pipe: *sphinx, gis*, a poetical monster. And perhaps some others, taken either from the Greek, or from a verb in *go*, as *aquilex, aquilegis*, he that maketh conveyance of water by pipes, or he that findeth springs, taken from *lego*, to gather. And this analogy is more general than one would imagine. For *lex* itself makes *legis*, only because it comes from *lego*, to read, according to Varro and St. Isidore. Which we may also say of *grex*, taken from *grego*, from whence comes *congrego*: of *rex* taken from *rego*, &c. But those which come from a verb in *co* make *cis*, as *dux, ducis*, from *duco*; *lux, lucis*, from *luceo*; (the pure termination

tion following the impure). And if the verb hath an *i* before *go* or *co*, this *i* is likewise continued before *gis* or *cis* in the genitive of the noun, which seldom happens except in words of more than one syllable, as appears in the following, taken from *remigo, judico, indico, plico, supplico*, &c. For which reason we say that

3. *Remex*, a rower, makes *rémigis*, changing E into I, because it has more syllables than one.

4. The other nouns in EX, that have more syllables than one (except *halex* and *vervex, écis*, already mentioned) also change E into I, and make ICIS. *Judex, júdicis*, a judge : *index, índicis*, a discoverer, a shewer, the forefinger, a mark or token, an index or table of a book : *simplex, ícis*, simple : *supplex, súpplicis*, humble : *duplex, dúplicis*, double, &c.

ANNOTATION.

The analogy of these genitives is owing likewise to this, that all these nouns were heretofore terminated in *is* in the nominative as well as in the genitive : thus the *x* being a double letter, in some is equivalent to *cs*, for which reason they make *cis*; and in others to *gs*, for which reason they have *gis*; see the preceding annotation.

Rule XXXIV.
Exception to the preceding rule.

Senex, nox, nix, onyx, supéllex, *make* senis, noctis, nivis, ónychis, *and* supelléctilis.

EXAMPLES.

These form their genitive in a different manner, viz. *senex, senis*, an old man; *hæc vox, noctis*, night : *hæc nix, nivis*, snow : *hæc onyx, ónychis*, a sort of marble or alabaster, but taken for a vase or box of that sort of stone it is masculine. See p. 53. *Hæc supéllex, supelléctilis*, houshold stuff. But we say also *supelléctilis, hujus supelléctilis*.

ANNOTATION.

Greek nouns in AX make ACTIS, as *Astyanax, actis*; Virg. the name of a man : *Bibrax, actis*, the name of a city : *Hipponax*, the name of a man : *Hylax*, the name of a dog.

Despauter excepts *Bryax*, which, as he pretends, does make *Bryaxis*. But it appears from several passages in Pliny, that the nominative is BRYAXIS : *hos deorum quinque colossos fecit Bryaxis*, lib. 34. c. 7.

Bryaxis

OF DECLENSIONS.

Bryaxis Æsculapium fecit, cap. seq. and it appears likewise that it makes *Bryaxidis* in the genitive. *Sunt alia signa illustrium artificum; Liber pater, Bryaxidis, & alter Scopæ,* ibid. Hence it makes *Bryaxin* in the accusative, as we shall take notice hereafter, p. 92.

The analogy of these genitives consists in this, that the nominatives are syncopated, having been heretofore like their genitives. It may also be said that *x* being a double letter, *nox* stands for *nocs,* which inserts a *t* with an *i, noctis*; and that *nix* standing for *nics,* it takes the Æolic digamma in *nivis,* for which reason it loses the *c,* lest the pronunciation should be too harsh. On the contrary *Onychis* assumes the aspiration *h* to strengthen the sound.

RULE XXXV.
General for the accusatives.

The accusative case is in EM, *as* dux ducis, *makes* ducem.

EXAMPLES.

The other cases are formed from the genitive, taking the termination that properly belongs to them, as that of EM for the accusative: for example, *hic sermo, sermónis,* accusative *sermónem,* speech, discourse: *hic labor, labóris, labórem,* labour: *dux, ducis, ducem,* a leader, a commander.

RULE XXXVI.
Of the accusatives in IM.

The following nouns, tussis, amussis, sitis, securis, decussis, vis, pelvis, ravis, buris, A'raris, Tigris, Tiberis, *form their accusative in* im.

EXAMPLES.

All these nouns have the accusative in IM. *Hæc tussis,* accusative *tussim,* a cough: *hæc amussis, amussim,* a mason's or carpenter's rule or line: *hæc sitis, sitim,* thirst: *hæc securis, securim,* an ax or hatchet: *hæc decussis, decussim,* a coin of the value of ten asses; and in like manner *centussis, centussim,* a coin of the value of one hundred *asses: hæc vis, vim,* force, violence, plenty: *hæc pelvis, pelvim,* a bason: *hæc ravis, ravim,* hoarseness: *hæc buris, burim,* Virg. the plowtail: *Arar,* or *A'raris,* accus. *A'rarim,* the river Saône: *Tigris, Tigrim,* the river Tiger: *Tiberis, Tiberim,* or *Tibrim,* the Tiber.

ANNO-

ANNOTATION.

Cannabis forms also the accusative in IM; we likewise meet with *cucumim, pulvim,* and some others.

Hereto we must also refer a multitude of Greek nouns, which take *n* for *m,* as *genesis,* accusative *genesin,* or *genesim*; *erynnis, erynnin*; *syrtis, syrtin,* and the like, which may be learnt by the use of authors. And all the names of rivers form likewise their poetical accusatives in *in, Albin, Bætin,* &c. Which is of great service to poets, because the M suffers an elision before a vowel, but the N may stand.

RULE XXXVII.
The accusative in EM or in IM.

Turris, seméntis, febris, restis, clavis, aquális, puppis, *and* navis, *form the accusative either in* EM *or* IM.

EXAMPLES.

These form the accusative in EM or in IM. *Hæc turris,* accusative *turrem,* or *turrim,* more usual, a tower: *hæc seméntis, seméntem,* or *seméntim,* a sowing, seed time, also corn sown; *hæc febris, febrem,* or *febrim,* a fever: *hæc restis, restem,* or *restim,* more usual, an halter, a rope: *hæc clavis, clavem,* or *clavim,* a key: *hic aquális, aquálem,* or *aquálim,* more usual, an ewer, a water pot: *hæc puppis, puppem,* or *puppim,* more usual, the hind deck of a ship, the poop: *hæc navis, navem,* or *navim,* a ship; the former in *em* is more usual.

ANNOTATION.

Cucumis in ancient writers, makes rather *cucumim* than *cucumerem.* We meet also with *cutem* and *cutim* in the accusative, *præsepem* from the noun *præsepis.* Strigilim, sentim, gummim, cannabim, avim, cratim, lentim, messim, ovim, ratim, and some others: even, some belonging to the precedent rule will be found to have *em* or *im.* And if we may believe Scioppius, all nouns in IS that have no increase in the genitive, had heretofore two terminations; for which reason, he adds, we say not only *partem,* but also *partim,* which has been made to pass for an adverb, but is a real accusative, for heretofore they said *hæc partis, hujus partis.*

There are a great many more Greek nouns, which increasing in the genitive, form the accusative in EM with increase, and in IN without increase, as *Iris, Iridis,* accusative *Iridem,* and *Irin: Bryaxis, idis,* accusative *Briaxidem* and *Bryaxin.* And then they have hardly any other than the ablative in E, as we shall shew hereafter, p. 97.

OF DECLENSIONS.

Rule XXXVIII.
General for the ablative.

1. *The ablative of substantives is in* E.
2. *That of adjectives in* E *or in* I.

EXAMPLES.

The ablative of the third declension may be considered according either to substantives, or to adjectives.

1. Substantives generally form the ablative in E, as *hic pater, patris,* ablative *patre,* a father: *hoc corpus,* genitive *córporis,* ablative *córpore,* a body: *hoc stemma, ătis,* ablative *stémmate,* a garland, a stem or pedigree, a noble act or atchievement; but to make it stand for a *coat of arms,* as is commonly done, I question whether this can be defended by ancient authority.

2. Adjectives generally form the ablative in I or in E, as *felix, felíce* or *felíci,* happy: *fortior* and *fortius, fortióre* and *fortióri,* stronger: *vetus, vétere* or *véteri,* old: *victrix, victríce* or *victríci,* victorious: *amans, amánte* or *amánti,* loving.

ANNOTATION.

Of some adjectives that have been doubted of, and which follow nevertheless the general rule.

Uber, which several grammarians except from this rule, forms nevertheless E or I. The former is usual, the latter we read in Q. Curtius, *uberi et pingui solo*; and in Seneca, *uberi cingit solo,* in Hercul. fur.

Degener makes *degeneri* in Lucan, lib. 4. *Dives* makes *divite* in Hor. and *diviti* in Pliny. *Locuples* makes *locuplete* in Hor. and *locupleti* in Cic. *Inops* makes *inope* or *inopi. In hac inope lingua,* Cic. *Plus* makes *plure* and *pluri* according to Charis. though Alvarez ranks it among those which make only *i*.

Of Par *and its compounds.*

Par makes *pare* and *pari,* but with some distinction. For being taken substantively in the masc. or fem. for *like, equal,* or *companion,* it has *pare,* as we read it in Ovid, 3. & 4. Fast. But when taken for couple, or a pair, as it is then neuter, it has *pari* by the following rule; hence it makes *paria* in the plural. *Ex omnibus sæculis, vix tria aut quatuor nominántur paria amicorum,* Cic.

While it continues adjective, it makes generally *pari*.

Ergo pari voto gessisti lella juventus, Lucan.

Its compounds retain both terminations, and are adjectives.
———*Atlas cum compare multo*, Mart.

And yet *impari* and *dispari* seem to be more usual. Wherefore upon this passage of the 8th eclogue, *numero Deus impare gaudet*, Servius says, *impare autem propter metrum; nam ab hoc impari dicimus*. And herein the analogy favours him, because heretofore they said, *hic et hæc paris, et hoc pare; accessit ei fortuna paris*, Atta. apud Prisc.

Of the adjectives in IX, fem. and neuter.

Victrix, and the like nouns in IX, are adjectives; and sometimes we find them even in the neuter, not only in the plural, as Servius believed, *victricia arma*; but likewise in the singular *victrix solum*, Claud. *Victrix trophæum*, Min. Felix; and then their ablative is in E or in I, *dextrâ cecidit victrice*, Ovid. *Victrici ferro*, Lucan.

This shews that Joseph Scaliger had no more reason than Servius, to declare in a letter to Patisson, that it was ridiculous to think we might say, *victrix genus*, as we say *victricia arma*.

But we have further to remark, that in these adjectives, the termination OR, as *victor*, serves for the masculine, and that in IX, as *victrix*, for the feminine and the neuter. Hence it is a mistake that has been censured in Virgil Martyr, to say *victrix triumphus* for *victor*. Which cannot be excused, says Vossius, but by allowing for the age he lived in, when the language was quite corrupted.

Of the names of countries in AS.

The names of countries in AS are also adjectives, and of course may have E or I. Though Frischlinus says that Priscian leads us into an error of making false Latin, by establishing this rule. But we read *Frusinati* in Cic. ad Attic. and *Aletrinati* in the oration pro Cluentio, according to Lambinus.

It is true that the termination *e* is perhaps more usual; for we find in the same author, *in Arpinate, Atinate, Capehate, Casinate, Fulginate, Pitinate*, and the like. And yet this does not seem to be so agreeable to analogy, since according to Priscian himself, these nouns were heretofore terminated in *i*., and instead of saying *Arpinas*, which serves now for the three genders, they said *Arpinatis* and *Arpinate*, from whence it would be more natural to form *Arpinati* in the ablative according to the 44th rule; the same may be said of the rest.

EXCEPTIONS TO THE RULE OF THE Ablative, relating to Substantives.

RULE XXXIX.

Exception 1. of nouns that make I in the ablative.

1. *The neuter in* AR *makes the ablative in* I.
2. (*Except* nectar, jubar, far, *and* hepar.)
3. *The*

OF DECLENSIONS.

3. *The neuters in* AL, *except* fal ;
4. *And those in* E, *except* gausape, *make also* I.

EXAMPLES.

1. The neuters in AR form the ablative in I, as *calcar, calcáris,* ablative *calcári,* a spur.

2. These four are excepted, which have E. *Jubar, júbare,* a sun beam: *nectar, néctare,* the drink of the gods: *far, farre,* all manner of corn, also meal or flour: *hepar, hépate,* the liver.

3. The neuters in AL form also the ablative in I ; *ánimal, animális, animáli,* a beast or animal. Except *sal,* salt, which makes *sale,* because it is more usual in the masculine.

4. Those in E form also the ablative in I ; *hoc mare, mari,* the sea: *hoc cubile, cubíli,* a bed: except *gausape* a furred coat, an hair mantle ; ablative *gausape,* in Hor. Plin. and Lucil.

ANNOTATION.

The dictionaries all in general * mark *gausape* as indeclinable, which in all probability is owing to this passage of Pliny, book 8. c. 48. *Nam tunica laticlavi in modum gausape, texi nunc primùm incipit:* taking *gáusape* in the genitive, as may be seen in Calepin. But Vossius pretends it is there an ablative, pointing it thus ; *lati clavi in modum, gausape texi incipit.* And indeed Priscian does not give it an E in the ablative because of its being indeclinable, but because all those nouns having heretofore had E (as well as I) this is one of those that retained this single termination. For which reason, he says, it is that *Persius* does not use *gausapia,* in the plur. but *gausapa,* which we find also in Ovid and in Martial. This is better than to derive it, as some do, from *gausapum,* which Cass. Severus made use of; but it never obtained, nor do we find it in any author extant.

Calepin likewise quotes *gausapia* from Varr. 4. de L. L. but I could not find it there, nor in any other author. Nor do we read any where *hæc gausapis,* from which several would fain derive the ablative *gausape.* For the Greeks saying ἡ γαυσάπης, the Latins have thence formed *hæc gáusapa,* according to the opinion of Varro, Char. and Prisc. in the same manner as of ὁ χάρτης they have made *hæc charta,* and others of the like sort, of which we took notice, when treating of the genders, p. 26.

* It is not marked so in Ainsworth's.

Of the analogy of the terminations included in this rule.

No wonder that the neuters in AL should follow those in E, for they are often formed from thence by syncope. Thus *animal* comes from *animale*, *autumnal* from *autumnale*, &c.

In regard to those in AR we may here observe a beautiful analogy, namely, that those whose ablative is in *i*, have the penultimate long by nature. For which reason those that have it short, make it in *e*, as *nectare*, *jubare*, *hepate*. Even *far* itself makes *farre*, because the penultimate is long only by position. From thence one should conclude that *lucar* must make also *lucare* and not *lucari*, because it is short in the penultimate. But I could find no authority for it. The same must be said of *cappar*, capers, which we read in Palladius; but we likewise meet with *capparis* in Colum. from whence comes *cappare*, the same as *baccharis*, *bacchare*, the herb called *lady's gloves*.

Of the proper names in AL *or in* E.

Proper names form always the ablative in E, *Annibal, Annibale*; *Amilcar, Amilcare*. And in like manner the names of towns, though neuter, as *Præneste, Cære, Reate, Bibracte*. The same may be said of *Nepete, Soracte*, and other proper names.

Poetical licence in regard to other nouns.

It is a licence hardly ever suffered but in verse to make the ablat. of appellatives in *e*, as the poets say in the ablative *laqueare, mare*, and the like. But here we must observe that the nominative is sometimes twofold, which will occasion two different ablatives. For we say *rete* and *præsepe*, which have the ablative in I. We likewise say *retis* and *præsepis*, which have the ablative in E. There shall be a list of these different terminations at the end of the heteroclites.

RULE XL.

Exception 2. of substantives that have E or I in the ablative.

From the accusative in EM *or* IM *the ablative is formed by dropping* M.

EXAMPLES.

The ablative is formed of the accusative, by dropping M; such therefore as have the accusative in IM, form their ablative in I; as *hæc sitis, sitim, siti*, thirst: *hæc vis, vim, vi*, force, violence, plenty.

And those which have the accusative in EM or in IM, form likewise their ablative in E or in I; as *hæc navis, navem* or *navim*; ablat. *nave* or *navi*, a ship: *hæc clavis, clavem* or *clavim*, ablat. *clave* or *clavi*, a key.

OF DECLENSIONS.

ANNOTATION.

It is obfervable that moſt of the Greek nouns which increaſe in the genitive, drop the augment in the accuſative in IN; but taking it up again in the ablative, they generally form it in E and not in I. As *avis, eridis*, accuſative *eridem* and *erin*, ablative *eride*, and not *eris: iris, idis, iridem* and *irin*, ablative *iride*, and not *iri*: **Daphnis,** *idis,* **Daphnin,** ablative **Daphnide,** and not *Daphni*.

And the reaſon of this is becauſe the dative and the ablative being the ſame thing in the Greek, they ought to conſiſt of an equal number of ſyllables, when they go over to the Latins. But we ſhall treat more largely of theſe nouns at the end of this third declenſion, where we ſhall ſhew that they are ſometimes declined without the augment, and then they may form their ablative alſo in I.

The nouns in YS have their ablative in E or in Y; as *Capys, Atys, Catys,* and ſuch like proper names. Ablative *Capye* or *Capy, Atye* or *Aty,* &c. The former is according to the Latins, who ſay in the dative *Apyi,* and even according to the Greeks in the common tongue, τῷ Κάπυι: but the latter comes from the Dorians, who decline ὁ Κάπυς, τῦ Κάπυ, for Κάπυος; τῷ Κάπυ for Κάπυι, &c.

RULE XLI.

Of ſome nouns which do not intirely conform to the analogy of the preceding rule.

1. A'raris *chuſes to make* A'rare, *and* reſtis *has only* reſte.
2. *On the contrary* vectis, ſtrigilis, canalis *form the ablative in* I.

EXAMPLES.

1. This rule is only an appendix to the former. For *A'raris,* the Saone, has ſcarce any other accuſative than *A'rarim,* as we have above obſerved, rule 36. And yet its ablative is generally *A'rare,* though we ſometimes meet alſo with *A'rari: reſtis,* a rope or cord, has only *reſte* in the ablative, though in the accuſative it has *reſtem* and *reſtim*.

2. On the contrary, *ſtrigilis,* a curry-comb, makes always *ſtrigili,* though we ſeldom ſay *ſtrigilim,* in the accuſative. It is the ſame with *vectis,* a bar, a lever, which makes *vecti*; and *canalis,* any fall or ſpout of water, a trunk or pipe for the conveyance of water,

which has *canáli*, though perhaps we shall not be able to find their accusative in IM.

ANNOTATION.

To these may be added *Bætis*, which makes *Bæte* or *Bæti*, though it has *Bætim* only in the accusative. The former we find in Livy, *superato Bæte amni*; and the second is in Pliny. The reason hereof is because all these nouns had heretofore both terminations in the accusative and the ablative: but custom has deprived them of one in the one case, while for the other it has reserved the other.

RULE XLII.

Third exception. Of other substantives whose ablative is in E or in I.

These have either E *or* I *in the ablative, viz.* unguis, amnis, rus, civis, imber, ignis, vigil, avis, tridens, supéllex, *with some others.*

EXAMPLES.

The following also form the ablative in E or in I. *Hic unguis*, ablative, *ungue* or *ungui*, a nail, or talon: *hic amnis, amne,* or *amni,* a river: *hoc rus, ruris,* the country; ablative *rure* and *ruri,* Charis. *hic et hæc civis, cive* or *civi,* a citizen: *hic imber, imbris, imbre* or *imbri,* a shower of rain: *hic ignis, igne* or *igni,* fire: *vigil, vigile* or *vigili,* a watchman, a sentinel: *avis, ave* or *avi,* a bird; the latter is more usual: *tridens, tridénte* or *tridénti,* a trident, any instrument that hath three teeth: *hæc supéllex, supelléctile* or *i,* household stuff, or furniture.

ANNOTATION.

There are some other nouns which have I or E in the ablative, and may be easily learnt by practice. Those of most frequent use and best ascertained are mentioned in the rule; the greatest part of the rest are thrown together in the following list, in which the learner will also find authorities for those mentioned in the rule.

A list of nouns substantives that form the ablative in I *or in* E.

AFFINITATI, *nisi ita conjunctus est affinitati,* Venul.

AMNI, which Frischlinus rejects, is in Horace;

―――*rapido ferventius amni.*

And in Virg.

―――*prono rapit alveus amni,* according to Pierius and all the antient copies; as also according to Charisius and Priscian.

But we meet likewise with AMNE in Hor.

Phœbe qui Xantho lavis amne crines, in Lucan, Martial, and others.

ANGUI

OF DECLENSIONS.

ANGUI is¹ absolutely rejected by Frischlinus, though Priscian has endeavoured to establish it by means of this passage of Horace; *cane pejus & angui.* But all the antient and modern editions have *angue.* And we meet with it also in Propertius.

Tisiphones atro si furit angue caput.

In Statius, *angue ter excusso,* and in Andronicus.

AVI;——*Malâ ducis avi domum,* Hor. *Avi incerta,* Cic. de Augur. ex Charis. And heretofore *avim* in the accusative in Nævius.

AVE is to be found in Varro, *ave sinistrâ,* 6. de L. L. And he himself also admits it in his 2d book de Anal. as does also Priscian, lib. 7.

CANI or CANE were both used, according to Charis. But the safest way is to use only the latter.

CIVI occurs constantly in Plautus, *in Persa,* Act 4. sc. *Cui homini.*

——*qui Atticam hodie civitatem,*

Maximam majorem feci, atque auxi civi fœminâ.

In Cicero it is the same, *ut nunc in uno civi res ad resistendum sit,* ad Atticum, lib. 7. ep. 3. *De clarissimo civi,* lib. 14. ep. 11. according to all the ancient copies, as Malaspina and Vossius maintain, and as Lambinus and Gruterus read it, though in several editions the passage be corrupted.

But CIVE occurs in Juvenal and in other writers.

——*Quid illo cive tulisset*

Natura in terris, quid Roma beatius unquam? sat. 10.

CLASSI is in Virg.

Advectum Æneam classi, victosque penates   *Inferre.* Æn. 8.

COLLI;—— *in colli tundentes pabula lœta.* Lucret.

FINI is very common: but

FINI frequently occurs in Gellius and in Papinian. It is even in Hirtius 1. *De bello Alex.* as Scipio Gentilis observes. We find it likewise in Terentianus and in Manilius, lib. 1.

FURFURI;——*qui alunt furfuri sues.* Plaut.

FUSTI, of which Alvarez doubted, is in Plautus.

Nihil est: tanquam si claudus sim, cum fusti est ambulandum.

Asin. act 2. sc. *Quod hoc est negotii.* It is also in the Captives: in Tacitus, and in Apuleius.

IGNI——*Igni corusco nubila dividens.* Hor.

IGNI——*commissis igne tenebris.* Virg. And the last was the best according to Pliny.

IMBRI. *Imbri frumentum corrumpi patiebantur.* Cic. in Verr. 5.

Nec minus ex imbri soles & aperta serena Prospicere. Virg. 1. Georg.

IMBRE. *Romam petit imbre lutoque Aspersus.* Hor.

LABI. *Nec novitate cibi, nec labi corporis illa.* Lucret.

LAPIDI. *Cum lapidi lapidem terimus.* Idem.

LUCI——*In luci quæ poterit res Accidere.* Idem.

MELLI. *Aut pice cum melli, nitrum Sulfur & acetum.* Seren.

MESSI also occurs in Varro 1. de R. R. where some however read *masse factâ.*

MONTI, FONTI. Vossius quotes them both from Varro. But on the contrary Varro condemns them, which Vossius does not seem to have sufficiently observed. It is in the 8th book de L. L. n. 64. where intending to shew that an erroneous custom does not at all make against the truth of analogy, he says that whoever makes use of Hoc MONTI and Hoc FONTI, where others read Hoc MONTE and Hoc FONTE, *and the like, which are said two ways, one true, the other false, does no manner of hurt to the analogy; but that the other on the contrary who follows this analogy, establishes and confirms it.* Whereby we see that Varro rejects the ablative in *i*, and admits only of that in *e*, as most agreeable to analogy.

MUGILI, which some pretend to prove by the 17th chapter of the 9th book of Pliny, occurs only in the title, which is indeed, *de mugili*; but not in the text of the author. Therefore Charisius chuses rather to say *mugile.* And thence it is that in the genitive plural in this same chapter of Pliny, he has *mugilum* and not *mugilium.*

NAVI.——*Navi fractâ ad Andrum ejectus est.* Ter.

Quò enim tibi navi opus fuit? Cic.

NAVE; *At mediâ Mnestheus incedens nave per ipsos Hortatur socios.*——Virg.

NEPTI, is in Priscian, but without authority.

OCCIPITI. *Occipiti cæco, posticæ occurrite sannæ.* Pers.

Occipiti calvo es. Auson.

ORBI. *Pectora, terrarum qui in orbi sancta tuetur.* Lucret. as Lambinus, Giffanius, and Vossius read him. And Charisius affirms that this is a very good word, being found in Cicero, *Orbi terrarum comprehensos.* 5. de Rep. and that it is ascertained by Pliny, lib. 5. *de sermone dubio.* Varro frequently uses it, *aquâ frigidâ & orbi ligneo.* 3. de R. R. c. 5. *in orbi rotundo ostendunt.* c. 16. and the like.

OVI is admitted by Charis. and Prisc. Even Varro acknowledges that they commonly said without a mistake OVI or OVE, AVI or AVE.

PARTI ——*loquitur de m^e et de parti mea.* Plaut. And in Lucretius we often meet with it. Some read it even in Cicero. *Parti miscentur in una.* in Arat. But others read, *Partem admiscentur in unam :* very likely because they were of opinion that *parti* was not used.

POSTI. *Raptáque de dextro robusta repagula posti.* Ovid.
POSTE. *Tum poste recluso.* Lucan.
RURI. Charis. *Esse rure* or *ruri,* to be in the country. *Ruri veneunt rustici.* Plaut. they come from the country.

SEGETI. *Ex segeti vellito ebulum, cicutam,* &c. Cato de R. R.
SORDI. *Visceribus cæcis, prope jam, sordiquæ spuliis.* Lucret.
SORTI. *Sorti sum victus.* Plaut.
STERCORI, occurs frequently in the Florentine Pandects. It is also in Apuleius according to Scioppius.
SUPELLECTILI. *In instrumento & supellectili C. Verris.* Cic.
VECTI. —— *In medium huc agmen cum vecti Donax.* Terent. Priscian pretends that *vecte* was likewise used, but he gives no authority for it.
UNGUI ——*acuto ne secer ungui.* Hor. For although this does not prove enough, being at the end of the verse, where he might have put *ungue ;* yet this is the established reading in all the ancient copies. And Charisius takes notice that Calvus had used it thus: but we meet likewise with UNGUE in Propert.

Ungue meam morso quærere sæpe fidem. It is also in Ovid, Martial, and others.

ANNOTATION.

The foregoing are the ablatives given by Vossius. However there is no manner of doubt of their having had formerly a great many more, since we find *vesperi, tempori, luci,* &c. marked as adverbs, which are indeed no other than ablative cases.

Hence Sanctius, after Consentius Romanus, affirms, that all the nouns of the third declension had formerly the ablative in E or in I: this is owing entirely to the affinity of these two vowels, E and I, which is so great, that in almost all languages they are changed for each other, as we shall observe in the treatise of letters, and a great many nations frequently confound them in the pronunciation. Though in practice we should always consult the antients, which Pontanus perhaps omitted, when he said :

—— *Cinerique maligno.* 1. Meteor.

But we have elsewhere taken notice of some other expressions of this author, which can hardly be defended.

That the dative and the ablative were always alike ; and that the Greeks have an ablative.

But what is most remarkable upon this head, is that heretofore the dative and the ablative of this, as well as of every other declension, were always alike in the singular, as they are still in the plural, whence it is that we find *insultet morte meæ,* Propert. for *morti. Quæ tibi sene serviet,* Catùll. as Scaliger reads it for *seni.* And

And other like phrases, of which we shall take more particular notice in the remarks.

From hence, say Sanctius and Scioppius, proceeds that mistake of the grammarians, who imagined that the Greeks had no ablative, because in their language the resemblance was general and without exception. Not at all considering that this is not what properly constitutes the difference of cases, but it is their different properties and offices in expressing and marking every thing whatsoever, and that it is natural and reasonable they should always retain the same properties whether in Greek, Latin, or in any other language.

EXCEPTIONS TO THE RULE OF Ablatives in regard to the Adjectives.

RULE XLIII.

First exception. Of adjectives that have only the ablative in E.

1. Hospes, pubes, senex, pauper, sospes, *form the ablative only in* E.
2. *The same happens to adjectives ending in* NS, *especially when they are put in an absolute sense.*

EXAMPLES.

1. These five nouns are adjectives; and yet they always form their ablative in E only, like that of substantives.

Hospes, a guest, an host, ablative *hóspite*: *pubes, ĕris*, of ripe age, full grown, ablative *púbere*: *senex*, old, *sene*: *pauper*, poor, *páupere*: *sospes*, safe, *sóspite*.

2. In like manner the participles or nouns adjective in NS generally form their ablative in E. And in the first place when they are put in an absolute sense, they never form it otherwise: *Deo volénte*, God willing: *regnánte Rómulo*, in Romulus's reign. So that it would be a mistake to say *volénti* or *regnánti* in this sense.

And even exclusive of this upon the whole they more frequently form the ablative in E. *Pro cauto ac diligénte*, Cæs. like a wary and diligent man.

—— *Illum déperit impoténte amóre.* Catul.
He is most passionately fond of him.

But then they may have I. *Excellénti ánimo.* Cic. Of an excellent disposition.

ANNOTATION.

Priscian says that the reason why *hospes* and *sospes* do not form the ablative in I, is because they have not the neuter in E, and therefore follow a different analogy from the rest. In general it may be said of the five nouns mentioned in the rule, that it is because they are seldom used in the neuter, though we sometimes meet with them, as we shall observe in the remarks, and most frequently they are taken substantively, and therefore they have followed the rule of substantives.

For which reason Vossius is of opinion we ought not intirely to reject *hospiti*, when it is a real adjective, and he thinks that from thence comes the genitive plural, *hospitium*, as he would have it taken in the description of Ætna.

Quod si diversas emittat terra canales,
Hospitium fluviorum, aut semita nulla, &c.

Though Ascensius reads *hospitium* here in the nominative by apposition. But this genitive we also meet with in Nonius on the word *cluet* in the following verse of Pacuvius.

Sed hæc cluentur hospitium irfidelissimi.

For this is the reading in the old editions and in several manuscripts, although some others have *hospitum*.

For the adjectives in NS.

Charisius, after Pliny and Valerius Flaccus, an excellent grammarian, lays down this general rule for the adjectives in *ns*, of having only E in the ablative; nor can it be denied but they have it very often; yet we meet with some also in I, when they are not taken in an absolute sense. *In terra continenti,* Varro, in Charis. *Primo insequenti die,* Asin. Pollio in the same author: *ex continenti visi,* Cæs. 3. B. Civ. *Gaudenti animo,* Cic. *Candenti ferro,* Varro. This is what Alvarez thought to reconcile, when he reduced this principle to the participles only, adding that whenever they occurred in I, they became mere nouns adjectives, that is, they no longer expressed any difference of time. But not to mention that it is difficult to fix this in several examples, as in the two just now quoted, *candenti ferro, gaudenti animo,* where the present time is evidently expressed, it is certain that the analogy of the language absolutely requires they should have *e* or *i*, it being impossible to give any other reason why the plural of these participles is in *ia,* and the genitive in *ium,* as *amantia, amantium,* but because they admit of I in the ablative, *amante* vel *amanti*: and therefore this is general only in regard to the ablatives absolute, as Vossius hath observed.

Rule XLIV.

Second exception. Of those adjectives which have the ablative only in I.

1. *All adjectives in* ER *or in* IS *reserving* E *for the nominative neuter, have* I *only in the ablative.*

2. The

OF DECLENSIONS.

2. *The same extends to the names of months.*

EXAMPLES.

1. Adjectives in ER or in IS form the ablative in I, to distinguish it from the nominative neuter in E.

Those in ER; as *hic et hæc acer*, and *hoc acre*, sour, sharp, ablative *acri: celeber* and *célebre*, ablative *célebri*, famous, celebrated.

Those in IS; as *dulcis et dulce*, sweet, ablative *dulci: fortis et forte*, ablative *forti*.

2. We include also the names of months which are real adjectives, as *September*, the month of September, ablative *Septembri: October*, the month of October, abl. *Octobri*.

Aprilis, April, ablative *Aprili: Quintilis*, July, ablative *Quintili: Sextilis*, August, ablative *Sextili*.

ANNOTATION.

To this rule a number of nouns may be referred, which being of their nature adjectives, follow this same analogy, because though they are very little, if at all, used in the neuter, yet they might have been used.

Such are the names of months, which even children themselves cannot but know to be adjectives, since they are made to say *mense Aprili, kalendas Octobres, nonas Novembres, idus Decembres*, &c.

Such are a great many nouns which agree to inanimate things, as *bipennis, biremis, triremis, annalis, natalis, rudis*, and the like, all which form the ablative in I.

Such are also a great many others which agree to man, as *sodalis, rivalis, familiaris, affinis, ædilis, popularis, patruelis*, &c.

To distinguish the ablative, according as the noun is taken either adjectively or substantively.

But we should take particular notice that as these nouns frequently assume the office of substantives, they follow likewise the analogy of the latter, forming only E in the ablative. Which is general, even in regard to all the other adjectives, as hath already appeared by examples.

Thus we find, as an adjective, *in Æsopo familiari tuo*, Cic. though in other places *familiaris* taken as a substantive forms likewise E. *Pro L. familiare veniebam*, Varro. *A Lare familiare*, Id.

Thus you may say, with the adjective, *volucri sagittâ, homine rudi*; and with the substantive, *à volucre comestus, rude donatus*, and the like.

Thus proper names derived from adjectives, have E only, as Pliny and Charisius observe. *Summa in Lateranense ornamenta esse*, Cic.

Cic. *Cum Juvenale meo*, Mart. though this name was heretofore in use for *juvenilis*. In like manner *Cerealis*, *Vitalis*, *Apollinaris*, and others, form all of them E, when they become proper names.

But the ablative of adjectives, or even of the nouns common in IS, is sometimes also terminated by the poets in E, as we have seen them give this termination to the substantives neuter in E. Thus they say, *cœleste sagittâ*, Ovid. *De porcâ bimestre*, Ovid. *Letale ferro impresso*, Sen. and in like manner *Tricuspide telo*, Ovid. *Cognomine terrâ*, Virg. Æn. 4. though in this passage it comes from *cognominis*, which is also in Festus and even in Plautus, *illa mea cognominis fuit*; and ought to make the ablative in I according to our 44th rule. This is what Servius clearly shews, where he says, *Quod autem communi genere, in E misit ablativum, metri necessitas fecit*; whereby we see that this ablative does not come from *cognomen*, as some have imagined, who find fault with this example; but from *hic et hæc cognominis*, and that the usual custom of those common nouns (which is very remarkable) as well as of the adjectives, was to have *i*, since he will have it that the poet departed from it only to serve the measure of the verse.

Memor makes in like manner *memori*, and may be referred to this rule; because its having only I in the ablative, is owing to the antient use of *memoris* and *memore* in the nominative, as may be seen in Caper and in Prisc.

OF THE PLURAL OF THE THIRD
Declension.

The nominative plural of the masc. and fem. is generally well enough known by the rudiments, where it is marked in *es*; *patres*, *fortes*, &c. Nevertheless they sometimes inserted an *i*, *forteis*, *puppeis*, *Aresteis*, which Varro affirms to be as proper as *puppes*, *Arestes*, &c.

This happened particularly in Greek words, whose contraction was in ης, as *Syrteis*, *Tralleis*, *Sardeis*, *Alpeis*, which were sometimes wrote with 1 long.

Smyrna quid, & Colophon? quid Cræsi regia Sardis?

because this I long and this diphthong EI were almost the same thing, as we shall make appear elsewhere.

Now, in order to know when the termination in EIS or in IS is best received, see what shall be said hereafter concerning the accusative.

We have only to give a rule here in regard to the neuters, some of which have the plural in A, and others in IA.

RULE XLV.
Of the plural of nouns neuter.

The nominative plural of neuters depends on the ablative singular:

1. If this be in E, they form the plural in A;

2. But

2. But if it be in I, or in E and I, they form IA.

3. All comparatives make the nominative plural in RA.

4. Plus *makes* plura; and sometimes plúria. But vetus *makes only* vétera.

EXAMPLES.

The nominative plural of neuter nouns depends on the ablative singular.

1. If the ablative be only in E, they form their plural in A, as *hoc corpus*, the body, ablative *córpore*, plur. *córpora*, bodies: *caput*, *cápitis*, the head, ablat. *cápite*, plur. *cápita*, heads: *hoc gaúsape*, ablative *gaúsape*, plur. *gaúsapa*, a furred coat, an hair mantle.

2. But if the ablative be in I only, or even in E and I, the nominative plural is always in IA: *mare*, the sea, *mari*, plur. *maria*, the seas: *dulcis, et hoc dulce*, sweet, abl. *dulci*, plur. *dulces, & hæc dulcia*. *Animal*, an animal, ablative *animáli*, plur. *animália*: *felix*, happy, ablative *felice et felici*, plur. *felices & felicia*: *amans*, loving, ablat. *amánte & amánti*, plur. *amántes & amántia*, &c.

3. The comparatives form the ablative in E or in I, because they are adjectives. *Púlchrior, & hoc púlchrius*, more handsome, ablat. *pulchrióre, & pulchrióri*; but by reason their ablative in E is the most usual, they form the neuter plural in A only; *pulchrióres, & pulchrióra*, and not *pulchriória*: *sánctius*, more holy, *sanctióra*: *fórtius*, stronger, *fortióra*.

4. *Plus*, more, makes *plure & pluri*; hence in the plural it has *plura*, and sometimes *plúria*. *Vetus*, old, makes, *véteri*; but in the plural it has only *vétera*.

ANNOTATION.

Aplustre, an ornament put on the masts of ships, a flag, or streamer, has a double nominative plural according to Priscian, whom Despauter has followed, giving it *aplustra* and *aplustria*. But the former may be said to come from *aplustrum*, of the second declension, according to Lucretius, when he says,

Navigia aplustris fractis obnititer undis.

And thus that *aplustre* simply follows the rule, making *aplustria*, because it forms the ablative in *i*. We find *aplustria* in *bus*, and not *aplustra*.

Plus

Plus makes *plura* and *pluria*, from whence comes *complura* and *compluria*, as is fully shewn in Gellius, book 5. c. 21, *Pluria mista*, Lucr. *Nova compluria*, Ter. which Voſſius has ventured to imitate in different parts of his works; but theſe nouns are comparatives, let Gellius ſay what he will in the place abovementioned. For which reaſon Chariſius, after Pliny and I. Modeſtus, excepts them from the rule of the reſt merely by cuſtom, which is the miſtreſs of languages; *conſuetudo tamen & hos plures dicit, & hæc pluria*, Chariſ. lib. 1. And yet the plural in *a* is the moſt uſual according to Priſc. *Plura dicam*, Ter. *Plura venena*, Juv. And indeed this noun is not one of thoſe whoſe ablative is only in I, as Alvarez fancied. It has alſo E; *plure tanto altero*, Plaut. *Plure venit*, Cic. as may be ſeen in Chariſius, book 1. and 2.

Hereto others refer alſo *bicorpor, tricorpor*, and the like compounds of *corpus*; but ſince Lucretius has ſaid in the feminine *tricorpora vis Geryonaï*, we may ſay likewiſe that the plur. *tricorpora* comes from *tricorporus, a, um*: or at leaſt that being part of the nouns compounded of *corpus*, they follow their ſimple, as we ſhall obſerve hereafter.

Rule XLVI.

General rule for the genitive plural.

1. *The ablative ſingular in E makes the genitive plural in* UM:
2. *But if the ablative ſingular be in* I, *the genitive plural is in* ïUM.
3. Plus *alſo makes* plurium.

Examples.

1. The genitive is formed of the ablative ſingular, ſo that if the ablative be in E, this genitive is in UM. *Hic pater*, the father, abl. *patre*, gen. *patrum: hæc áctio*, an action; *actióne, actiónum: hoc ænigma*, a riddle, *ænigmatum: hæc virtus*, virtue, *virtútum*.

2. But if the ablative ſingular be in I, whether I only, or E and I, the genitive plural is in ïUM, as *hoc láquear*, a ceiling, abl. *laqueári*, gen. *laqueárium: amans, amántium*, loving: *hic amnis, ámnium*, a river: *hæc avis, ávium*, a bird: *dulcis & dulce*, ſweet, *dúlcium: hic imber*, a ſhower, abl. *imbre*, or *imbri*, gen. plur. *imbrium*.

3. *Plus* alſo, though a comparative, makes *plúrium*, becauſe it has *plure* and *pluri*, in the ablative ſingular.

OF DECLENSIONS.

EXCEPTIONS TO THE RULE OF THE Genitive.

Rule XLVII.

Exception 1. Of comparatives and others which make UM.

1. *But all other comparatives,*
2. *As likewise* primor *have the genitive in* UM;
3. *Add to these,* vetus, supplex, *and* memor, *though their ablative is in* I.
4. *Add also,* pupil, dégener, celer, compos; impos, pubes, uber, dives, confors, inops.
5. *With the compounds of* pes;
6. *The derivatives of* facio *ending in* fex;
7. *And the derivatives of* capio *ending in* ceps.

Examples.

1. As the comparatives form the nominative plural in A, so they have the genitive in UM, and not in IUM. *Major et hoc majus,* greater; plur. *majóra, majórum: fórtior & fórtius,* stronger, *fortióra, fortiórum.*

2. *Primor, óris,* the first, the foremost, plur. *primóres, primórum.*

3. The following make also the genitive in UM, though they have the ablative in I: *vetus,* old, gen. *véterum: supplex, súpplicum,* suppliant: *memor, mémorum,* mindful; in like manner *immemor, immémorum,* unmindful.

4. *Pugil, púgilum,* a champion: *dégener, degénerum,* degenerate; in like manner, *cóngener,* one of the same kind or race: *celer, célerum,* swift, light; *compos, cómpotum,* one that hath obtained his desire or purpose: *impos, ímpotum,* unable, without power: *puber,* or rather *pubes, púberis,* plur. *púberum,* of ripe age: *uber, úberum,* fertile: *dives, divitum,* rich: *confors, consórtum,* a companion, or that partakes of a thing: *inops, ínopum,* poor.

5. The compounds of *pes, pedis,* as *álipes, alípedis,* abl. *alípede, i,* plur. *alípedes, alípedum,* swift of foot: *quádrupes, edis,* plur. *quádrupes, um,* four footed.

6. The

6. The derivatives of *facio*, ending in *fex*, have also UM; as *ártifex, ícis*, plur. *artíficum*, an artist: *ópifex, opíficum*, one that worketh, the maker or framer of: *cárnifex, ícum*, an executioner, a villain.

7. The derivatives of *cápio*, ending in CEPS, as *múneceps, ípis*, plur. *municípum*, one of a town whose inhabitants were free of the city of Rome, a burgher: *princeps, príncipum*, the foremost, the prince.

ANNOTATION.

The reason why the comparatives form the genitive in UM, is because their ablative in E is most usual. Hence it is that they have the nominative likewise in A and not in IA. And this reason may hold for most of the nouns of this rule, which have more frequently E than I in the ablative. This is so far true that Charis. pretends they never say *vétrri, majóri, melióri*, though he is in the wrong to exclude them absolutely.

Primor, though it has in the ablative *primore* or *primori*, makes also *primórum*, either because it partakes of the nature of comparatives, *primor, quasi primior*; or because it is oftener in the nature of a substantive in the plural, *primores*, the nobles, or the chief men of a place.

To these we may add also the derivatives of *corpus*, which beyond all doubt are terminated in *or*, since *tricorpor* is from Accius in Prisc. and an ancient poet makes use of *tricorporem* in Cic. Tusc. 2. and we meet with *tricorporis* in Virg. Æn. 6. And then we may take for a rule that they follow the analogy and the declension of the simple, forming in the ablative, *córpore*, in the plur. *córpora, corporum*, though, as we have above observed p. 106. they followed also another declension.

To these Despauter, and after him Verepeus, join also *vigil*. And it is true we find

—— *Vigilum excubiis obsidere portas*, Æn. 9.

but there it is taken substantively, and then it would make *vigile* in the ablative: whereas when we find Juvenal using adjectively *vigili cum febre*, and Statius *vigili aure*, one would think that we should likewise say in the plural *vigilium aurium*. This is at least the opinion of Vossius. And yet Horace has it otherwise where he says ———— *Et vigilum canam tristes excubiæ*, lib. 3. od. 16. But this may be a syncope, since in the civil law where it is taken substantively, we read *præfecti vigilium*. The reason hereof is that *vigil* is only a syncopated word for *vigilis, hujus vigilis*, which would make *ium* in the plural by the following rule. Be that as it may, it is always better in prose to say *vigilum*, when it is a substantive, and *vigilium* when it is an adjective, which coincides intirely with the general rules.

But it is not the same in regard to the compounds of *facio* and *capio*; for though as adjectives they have the ablative in E

or

or in I like the rest, yet they constantly form the genitive plural in UM and not in ïuM. Hence though Statius has *artifici pollice*, yet we must not say *artificium pollicum*, but *artificum*, and the rest in the same manner. The reason of this has been to distinguish these genitives from the substantives in ïuM, which resemble them: as *hoc artificium, principium*, &c. We meet even with *carnificium* in Plautus, and in like manner the others.

This reason must be extended also to *consors*, which makes *consortum*, to distinguish it from *consortium* the substantive: to *supplex*, to distinguish it from *supplicium*, punishment, in Cic. or a prayer or supplication in Sallust, and to some others.

Rule XLVIII.

Exception 2. Of nouns of more than one syllable in AS, ES, IS, and NS, which have ïuM in the genitive.

1. *Nouns in* ES *and* IS *that do not increase in the plural.*
2. (*Except* júvenis, vates, canis, strígilis, vólucris, panis.)
3. *Also nouns in* AS.
4. *With those in* NS, *all these make the genitive plural in* ïuM.

Examples.

1. Nouns in ES and in IS, that have no more syllables in the plural than in the singular, form the genitive plural in ïuM, though their ablative singular is in E, as *hic enfis*, a sword, plur. *enfes, énfium: hæc clades*, a defeat; *clades, cládium: hic vermis*, a worm; *vermes, vérmium: hic collis*, a hill; *colles, cóllium*.

2. These are excepted, and form their genitive in UM: *júvenis*, a young man, plur. *júvenes, júvenum: vates, vatum*, a prophet, a poet: *canis*, a dog or bitch, *canes, canum: hic strígilis, strígilum*, a curry-comb: *vólucris, vólucrum*, a bird, any winged creature: *hic panis, panum*, bread.

3. To these may be joined those in AS, which also make ïuM: as the names of countries, *Arpínas, átis, Arpinátium*, one that is of *Arpínum: nostras, átis, nostrátium*, one of our country: *vestras, vestrátium*, one that is of your country.

And sometimes even the other nouns in AS, as *utílitas,*

litas, átis, utilitátium, Liv. utility : *cívitas, civitátium*, a city, a state, a corporation. Though in these the genitive in *um* is the most usual, *civitátum, utilitátum*, &c.

4. Those in NS form their genitive in the same manner, as *infans, infántis*, plur. *infántium*, an infant : *adoléscens, adolescéntium*, a young man or a young woman : *rudens, rudéntium*, a cable rope : *torrens, torréntium*, a torrent of water. Though they oftentimes admit of a syncope of the I, *paréntum, prudéntum*, &c. as we shall observe hereafter.

ANNOTATION.

Volucris heretofore made *volucrium*, as we find in Varro. And Charis. quotes it also from Quintilian, and even from Cicero, 2. de fin. as Gruterus likewise reads it. *Videmus in quodam* VOLU-CRIUM *genere nonnulla indicia pietatis*. Nevertheless the custom of saying always *volucrum* had obtained even so early as the time of Pliny, as may be seen in Charis. lib. 1. And thus it has been used not only by Pliny but by Virgil and Martial. Which must be always followed when this noun is a substantive. But when it is taken for an adjective, as we have mentioned above, p. 103. that then it made *volucri* in the ablative, so it must have *volucrium* in the genitive plural.

Concerning *panis* there have been disputes among the ancients. Cæsar would fain have *panium* ; on the contrary Verrius, preceptor to Augustus's nephews, was of opinion that we ought to say *panum*. Which Priscian indeed afterwards followed, so that it hath been almost universally received.

To these Despauter also joins *proles, soboles, indoles* ; but we shall plainly shew at the end of the heteroclites, that these nouns have no plural.

Apes or *apis*, a bee, makes *apium* by this rule, and *apum* by syncope. The former occurs frequently in Varro and in Columella, and we find it also in Juvenal. The latter we often meet with in Pliny and in Columella.

Of the nouns in AS and in NS.

The reason why the nouns in AS and in NS form also ĭUM, is because they formerly terminated in ES or in IS. For they said *Arpinatis* and *nostratis*, from whence have been formed *Arpinas* and *nostras*, and so on. Hence *Arpinatium* is in Cic. ad Att. *Fidenatium* and *Capenatium* in Livy. *Optimatium* is also in Cic. and by syncope *optimatum* in Corn. Nepos.

Ætatium is in Velleius, lib. 2. *Affinitatium* and *calamitatium* in Justin. *Civitatium* occurs frequently in Livy, Cato, Justin, Censorinus, and others, and generally appears on ancient inscriptions. Thus Varro, lib. 7. de L. L. mentions that they said indiscriminate-

ly

ly and both equally good, *civitatum* and *civitatium*; the same as *parentum* and *parentium*, though the syncope is now more usual.

We meet also with *facultatium*, *hæreditatium* in Justin, *utilitatium* in Livy, and such like.

With regard to the nouns in NS, we have already shewn that they are derived from those in ES and in IS, so that they had no increase in the genitive; and hence it is that they have frequently the plural in ïum, even when taken substantively.

Rule XLIX.

Exception 3. Of monosyllables that make ïum.

1. *The following monosyllables have* ïum *in the genitive, viz. those ending in* AS,
2. *And those in* IS;
3. *Those also which end in two consonants:*
4. (*Except* gryps, linx, sphinx,)
5. *To which add* mus, sal, cor, cos, *and* dos,
6. *Also* par, lar, faux, nix, nox, *and* os.

Examples.

There are a great many monsyllables that make ïum in the genitive plur.

1. Those in AS, as *hic as, assis*, a pound weight, also a Roman coin worth about three farthings of our money, gen. plur. *assium: hic mas, maris*, the male in all kinds of creatures, *márium: hic vas, vadis*, a surety or bail, *vádium*.

2. Those in IS, as *dis, ditis*, rich, *ditium: hæc lis, litis*, a dispute, a law suit, a quarrel, *litium*, Cic. Hor. *hæc vis*, force, plur. *vires, virium: hic glis, gliris*, a dormouse, *glirium*, Plautus.

3. Those ending in two consonants, as *hæc ars, artis*, an art, a trade, plur. *ártium: hæc gens, gentis*, a nation, *géntium: hic dens, dentis*, a tooth, *déntium: hic aut hæc stirps, stirpis*, the root or stock of a tree or plant, *stirpium: hic fons, fontis*, a fountain, *fontium: hic mons, montis*, a mountain, *móntium: hæc urbs, urbis*, a city, *úrbium: hæc merx, mercis*, merchandise, plur. *merces, mércium*.

4. Of these we must except *gryps, gryphis*, a griffon, plur. *gryphes, gryphum*; but they say likewise
gryphus,

gryphus, a griffon: *lynx, lyncis*, a spotted beast of the nature of a wolf, an ounce, *lyncum: sphinx, sphingis, sphingum*, a fabulous monster. In like manner all nouns latinised from the Greek, as we shall shew hereafter.

5. There are moreover divers monosyllables that make ĭUM, and are mentioned in the rule; namely, *hic mus, muris*, a mouse, *múrium: hoc cor, cordis*, the heart, *córdium: hæc cos, cotis*, a whetstone, *cótium: hæc dos, dotis*, a portion or dowry, a property, an advantage, *dótium* frequently in the civil law.

6. *Par*, not only the adjective which signifieth *equal*, but moreover the substantive signifying *a pair*, makes *párium*, though it has then only *pare* in the ablative: *hic lar, laris*, a houshold god, the chimney or fireside, *lárium*, Cic. *hæc faux, faucis*, the throat, *faúcium*, Plin. *hæc nix, nivis*, snow, *nívium: hæc nox, noctis*, the night, *nóctium: hoc os, ossis*, a bone, *óssium*, Plin. *hoc os, oris*, the mouth, the countenance, *órium*. Idem apud Verep.

ANNOTATION.

What we have here seen concerning the monosyllables in AS, confirms the analogy of this very termination, which I have already taken notice of, for nouns of more syllables than one.

Even those in IS make ĭUM for no other reason, but because they had heretofore an equal number of syllables in the nominative and the genitive. For they said *viris, hujus viris*, force; *litis, hujus litis*, &c. They said also *hic paris, hujus paris*, instead of *par*, from whence comes *párium*.

Greek monosyllables. LINX.

But there has been always so great an uncertainty in regard to this genitive in monosyllables, that Charisius mentions even from the authority of Pliny, that the ancients could lay down no certain rule concerning them. However, it may be said that those which have been latinised from the Greek, frequently changed the termination ὧν into *um*, and thus that *Phryx* will make *Phryges, Phrygum*; *Thrax, Thraces, Thracum*, because the Greeks say τῶν Φρυγῶν, τῶν Θραχῶν, and the rest in the same manner.

For this reason Vossius censures those who will have it that *lynx* makes *lyncium*, because it is contrary to this analogy.

The lynx is a kind of spotted deer, which some take to be the ounce; it is a very quick-sighted animal, whence it is commonly said to see through mountains and walls. Perot mentions it, and Pierius in his hieroglyphics quotes it out of Pliny, book 8. c. 38.

though

though Pliny says no such thing. However, from its piercing sight comes Λυσχικὸς ϐλέπειν in Hom. and the like, to denote quickness of sight.

Of Lar, mus, crux, *and some others.*

In regard to the other monosyllables, the following are such remarks as can be most depended upon.

Lar makes *larium* in Cicero and in Pliny. And yet in Varro, 8. de L. L. we meet with *maniam matrem larum.*

Mus makes *murium. Murium fetus,* Pliny and others. Nevertheless *murum* is in Cic. as quoted even by Charisius. *Nec homines murum aut formicarum causâ frumentum condunt,* 2. de Nat. Though Charisius owns that Pliny did not approve of this passage of Cicero, because he says the genitive in UM was particularly for the nouns in R, as *fur, furum.* Hence he likewise condemned Trogus for having said *parium numerorum & imparium.* It is true the genitive *murum* is no where else to be found. But Pliny's reason of the nouns in R is groundless, because from *calcar* we make *calcarium,* and a great many more; so that he had no sort of reason to find fault with Trogus for saying *parium et imparium.*

Crux makes *crucum* according to Charisius. And thus it is in Tertullian's apology, according to Rigaut's edition. Pamelius reads *crucium,* and yet he confesses that all the MSS. have *crucum.* This was not sufficiently observed by Vossius, when he sets Tertullian against Charisius.

Of those monosyllables that make UM.

The other monosyllables not included in the particular rules, more frequently make UM according to the general rule, as *ren,* plur. *renes, renum,* Plin. *fur, furum,* Hor. Catull. *pes, pedum,* Cic. in like manner its compounds, *bipes, bipedum,* Cic. *mos, morum; flos, florum; crus, crurum,* Virg. *grus, gruum; sus, suum; thus, thurum,* Charis. *fraus, fraudum;* though Apuleius has *fraudium; laus, laudum,* though in Sidonius we find *laudium; prex,* unusual, plur. *preces, precum; frux,* unusual, plur. *fruges, frugum; nux, nucum,* Plin.

Monosyllables unusual in the genitive plural.

But many of these nouns are very little or not at all used in the genitive plural. Hence we should be very cautious how we use in this case the following words, viz. *pax, fax, fæx, nex, pix, lux, mel, fel, sol.* To these we must join *plebs,* though Prudentius has *coronam plebium.* We may add *glos, pus,* and *ros,* though the grammarians insist upon their having a genitive in ïUM, according to Scioppius, but without authority.

Jus makes *jurium* in Plautus; *legum atque jurium fictor,* in Epidic. But Charisius quotes from Cato, *jurum legúmque,* though neither of them are much used. The same Charisius acknowledges that *maria, rura, æra, jura,* are not to be found but in the nominative, accus. and vocat. However, if we were obliged to make use of them

them, it would be better to say *jurum* than *jurium*, *rurum* than *rurium*, *ærum* than *ærium*, because, says Vossius, they have their nominative in A and not in īa.

With regard to *mare* it is a different thing; for as it has the ablative in I, it has also the plur. in īa, *maria*; though its genitive be unusual according to Charisius. But its ablative plural, which this author fancied was no where to be found, is in Cæsar. *In reliquis maribus*, 5. bel. Gal. which Priscian also quotes. And in Quintus Curtius, l. 6. it is plainly implied, where he says, *Mare Caspium, dulcius præ cæteris*, sup. *maribus*.

Mas, maris, the male in all kinds of creatures, makes also *marium, maribus*; and is very common, according to the rule of monosyllables in AS.

Rule L.
Exception 4. Of some other nouns that make īum.

1. *The following nouns have likewise the genitive in* īum, *namely the derivatives and compounds of* AS:
2. *Also* linter, caro, cohors, uter, venter, palus, fornax, Quiris, Samnis;
3. *Unless they are used with a syncope.*

Examples.

All these nouns have likewise īum in the genitive; though they form the ablative in E.

1. The derivatives and compounds of *As* (which has been already included in the rule of the monosyllables in AS) *hic quincunx, úncis*, five ounces, *quincúncium: hic sextans, sextántis*, two ounces, *sextántium: hic bes*, or *bessis, hujus bessis*, the weight of eight ounces, *béssium*, &c.

2. These nouns in particular; *hæc linter, líntris*, a cock-boat, a sculler, *líntrium: hæc caro, carnis*, flesh, *cárnium: hæc cohors, órtis*, a barton or coop, a pen for sheep, a band of men or soldiers, an assembly or company, *cohórtium*, Cæs. *hic uter, utris*, a bottle, a bag of leather made like a bottle, *útrium: hic venter, tris*, the belly, *véntrium: hæc palus, údis*, a morass, *palúdium*, Colum. *hæc fornax, ácis*, a furnace, *fornácium*. Plin.

Thus *Quiris, Quirítis*, a Roman, *Quirítium: Samnis, ítis*, a Samnite, *Samnítium*.

OF DECLENSIONS.

ANNOTATION.

Moſt of theſe nouns follow likewiſe the analogy above mentioned. For as it was cuſtomary to ſay *Samnitis* in the nominative, alſo *Quiritis, cohortis, carnis, beſſis*; they ranked among thoſe which had no increaſe in the genitive, and therefore made ĭUM. And very likely *linter, fornax,* and the others here mentioned, followed the ſame analogy.

A great many more nouns heretofore made ĭUM.

There were a great many more nouns which had ſometimes the genitive in ĭUM, though they are not to be followed, as *radicium*, which we find in Varro, though Colum. ſays *radicum,*; and Chariſius is more for the latter, while Pliny pretends we ought to ſay *radicium* and *cervicium*.

As alſo *hominium* for *hominum*, which is found in Salluſt, *in Jugurth.* according to Joſeph Scaliger. *Meretricium* in Plautus's *Bacch.* according to Duza, and in his *Caſſina* according to Lipſius. *Servitutium & compedium,* in the ſame poet's *Perſa,* Act. 3. ſc. *Curate iſtuc intus,* according to Scaliger and Colerus, though a corrupt word *ſervitricium* is generally read in the ſtead. *Judicium* for *judicum* in the civil law; *virtutium* for *virtutum* in S. Paulinus epiſt. ad Auſon.

And ſome others, which we may learn perhaps by obſervation. This may be owing, as we have already taken notice, to all the ablatives having been heretofore in E and in I in this declenſion, whence-ſo many genitives in ĭUM have remained.

3. But there is ſometimes a ſyncope of the I in this genitive in ĭUM, not only in the nouns of this rule, but in all the reſt. Thus they ſay *apum*, Plin. for *ápium*, bees: *Quirĭtum* for *Quirĭtium*, Romans: *loquéntum* for *loquéntium*, of thoſe who ſpeak, &c.

ANNOTATION.

We find *paludum* in Mela, inſtead of *paludium*, which is in Colum. *fornacum* and *fornacium* are both in Pliny.

Parentum and *parentium* are both good Latin according to Varro, 7. L. L. The latter is alſo in Horace. Chariſius and Priſcian quote it even out of Cic. Nevertheleſs *parentum* at preſent is more uſual in proſe.

What nouns moſt frequently admit of this ſyncope.

This ſyncope is particularly to be obſerved in nouns ending in NS; as *adoleſcentum* for *adoleſcentium*; *infantum*, *rudentum*, &c. And eſpecially in participles, which we find as often in UM as in ĭUM; *cadentum* for *cadentium*, likewiſe *faventum, furentum, loquentum, monentum, natantum, precantum, recuſantum, ſequentum, ſilentum, venientum,* and the like, in Virgil and others.

It is also very usual in nouns in ES and IS ; *cædûm* for *cædium*, Silius : *cladûm* for *cladium*, Id. *Veronensûm* for *Veronensium*, Catul. *mensûm* for *mensium*, Seneca, Ovid, Fortunatus, and other later poets. It is also frequently to be seen in the writings of civilians, as in Paulus the civilian, in the Theodocian code, and elsewhere.

What nouns seldom admit of this syncope.

On the contrary this syncope very rarely occurs in neuters that have the ablative in I. For we do not say *cubilum* instead of *cubilium*; *animalum* instead of *animalium*, &c. And if Nævius calls Neptune *regnatorem marum*, this was never followed, and doubtless he did it to distinguish it from *marium*, coming from *mas*. But this genitive of *mare*, as we have already mentioned, is unusual.

It occurs also very rarely in adjectives of one termination ; for of *atrox* we do not say *atrocum* ; nor of *felix*, *felicum*. However *locupletum* is said for *locupletium*, and we read it even in Cicero.

Of the epenthesis.

But it is observable, that as these genitives sometimes admit of a syncope or diminution of a letter, on the contrary they sometimes also admit of an epenthesis or a letter added. Thus we find *alituum* in Virgil for *alitum* : *cælituum* for *cælitum*, and such like, which are owing perhaps to some ablatives in U, as we still say *noctu* and *diu* for *nocte* and *die*. Or else it must have been a change of I into U, for *alitium*, *cælitium*, which were used as well as *hominium*, whereof mention has been made above.

OF THE ACCUSATIVE PLURAL.

The accusative plural (excepting neuters which have it in *a* or in *ia*, like their nominative) generally ends in *es*, *Pater*, *patres*. But antiently it oftentimes ended in *eis* or in *is* long, which were almost the same thing.

And this termination was particularly received in nouns that had ïuм in the genitive, as *montium*, *monteis* ; *omnium*, *omneis* or *omnis*, though grammarians could never give us any fixed rule concerning this matter. For as from *mercium* they said *merces* ; from *axium*, *axes* ; so from *fortiorum* they said *fortioreis* ; from *sanctiorum*, *sanctioreis*, and the like.

In what manner the antients judged of their language.

This shews that these variations were intirely owing to the delicacy of the language. Hence we learn of Gellius, lib. 13. c. 19. that Probus, upon being asked whether it was proper to say *urbis* or *urbeis*, made no other answer, but that the ear should be consulted, without giving one's self any further trouble about all those musty rules of grammarians ; affirming that he had seen a copy of the Georgics, with corrections in Virgil's own hand writing, in the first book of which there was *urbis*, with an I.

—— *urbisne invisere, Cæsar.*

because the verse would not have run so smooth with *urbes*. And
on

OF DECLENSIONS.

on the contrary that in the 3. book of the Æneid, he had put *urbes* with an E,

—— *Gentum urbes habitant magnas*;

to render it more swelling. And this author recommended the same rule for the accusatives in EM or in IM. But as we have not at present so nice an ear as to be able to judge exactly of this cadence, it is more incumbent upon us to abide by what the antients have advanced concerning this point, and to insert nothing without authority.

Rule LI.

Of nouns that have no singular, and of the names of festivals in ïA.

1. *Plural nouns are to be regulated by supposing their singular, as* manes, mánium,
2. Tres, trium.
3. *But we say* opum, cœ'litum.
4. *The names of festivals in* ïA *follow the second and third declension.*

Examples.

1. The genitive of plural nouns ought to be regulated, by supposing their singular. Thus *manes*, a spirit or ghost, the place of the dead, dead bodies, makes *mánium*, because heretofore *manis* was used in the singular, whence we have *immánis*, cruel.

2. Thus *tres*, three, makes *trium*, by reason that though it cannot have a singular, yet it follows the analogy of the other adjectives, and therefore makes the neuter in ïA, *tria*, and the rest in like manner.

3. We must except *opes*, riches, which coming from *ops, opis*, makes *opum*, and not *opium*, as it should naturally by the rule of monosyllables: and *cœ'lites*, the gods or saints above, which has *cœ'litum*, though it seems to be an adjective, or at least that it ought to come from *cœlis, cœ'litis*, and therefore should follow the analogy of *dis, lis, Quiris, Samnis*, &c. which make ïUM.

The neuter nouns follow this same rule: for we say *mœ'nia, mœ'nium*, the walls or ramparts: *ilia, ilium*, the flank, the small guts; because were they to have a singular, their ablative would be in I, as their nominative plural is in ïA.

I 3   4. The

4. The names of festivals in ÏA follow the second and third declension, *Saturnália*, a festival in honour of Saturn, genit. *Saturnálium* and *Saturnaliórum*. In like manner *Bacchanália*, *Compitália*, *Florália*, and others, though in the dative and ablative they are only of the third, *Saturnálibus*, *Terminálibus*, &c.

ANNOTATION.

From this rule we must not except *proceres*, *procerum*, nobles or peers: *lemures*, *lemurum*, hobgoblins: *luceres*, *lucerum*, one of the three centuries, into which Romulus divided the people: *celeres*, *celerum*, the light horse, 300 in number, chosen out of the rest of the cavalry by Romulus for his body guard: because their antient nominative was *porcer*, *lemur*, *lucer*, *celer*, which made UM, the same as *furfur*, *furfurum*; *carcer*, *carcerum*, &c.

Nor must we except *fores*; for *forum* in Plautus is a syncope, instead of which we meet with *forium*, as coming from *hæc foris*. It is also by syncope that the same author said *summatum* in Pseud. as Cornelius Nepos said *optimatum* for *optimatium*, which we read in Cicero, by the 48th rule of the nouns in AS.

Of the names of festivals in ÏA.

In regard to the names of festivals, the true reason of their having a double genitive, is because heretofore they had two nominatives singular, so that they said *hoc agonale*, and *hoc agonalium*; *hoc Saturnale*, and *hoc Saturnalium*, &c. as we still meet with *exemplare* and *exemplarium* among the Civilians; with *milliare* and *milliarium* in Cicero, and the like. Wherefore this ought to serve as a rule for a great many other nouns, which have two genitives, as *vectigaliorum* in Macrobius for *vectigalium*; *anciliorum*, in Hor. for *ancilium*; *sponsaliorum* in Suet. for *sponsalium*, and the like. In the same manner those in MA, *diadematorum*, for *diadematum*, of which we shall take notice in the following rule.

RULE LII.

Of the dative plural; and of some particular cases borrowed from the Greeks.

1. *The dative plural is in* IBUS.
2. *But those in* MA *make also* TIS.
3. *Of the Greeks three cases are borrowed in this declension; the genitive singular in* OS.
4. *The accusative singular in* A.
5. *And the accusative plural in* AS.

EXAMPLES.

1. The dative plural of the third declension is in IBUS, as *pater*, *pátribus*, to the fathers.

2. But

2. But nouns in MA like to form this case in IS rather than in IBUS. *Hoc thema,* a theme or subject of discourse; dative and ablative *thématis* rather than *themátibus: hoc poêma,* a poem; dative and ablative *poëmatis* or *poëmátibus.*

ANNOTATION.

Priscian takes notice that these neuter nouns in *ma,* were formerly feminines of the first declension, hence we read in Plautus, *cum servili schemâ* in the ablative, for *schemate,* and Pomp. *diademam dedit.* Celsus also observes that they formerly ended in *tum, thematum, diadematum, dogmatum,* being declined by the second, *diadematorum,* &c.; so that it is no wonder they have still retained their dative and ablative plural in IS.

The Greeks moreover give us three cases in this declension, which are very usual among poets, namely the genitive singular in OS, the accusative singular in A, and the accusative plural in AS.

3. The genitive, as *Pallas, Pálladis* or *Pállados,* the goddess Pallas: *génesis, génesis* or *genéseos* and *genésios,* genesis, generation: *pyxis, py'xidis* or *py'xidos,* a box: *Æneis, Ænéidis* or *idos,* the Æneid.

4. The accusative, as *Hector, Héctorem* and *Héctora,* a proper name: *Laïs, Lâidem* and *Lâida,* a famous courtezan: *hic aër, aërem* and *aëra,* the air. Some have even three, as *Mæótis,* gen. *Mæótidis* or *Mæótidos,* accus. *Mæótidem* or *Mæótida,* and also *Mæótin.* See the following remarks.

5. The accusative plural; as *Tros, Troïs,* a Trojan; plur. *hos Troës* or *Troas: crater,* a great cup or bowl, plur. *hos cratéras; rhetor,* a rhetorician, *hos rhétoras,* and so on.

CONSIDERABLE OBSERVATIONS ON the Greek nouns of this declension.

Of the genitive in OS.

The genitive in OS may be used without any scruple in Latin, especially in verse. But it must be observed that these nouns being in Greek of the fifth declension, which increases in the genitive, they are generally adopted by the Latins together with their augment, *Pallas, Palladis* or *Pallados; Bryaxis, Bryaxidis,* as we read in Pliny, and not *Bryax, Bryaxis,* as Despauter gives it us, without authority.

And yet these nouns are sometimes declined without increase, as Charisius observes that Varro, Cicero, and Cincius had wrote *hujus Serapis, hujus Isis:* which shews that it is not so gross an error in that great Italian poet, to say *Ianthis* for *Ianthidis* or *Ianthidos*, and *Adoni* for *Adonidi*, though he is censured for it by Vossius; since we read in Plautus

——— *tum ille prognatus Theti*
Sine perdat, &c. Epidic. Act. 1. sc. 1.

whereby Priscian shews that *Thetis* heretofore made *hujus Thetis* in the genitive, instead of *Thetidis* or *Thetidos*, both of which are in Horace.

Therefore it is always the safest way to take these nouns with their augment, if they be not declined in OS pure in Greek.

But if they are declined in OS pure, that is with a vowel before OS, then the Latin genitive in IS is without any increase, as *poësis, hujus poësis:* whereas the genitive in OS is always with an increase as in the Greek itself. Therefore these nouns have a double genitive in OS; for as the Greeks say τῆς ποιήσιος or ποιήσεως, so the Latins say *hujus poësios* or *poësios*, and in like manner the rest.

The genitive of proper names in ES.

It is also to be observed that the genitive of names in ES is oftentimes in I, as well as in IS, as in Cic. *Verri,* for *Verris,* and so *Ariobarzáni, Aristóteli, Theóphani,* and in Virgil.——*Pellacis Ulyssi.* ——*Nunc acris Oronti.*——*Atque immitis Achilli.* In Terence, *Puerum ego convéni Chremi,* and the like.

This made Priscian believe, that heretofore they used the dative instead of the genitive. Just as if these changes of cases were not intirely contrary to the analogy of construction, and to the natural idea we ought to have of it. And Quintilian says nothing more about it than this, that these nouns heretofore formed the genitive in I. Charisius is of the same opinion, though Vossius seems to think the contrary.

The true reason ought therefore to be borrowed from the original language, because as the Æolians said Ἀχίλλης for Ἀχιλλεύς, Ὀδύσσης for Ὀδυσσεύς, Ὀρφῆς for Ὀρφεύς, in the same manner one might say, Ἀριστόλης and Ἀριστολεύς, Μωυσῆς and Μωυσεύς, and so on. Thus from the former nominative in ης shall be derived the noun in *es* which forms the genitive in *is*. *Aristoteles, Aristotelis; Moyses, Moysis*. And from the nominative in ευς comes a noun *eus,* which being of the second declension, forms the genitive in I, as *Orpheus, Orphei; Moyseus, Moysei,* and by contraction *Moysei,* then dropping the prepositive vowel, *Moysi;* the I long and the diphthong *ei* being, as we have often observed, generally exchanged for each other in Latin words. Therefore we so frequently meet with *Ulyssei, Periclei, Achillei,* and such like, written with a diphthong.

Hence it is easy to see why Tertullian, and the other fathers, use indiscriminately in the genitive, *Moysis* or *Moysi,* though we meet with *Moysi* also in the dative: and moreover by syncope

Mosis

OF DECLENSIONS.

Mosis and *Mosi*. Just as the Greeks say ὁ Μωσῆς, τῦ Μωσῦ, for Μωυσῆς, Μωυσοῦ, and ὁ Μωσεὺς, τῦ Μωσέος, for Μωυσεὺς, υσέος.

But here we should take notice that as the nouns in ης, according to the observation of Priscian, followed indifferently in Greek either the fifth or the first declension, so in Latin we decline them either by the first or by the third. Thus for instance as they said ὁ Κώμης, Κώμυ, or Κωμηίος: ὁ Ἀριςοφάνης, Ἀριςοφάνα, (whence likewise comes τὸν Ἀριςοφάνην) or Ἀριςοφάνεος, ες: so we may say, *hic Aristophanes, is*, and *hic Aristophanes, æ*, just as Virgil said, *Achates, Achatæ.*
———*Magnîque femur perstrinxit Achatæ.* Æn. 10.

Hence it is that some nouns having retained either entirely or more frequently the analogy of one of these declensions in Greek, are still more generally used in the other in Latin, because it is supposed that heretofore they had both: thus in Greek we say, ὁ Μωσῆς, τῦ Μωσοῦ, and in Latin *hic Moses, hujus Mosis*; and in like manner a great many others.

The accusative in A.

The accusative in A is used only by poets in Latin. Nor do they use it properly except in nouns, whose declension is formed upon the Greek analogy, as *Hectora, Amaryllida, Phyllida,* &c. And therefore it would be an error to say *hunc Ajaca*, because in Latin we say *Ajax, Ajacis*, whence should naturally come *Ajacem*; whereas in Greek they decline it Αἴας, Αἴαντος, which should make Αἴαντα; these two ways of declining being quite different and having no sort of connexion with each other. For which reason, in the rule I did not say merely that they formed it in A, but that they borrowed it of the Greeks, that is, after the manner that it is formed and declined in the Greek language.

Hence this accusative in A is very scarce in the masculines in IS, because in Greek they oftener form it in ιν than in α, Πάριν rather than Πάριδα. Which made H. Stephen believe that *Paridem* is not used in Latin, though we meet with it sometimes, and even in Virgil.
Solus qui Paridem suetus contendere contra.
It is also to be found in Persius, Suetonius, Juvenal, &c.

The accusative of nouns in IS and in YS.

A great many learned men have been mistaken in regard to the nouns in IS and in YS, by not distinguishing sufficiently those which have only A, or IN only, from those which have both terminations. For those which in Greek have the accusative in A, form it simply in A and in EM in Latin; such are those which have the acute on the last syllable; as Λαΐς, ίδος, ίδα, *Laïs, ïdos,* accusative *Laïdem* and *Laïda,* and not *Laïn,* which some writers however have made use of. In like manner *chlamys, ydos, chlamyda* or *chlamydem,* and not *chlamyn.*

But the barytons that are not declined in OS pure, have in Greek the accusative in A and in N, as Μαιῶτις, ιδος, Μαιώτιδα, and Μαιῶτιν.

Μαιώτιν. Hence in Latin we say *Mæotida* and *Mæ tidem*, as also *Mæotin* or *Mæotim*. Thus we find *Serapidem* in Tertullian's apology; *Serapim, Isimque*, in Cic. and *Serapin*, in Martial.

And such as are not declined in OS pure, whether they be acutes or barytons, have only N and not A; and therefore they make only the Latin accusative in IN or in IM, as *genesis, hujus genesis*, or *genesios, hanc genesin*, or *genesim*.

But after all, to know which are better in IM, we must refer to what has been above said concerning the rule of accusatives, p. 91, 92.

The accusative in O *and* UN *or* UM.

There are moreover nouns of the fourth declension of contracts, which form also the accusative O in Latin, according to the Greek contraction, as

——————*Miseramque relinquere Dido*, Ovid.

which comes from Διδόα, Διδώ. Hence the Ionians having said Διδῶν, the Latins have also made it *Didun* or *Didūm*, which does not at all hinder but, according to the Latin analogy, we may say also *Dido, Didouis, Didoni, Didonem, Didone*.

The accusative in YS.

But before we quit the accusative, it is to be observed that there are some in YS, as *has Erinnys*, which comes from the contraction *Erinnyes* or *Erinnyas*, as the Greeks say Ἐριννύας, Ἐριννῦς.

——————στυγερὰς δ' ἐπικίκλητ' Ἐριννῦς.
Odiosas verò invocabat Furias. Iliad. 1.

This appears also in Seneca's Oedipus.

Et mecum Erinnys pronubas thalami trahas.

For not only Farnaby and Vossius read it thus, but there is no possibility of reading it otherwise, since *Erinnes*, as Delrio reads it, is a word that is neither Greek nor Latin; and *Erinnyas*, which would agree with the analogy, is inconsistent with the verse.

Of the vocative.

I have already observed, that the Greeks form it of the nominative, by dropping S. *ô Ænéa, ô Chalcha, ô Pari*, and even *ô Hercule* in Plaut. *ô Socrate* in Cic.

But those in ES sometimes retain the S. in this declension, *ô Socrates, ô Chremes*. See what has been said upon this subject at the entrance of the first declension, p 62. as also the remarks at the beginning of the second declension, p. 65.

Of the genitive plural.

The Greeks, as hath been already mentioned, always form this genitive in ων; a termination which has been often adopted by Latin authors, as *hebdomadôn, epigrammatôn, hæreseôn*, &c. And sometimes they preserve even the Greek ω, *hæreseωn*, &c.

Of the dative plural.

The Latins have also sometimes borrowed the Greek dative in ιν, as in Propertius, *Dryasin* for *Dryadibus*, &c. But this has been
followed

followed by profe writers only, except in nouns that had no Latin declenfion, as when they fay *in ethefin*, and the like.

This much, I think, and what has been abovementioned, may be fufficient to fhew the analogy and ufe of words latinized from the Greek. But if I fhould ever, with the divine affiftance, have time to write more copioufly upon this language, I fhall endeavour to reduce its rule to a new method like the prefent, and perhaps full as eafy, and as ufeful.

THE FOURTH DECLENSION.

THIS declenfion intirely follows the rudiments, except fome nouns that have the dative plural in UBUS, inftead of IBUS, as we fhall prefently fhew.

And yet it is obfervable that heretofore a great many nouns were of the fecond and the fourth declenfion; hence we ftill find the genitives, *fructi, tumulti*, &c.

But in the fourth they formerly faid *fructuïs, exercituïs, anuïs, domuïs*, and the like; whence came the contraction, *us, fructûs*, &c.; as in the dative we fometimes meet with *û* inftead of *uï, metû* for *metuï*. *Parce metû Cytheréa*, Virg. *Victû invigilant*, Virg. Which is very ufual in this poet. And this we fee even in Cic. *quibus fubito impetû, & latrocinio parricidarum refiftat*: being alfo an imitation of the Æolians, as hereafter fhall be fhewn.

This contraction has always continued in the other cafes; fo that it may be faid that this declenfion is only a branch of the third, which bears fome relation to the contracted declenfions of the Greek. And for this reafon it is that the termination *us*, as *fructûs*, is long in the genitive fingular and in the plural cafes, as we fhall further obferve, when we come to treat of quantity, becaufe every contraction makes the fyllable always long.

The genitive plural has fometimes its contraction here alfo, as well as in the three preceding declenfions, though not fo often; as *nurûm* for *nuruum*: *pafiûm* for *paffuum*: *quæ gratia currûm*, Virg. for *curruum*, &c.

Rule LIII.
Of the dative plural in UBUS.

The dative plural is in IBUS. *But* lacus, arcus, fpecus, artus, tribus, portus, veru, partus, *make* UBUS.

Examples.

The dative plural of this declenfion is regularly in IBUS, as *fructus*, fruit, dat. plur. *fructibus*: *manus*, a hand, *manibus*.

Thefe

These here form it in UBUS; *lacus,* a lake, dat. plur. *lácubus: arcus, árcubus,* a bow: *specus, spécubus,* a cavern, a grotto: *artus, ártubus,* a joint, the limbs: *tribus, tríbubus,* a tribe or family: *portus, pórtubus,* or even *ibus,* a port: *hoc veru,* a spit, *vérubus* or. *ibus:* in like manner, *genu,* the knee, *génubus,* or *ibus: partus, pártubus,* the birth or act of bringing forth.

ANNOTATION.

In all these nouns the ablative is in UBUS, like the dative, because these two cases are always alike in the plural.

In this class Despauter ranks *acus,* a needle; *quercus,* an oak tree; and *ficus* a fig or fig tree: but he has no authority for it.

THE FIFTH DECLENSION.

EVERY body may see that this declension is also a branch of the third; hence we find so many nouns which are declined both ways, as *plebes, is,* and *plebes, ei; quies, quietis,* and *quies, quiei; requies, etis,* and *requies, requiei;* &c. and others of which we shall take notice hereafter.

It has only one termination in the nominative, and the rudiments alone may be sufficient for children to learn, and to decline it. But formerly it had four terminations in the genitive, of which we must take particular notice.

The first is *ei,* which at present is the most usual, *diei, rei,* &c.

The second is *ii,* as *pernicii,* or *i* alone, when the termination of the nominative is not pure; as *fides, fidi,* for *fidei; nihil pernicii causa,* Cic. *munera lætitiamque dii,* Virg. for *perniciei,* and *diei,* according to Gellius.

The third is ES. *Equites daturos illius dies, pœnas,* Cic. pro *Sextio,* according to Gellius, who may be consulted at full upon this subject, lib. 9. c. 14.

The fourth is E. *Hujus die, hujus specie,* as marked by Cæsar, 2. *de Analog.*

Libra die somnique pares ubi fecerit horas, Virg. as Servius, Priscian, and others read it.

The dative of this declension was also formed heretofore in E as well as the ablative.

Prodiderit commissa fide, *sponsumve negarit,* Hor. lib. 1. sat. 3.

Fide *censebam maximam multo fidem,* Plaut. for *fidei,* says Charis.

And Priscian does not at all doubt of it. *Veteres* (says he, in his 8th book) *frequentissimè inveniuntur similem ablativo protulisse in hac declinatione, tam genitivum quàm dativum.* But as some gentlemen eminent for their taste in polite literature, have started objections against me upon this very head; I shall therefore add here

the

the authority of Gellius, lib. 9. c. 14. *In casu autem dandi*, says he, *qui purissimè locuti sunt, non* faciei, *uti nunc dicimus, sed* facie *dixerunt*. Whereby it appears that this termination of the dative was not only received; but what is more remarkable, that it was more usual than that in *ei*, which obtains at present.

That the Æolians dropped the I *subscribed in all the datives, and that in this they were followed by the Latins.*

But the latter termination in E, which was for the genitive and the dative, is plainly owing to the Æolians, who, as hath been observed already, dropped the ι subscribed in all the datives, saying, Αἰτία, μούση, λόγω; for Αἰτίᾳ, μούσῃ, λόγῳ: whence the Latins have taken not only *agro* for *agroi*, *metu* for *metui*, and in the same manner *die* for *diei*; but what is more remarkable, they have said also *musa* in the dative, for *musai* or *musæ*, as we shall prove in the remarks after the syntax.

Some cases unusual in this declension.

The genitive, dative, and ablative plural of this declension, are seldom used except in *dies*, and in *res*; most of the other nouns are without them. Aldus nevertheless attempted to comprize in the following verse such as happen to have these cases in the writings of the antients.

Res, speciésque, dies, facies, spes, progeniésque.

And it is true, for instance, that we meet with *facierum* in Cato, and with *specierum* in Celius Aurel. Which Joseph Scaliger made no difficulty to follow, though Cicero in his topics seems more scrupulous about this word, as well as about that of *speciebus*.

BOOK

BOOK III.

THE HETEROCLITES,

OR

IRREGULAR NOUNS.

WE call heteroclite or irregular nouns, such as are declined differently from the rest, of which there are two sorts.

The first are variant in their gender, not retaining the same in the singular as in the plural; and the second are variant in their declension. Thus, for instance, we say *locus* masculine in the singular, and *loca* neuter in the plural. We say *vas*, *vasis*, of the third declension in the singular, and *vasa*, *vasorum* of the second in the plural.

But take notice that this irregularity was gradually introduced by custom, whereas, these nouns in the beginning were as regular as the rest; because they said not only *hic locus*, from whence came the plural *hi loci*, but likewise *hoc locum* (as we find in Varro and Macrobius) which made *hæc loca*. In like manner they said not only *vas*, *vasis*, but also *vasum*, *vasi*, (which is still in Plautus and in Aulus Gellius) whence has remained the plural *vasa*, *vasorum*. And the rest in the same manner.

For which reason, as Sanctius judiciously observes, there are strictly speaking no irregular nouns; and if we would treat of these nouns, we ought rather to divide them into two other branches, one of those that are redundant either in the termination of the nominative, or in the declension; and the other of those that are defective, viz that want something, whether it be that they are defective in number or defective in case.

This is the method we propose here to follow in treating of these nouns, and we shall give particular lists of them for the use of those who write in Latin. But first of all let us comprise in a few rules, such remarks as are most necessary for beginners.

OF NOUNS IRREGULAR IN THEIR GENDER.

THERE are six sorts of nouns, that are called irregular in their gender, which shall be comprised in the six following rules.

Rule I.
Of those that are masculine in the singular and neuter in the plural.

Hic Tártarus *makes* hæc Tártara; *as* hic Avérnus, hæc Avérna.

Examples.

Hic Tártarus, Hell, or the very bottom of Hell. *Tum Tártarus ipse ——— Bis patet in præceps*, Virg. *Nigra Tartara*, Virg. *Tristia*, Id. the dark and dismal prison of Hell.

Hic Avérnus, a lake of Campania in Italy, taken by the poets for Hell. *Grave olens Avérnus*, Virg. stinking: *Avérna alta*, Id. deep.

Annotation.

Infernus, placed here by Despauter, is an adjective, for we say *infernus carcer, infernæ aquæ, inferna loca*, &c.

But we rank in this same class the following names of mountains, *Dyndimus, Ismarus, Mænalus, Pangæus, Tænarus, Taygetus,* which were also terminated in UM in ancient writers, and on this account have the plural in A.

Rule II.
Of those that are masculine in the singular, and in the plural are masculine and neuter.

Jocus *makes* joci, joca; locus *has* loca, *and sometimes* loci.

Examples.

Jocus, a jest, a joke, raillery; in the singular is masculine, *illiberális jocus*, Cic. a clownish jest; in the plural we say, *joci*, and *joca*; *ridiculi joci*, Plaut. pleasant jests or raillery; *joca tua plena facetiárum*, Cic. thy pleasant and facetious raillery.

Locus, masculine, *locus amæ'nus*, Cic. a pleasant place. In the plural it is neuter; *loca opulénta*, rich places; *ábdita*, Cic. secret, private.

ANNOTATION.

We say likewise *loci*, especially to signify the topics or common places, *loci argumentationum*. To denote places or parts, we generally make use of *loca*, though Virgil has *devenere locos*, &c. they came to those places.

As to *Eventus* and *Sibilus*, see the list of the nouns in US and in UM hereto annexed.

RULE III.

Of nouns that are feminine in the singular and neuter in the plural.

Hæc Cárbasus *makes* cárbasa, *as* hæc supéllex *makes* supellectília.

EXAMPLES.

Cárbasus, fine linen, a sail of a ship, is feminine in the singular; *cárbasus inténta*, Lucr. In the plural it is neuter, *dedúcere carbasa*, Ovid, to lower the sails.

Supéllex, and formerly, *supelléctilis, is*, is feminine in the singular; *Campána supéllex*, earthen ware made in Campania: in the plural it is neuter, *supelléctilia, ium*, though it is not much used in this number.

ANNOTATION.

Cárbasus, which Despauter makes doubtful in its genders, and which he places here among those that are only masculine in the singular, has no other authority for this gender than a passage of the 1st book of Valerius Maximus, where he is speaking of the vestal Æmilia: but the best copies make it feminine in this very passage: *carbasus quam optimam habebat*, &c. Which Pighius himself has followed, though he mentions his having found it masculine in two MSS. See the genders above, p. 45.

Of the word Pergamus.

Diomedes, and after him Despauter and others, rank in this class also *hæc Pergamus*, plur. *hæc Pergama*. And yet Vossius in his grammar thinks that *Pergamus* is properly the city of Pergamus in Asia, the capital of king Attalus, and says that we shall not perhaps be able to find it any where signifies the fort of Troy, which is called *Pergama*, and is oftentimes taken for the whole town. But it is without foundation he says this, it being certain that this noun is common to both these towns, and that as Ptolemy calls that of Attalus Πέργαμος, so Hesychius says of this very same word that it signifies the fort of Troy, as it is also marked in the description of mount Ætna.

Quis non Argolico deflevit **Pergamon** *igni*
Impositam? &c.

And on the contrary we find *Pergamum* in Pliny, and Πέργαμος neuter in Strabo, to signify the *town of Pergamus*.

The reason hereof is that this noun is properly an adjective; for as Suidas and Servius observe, all high places were called *Pergama*. So that Pergamus was so called merely on the account of its situation, being only a fort in the time of Lysimachus, as Strabo takes notice, which he pitched upon to lodge his treasures, because of its situation and strength. It is true it was afterwards improved by Eumenes, who made it one of the beautifullest cities in Asia; it was he also, who, according to the testimony of Pliny, invented parchment in that city, or rather who extended the use of it, and therefore it is that from the name of the town it has been called *Pergamenum*.

It is more remarkable concerning this noun, that Πέργαμος agrees to both places, and supposes πόλις, *urbs*; whereas Πέργαμον supposeth φρέριον *propugnaculum*, and is taken particularly for Pergamus in Asia, though there was also another *Pergamum* in Crete, of which mention is made in Pliny and in Virgil, who affirms it to have been built by Æneas. As on the contrary *hæc Pergama*, in the plural, is taken for the forts and towers of Troy, because there were several of them; for as we have already observed, p. 23, no proper name can of itself be in the plural, because this number in its primary signification always denotes a multitude.

RULE IV.

Of those that are neuter in the singular, and masculine in the plural.

Cœlum, *though a neuter, makes* hi cœli; *and* Ely′sium *makes* Ely′sii.

EXAMPLES.

Cœlum is of the neuter gender in the singular, *cœlum rotúndum*, the round heavens; *liquidum cœlum*, Virg. the clear heavens, fine weather. The plural is *hi cœli: cœli cœlórum, laudáte Deum*, O ye heavens, praise the Lord.

Hoc Ely′sium, the place assigned by the poets for the habitation of the souls of good men.

———*sed amæ′na piórum*
Concilia Elysiúmque colo, Virg.
I am in the agreeable company of the virtuous, and in the habitation of the blessed. In the plur. we say *hi Ely′sii*, masculine.

Tu colis Ely′sios, Mart.

ANNOTATION.

The plural *cæli* comes from *cælus*, which Ennius made use of according

according to Charisius; *cælúsque profundus*. It hardly occurs any where but in the vulgate, and in this passage of Lucretius,

Quis potis est cælos omnes convertere?

Which Vossius attributes to a poetical licence. And indeed *cælum* was not used in the plural, according as Gellius mentions that Cæsar had expressly observed in his books of analogy, which he sent to Cicero. And Charisius tells us the same thing. For which reason Cicero did not care to express it himself in his last epistle of the ninth book, where he has: *ille baro* (that is, that blockhead) *te putabat quæsiturum, unum cælum esset an innumerabilia*.

Elysium comes from λύω *solvo*, because when the souls got thither, they were thought to be freed from all care. This noun is properly an adjective; for we say *Elisii campi*, Virg. the Elysian fields near Thebes in Bœotia; *colle sub Elysio*, Ovid. *Dominus Elysiæ*, Id. So that even in the singular, when we say *Elysium*, the ancient word *locum* is always to be understood.

Of the word Argos

To these we might join *Argos*, which being of the neuter in the singular, because it comes from τὸ Ἄργος, εος, (as hath been already observed, p. 17) is masculine in the plural, *Argi, Argorum*.

Si patrios unquam remeassem victor ad Argos, Æn. 2.

The reason of this is because, as we have taken notice in another place, when the Romans borrowed the Greek nouns, they sometimes gave them a termination intirely Latin, which they declined like the other Latin nouns. So that this plural *Argi* must come from the singular *Argus*, taken simply from Ἄργος. Now this noun is used only in three cases in the singular, namely, the nominative, vocative, and accusative, which are alike. But in the plural *Argi* is declined through all cases. And it is observable that out of four principal towns which take this name (one in Peloponnesus, the other in Thessaly, the third in Acarnania, and the fourth in Apulia, built by Diomedes, out of regard to his antient country *Argos*, and which was heretofore called *Argyrippa*, as Virgil testifies, 9 Æn. instead of *Argos Hippium*, and by a word still more corrupt, *Arpi*, as Servius informs us upon this same book of Virgil, and Strabo in the sixth book of his geography) nor even out of any of the rest, for Stephanus, an antient geographer, mentions no less than eleven of this name, this is perhaps the only one that has this plural, *Argi, orum*, which should be taken for the people as much as for the city, according to what we have said concerning the genders, p. 24.

RULE V.
Of nouns that are neuter in the singular, and masculine or neuter in the plural.

Frænum *has* fræni, *or* fræna;
And so raftrum *has* raftri, *or* raftra.

OF HETEROCLITES.

EXAMPLES.

Hoc frænum, a bridle, or the bit of a bridle. *Frænum mordére*, Cic. to receive the bridle, to submit: *dare fræna*, Sen. to subdue. *Frænos injícere alícui*, Val. Max. to stop a person in the midst of his career.

Rastrum curvum, a crooked harrow; *graves rastri*, Ter. the heavy harrow; *rastra coquere*, Juv. to make harrows.

ANNOTATION.

Rastra is not near so much used as *rastri*; hence Stevech condemns it as bad Latin. And yet we find it in Celsus, according to Nonius, *Omnes rastra attollunt & adigunt*. And in Juv. sat. 15.

—— *Cùm rastra & sarcula tantùm*
Adsueti coquere.

It is also in S. Isidore, book 20. c. 14. *de instrum. rustic.* Now *rastri* comes from *raster*, which we meet with in Philoxenus's glossaries for δίκελλα. And the old glossary published by H. Stephen, as that also of S. Cyril, have *raster*, and *rastrum*, adding for a third synonymous word *videns* for *bidens*.

To these Despauter adds also *claustrum*, an inclosure ; *capistrum*, an halter ; *filum*, a thread ; but without authority. For it would be a mistake to say *hi claustri, hi capistri*, and perhaps even *hi fili*, of which we shall take notice hereafter in the list of nouns in US and in UM.

RULE VI.

Of nouns that are neuter in the singular, and feminine in the plural.

E'pulum *makes* épulæ; delícium, delíciæ; *But* bálneum *has* bálneæ *and* bálnea.

EXAMPLES.

These nouns being of the neuter gender in the singular, take the feminine in the plural : *epulum fúnebre*, a funeral banquet : *dare épulas*, to give an entertainment.

Delícium domûs, the delight of the family ; it is seldom used in the singular : *Tulliola deliciæ meæ*, Tulliola my delight.

Hoc bálneum, a bath ; plur. *hæ bálneæ*, or *hæc bálnea*. *Bálnea conjúncta* ; *bálneæ Palatínæ*.

ANNOTATION.

Epulæ comes from *epula*, which is in Nonius according to Stevech, who would have us read the following passage of Lucilius thus ; *idem epulo cibus, atque epulâ Jovis*. The accusative *epulam* is in Paulus Diaconus. *Deliciæ* comes from *delicia*, which is in Plautus, Solinus, and Nonius.

As for *balneum*, it is to be observed that we say also *balneum*, plur. *balineæ* and *balinea*. But *balneum* or *balineum* in the singular, signified a private bath, because there was only one in each house. And *balineæ* or *balinea* in the plural, signified public baths, because there were several of them; the place where the women bathed being always distinct from that of the men. See Varro book 8. de L. L.

OF NOUNS IRREGULAR IN THEIR DECLENSION.

NOUNS, irregular in their declension, are of three sorts: the first are of one declension in the singular, and of another in the plural. The second partake of both declensions, as well in the singular, as in the plural. And the third deviate in the whole or in part from the analogy natural to their nominative. Which we shall shew more particularly in the following rules.

Rule VII.

Of *jugerum* which is of the second in the singular, and of the third in the plural.

Júgerum, júgeri, *borrows of* juger,
Júgera, júgerum, *in* the plural.

Examples.

Hoc júgerum, júgeri, of the second in the singular. *Júgerum vocatur, quod uno jugo boum in die exarári possit,* Plin. They give this name to as much ground as can be ploughed by a team of oxen in one day. In the plural it is of the third, *júgera, júgerum, jugéribus;* which is taken from the old word *juger,* whence comes also *júgeris* in Mela, and *júgere* in Tibullus. See the list here annexed of neuters plural.

Rule VIII.

Of *vas,* which is of the third in the singular, and of the second in the plural.

From the singular vas, vasis, *comes* vasa, vasórum, vasis.

Exam-

OF HETEROCLITES.

EXAMPLES.

Hoc vas, vasis, a vessel, of the third declension. In the plur. *vasa, vasórum,* of the second. *In aureo vase,* in a golden vessel. *Vasórum appellátio commúnis est,* Ulpian. the name of vessel is general.

RULE IX.

Of *domus,* which follows the second and fourth.

Domus *makes* domûs, dómui, *as also* domi, domo.

EXAMPLES.

Hæc domus, a house. This noun is partly of the second, and partly of the fourth, and is thus declined.

DOMUS.

Singular	Plural
N. V. *Domus.*	N. V. *Domus.*
Genit. *Domi,* only in answer to the question UBI, every where else *domus.*	Genit. *Domórum* for the second; and sometimes *domuum* for the fourth.
Dat. *Dómui,* only.	Dat. *Dómibus,* only.
Accus. *Domum.*	Accus. *Domos* and *domus.*
Ablat. *Domo,* and heretofore *domú.*	Ablat. *Dómibus,* as in the dative.

The several cases unusual in either declension are included in this verse of Alstedius:

Tolle *me, mi, mu, mis,* si declinare *domus* vis.

Where he rejects *domi,* as well because it is not used in the plural, as even in the genitive singular it is used only in answer to the question UBI: and *domú,* because it is obsolete.

RULE X.

Of *vis* and *bos,* which are irregular in some cases.

Vis, vis, *makes* vires, viribus; *and* bos, bovis, *makes* boum, bobus.

EXAMPLES.

The noun *vis* is irregular, in as much as it has no increase in the singular, though it increases in the plural. It is therefore declined thus:

Nom. *vis,* gen. *vis.* It wants the dative. Accus. *vim,* Abl. *vi.*

In the plural it should naturally make *ves*; but we say, *vires*: gen. *virium*: dat. *viribus*: accuf. *vires*: voc. *vires*: abl. *viribus*.

Bos, bovis, an ox. Plur. *boves*: genit. *boum*: dat. and abl. *bobus* or *bubus* by syncope, instead of *bovum*, *bóvibus*.

ANNOTATION.

The plural *vires* proceeds, as Vossius observes, from their having heretofore used *viris, hujus viris*. Hence as *vis* in the singular is only a contraction for *viris*, so they have used the same word now and then in the plural, *vis* for *veis* or *ves*, instead of *vires*.

Et quo quisque magis vis multas possidet in se,
Atque potestates, Lucret. 2.

And in Sallust, according to Priscian, *male jam adsuetum ad omnes vis controversiarum*, Histor. 3. The genitive *vis*, which has been doubted of by some, is in the civil law: it is also in the dialogue about orators, attributed to Tacitus. *Quanquam in magna parte librorum suorum plus habent vis quàm sanguinis.*

Bos makes *bovis*, merely because of the Æolic *digamma*, whose place is supplied by the V consonant, as we have already taken notice, p. 83. But it drops this letter in the genitive and dative plural, *boum, bobus*, as it ought naturally to make *bos, boïs*, in the singular.

We might take notice in this place of other irregularities, which are as contrary to analogy as this; such are *iter, itineris; jecur, jecoris; Jupiter, Jovis*. But you may see these nouns each in their particular rule above, and what we have said of them in general, p. 70.

OF DEFECTIVE NOUNS, OR IRREGULARS
that want something.

Of these we reckon three sorts; the first are defective in number, either singular or plural; the second are defective in declension, that is, are not declined at all; and the others are defective only in some cases.

Of those that have no plural.

1. Proper names have no plural; as *Petrus, Lutetia, Rhodanus*.

We must except such as have the plural only, as *Delphi, Parisi, Athenæ*; concerning which we refer to what has been said when treating of the genders, p. 24.

Even the others admit of a plural on different occasions, as when we say with an emphasis, the *Alexanders*, the *Cæsars*, &c.

Or when the same name is common to many, as when I say, *complures fuerunt Socrates*, there have been a great many Socrates's. *Octodecim numerantur Alexandriæ*, they reckon eighteen cities of the name of Alexandria. But then they are rather appellatives than proper names, since they agree to many.

2. The

OF HETEROCLITES.

2. The names of age or time of life are also without the plural, as *pueritia, juventus, senium*; but concerning this there is no difficulty, since it is the same analogy in the French language.

To these two rules the generality of grammarians add three more, one of the names of metals, as *aurum, argentum*; the other of the fruits of the earth, as *oleum, acetum, butyrum*, &c. This remark may hold good in regard to a great many of those nouns: but we intend to examine these rules more particularly hereafter, and shall make it appear that they are not general.

Of nouns that have no singular.

The grammarians have likewise collected here an infinite number of nouns, which they pretend have no singular number at all. But tho' they are mistaken in this as much as in any one thing, by maintaining it absolutely; yet it is certain that a great many of these nouns are used but very little or scarce at all in the plural, and others only in some particular cases. So that they can be used only in the very cases that are found in writers, and even then very cautiously, if they do not frequently occur. I shall content myself with mentioning a few in the following rule, reserving the rest for the lists hereto annexed.

RULE XL.

General for nouns that have no singular at all, or but very seldom.

Many plural nouns seldom or never are used in the singular, as arma, nugæ, nuptiæ, grates, vepres, divitiæ, *and a multitude of others, which use will make familiar.*

EXAMPLES.

There are a great many nouns used in the plural, that never have a singular, or at least but very seldom, and only in particular cases; as *arma impia*, impious arms: *meræ nugæ*, mere trifles: *rependere grates*, to return thanks: *vepres multi*, a quantity of briars: *multæ divitiæ*, great riches.

Those which are sometimes found in the singular, as *vepre* in the ablative in Ovid, must be learnt by use, and by what we shall say concerning them in the subsequent lists.

THE FIRST LIST.

Of nouns that admit of different terminations in the nominative.

THIS and the following list may give a sufficient idea of whatever is remarkable concerning irregularity in gender or declension, since, as we have already taken notice, this difference is intirely owing to the nominative's having been formerly different.

But they are moreover particularly necessary for those who write in Latin, because the gender frequently changing with the termination, it is so much the easier to be mistaken on this article, as a person is apt to imagine he has authority for the gender of a noun, which gender belongs nevertheless to another noun. Thus, though we find *de optimo papyro*, yet we must not believe we have a right to say *optimus papyrus*, the latter being always feminine, whereas the ablative in the foregoing example comes from *papyrum*, which is neuter. And in like manner a great many others.

Of those whose double termination is in vowels.

A and E.

Cepa, æ, *Plin. Colum.* an onion.
Cepe, *indeclin Prisc.* Cepe succum melle mix. m, *Appul.*
Cepe, is; *Quis usus cepis putridi*, an old proverb.
Circa, æ, *Plaut.* Circe, es, *Hor.*
Epitoma, æ; epitome, es, *Cic.*
Gausapa, æ, *Varro.*
Gausape, is, *Voss. ex Plin.*
Gausapum, i, *Cass. Severus* in *Prisc.*
Charisius quotes also *gausapes*, in the plural, from Augustus Cæsar's will. But Vossius thinks we should read GAUSAPAS. See the declensions, p. 95.
Grammatica, æ; grammatice, es, *Cic. et alii.* In like manner the other names of arts, which are oftentimes used even in the neuter plural, *grammatica, orum*, &c.
Helena, æ; Helene, es, *Virg. Hor.* And a great many more proper names. Concerning which see what has been said, p. 62.

A and O.

Hæc Narbona, *Isid.*
Hic Narbo, *Cic.*

Hæc missa & missio, *Alcim. Avit.* and *Isid.*
Remissa et remissio, *Cyprian.*

Of those which have their termination in a consonant.

A and UM.

Acetabula, æ; *Voss.*
Acetabulum, i, *Plin.* a saucer or little dish, a measure of two ounces and a half, the pan in the joint of the bones, the clay in lobsters and such fish, jugglers cups, the herb pennyworth.
Alimonia, *Macrob.*
Alimonium, *Varro*, the same as *alimentum.*
Amygdala, *Plin.*
Amygdalum, *Pallad.* an almond: but for the almond tree they say only *Amygdala.*
Arteria, *Cic.*
Arterium, i, *Plin.* a saucer or rather *Arteria, orum*, *Lucret.* the arteries.
Arva, *whence* arvas *in Pacuv. and Non.*
Arvum, *Cic. Virg.*
Buccina, *Cic.* um, *Plin.*
Cæmenta, *Enn.* um, *Cic.* rubbish, shards, or pieces of stones to fill up walls with; in the scripture it is taken also for mortar or cement.

Castra,

Of Nouns of Diverse Terminations.

Castra, *Acci.*
Castrum, *Cic.* a castle, or citadel. In the plur. it signifies a camp.
Cichorea, *Hor.*
Cichoreum, *Plin.*
Colustra, *Non,* Colustrum, *S. Isd. the first milk or beestings.* The former is in Plin. and the latter in Martial, only that some read *colostra* and *colostrum.*
Decipula, *Sipont.* um, *Appul.* a snare, or gin to catch birds, a trap.
Delicia, *Plaut.* um, *Cic.* See p. 131.
Fulmenta, *Plaut.* um, *Non. ex Varr.*
Ganea, *Col.* um. *Ter.* Cicero has used it in the plur. *ganea, orum,* a bawdy house or stew.
Horrea, & um, *Cic.* a granary, a barn, a warehouse.
Insomnia, *Cæcil apud Non.*
Insomnium, *Virg.*
But there is a difference between these two words, which seems to have escaped Nonius's observation. For *insomnia, æ,* signifieth watching, or difficulty to sleep, as Servius observes: whereas *insomnium* signifieth dreams.
——— *Quæ me suspensam insomnia terrent?* Virg.
Lahia, æ, *Plaut.*
Labium, i, *or rather* labia, orum, *Ter.*
Labrusca, *Virg.* um, *in Culice,* the weed called wildvine.
Lania, or Lanea, *Liv.*
Lanicia, *Laber. apud Non.*
Lanicium, *Virg.* the commodity of wool, the increase or gain of it, the dressing or ordering of it.
Lixivia, *and* um, *Colum.*
Mandibula, *Isd.* um, *Macrob.*
Macella, *and* um, *as we may conclude from Plutarch in his Roman questions.*
Margarita & Margaritum.
Though the ancients were in doubt about it, and Charis. contradicts himself upon this article, as may be seen in the 1st book, chap. of analogy, and in the chapter of defectives. But this neuter is in Varro, in Valgius, and frequently occurs in Tertull.
Menda, *Gell.* um. *Cic.*
Mulctra, *Virg.* um, *Hor.*
Myrteta, æ, *Prisc. ex Plauto.*
Myrtetum, *Virg.* a myrtle grove.
Ostrea, *Gell.* um, *Plin. The dative* ostreis *is in Cic. 2. de Divin.*
Palpebra, *Cic. & alii.*
Palpebrum, *Nonius,* who assures us that the latter was more usual in his time.
Pistrina, *Lucil. Plin.*

Pistrinum, *Plaut. Ter. & alii.* I comes from *pinso,* and was properly the place where they pounded their corn before the invention of mills. It has been since taken for the mill, and for the bakehouse itself. Charis. says that Lucilius never used it in the feminine, but when he referred it to *taberna.* And the same must be said of *sutrina, medicina, tonstrina, textrina,* according to Donatus; which sufficiently proves that they are adjectives.
Postica, *Varr.* um, *Hor.*
Prosecta, *Lucil.* um, *Lucan.* the haslets, that which is to be cut out of the bowels of beasts to be sacrificed to idols.
Proficia, *Macrob. Arnob.*
Proficium, *Paul. Diac.* and *even* Proficies, *Varro.* a chop of the meat of a sacrifice.
Prostibula, *and* um. *Whence some read* prostibulam in Plautus, *for* prostibulum, *which is in Pers. Act.* 5. *sc.* 2. *vers.* 56.
Ramenta, *Plaut.* um, *Plin.* a chip, a shaving, a filing.
Rapa, *Colum.* um, *Plin.*
Seplasia, *Cic.* um, *Varro,* a place in Capua, where perfumes were sold, whence comes *seplasiarius,* a seller of perfumes, also a gallant that goeth powdered and perfumed.
Sesama, *Plin.* um, *Colum.* sesame, a white grain or corn growing in India, whereof oil is made.
Terricula, *Sen.* um, *Liv.*
Testa, *Cic.* um, *Non.* but the former is almost the only one used.
Tribula, *Colum.* um, *Vir.* a little cart or dray made of rough boards, which they used before flails for the threshing of corn. It comes from *tero,* from whence also comes the word *tribulation.*
Vestibula, *Non.* um, *Cic.*
Vigilia & um, *Non. ex Varr.* and thence *pervigilium,* according to Vossius.

A, EN, ON.

Hæc Attagena, *Mart.*
Hic Attagen, enis, *Plin. Her.*
Hæc Narbona, *Isidor.*
Hic Narbon, *or rather* Narbo, *Cic.*
Sirena, *Isd.*
Siren, enis, *Virg. Hor.*

A and ER.

Æthra, æ, for æthera, *Cic. Virg.*
Æther, eris, *Cic. Virg.*
Cratera, *Cic. in Arat. Pers.*

Crater,

Crater, *Virg.*
Panthera *and* Panther; *see the genders.* p. 58.
Statera, *Cic.* stater, *Bud.* though with this difference, that *statera* is a balance, and *stater* is a kind of coin.
Vespera, *Plaut.* vesper, *Cæs.*

In all these nouns ER is the original termination, that in A having been almost generally formed from the Greek accusative of the other termination, except it be *Vespera*, because the Greeks said in the nominative, not only ἕσπερος but also ἑσπέρα. And it is very likely that heretofore they said *Vesperus*, which followed the second declension, whereas *Vesper* rather followed the third. Hence we have still cases in both these declensions, *Vespero surgente*, Hor. *Primo Vespere*, Cæs.

Hereto we may join the termination OR; as lympha (from νύμφη) lymphor, *Non. ex Lucilio.*
Pigritia, *Cic.* pigror, *Non.*

A and AS.
Hebdomada, æ; hebdomas, adis, *Cic.*
Lampada, æ, *Manil.*
Lampas, adis, *Cic.*
Hæc tiara, æ, *Serv.*
Hic tiaras, æ, *Virg.*

A and ES.
Of the same declension.
Hic cometa, æ, & cometes, æ. *See the genders,* p. 26.
Geta, *Ter.* Getes, æ, *Ovid.*
Epirota, Epirotes, *Cic.*
Geometra, geometres, æ, *Cic.*
Propheta, æ, *Isid. Fest.*
Prophetes, æ, *Voss.*

A and ES.
Of different declension.
Avaritia, æ, *Cic.* avarities, ei, *Lucr.*
Barbaria, æ, *Cic.* barbaries, ei, *Cic.*
Blanditia, æ, *Cic.* blandities, ei, *Cic.*
Canitia, *Lucret.* canities, *Virg.*
Delitia, æ, *Plaut.* delities, *Appul.*
Desidia, *Cic.* desidies, *Lucret.*
Duritia, *Cic.* durities, *Cic.*
Effigia, effigies, *Cic.*
Fallacia, *Ter.* es, *Appul.*
Luxuria, & es, *Cic.*
Maceria, *Cic.* es, *Appul.* any wall or mound about a ground.
Maceries, *in antient writers signified leanness*, Non.
Materia & es, *Cic.*
Mollicia & es, *Cic.*
Munditia, *Cic.* es, *Catul.*
Nequitia, *Cic.* es, *Hor.*
Notitia, *Ter.* es, *Lucret.*
Pinguitia, *Arnob.* es, *Appul.*

Planitia, *Hygin.* es, *Liv.*
Prosapia, *Cic.* es, *Lucret.*
Scabritia, *Plin.* scabrities, *Colum.* scabbiness, roughness.
Sævitia, *Cic.* es, *Voss.*
Segnitia, *Ter.* segnities, *Virg.*

To these some add *provincia*, and *es*; but for the latter they have no authority.

Pauperia is in S. Cyril's glossary for *œvia*, but perhaps it is to be found in no other place. For *œvia* is rather *paupertas*, the inconvenience of poverty; and *pauperies*, the accident or misfortune that impoverishes us. And thus it is that Caper distinguishes them in his orthography.

We must not however believe what some grammarians have ventured to advance, that there was a difference between all these nouns in A and ES, as Cornelius Fronto, who imagines that *materia* is said of material things, on which artificers work; and *materies* of intellectual things that relate to the mind. For if we consult the authors here quoted, we shall find that all these nouns are indiscriminately taken for the same thing.

A and IS.
Absida, æ, *in later authors for*
Absis, idis, *which we find in Isidorus*, 3 Orig. cap. 68. where he takes it for the circles of the stars, just as Pliny does, lib. 2. c. 15. But the same Isidorus, lib. 14. c. 8. takes notice that the learned (in his time) doubted whether it was best to say *absidem* or *absidam*. Others write also *apsis*, because it comes from the Greek ἁψίς. In ecclesiastic writers this word is taken for the gallery of a church, for an episcopal chair, or for the inclosure of a chair. It is also taken for the bowing of an arch, and for the ring of a cart-wheel.
Bura, *Varr.* buris, *Virg.* the ploughtail or handle.
Cassis, idis, *Cæs.* cassida, æ, an helmet, *Charis. Prisc. Propert.* as also Virg.

Aureus ex humeris sonat arcus & aurea vati
Cassida ———————— Æn. 11.
Where Servius pretends it is a Greek accusative for a Latin nominative. It would have been much better if he had said that it is a real Latin noun, but derived from a Greek accusative, as we have above shewn that this also happens to nouns in ER and in A.

A and

A and US.

Aranea, æ, *Virg.* **Araneus,** i, *Lucret.* a spider. They say also **Aranea,** æ, *Ovid*, and **araneum,** i, *Phædr.* for a cobweb. Pliny useth both of them for a rime or dew, like a cobweb, which spoils olives and grapes.

Acina, æ, *Catul.* **acinus,** i, *Cic.* and also

Acinum, i, *Non.* the stone of grapes and other fruit.

Baptisma, atis; **baptismus,** i; and likewise, **baptismum,** i, *in ecclesiastic authors.*

Clavicula, æ, *Plin.* and **claviculus,** i, *Colum.* the tendrel, or young twig, or shoot of a vine, wherewith it takes hold of every thing, and climbs up by it.

Juventa, æ, *Virg. Hor.* **juventus,** utis, *Id. & Cic.*

Syngrapha, æ, *Cic.* **syngraphus,** i, *Plaut.* also **syngraphum,** *Plaut.* a writing or deed under the hand of both parties, an obligation, bill, or bond.

The following generally differ in sense.

Mercatura, *Cic.* traffic, merchandise.

Mercatus, *Cic.* the market, though in *Plautus* it signifies also a buying and selling, the trade of merchandise.

Venatura, *Voss.* venison.

Venatus, *Cic.* **venatio,** *Id.* hunting.

Usura, *Cic. Liv.* use, usage, enjoyment of a thing, usury, or money given for the use of money, interest, *Cic.*

Usus, *Cic.* use, exercise, profit, experience, usage, custom.

A and YS.

Chlamys, *Virg.* **chlamyda,** æ, *Voss.* a soldier's coat.

E and AL.

Autumnale, *Varro.*

Autumnal, *Id. apud Charis.*

Capitale, *Cic.* ——tal, *Cic. Varr.*

Cubitale, *Cic.* ——tal, *Hor.* a fore sleeve for the arm to the elbow downwards.

Penetrale, *Claud.* ——tral, *Propert.* the recess, or inmost part of any place.

Puteale, *Cic.* ——tral, *Cic. Hor.* the cover of a well or pit.

It is also taken for a place near the *palatium* in Rome, so called from a well that was there, in which they had a seat of justice and oaths were administered. This was the well over which was seen the statue of Accius Nævius; and hard by the altar where they preserved the razor with which king Tarquin made him cut a stone in his presence.

Quadrantale, *or* ——tal, *Festus*, a figure square every where like dice; also a vessel a foot square every way.

Sale *or* **sal,** *Charis.* This author prefers the former, which makes Muretus believe that in Terence's Eunuchus we ought to read.

Qui habet sale quod in te est.

Where others read *salem qui*: and others by synecdoche *salem, quod in te est.*

Torale, *Varr.* ——ral, *Hor.* the furniture of a bed or table, as sheets, blankets, coverlets.

E and R, or ARE and AR.

Altare, *Cic.* altar, *Præd.*

Alveare, *Colum.* ear, *Voss.* a bee hive.

Calcare, *Voss.* car, *Cic.* a spur.

Cochleare, *Mart.* ear, *Colum.* a spoon.

Exemplare, *Lucr.* ar, *Cic.* a sampler, a resemblance or model, a copy.

Lacunare *or* nar, *Hor.*

Laqueare *or* ar, *Virg. Plin.*

Pugillare *or* ar, *Auson.* also hæ **pugillares,** *Plin.* a table book.

Pulvinare *or* ar, *Ovid*, a bolster of a bed, a pillow, a cushion.

And these nouns often change their termination into ium, for we say,

Altarium, *Sever. Sculp.* **pugillarium,** *Plin.* **lupanarium,** *Ulp.*

Some grammarians (and among the rest L. Valla, book 6, c. 33.) add here **exemplarium,** pretending it is from Pliny, lib. 6. c. 29. *Omisit in hoc tractu (nisi exemplarium vitiosum est)* Berenicen alteram. But the best editions, as the earliest of Paris, that of Parma, and that of Delecampius, have, *nisi exemplarium vitium est.* For as it cannot be denied but this word was received in later ages, so there is no probability at all of its having been current in Pliny's time: but we find it in Ulpian; *si in duobus exemplariis scriptum sit testamentum,* according to Haloander and the Florentine Pandects.

E and ES.

Hoc tapete, *Non. from whence comes* **tapetia** *in Pliny.* **Hic tapetes,** *or* **tapes,** etis, *Virg.* also **tapetum,** i, *Virg.* tapestry.

E and IS.

Hoc conclave, *Ter. Cic.*

Hæc conclavis, *Voss.* and also

Hoc conclavium, *Plaut.*

Præsepe, *Cic. Virg.* **præsepis,** *Varro.*

Præse-

Præsepium, *Appul.*
Rete, *Virg. Ter. Cic.* retis, *masc.* Albo rete, *Plautus.* For if it came from *rete*, neuter, he would have said *albo reti.* See the declensions, p. 106. and the genders, p. 41. Hence it is that Plautus in his *Rudens* has also *uvidum retem*, according to Priscian and the antient copies; which perhaps has not been duly considered by those who have corrected *uvidum rate.* But Charisius has likewise taken notice of *retes*, feminine in the plural. *Nam et in consuetudine*, says he, *dicimus* ; *in retes meos incidisti:* which he places among nouns that have no singular, whereas there can be no objection against taking it from *retis* itself, as Vossius hath observed.

I and IS.

Hoc gummi, *Plin.* hæc gummis, *Col.*
Hoc sinapi, *Plin.* hæc sinapis, *Plin.* and *Plaut.* See the genders, p. 23.

O and UM.

Adagio, *Varr.* gium, *Plaut.*
Alluvio, *Cic.* ium, *Voss.* ies, *Liv.*
Consortio, *Liv. Cic.* ium, *Celf. Ulp.*
Contagio, *Cic.* ium, *Virg. Mart.* both are taken for a touch or contact, and for an infection or pestilence.
Oblivio, *Cic.* oblivium, *Tacit.*
Postulatio, *Cic.* atum, *Cæs. Tacit.*
Proluvio, *Voss.* ium. *Ter. Gell.*
Proluvies, *Virg. Cic.*
Supplicatio, *Cic.* supplicium, *Sallust. Tacit.* supplication, prayer, a solemn procession.

O and EN.

Anio, *Hor.* Anien, *Stat.*
Anio made *Anionis* according to Prisc. So that *Anicnis* in Catullus, and *Anienem* in Virgil, properly come from *Anien*, though they have been attributed to *Anio.* The same must be said of
Nerio, onis, *and* Nerien, enis, *Plaut.*
Turbo, onis, *and* Turben, inis, *Tibull.*

O and ON.

Agamemno, *Stat.* Agamemnon, *Voss.*
Antipho, *Ter.* on *Ter.*
Amazo *or* on, *Voss.*
Demipho, *Ter.* on, *Ter.*
Palemo *or* on, *Virg.*
Plato, *Cic.* on, *Manil.*
Simo, *Ter.* on, *Plin.*
And others of the like sort which have often dropped their *n* at the last syllable, as may be seen in Terence and other writers.

O and OR.

Squalitudo, *Acc.* squalor, *Cic.* filthiness, roughness, the sorrowful estate of those that be arraigned or accused.

O and AS.

Beatitudo *and* beatitas, *Cic.* 1. de *Nat.* He takes notice that both these words were with difficulty established in his time: *Utrumque enim durum*, says he, *sed usu verba mollienda sunt.*
Concinnitudo, *Cic.* itas, *Cic.*
Cupido, *Virg. Hor.* ditas, *Cic.*
Necessitudo, *Cic.* itas, *Cic. Cæs.* They are both taken for necessity, or for the tie that one has, whether of kindred or friendship. However, *necessitudo* is oftener in the latter signification; *necessitas* in the former.
Teneritudo, *Cic.* ritas, *Appul.*

O and ES.

Alluvio, onis, *Cic.*
Alluvies, ei, *Colum.*
Colluvio, *Cic.* vies, *Colum. Plin.*
Proluvio, *Voss.* vies, *Cic. Virg.*
Contagio, *Cic.* contages, *Lucret.* They say also *contagium*. See above.
Compago, inis, *and* ages, is.
Servius (1. *Æn.*) allows of both; but he says that the first is indeclinable, and that there is no such word as *compaginis.* It is indeed very scarce, yet we read in Ovid
———*disparibus calamis compagine cerae,* Metam. 1.
Propago, inis, *Virg.* ages, agis, *Enn.*

O and IS.

Apollo, inis.
Apollinis, hujus Apollinis, *Voss.*
Caro, carnis, *Cic.*
Carnis, hujus carnis, *Liv. Andronic.* apud Prisc.

O and US.

Abusio, *Cic.* abusus, *Cic.*
Admonitio *Cic.* itus, *Cic.*
Affectio, *Cic.* tus, *Cic.*
Which is very usual with verbal nouns derived from the supine. But it is observable also in others; as
Architecto, *Plin.* ctus, *Cic.* also Architector, oris, *Plaut.* an architect.
Capo, onis, *a capon. Mart.* capus, *Varr.*
Gobio, *Plin.* gobius, *Mart.* a gudgeon.
Lanio, *Voss.* lanius, *Ter. Phædr.*
Pavo, *Plin. Cic.* pavus, *Gell.* a peacock.
Scorpio, *Plin. Cæs.* pius, *Virg.*
Strabo, *Cic. Hor.* bus, *Voss.* goggle-eyed, one who looketh asquint.

U and US.

Artu, *Plaut.* artus, *Cic.* a joint, the limbs.

Hoc

Of Nouns of Diverse Terminations. 141

Hoc cornu, *Cic.* hic cornus, *Cic.*
Also hoc cornum, *Prisc.* a horn.
Tonitru, *Virg.* tonitrus, *Stat.*
Tonitruum, *Plin.*

Of those whose terminations end both in consonants, viz. in L, M, N, R, S.

L and S.
Debil *for* debilis, *Ennius.*
Subtil *for* subtilis, *Prisc.*
Facul *for* facilis, *Voss.*
Difficul *for* difficilis, in Plaut. and in the antients, Pacuvius, Accius, Lucilius, as Nonius relates.

The same changes of termination happen to the substantives, as
Mugil, *Prisc.* mugilis, *Juv.*
Strigil, *obsolete*, striligis, *Plaut.*

There is great probability that the word *strigil* was in Non. chap. 3. in this corrupted passage where we read, *strigilim manifestum est esse feminini, neutri, Varro Bimargo,* &c. For the sense would be complete, as Vossius observes, were we to read *strigil neutri*; because these nouns by changing their terminations, also change their genders. Now it appears from hence that as Nonius evidently maketh *strigilis* a feminine, according to the general rule of the nouns in IS, we ought not to mind either Aldus, who took it for a masculine, or Isidorus, who in the last chapter of his last book of Origins, makes use of it in this gender; *strigiles nuncupati à tergendo*; besides that it would have been better if he had said *à strigendo*; for *strigo* was formerly used for *stringo*, whence comes also *strictus*, close or narrow; *strigosus*, lean, thin, barren; and *strigilis*, a curry-comb, an instrument used in bathing, to rub filth and sweat from their bodies, also a kind of long vessel: likewise *striglis* which is formed by syncope from *strigilis*, and properly signifies a furrow or gutter in carpenter's or mason's work, a chamfering or channelling; as *stria* (which is also derived from thence) is taken rather for a passage or outlet and its entrance, though they are sometimes confounded one for the other.
Famul *for* famulus, *Enn. Non. Lucret.*

MENTUM & MEN.
Augmentum, *Varr.* augmen, *Lucret.*
Carmentum, *Voss.* ——men, *Cic.*
Momentum, *Cic.* ——men, *Lucret.*
Limentum, *Varr.* ——men, *Cic.*
Sublimentum *or* ——men, *F.st.*

UM and R.
Alabastrum, *Mart.*
Alabaster, *Cic.* a vessel made of alabaster to keep sweet ointments in.
Calamistrum, *Cic.* ——ter, *Varr. Cic.*
Candelabrum, *Cic.* ——ber, *Arnob.*
Canistrum, *Cic.* ——ter, *Pallad.*
Cochlearium, *Varr.* Cochlear, *or* Cochleare, *Mart.*
Jugerum, i, *or* juger, jugeris, see above, p. 132.

UM and S. Whether
In ES, contagium, *Plin.*
Contages, *Lucret. also* contagio, onis, *Plaut.* the touch, infection, pestilence.
Diluvium, *Virg.* vies, *Hor.*
Tabum, *Virg.* tabes, *Virg.*
Tapetum, i, *Virg.* hic tapes, etis, *Virg. also* tapete, is, *Plaut.*
In OS, Ilium, *Virg.* Ilios, *Hor.*
In US, Buxum *and* Buxus: and a great many of which we shall take particular notice at the end of this list.

UM and T.
Occiput, *Auson.* occipitium, *Plaut.*

N and M.
Momen *or* momentum, *and others of which mention has been made above.*

N and IS.
Fulmen, *Cic. Plin.* fulminis, *Voss.*
Oscen, *Auson.* oscinis, *Cic.*
Sanguen, *Lucret.* sanguis, *Cic.*

Giffanius adds also *vermen* for *vermis*, a worm, because Lucretius has,

Donicum eos vitâ privarent vermina sæva.

But he did not know that *vermina* in this passage signifies only *tormina*, as Festus observes; *the griping of the guts, the wringing of the belly*; which is derived however from VERMES, *quid facilè se torqueant*, says Nonius.

N and US.
Titan, *Virg. Cic.* Titanus, *Plaut.*
Delphin, *Ovid*, *Virg.* delphinus, *Cic. Hor.*

But here the latter nominative comes from the genitive of the former, as from τῦ Τιτᾶνος is formed *Titanus, ani*, For it often happens that of the genitive or other Greek case, they form a new Latin noun, which follows a different declension.

Diacon *and* diaconus *in the sacred writings.*

R and M
Alabaster *and* alabastrum; *see above the title,* UM, R.

R and

R and S.

Arbos *and* arbor, *Cic.*
Honos *and* honor.
Impubes *and* impuber, are generally placed here. But Vossius thinks that *impuber* is to be found no where but among the grammarians, who produce no authority for it, though Joseph Scaliger in Catullus. *in Galliam*, chose to read *puber* instead of *mulier.*
Ligus *and* Ligur, *Virg.*
 Also
Ador *and* Adus, *Voss.*
Algor *and* Algus, cold, great cold.
 Tu vel suda vel peri algû, Plaut.
Decor *and* decus, where the vowel changes together with the R; see the genders, pages 34, 43. And here by the way we may observe, that it is not true, strictly speaking, that *decor* and *decus* are two words of an intire different meaning, of which the former signifies *beauty* only, and the latter *honour*, according to the opinion of some. For in Virgil,

——— *Tantum egregio decus enitet ore.*

 Hunc decus egregium formæ movet atque juventæ, and the like; *decus* as plainly expresses *beauty* as *decor*, though there may be some other difference in the application of these words.

R and IS.

Arar, *Lucan. Sil.* Araxis, *Virg. Prisc.* the river Saone.
Hoc bacear, *Plin. Prisc.* hæc baccaris, *Plin.* βάκκαρις, *Hesych.* a kind of herb or flower. See the genders, p. 32.
Celer, *Virg.* And celeris, *even in the masculine*, *Voss.*
Sacer *and* sacris, *Porci sacres,* Plaut.
Memor *and* memoris, *Cuper apud Prisc.*
Indecor *and* indecoris, *Non.*
Turtur *and* turturis, *Mariangel. Accurs. ex Auson.*
Vultur *and* vulturis, *Enn. apud Charis. ex Prisc.*

 Vulturis in silvis miserum mandabat Hemonem.

Unless we are obliged to read *vulturus*, as it is in the manuscript copies according to Vossius and Giffanius. But we say also *vulturius*, a vultur, which is in Ovid, Livy, and Phædrus.

ER and US.

These two terminations are found more particularly in nouns latinised from the Greek, as
Evander *and* Evandrus, from Εὐάνδρος.

Mæander *and* Mæandrus, from Μαίανδρος.
Also in the others, as
Acer *or* acrus, according to *Charisius.*
Exter *and* exterus.
Infer *and* inferus.
Ister *and* Isterus, *Gell.*
Pestifer *and* Pestiferus.
Prosper *and* prosperus.
Uter *for* uterus, *Cæcil.*

AS and US.

Elephas, *Cic.* elephantus, *Plin.* and *Phædrus.*

ES and IS.

Apes, *Probus,* apis. *Colum. Ovid.*
Feles, *Phædr.* felis, *a cat.*
There are some who scruple to make use of *feles* in the singular. And yet we read it in Phædrus, lib. 2. fab. 4. *Feles cavernam nacta.* And in that passage of Pliny where some read *Felis aurea pro Deo colebatur,* lib. 6. cap. 28. the MSS. vary, most of them having *feles*: and in the 3d book of Varro de R. R. which Calepin quotes for *felis,* Grifius's and all the best editions have, *ne feles ad nocendum intraire possit.*
We meet with this word also in Plautus, *feles virginaria,* meaning a ravisher of young girls, and a corruptor of virginity. As in Ausonius, *feles pullaria,* for one that carried off the children, whom the ancients called *pulli.* Besides Charisius expresly informs us that they said *hæc feles,* in the same manner as *hæc moles.*
Hence it appears that so far from being authorised to reject *feles,* on the contrary we have great reason to suspect *felis*; and still more so to suspect the gender given it by most dictionaries, without producing any authority. For the great thesaurus of the Latin tongue, Morel, Pajot, and other late dictionaries, make it common: but Stephens, Calepin, and the little dictionary mention it only as masc. yet it is difficult to make it pass under this gender, though Cicero has, 1. *de Nat. As ne fando quidem auditum est Crocodilum aut Ibim, aut felem violatum ab Ægyptio*; which ought to be referred to a syllepsis, because of the masculines that go before, as we shall observe when we come to treat of this figure.
Puppes, *Prob.* puppis, *Ovid.*
Torques, *Cic.* torquis, *Plin.*
Valles, *Prob.* vallis, *Cic.*

ES and UM.

Whether the ES follows the fifth, as

Pro-

Proluvies, ei, *and* proluvium.
  See the title UM and ES.
Or whether it follows the third, as Tapes, etis, *Virg.* tapetum, i. *Virg.*
Also hoc tapete, *Plaut.*

ES and US.

Achilles, is, *and* Achilleus, i.
Perses, is, *and* Perseus, i.
  And then the termination ES comes from the Æolians, who for 'Οδυσσεὺς say 'Οδυσσευς, whence comes Ulysses. See the declensions, p. 120.

ES and BS or PS.

Adipes, *Varro*, adeps, *Pliny.*
Plebes, is, *Liv. Tac.* plebs, ebis, *Cic.*
  But heretofore they said also plebes, plebei, *Plin.*
Sepes, *Colum. Varro,* seps.
  We find it likewise in Lucan, where it signifies a serpent.
  Ossáque diſſolvens cum corpore tabificus sepis.
  But for its signifying a hedge I know of no authority. It is true that Ausonius attributes it to Cicero.
  Bucolico ſæpes dixit Maro; cur Cicero sepes?
  But we meet with no such word now in Cicero.
Satraps, *Sidon.* satrapes, *Ter.* The grandees of Persia. *But we say also* satrapa.
Trabes, *Cic.* trabs, *Virg.*

IS and S. with a consonant.

Scrobis *and* Scrobs.
Scobis *and* scobs.
Stipis *and* stips.
Glandis *and* glans.
Mentis *and* mens.
Concordis *and* concors.
Discordis *and* discors.

See the genders, p. 49. declensions p. 70.
  We find also *Tiburs* in Cato, and *Tiburis* in the old inscriptions.

IS and US.

Gruis, *Phædrus*, grus, *Virg.*
Hilaris, *Hor.* hilarus, *Ter. Plaut.* whence comes *hilara* in Rud. *hilara vita*, *Cic.*
Improbis, *Feſtus*, improbus, *Virg.*
Pronis, *Varr.* pronus, *Cic.*
  But this happens particularly to nouns in

ARIS and ARIUS.

Auxiliaris, *Cæſ.* auxiliarius, *Cic.*
Jocularis, *Cic.* —arius, *Ter.*
Singularis, *Cic.* —arius, *Plaut.*
Vulgaris, *Cic.* —arius, *Non.*
  And others of the same sort.

OS or US, and UM or ON.

Ilios *and* Ilion.
Melos *and* Melus, *Non.* See the genders, p. 32.

US and NS.

Violentus *and* violens, *Hor.*
Opulentus *and* opulens, *Nepos.*

US and UR.

Ligus *and* Ligur, *Virg.*

X and ES.

Fax *and* faces, *Feſt.*
Pollux *and* Polluces, *Plaut.*

X and CIS or GIS.

Nucis *and* nuceris, is.
Regis *and* regeris, *according to Chariſius.*
  Of which by syncope they have formed *rex, regis : nux, nucis.*

X and IS.

Senex *and* senecis, whence comes *seneciór, ſeneEtus*, and *ſenecitus.*
Supellex *and* ſupellectilis. *See above* p. 128.

US and UM.

As these two terminations occur oftener than any of the foregoing, I have deferred to treat of them more amply by themselves. Sanctius, after John Pastranes, observes that heretofore all the nouns in US were terminated also in UM; and the great number of those that are left, seems to render this probable.

These nouns of their nature are either adjectives, as *effectus* and *effectum, eventus* and *eventum, inteſtinus* and *inteſtinum, juſſus* and *juſſum, ſuggeſtus* and *ſuggeſtum, textus* and *textum, tributus* and *tributum*, or substantives; and it is the latter that we shall examine more particularly in the following list.

Abſinthius,

A.

Absinthius, *Varro.*
Absinthium, *alii.*
Acinus, *Cic.* acinum, *Col.*
Actus, *Cic.* actum, or rather acta, orum, *Id.*
Admonitus, us, *Cic.* admonitum, *Id.* also admonitio, *Id.*
Ærarium, *the treasury or exchequer.* But *ærarius* was quite another thing, which Nonius does not seem to have sufficiently considered. For this as a noun adjective always supposeth its substantive, and is taken either for him who works in brass, as in Pliny: or for a clerk of the exchequer, as *ærarium facere*, according to Budeus: or for a person who was deprived of the privileges of a Roman citizen, as in Cic. *inter ærarios referre.*
Amaracus, *Catul.*
Amaracum, *Plin.*
Angiportus, and angiportum, *Plin.* and after him Priscian, who proves it to be of the neuter gender by this passage of Ter. *Id quidem angiportum non est pervium*; in Adelph. And to be of the masculine by this other; *sed hinc concedam in angiportum hunc*; in Phorm. And thus we read it in Gryphus's, Heinsius's, and all the best editions. And indeed Priscian himself, let Vossius say what he will, brings no more than these two examples to prove the two genders.
Anfractus, *Cic.* um, *Varr.*
Antidotus, *Gel.* um, *Curt.* This is properly a noun adjective, the neuter being referred to *medicamentum.*
Autumnus, *Cic.* um, *Varr.*

B.

Baculus and um, *Ovid.* Whence comes *bacillum* in *Cic.*
Balteus, *Sen.* um, *Varr.*
Barbitus, *masc.* in *Hor. fem.* in *Ovid.*
Barbitum, *Auson.*
Blitus and um, *Plin.*
Buxus and um, *Ovid.* See the genders, p. 20.

C.

Calamistrus, *Cic.* um, *Plaut.*
Calcaneus and um, *Virg.*
Callus and um, *Cic.* The neuter is most used.
Candelabrus for candelabrum, *Non.*
Capillus, *Cic.* um, *Plaut.*
Carbasus, *fem.* carbasum, *neuter.* See above, p. 128.
Carrus, *Hirt.* um, *Cæs.*
Catinus, *Hor.* um, *Varr.*

Catillus and um, diminut. *Plin.*
Currus, *Cic.* um, *Liv.*
Caseus, *Virg.* um, *Plaut.*
Census and um, *Cic.* Fortunæ censa peredit, *ut est apud Non.*
Cerasus and um, *Plin.* Carne & succo mora constant, cute et succo cerasi, lib. 15. c. 25. Though generally speaking the noun in US signifies the tree, and that in UM the fruit. See the genders above, p. 21.
Chirographus, which Vossius says is not Latin, we find in Quintilian. *Fulvius legato interroganti an in tabulis chirographus esset? Et vetus,* inquit, *Domine,* l. 6. c. 4.
Chirographum, *more usual*, *Cic.*
Cingulus, *Cic.* um, *Varr.*
Cingula is also used for a girth, according to Beda in his orthogr.
Et nova velocem cingula lædat equum, *Ovid.*
Clivus, *Cic.* um, *Cato.*
Clypeus, *Cic.* um, *Varr.*
Cœlus and um, *Arnob.* See above, p. 129.
Collus, *Varr.* um, *Cic.*
Commentarius and um, *Cic.*
Compitus, *Varr.* um, *Cic. Virg. Hor.*
Corius, *Plaut.* um, *Cic.*
Cornus, *masc.* and cornua, *neuter* for cornu, according to Priscian, book 6. The first is from Cicero himself, 2. *Nat. Deor. Cornibus iis qui ad nervos resonant in carnibus*, according to the best editions, as of Robert Stephen, Colinet, Santandré, Elzevir, Gruterus, &c. Which shews the little reason that Lambin had to doubt of this passage, as well as of a great many others which he wanted to correct. The second is of Ovid, *flexibile cornum*, in Prisc. and the third is commonly used.
Costus, *fem. Plin.* um, *Hor.* a kind of shrub.
Crocus, *Virg.* um. *Plin.*
Crystallus, *fem. Propert.* um, *Plin.*
Cubitus, *Cic.* um. *Plin.*
Culeus, *Cic.* um. *Varr.*

D.

Denarius, *Cic.* um, *Plaut.*
Dictamnus or dictamnum, *Stat.*
Dictamnum, *Virg.*
Dorsus, *Plaut.* um, *Virg.*

E.

Effectus, *Cic.* um, *Quintil.*
Eventus, *Cic.* eventum, *Lucret.* l. 1. *Eventum dici poterit quodcunque erit actum.*

OF NOUNS OF DIVERSE TERMINATIONS. 145

The plural *eventa* we frequently meet with in Cicero.

F.

Filus, which they place here, is hardly Latin; for the verse which they quote from Lucan,
Texerunt torti magica vertigine fili, lib. 6.
proves nothing at all; *torti fili* being a genitive governed by *vertigine*. And yet heretofore they said also *filus*, according to Arnobius, lib. 6. But *filum* is very common in Cicero and other writers; and no other ought to be used.

Fimus *and* um, *Plin.*
Forus, *Non. Isid. Charis.*
Forum, *Cic. & alii.*
Fretus, *Lucret.* um, *Virg.*
  Perangusto fretu divisa, Cic. 5. in Verr. apud Gell.

G.

Galerus *and* um, *Stat.* a little hat.
Gladius, *Cic.* um, *Plaut. Varr.*

H.

Hebenus *and* um, *Plin. Virg.*
Helleborus, masc. *Virg. Colum.*
Helleborum, *Plin.*
Hyssopus, *fem.* um, *Colum.*

I.

Incestus, us, *Cic.* incestum, i, *Cic.*
Intubus, *Lucil.* um, *Virg.*
Jugulus, *Lucan,* um, *Cic.*
Jocus *and* jocum, see above, p. 127.
Jussus, *whence comes the ablative* jussu, *Cic.*
Jussum, i, *idem.*

L.

Lacertus, *Cic.* um, *Acci.*
Lectus *and* um, *in the civil law.*
Libus, *Non.* libum, *Virg.*
Locus *and* locum, see p. 127.
Lucrus, *Plaut. apud Non.*
  Pergrandem lucrum facias.
Lucrum, *Cic. & alii.*
Lupinus *and* um, *Plin.* the former more usual.
Lupus, *Cic.* um, *Non. ex Varr.*

M.

Mandatus, *whence comes the ablative* mandatu, *often used in the civil law.*
Mandatum, i, *Cic. & alii.*
Medimnus, *Lucil.* um, *Cic.*
Modius, *Colum.* um, *Plin.*
Mundus *and* um, *women's ornaments.*
  Negavit quidam uxori mundum omne penumque, Lucil.

N.

Nardus, fem. *Hor.* nardum, N. *Plin.*
Nasus, *Cic.* um, *Lucil. Plaut.*
Nuntius, *Cic. Virg. & alii.*

Nuntium, *apud aliquos non acceptæ authoritatis*, says Nonius: because Nuntius is taken both for the messenger and the news. And though we find *lepidum nuntium* in Plautus, *nova nuntia referens* in Catullus, there is reason to mistrust the reading, for the best copies vary upon this article. The great *thesaurus* quotes also from Tibullus, lib. 3. eleg. 4. *Nuntium de cælo*, but we can find no such passage. We say also in the fem.

Nuntia, *a female messenger*, Virg. Plin. and even in Cicero in verse.

O.

Ocimus *and* um, *Sosipat.* the herb basilroyal. The neuter is more usual.
Oestrus, *Plin.* um; *Virg.* a gad-bee, a dun-fly.

P.

Pagus, *Cic.*
Pagum, *Sidon.* and other later writers.
Palatus, *Cic.* um, *Hor.*
Palus, *Plin.* um, *Varr.*
Pannus, *Hor.* um, *Non.*
Papyrus, i, fem. *and* papyrum, N. *Plin.*
  Papyrus nascitur in paludibus Ægypti.
Patibulus, *Licin.* um, *Cic.*
Peccatus, *Cic.* manifesto peccatu. *Verrin.* 2. as Gellius observes.
Peccatum, *Id. & alii*, more usual.
Penus, oris, N. *Hor.* Penus, us, masc. and fem. *Plaut.*
Penum, i, *Ter.* also hoc penu, indeclinable.
Pergamus, *Prol.* um, *Plin. Strabo.* See above, p. 128.
Pileus *and* um, *Plaut. Pers.*
Pistillus, *Nœv.* um, *Plaut.*
Portus, *Cels. Plin. Pallad.*
Portum, *Plin.*
Prætextus, us, *and* prætextum, i, *Sueton. Sen.*
Punctus *and* um, *Plin.* Omne tulit punctum, *Hor.*
Puteus, *Cic. Virg.* um, *Varr.*

Q.

Quasillus, *Fessus,* um, *Cic.*

R.

Rastrus, or rather, raster and um, see p. 131.
Reticulus, *Varr. Plin.*
Reticulum, *Hor. Plin.* The former comes from *retis* masc. and the latter from *rete* neuter.
Rictus, *Cic. & alii.*
Rictum, *Cic. apud Non.* Lucret. l. 6.

S.

Saguntus, *Strabo,* um. See the genders, p. 16.

Sagus, *Varr.* um, *Cic.*
Salus, *Enn.* undantem falum.
Salum, i, *Cic. et alii.*
Scutus, *Non.* Turpill. um, *Cæf. Cic. & alii.*
Senfus *and* um, *Cic.*
Seftertius *and* um, *Agricola.*
Sexus *and* um, *Sanctius.*
Sibilus, *Cic.* fibilum, *Seren. apud Non.* The plural *fibila* is likewife in Ovid, Lucan and others. But this noun is of its nature an adjective; hence Virgil has *ora fibila, colla fibila,* &c. fo that even when we fay *fibilus,* we fuppofe *fonus.*
Sinus, *Plaut.* um, *Virg.* a milk pail.
Sparus, *Virg. Sal. & alii.*
Sparum, *Lucil. Stat.* a fmall dart. But for a kind of fea fifh we fay only *fparus.*
Spicus *and* um, *according to Servius.* Spicum illuftre, *Cic. in Arat.* Tho' the neuter is not ufed in the plural, according to the fame grammarian Servius. But generally fpeaking they prefer the ufe of
Spica, æ, *Cic. & alii.*
Stadius, *Macrob.* um, *alii.*
Suggeftus, *Plin.* um, *Cic.*
Supparus, *Varr.* um, *Lucan.* a linen upper veil, any garment of linen.
Symbolus, *Plaut.* um, *Plin.* a fign, a mark. But
Symbola *fem.* in Plaut. and in Ter. is a different thing, *fymbolam dedit,* he has paid his club.

T.

Tartarus, *fee p.* 127.
Tergus, um, *Plaut. Cic.*
To thefe fome add *thefaurus & thefaurum,* grounding their opinion upon the following paffage of Plautus in his Aulularia, Act. 2. fc. 2.
  Credo ego, jam illum inaudiffe mibi effe thefaurum domi.
  Id inhiat, eâ affinitatem hanc obftinavit gratiâ.

But *id* is there for *ideo* or *propter id,* juft as in his Amphitryo he fays,
  Et id huc revorti, uti me purgarem tibi.
Thymus *and* um, *Plin. Colum.* either for the herb called thyme or time, or for little warts that grow upon the flefh, and which look like the leaves of thyme.
Tignus, *Ulp.* um, *Cæf.*
Tributus, *Gell. Plaut.*
Tributum, *Cic. & alii.*

V.

Vadus, *Sal. apud Non.*
Vadum, *Cæf.*
Vallus *and* um, *Cic.*
Vinaceus, *Varr.* vinaceum, *or rather* vinacea, orum, *Colum.*
Vifcus, *Cic.* um, *Plin.*
Uterus, *Virg.* um, *Plaut.*

To thefe we may add a great number of Greek nouns, which end in OS or in ON, as

Gargaros *and* on; tympanos *and* on, and the like.

US which drops U.

We meet with a great many nouns in US, which receive a different termination by dropping the U, as
Abacus, *Cic.* abax, *Colum.* For the *x,* and the *cs,* are the fame thing.
Arabus, *Virg.* Arabs, *Hor.*
Æthiopus, *Lucil.* Æthiops, *Plin.*
Cappadocus, *Colum.* Cappadox, *Cic.* and fuch like.

But in regard to thefe nouns the fecond is rather the original termination, while the other is only borrowed from the genitive of this. For Ἄραψ makes Ἄραβος, whence comes *Arabus,* and the reft in the fame manner.

Thus becaufe the Greeks fay γρὺψ, γρυπὸς, the Latins have thence formed *gryps, gryphys,* Virg. only afperating the fmooth confonant. And of this fame genitive, they have alfo formed *gryphus,* i.

THE SECOND LIST.

Of Nouns that follow different declensions, whether in one or in different numbers.

IN the preceding list we have shewn that nouns may frequently admit of different terminations, and among these we find some that frequently change their declension as well as their gender. But our intent here is to point out such as under one termination are differently declined.

Of these we may reckon five sorts, which shall be comprised under the following heads.

I.
Of the first and third declension.

AS, *as* Calchas, antis, *Virg.*
Calchas, æ, *Plaut.*
ES, Ganges, æ, *and* is, *Papin. Plin.*
Euphrates, æ, *and* is, *Lucan. Plin.*

And in the same manner, Thucydides, Mithridates *or* Mithradates; *for we meet with both in ancient monuments,* Orontes, Tigranes, Heraclides, Timachides, Æetes, Herodes, Euripides, *and others which may be seen in Prisc. lib.* 6.

MA. Those in MA, as we have already observed, p. 119. were heretofore of the first declension, whereas they are now of the third.
Dogma, æ, *Laber.*
Glaucoma, æ, *Plaut.*
Sacoma, æ, *Vitruv.*
Schema, æ, *Plaut.*

II.
Of the second and third declension.

ER, *as* cancer, cancri *and* canceris.
Canceris ut vertat metas se ad solstitiales,
   Lucret.
Where he is speaking of a heavenly constellation. Arnobius uses it in the same manner for a distemper.
Mulciber, mulciberi, *or* mulcibri, *and* mulciberis.
Mulciberis capti Mársque Venúsque dolí.
   Ovid.
Mulcibri is quoted in verse by Cicero, 2. *Tusc.* And *mulciberi* in Capella.
Sequester, sequestri, *Plaut. Virg.* sequestris, *Cic.*
EUS, *as* Perseus, Persei, *and* eos. See p. 119.

US. Glomus, glomi, *and* glomeris.
But a great many are mistaken in placing GIBBUS among this number; because it is true we say *gibbi*, but not *gibberis*, as they pretend, though R. Stephen has fallen into this mistake in his great thesaurus and in his dictionary. The passage he quotes from Juvenal, *Attritus gibbere naso* is not to be found; we read only in the 6th satyr.
Attritus galea mediisque in naribus ingens gibbus.

They are also mistaken in regard to GIBBER, of which they pretend to make *gibberis*. For this noun, whether it be an adjective or a substantive, is always of the second declension. *Gibberi spina leviter remissa,* Varr. *Gallinæ Africanæ variæ, grandes, gibberæ,* Id. *Gallinarum genus gibberum,* Plin. lib. 19. c. 26. But in the passage they quote out of the 8th book, chap. 45. there is only the nominative: *Syriacis (bobus) non sunt palearia, sed gibber in dorso;* from which they can infer nothing. This shews that these great thesaurus's and these dictionaries are not free from mistakes, even in the late editions, as we have elsewhere more than once observed.

Compounded of pater.

Those compounded of pater, which are all latinised from the Greek, follow the second declension; as
Antipater, antipatri, ὁ Ἀντίπατρος, υ.
Sosipater, tri, ὁ Σωσίπατρος, υ.

Those which are purely Latin, follow the third; as,

Diespiter, itris ; Marspiter, itris.
Semipater, atris. *Ad sanctum semipatrem.* In vet. carm.

III.
Of the second and fourth declensions

Angiportus, us, *Hor.*
 Flebis in solo levis angiportu.
Angiportus, i, *Cic. Catull. Ter.*
Arcus, us, *Hor.* more usual.
Arcus, i, *Varr. apud Non.*
Cibus, i, *heretofore of the fourth*, *Plaut.*
Colus, i, *and* us, *Charis. Prisc.*
Cornus, i, *and* us, *Stat.*
Cupressus, i, *Hor. Virg.*
Cupressus, us, *Colum.*
Domus, *see p.* 133.
Fagus, i, *and* us, *Virg.* For some read *fagus* for *fagos*, 2 Georg. v. 71. as we still find *umbrosæ fagus*, in Culice. Just as Scaliger insists upon our reading *aëriæ platanus*, in the very same work where others read *platani*.
Fastus, i, *and* us, *Hor. Claud. Varr. Colum. Qvid. Beda.* Though Servius condemns Lucan for saying.
 Nec meus Eudoxi vincetur fustibus annus.
We must own nevertheless that it is more usual in the second.
Ficus, fici, *and* ficus, *Voss.* signifying as well the tree, as its fruit. But to denote a distemper, it is only of the second, though Priscian says in plain terms, *Etiam hic ficus vitium corporis, quartæ est*, lib. 6. For which he is censured by L. Valla and by Ramus, because he proves it only by some verses of Martial which are of very uncertain authority. See the genders, p. 45.
Fructus, i, *Ter.* us, *Cic.*
Humus, i, *heretofore* us, *Non.*
Laurus, i, *Virg.* us, *Hor.* But Servius prefers the former.
Lectus, i, *heretofore* us, *Plaut.*
Ornatus, i, *Ter.* us, *Cic.*
Pannus, i, *heretofore* us, *Non.*
Pinus, i, *and* us, *Virg.*
Quercus, i, *and* us, *Cic.* Quercorum rami in terra jacent, *in sua Chorogr. apud Prisc.*
Somnus, i, *and* us, *Varr.* But the former is almost the only one now in use.
Sonus, i, *and* us, *Non.* The former more usual.
Succus, i, *always of the second declension.* Though Appul. has made it of the 4th, *Nutrimentis succuum*, &c.
Susurrus, i, *and* us. *The latter is in Appul.*

Ventus, i. *and* us, *Plaut.*
—— *Qui secundo ventu vectus est*, as Sosipate. and Charisius read it.
Versus, i, *and* us. *The latter more usual.* The former in Laberius.
 Versorum, non numerorum, numero studuimus.
Vulgus, i, *and* us, *according to Charis.*
Other nouns which are ranked in the same class as the preceding, but without foundation.

2. **Penus,** which Charisius and Cledonius will have to be of the second and fourth, is only of the fourth. What deceived them was the genitive *peni*, which comes from *penum* neuter.

5. *Specus*, likewise is never of the second; wherefore it would be an error to say *speci* or *speco*, though some grammarians have marked it thus.

2. *Sinus*, is indeed of the second and fourth, but in different meanings; for in the second it is taken for a milk pail, and in the fourth for the bosom, and metaphorically for the bosom or gulf of the sea.

1. *Centimanus*, which Priscian affirms to be of the fourth, the same as *manus*, is always of the second. He quotes from Horace
 Testis mearum centimanus Gyges Sententiarum notus.
Where *centimanus* is evidently in the nominative, and of course proves nothing.

3. *Sibilus*. He commits the same mistake in regard to this word, quoting from Sisenna, *Procul sibilus significare consuli cœpit.*

IV.
Of those that are of the third and fourth declension.

Acus, eris ; *and* acus, us, *Col.* chaff.
Penus, oris ; *and* penus, us, *whence comes* penu *in the ablative.*
Specus, oris ; *and* specus, us, *whence comes* specu *in the ablative.*

V.
Of those that are of the third and fifth declension.

Plebes (of which they have made *plebs*) gen. plebis, *Liv.* and plebei, *Varro, Tacitus.* Tribunus plebei, *Gell.* or plebi *by contraction*, according as H. Stephen reads it; just as we say *fami* for *famei* ; *pernicii* for *pernicii*, and such like, of which we have taken notice in the fifth declension, p. 124.

Quies,

Quies, etis, *Cic. & alii.*
Quies, ei, *Afran. & Næv. apud Prisc.*
Requies, ei, and *sometimes* etis, *Cic.* hence we find also *senectutis meæ requietem*, lib. de Senect. according to the old editions: *intervalla requietis*, 1. de fin. *ut tantum requietem bubeam*, ad Attic.
In like manner *quies*, *inquies*, and *requies*, were heretofore taken adjectively, and followed the third declension. *Jamque ejus mentem fortuna fecerat quietem*, Næv. apud Prisc. *Corpore & linguâ percitum & inquietem*, Sal. *Quod libet ut requies victu contentus abundet*, Virg. in Culice, as Scaliger reads it.

Whether there are any nouns of the first and fifth declension.

There are some who to these five sorts of nouns that follow different declensions, add another of those which are of the first and fifth, as *materia, æ,* and *materies, ei,* &c. But they change the termination in the nominative, and therefore belong to the preceding list; we have made mention of them, p. 138.

Of those which change declension in different numbers.

We have already observed, p. 126. that this difference of declension in different numbers was owing only to this, that the termination of the nominative had been formerly different: wherefore this also belongs to the preceding list.

Thus far may suffice for what concerns those nouns which are redundant either in the termination of the nominative or in the declension: we must now proceed to those which grammarians call defective either in regard to number, or case.

THE THIRD LIST.

Of those nouns which by grammarians are said to want the plural in sense.

We have already given some hints, p. 136. concerning these nouns in general, where we mentioned three or four different species of them. We shall now examine what further particulars may deserve our consideration upon this subject.

Of metals.

Grammarians observe indeed that metals have no plural, but they do not give us the reason, which is, as I apprehend, that every metal is generally considered not as a species containing several individuals under it, but as a whole, that has only different parts. Thus when in French we say *des fers*, it is to denote the chains, and not the metal called iron: in like manner in Latin, if we say *æra*, it is to signify the money or the instruments, and not the metal. Thus we find

——*Quid d'stent æra lupinis?* Hor.
Armati in numerum pulsarent æribus æra, Lucret.
The genitive *ærum equestrium*; the dative, *de æribus equestribus*; and the ablative *fundum æribus suis emptum*, are in Cato, as Priscian observes.

ELECTRUM, amber, which according to Isidorus is only a kind of gum, owing oozing from pines, that afterwards grows hard. This word is also taken for a mixture of gold and silver, whereof the fifth part was silver, according to Pliny. It has its plural in both these significations.

Inde fluunt lacrymæ, stillatáque sole rigescunt
De ramis electra novis, Ovid.
Vera minus flavo radiant electra metallo, Mart.
────── *In celsas surgunt electra columnas,* Claud.

ORICHALCA is in Vitruvius in the plural, as well as
STANNA.

Of the fruits of the earth.

The rule of grammarians is more erroneous in respect to this than to the other article; for as to the names of herbs, we may use them without any difficulty in the plural, and say *carduus, turicas, malvas,* and a great many more.

I own we do not find perhaps in this number *ador, anethum, cannabis, bissopus, piper, ruta, filigo,* and the like.

But we find FABÆ, Virg. FORNA, Appul. FRAGA, Virg. FRUMENTA, Virg. HORDEA, Virg. Though he was found fault with for the latter even in his life time, according to the testimony of Cledonius.

LUPINI, Virg.

We likewise meet with AVENÆ not only in Virg.
────── *Et steriles dominantur avenæ,* 1. Georg.
but also in prose in Tertullian; *fruticaverunt avenæ Praxeanæ.* Though in these several passages it is not taken for oats, but for a poor kind of seed, as spelt or cockleweed which Virgil calls *steriles,* because it produces nothing to signify.

Of liquids.

A great many liquids are without any sort of objection used in the plural.

CERÆ ────── *Pingues unguine ceras,* Virg. 3. Georg.
MELLA occurs often in Virg.
MULSA ────── *ut mulsa loquitur,* Ovid. It is also in S. Jerome. *Ep. ad Gaud.*
MUSTA, is also common in Ovid, Martial, and others. And it is properly a noun adjective; for as from ὄρχος comes *ortus* or *hortus;* so from μόσχος (which signifies whatever is young and fresh) they have made *mostum* or *mustum*; to signify *novum.* Hence we not only meet with *mustum vinum* in Cato, but also *mustam ætatem, mustam virginem* in Næv. according to Nonius. And *musta agna* in Prisc.

PICES. *Ideasque pices,* Virg.

VINA. *Tanquam levia quædam vina nihil valent in aqua,* &c. Cic. We meet also with *vina, vinorum,* and *vinis* in Pliny, who makes use even of the diminutive *villa,* for small wines; as Terence:
Edormiscam hoc villi.

In a word, Misus plainly declares in Charis. lib. 1. that we may elegantly and consistently with usage say, *mella et vina* when we desire to express them in their specie, as *Attica mella, Italica vina,* &c.

And therefore this rule of depriving liquids of the plural, cannot be always true.

THE FOURTH LIST.

Of those nouns which, as grammarians say, are not used in the plural, though we sometimes meet with examples to the contrary.

MASCULINES.

ADEPS. *Adipes tenuare,* Quint. *Detrahere,* Plin. *Adipes medicamentis apti,* Id. *Corporatura pecudis non adipibus obesa,* Colum.

AER. *Aëribus bonis,* Lucr. *Alternis,* Id. *Novisse oportet aëres locorum,* Vitr. which is borrowed of the Greeks, who say in the plur. περὶ ἀέρων, Hippocr.

ÆTHER in approved authors occurs only in the singular. But those who wrote in the times of the lower empire, have used this word, as well as
Aër,

OF NOUNS OF DIVERSE TERMINATIONS. 151

Aër, very differently, making them neuters in the plural. This was owing without any manner of doubt to their seeing in the accusative singular *aëra* and *aethera*, which is the Greek termination, and this made them believe it was a neuter plural.

Clausa diù referant credentibus aethera sæclis, Bede.
Aëra librantur, fluctuat Oceanus.
Orientius Illiber. Epist.

And in the hymn to the virgin attributed to Fortunatus, or to S. Gregory the Great.

Quem terra, pontus, aethera,
Colunt, &c.

ALVUS, *sapor ad eliciendos alvos*. Plin.
AUTUMNUS or AUTUMNUM.
————— *per inæquales autumnos*, Ovid.

CARCER, which Servius insists upon being always in the singular to signify a prison, and in the plural to signify a barrier or starting place at horse races, occurs also in the singular in this second signification (which Servius himself acknowledges in Virgil)

————*ruúntque effusi carcere currus*, Georg. 3.

And in the plural in the former signification, *plures carceres*, Sen. *Carcerum squaloribus premitur*. Jul. Firm.

CESTUS, with a simple *e*, signifies a marriage girdle, and must always be in the singular; but CÆSTUS, with *æ*, is taken for a thong of leather, having plummets of lead fastened to it, used in boxing, or wrestling, and is often in the plural.

CRUOR.————*Atros siccabat veste cruores.* Virg.

FIMUS is always singular, as Sosipater, Diomedes, and Phocas have observed. But

FUMUS is in the plural in Martial, *fumos*, lib. 2. *sumis*, lib. 3.

GENIUS. We find *genios* and *geniis* in Plautus, Censorinus, Festus and others.

JUBAR, without a plural, according to Sosipater, and Charisius.

LIMUS, according to the same Charis. according to Diomedes and Phocas.

MERIDIES, hence Ovid to express it in the plural has made use of a periphrasis.

Proveniant medii sic mihi sæpe dies, Amor. 1. el. 5.

METUS, *solve metus*, Virg. and this plural occurs also in Ovid, Seneca, Silius and others. I own indeed that perhaps we shall not meet with *metuum* nor *metibus*.

MUNDUS. *Innumerabiles esse mundos*, Cic. *Innumerabilitatémque mundorum*, Id. and such like. But signifying a woman's ornaments, it is never used but in the singular.

MUSCUS, *moss*, always singular according to Charis. Diom. and Prisc.

NEMO, *nobody*. But the word shews it sufficiently of its own nature, excluding not only plurality but unity.

PALLOR, always singular according to Charisius, though Lucretius has,

Quæ contage suâ palloribus omnia pingunt.

And Tacitus uses it in the same manner.

PULVIS. *Novemdiales dissipare pulveres*, Hor.

Though Charis. Diomed. Phocas, and Priscian mention it as a singular only.

ROS. *Rores* frequently occurs in Virg. Hor. Silius, and others. *Roribus* is in Colum. and in Pliny. But *rorum* or *rorium*, is not perhaps to be found.

SAL is current in the plural, even to signify salt, *carnem salibus aspersam*, Colum. *Emere sales*, in the writings of civilians.

SANGUIS, which the grammarians deprive of a plural, because, says Priscian, it would not signify more in this number than in the singular. And yet we meet with it among the Hebrews: *viri sanguinum; libera me de sanguinibus*, &c.

SILEX. *Validi silices:* Lucr. *Rigidi*, Ovid.

SITUS, is found in the plural to signify either situation, as *terrarum situs*; or filthiness, mouldiness.

————*Demptos Æsonis esse situs*, Ovid.

SOL and LUNA.

————*Visásque polo concurrere Lunas*,
Et geminos Soles mirari desinat orbis. Claud.

SOLES, is used by poets to signify either great heats, or the days. Juvenal has it even in the dative.

————*Ruptáque tandem*
Solibus effundit torpentis ad ostia ponti.

SOPOR, always singular according to Sosipater.

TIMOR————*Quas ille timorum*
Maximus haud urget lethi metus. Luc.

L 4

Hæc

—— *Hac dubios lethi precor ire timores.* Stat.

VIGOR, according to Charif.

VISCUS, masc. bird-lime, glue, has no plural; but *Viscus*, neuter, has *viscera*, bowels.

UNUS, ought to have no plural according to Phocas; but we find in Ter. *Ex unis geminas mihi conficies nuptias.* In Andr. *In unis ædibus*, in Eun. and in Cic. *Unis litteris unæ tabulæ: ab unis hostium copiis*, &c.

FEMININES.

ARENA, even in the opinion of Cæsar, in his books of analogy, as quoted by Gellius, was not used in the plural: and Fronton says the same. Yet Virgil has

—— *quàm multæ Zephyro turbentur arenæ.*

And Horace:

Tentabo & arentes arenas.

Propertius and Ovid speak in the same manner, the former using also *arenis*, as Seneca in his Medea. And this noun we also find in other authors. Though Ramus prefers Cæsar's opinion, and says we ought to leave the other number to the poets, as this word sufficiently expresses a multitude in the singular.

ADOREA, always singular, *fine corn*, like *ador*; hence it is taken for honour and glory, because it was a sign of wealth and grandeur to eat bread made of fine wheat.

Qui prædâ atque agro, adoreaque affecit populares suos. Plaut.

AVARITIA, and all other names of virtues and vices are deprived of their plural by the grammarians. And yet we read in Cic. *Nec enim omnes avaritias, si æquè avaritias esse dixerimus, sequitur etiam, ut æquas esse dicamus*, 4. de Fin.

BARBA. See the list of plurals lower down, p. 157.

BILIS, though Pliny has, *biles detrahere.*

CARITAS. *Imperatorum Caritates admodum raræ*, says Claud. Mamertinus in his thanksgiving to the emperor Julian.

CERVIX, for the hinder part of the neck is said to be always singular; and for pride or obstinacy it is plural. But this distinction, which has been remarked even by Servius, is without foundation, because, as Varro and Quintilian relate, Hortensius was the first that said *cervicem* in the singular (which must be understood of prose) and before his time, they always said *cervices*, in both significations, as indeed we find it constantly in this number, not only in Cato, but likewise in Cicero and others.

CONTAGIO. *Græciam cœvertit contagionibus malorum, quæ à Lacedæmoniis profecta manarunt latiùs*, Cic.

CULPA. *In hoc uno omnes inesse culpas*, Cic.

Palmas non culpas esse putabs meas, Auson.

CUTIBUS, is in Cælius Aurelianus and in Arnobius.

ELEGANTIA, has no plural, according to Charis. and Diomedes. So that if we were to believe them, it would not be right to say, *sermonis veneres & elegantias.*

ELOQUENTIA, according to the same author, has no plural. Which appears more reasonable than what they say of the preceding one.

FAMA is now very seldom used but in the singular. And yet Sallust made no difficulty to say, *Æqui boni famas petit*; and after his example Aruncius and Arnobius made use of it, but this example is not to be followed: hence it is that Seneca blames Aruncius for his affecting thus to make use of the most uncouth expressions that were to be found in Sallust.

FAMES, without a plural, according to Charisius and Phocas.

FIDES, signifying faith and loyalty. But for the strings of an instrument we say *fides, fidibus.*

FUGA. Though Tacitus says, *fugas & auxilia.* And Virgil,

Impediunt texúntque fugas. Æn. 5.

GALLA, a fruit called gall, or oak-apple.

GAZA, in Cicero, Livy, and in other writers of their time, is always singular. But those who wrote after them, as Lucan, Seneca, Justin, have also used it in the plural. In later ages they made it even a neuter plural; *gaza, gazorum*, in which, they are no more to be imitated, than when they say *feria, orum*, which we find in Corippus Gramm.

GLORIA. Though Cicero has *gloriæ dispares*; and Tacitus, *veteres gallorum glorias.* And Gellius, *has ille inanes cùm staret glorias.*

HALIC,

OF NOUNS OF DIVERSE TERMINATIONS.

HALEC, neuter, or HALEX, fem. if it be taken for a kind of fish, may have a plural, according to Vossius; if it be taken for a kind of brine or pickle, it has no plural, no more than a great many other names of liquids, as *lac, oleum, butyrum*, &c. concerning which see what has been said, p. 134, 150.

HARA. But we find *baras* in Varro; and *baræ* in Colum. an hog-sty, a goose-pen.

IMPURITIA, in Plaut. *tuas loqui impuritias nemo potest*.

INERTIA, according to Charisius.

INFAMIA, *si ad paupertatem admigrant infamiæ*, Plaut.

INIMICITIA, *nec me pœnitet mortales inimicitias, sempiternásque amicitias habere*, Cic.

INSANIA, according to Charisius, though Plautus has,
Larvæ hunc, atque intemperiæ, insaniæque agitant senem.

IRÆ, IRARUM, IRAS, current in Virgil, Ter. Livy.

JUSTITIÆ and JUSTITIAS in the sacred writings and ecclesiastic authors only.

LABES, ὄλισθος, without a plural, according to Charisius, Diom. and Phocas, though in Cicero we read, *Hunc tu quas conscientiæ labes in animo censes habuisse, quæ vulnera*. Which Arnobius has likewise imitated, *Quas labes flagitiorum*, lib. 4. Gellius and Symmachus have used it in the same manner.

LUCULENTIAS *verborum*, is also in Arnobius, lib. 3.

LUES. *Et confer alternas lues*, Prud. which you will not find perhaps in any classic author.

LUX, always singular when it signifies light, τὸ φῶς, says Charisius. But when it signifies time or a certain number of days, it is likewise used in the plural, as in Ovid, *Post septem luces*; in Horace, *Profestis lucibus & sacris*; and the like.

MOESTITIA, according to Charisius.

OBLIVIONES *lividas*; Hor. But it is much more usual to say *oblivia, orum*.

OLIVITAS, always singular in Varro; but in Colum. we read *Largissimis olivitatibus*, very plentiful harvests or crops of olives or oil.

PAUPERTATES, is in Varro. *Horum temporum divitias & illorum paupertates*, lib. 1. de vita pop. Rom.

PAX, always singular according to Charis. Diom. and Phocas, though in Plautus we read ——*pacibus perfectis*, in Pers. and in other passages he makes use of *paces*, which we find also in Lucret. Sallust and Horace, ep. 3. lib. 1.
Bella quis & paces longum diffundit in ævum.

For which reason Pliny, even according to Charisius himself, did not entertain the least doubt whether *pax* had a plural, but whether it made *pacum* or *pacium* in the genitive plural. *Pacium an pacum, lucium an lucum, dubitari etiam nunc ait Plinius*, says he. Where you may observe that the words *nunc* and *ait*, seem to indicate that Charisius wrote in Pliny's time, or a little after.

PERFIDIA: though we find in Plaut. *perfidias*.

PERNICIES, is in the plural in Arnobius, but this is not to be imitated.

PESTES and PESTILENTIAS, are not only in Tertullian, but moreover in Statius, Claudian, Gellius, Seneca and others, and even in Cic. Tusc. 2.
Perge, aude, nate, illacryma patris pestibus.

In regard to what Giffanius and some others have observed, that *pestis* was never taken for the distemper called the plague; the contrary appears from Columella, a most pure writer, who says somewhere *in morbis & pestibus*; and from this verse of Silius.
Et posuere avidæ mortis contagia pestes.

And from this passage of Seneca, *Non minores fuere pestes mortalium, quàm inundatio*, lib. 3. Nat. quæst.

PIGRITIA, without a plural, *Scipat*.

PITUITA. But Pliny uses it in the plural.

PLEBS, though in the code we read *plebes urbanæ*.

PROLIS; but Capella gives it *prolum* in the genitive plural; which Despauter has followed, though without authority.

PROSAPIA; yet Cato has, *veteres prosapiæ* in the plural. But Quintilian takes notice that it is obsolete even in the singular. *Ut obsoletæ vetustatis, universam ejus prosapiam dicere insulsum*. And Cicero has made an apology for using it: *fratres agnates-*

agnatósque appellare solemus, & eorum, ut utamur veteri verbo, prosapiam.

QUIETES *ferarum*, is in Lucret. to signify their dens; and *quietibus* in Cic. for the relaxations of the mind.

RABIES, according to Charisius and Diomedes.

SALUBRITATES, is in Censorinus, according to the MSS. *Quod in eo* (anno Chaldaico) *dicunt tempestates frugúmque proventus, ac sterilitates, item morbos salubritatésque provenire.* It is true that this word is not in some printed editions, but this is doubtless by reason of its having been omitted by those who thought it too modern; whereas they ought to have been no more surprized at it, says Vossius, than at *valetudines*, which is in the same author. Accordingly Scaliger made no difficulty to use it in his book *de emend. tempor.*

SALUTES, is found no where but in the sacred writings. *Magnificans salutes regis*, Psal. Though Marsilius Ficinus uses it without any scruple, as well as *salutibus*; but we should prefer the authority of Charisius, who says it wants the plural.

SANCTITAS, always singular, though we read *sanctitates* in Arnobius, as likewise a great many other nouns plural, which we ought not to imitate.

SANIES, corruption. SAPIENTIA. SEGNITIA. SITIS, always singular.

SOBOLES, which is commonly joined to these, we find in Cicero. *Censores populi, ævitates, soboles, familias, pecuniásque censento*, 3. *de leg. Sobolibus* is in Colum.

SOCORDIA, has no plural according to Sosipater and Diomed.

SORS, not only when it signifies the sacred oracles, but also when it stands for lot or destiny, occurs in the plural. *Dicendum igitur de sortibus: quid enim sors est?* &c. Cic.

SPES, which is placed here by the grammarians, we find every where in the plural, in Plautus, Terence, Cicero, Horace, Ovid, Quintilian, Pliny and others.

STERILITATES is in Censorinus. See *salubritates* a little higher.

STULTITIA has no plural according to Charisius. But since Plautus has said *insanias*, who can doubt but

with the same propriety he might have said STULTITIAS?

TABES, *hujus tabis*, sing.

TALIONES, and *talionum* in Gellius.

TELLURES may be said of different continents, as Corn. Gallus. *Uno tellures dividit amne duas.*

TERRA, to signify the whole earth, is always singular. But for different countries it has a plural; as when we say *orbis terrarum; loca terrarum ultima*, &c.

TUSSES, is used by Pliny several times.

VALETUDINES, in Censorinus, Tacitus, and Tertullian.

VECORDIA, always singular according to Charisius.

VELOCITAS, according to the same.

VIS, according to the same. But without mentioning *vires*, we meet also with *vis* in the plural in Lucretius, Sallust, and also in Varro, according to Probus, though this is not to be imitated. See p. 133.

VITA, which they rank in this class, is current in the plural in Virgil, Terence, Gellius, Appuleius, and others. And Gregory of Tours in his preface to the lives of the fathers, refutes this error by the authority of Pliny, *lib. 3. artis grammaticæ.*

NEUTERS.

ÆVUM, always singular according to Phocas; yet we meet with *ævis* several times in Ovid and in Pliny.

ALLIUM, though we read in Virgil, *Allia serpyllúmqua herbas contundit olentes.*

ALTUM——*tranquilla per alta,* Virg. which is not at all surprizing, because *altum* being an adjective, as it supposeth *mare* in the singular, so it refers to *maria* in the plural.

BARATHRUM, a gulf, a deep place; but is often taken for Hell.

CALLUM, ὁ τύλος, hardness of the skin by much labour.

COELUM, see p. 129.

COENUM, according to Diomedes and Phocas.

CROCUM, without a plural; according to Diomedes *crocus* has *croci*, hence we read in Ovid, *Ipsa crocos tenues*, 4. Fast.

FAS and NEFAS, though Lucilius said *Ob facta nefuntio*. For *nefas* is said for *nefans*, which should make *nefantia.*

FASCINUM.

FEL.

OF NOUNS OF DIVERSE TERMINATIONS.

FEL.
GAUDIUM.
Latonæ tacitum pertentant gaudia pectus, Virg.
GELU, according to Charisius.
GLUTEN.
HILUM.
INGENIUM, is placed here by Diom. But the plural is current in Cic. Ter. Quintil. and others.
JUBAR.
JUSTITIUM, the vacation, or time out of term.
LETHUM, death.
LUTUM. Though Nonius quotes *luta* and *limum* from Cic. And Caper *luta* from Cæsar.
MACELLUM, though the same Caper quotes from Memmius, *ista macellia*.
MARIA. See the declensions, p. 114.
MURMUR, without a plural, according to Charisius. But we find MURMURA in Virgil, Lucretius, Propertius, Ovid, and others.
NIHILUM.
NITRUM.
PASCHA, is ranked in this number by Aldus and by Verep. Yet Vossius thinks we may say *tria pascha*, or *tres paschas Christus celebravit*.
PEDA *duo*, may be said in the plural according to Priscian and Vossius, though Phocas affirms the contrary.
PELAGUS, neuter, has no plural according to Caper and Charisius; nevertheless as the Greeks say τὰ πελάγη, so Lucretius says *Pelagéque sonora*: and some where else, *At pélage multa*.
PENUM. For *penora* comes from *penus, oris*.
PUS, according to Diom.
SAL, neuter, has no plural: but the masculine has; thus *sales* in the civil law; *salibus* in Colum. See the genders, p. 29.
SCRUPULUM, without a plural according to Charis.
SENIUM, in the same manner.
SILER, SINAPI, SISER.
SOLUM, which is generally put here, has its plural, *sola terrarum ultima*, Cic. We meet with it also in Virgil, Martial, Statius, Ennius, Catullus, Lucretius, &c. And we find it in this number not only to denote the ground, but also the sole of the foot, or the sole of one's shoe.
SOLIA, *regum*, may be likewise said according to Vossius, since in Pliny we read, *soliis argenteis*, &c.
VER, always singular.
VIRUS, VISCUM.
VITRUM.
VULGUS, according to Charisius and Phocas, though Despauter pretends the contrary, alleding this passage from the third *de nat. Deor. Saturnum maxime colunt vulgi*. But the best copies have *colunt vulgo*, as Vossius observes.

※※※※※※※※※※※※※※※※※※※※※※※

THE FIFTH LIST.

Of those nouns which grammarians mention as wanting the singular, though we sometimes meet with instances to the contrary in authors.

MASCULINES.

ANNALES. This noun being an adjective of its nature, refers to *libri*, and of course may without any difficulty be used in the singular, referring it to *liber*, as Cic. Pliny, Gellius and others have done.
ANTES, *the fore ranks of vines*, masc. and always plural according to Charisius, Diomedes, and Phocas; and so Virgil has put it.

Jam canit extremos effætus vinitor antes.

Wherefore, though this noun comes from *ante*, as *postes* comes from *post*; yet we are not to infer that as *postis* is said, so we may say *antis* also: because we find indeed *postem* and *poste* in Cicero and other writers; but for *antis* we have no authority.

ARTUS

ARTUS in the singular is only for poets,
—*tunc artus palpitat omnis*, Lucan.

CÆLITES, always plural, according to Charifius; though we read *cælitem* in Tertull. *de Pallio*; and *cælite* in Ovid.

CANCELLI, always plural.

CANI. But this is a noun adjective, and fupposeth *capilli*.

CARCERES, for a barrier or starting place at races, though we read,
—*Cum carcere pronus uterque emicat*, Ovid.
Quafi fi quis ad Olympicum curfum venerit, et fteterit, et emittatur, impudentefque illos dicat effe qui currere cœperint, ipfe intra carcerem ftet. See CARCER in the preceding lift.

CASSES, *cum coffe victus*, Sen. in Agamemnon.

COELI. See p. 129.

FASCES. When it is taken for a badge of authority, it is always plural, because they carried twelve of them. But when it is taken for a faggot, or bundle of wood, we find *fafcem* in Cic. according to Charifius, *fafce* in Virg. &c.

FINES, for boundaries or limits.

FOCI, always plural in the fenfe in which Cic. has taken it, faying, *pro aris & focis pugnare*.

FORI, though Ennius faid, *multa foro ponens*, &c. as Defpauter gives it us after Ifidorus.

FRENI, always plural according to Charif. and Diomed. For we fay no longer *frenus*. But we find *frenum* in Virg. from whence comes alfo the plural *fræna*. See p. 130.

FURFURES, always plural, when it is taken for fcurf, dandruff; though Defpauter thought it to be alfo in the fingular in this fenfe in the following paffage of Serenus Sammonic. c. 15.
Additur excuffus niveâ fimilagine furfur.
where it is obvious that it fignifieth bran.

GABAMAS, is in Seneca, Claudian, and others.

GEMINI, plural, as the nature of the word fhews it, where we are to underftand *fratres*. And yet Plautus has *Geminus eft frater tuus*.

GRUMI, ἀ τῶν ὀρῶν λίθει, always plural according to Charifius. But Nonius quotes from Accius:
Quemcunque irftiteram grumum, aut præcifum jugum.

Grumus falis is in Pliny.

HORTI, taken for a park, or walks planted with trees, is always plural: for a garden it has its fingular. See Laur. Valla in his eleg. as alfo Erafmus in his paraphrafe on this author.

INDIGITES. *Jovem indigetem appellant*. Livy fpeaking of Æneas. See the declenfions, p. 79.

LARES; yet Charifius confeffes we may fay *lar*; and Plautus, Horace, Appuleius, and others have ufed it.

LEMURES, though we find *lemurem* in Appul. where he is fpeaking of the God of Socrates.

LENDES, for the nits of the head, κονίδες.
——*lendes deducis iniquas*, Seren.

LIBERI, children. And yet we find *liberi & parentis affectus* in Quintil. in *Decl.* and the fingular is ufed alfo in the civil law.

LOCI, in the plural, when we fay *loci argumentationum*, or *loci muliebres*, *ubi nafcendi initia confiftunt*, fays Varro.

LOCULI, generally plural, though we find *in loculum confcere*, in Varr.

LUDI, for public games, *Apollinares ludos*, fays Cicero.

LUMBI, is more ufual in the plural, though Martial has,
Cerca quæ patulo lucet ficedula lumbo.

MAJORES, anceftors; because in Latin, as well as in French, this word implies a multitude. And yet we find in Appul. *Major meus Socrates*.

MANES. But Appul. has *Deum manem vocant*. And the reafon is becaufe it is a noun adjective. For *Manis* fignified *good*, from whence comes alfo *immanis*. So that as with *fuperi* or *inferi* we underftand *Dii*, fo we are to underftand it alfo with *manes*: and in antient infcriptions it is generally expreffed DIIS MANIBUS.

NATALES, for extraction or birth, whether noble or mean. But to fignify a birth day, we fay

NATALIS, in the fingular.

NOMADES, and other like names of nations, are very unufual in the fingular. However as we have obferved GARAMAS in Sen. fo we find NOMAS in Martial.

PLERIQUE. But we read *plerus* in Cato, whence comes alfo *plera pars* in Pacuvius, and *plerum* in Sempr. Afcilin.

PRIMORES; but it fuppofeth *homines*, becaufe it is an adjective; hence Silius

SILIUS has *primori marte*. Tacitus, *primori in acie*; and Suet. *partem domus primorum*. Cic. *primoribus labris*, &c.

PROCERES; but in Juvenal, *Agnosco procerem*.

PUGILLARES. Yet we read in Ausonius, *bipatens pugillar expedit*. Which shews that the expression in the singular made use of by the antient interpreter, *postulans pugillarem*, is not unwarranted; for indeed this is a noun adjective, and supposeth *liber* or *libri*. Catullus has also in the plural *pugillaria*, where we are to understand *schedia*, or some such word.

QUINQUATRUS, the feast of Minerva. We find also *Quinquatria Minervæ*, in Suetonius. And these two nouns have *quinquatrium* and *quinquatribus* in the genitive and dative. But *quinquatriæ*, which we find in Diomedes, and *quinquatres* in Charisius and Priscian, are not in use.

QUIRITES. It is true we find *quiritis* and *quiritem* in Horace, but this should not be easily imitated in prose.

SALES. See *sal* in the preceding list p. 155.

SENTES, *nos sentem canis appellamus*, Colum. but this is very rare.

SINGULI, which Charisius, Priscian, Lambinus, and others affirm to be always plural, is in Plautus in the singular.

Atat, sirgulum vestigium video. according to Nonius, who in corroboration of his opinion, produces from two different passages of Varro; *semel unum singulum esse*.

SPIRITUS, to signify courage, and pride, is generally plural, as *res gestæ credo meæ, me nimis extulerunt, & mihi nescio quos spiritus attulerunt*, Cic. And yet in Cicero we read also, *Quem hominem? quâ irâ? quo spiritu?*

VEPRES. Though Ovid has, *vepre latens*. And Colum. *hunc veprem interimi non posse*. Whereby we may defend the old interpreter of Isaiah, who makes use of *veprem* and *spinam*.

FEMININES.

ÆDES, in the singular, says Servius, signifies a temple, in the plural a house. And this is the opinion of Charisius and Diomedes. Yet Plautus has

—*Ædis nobis area est, anceps sum ego*.

The same we find in Quintus Curtius and others.

ALPES. But *Alpem* is in Ovid, Lucan, and Juvenal. *Alpis* is in Livy; and *Alpe* in Claudian.

AMBAGE is in Ovid, Tacitus, Seneca, Claudian, and Prudentius.

ANGUSTIÆ. *Angustia loci*, Plin. *Angustia conclusæ orationis*, Cic.

ANTÆ, the posts or cheeks of the door: it is plural, because there are always two; yet Vitruvius uses it in the singular, *anta fixa*, and Vossius believes we may very well say, *dextram vel sinistram antam*.

ANTIÆ, the forelocks, women's towers or frowzes. But it is an adjective and supposeth *comæ*.

ARGUTIÆ. But in Appul. we find *Argutia Nilotici calami*. Gellius has made use of it in the singular, and even formed thereof the diminutive *argutiola*.

BALNEÆ, public baths. See p. 131.

BARBÆ, which Servius and Caper pretend is used in the plural, for the beard of brute animals, and in the singular for that of man, occurs in both senses in both numbers.

Stiriaque impexis induruit horrida barbis, Virg. 3. Georg.

Utque lupi barbam variæ cum dente colubræ, Hor.

BIGÆ, TRIGÆ, QUADRIGÆ, &c. But *quadriga* is in Valerius Maximus and in Pliny. *Triga*, in the civil law. *Unius bigæ* in Suetonius. Seneca and others have expressed themselves in the same manner. It is true that in Cicero's time this was not current in prose, which made Varro deny that we are allowed to say *biga* or *quadriga*. And Cæsar in Gellius says that *quadrigæ* has no singular. Yet we are informed by this very author, that Varro had made use of *quadrigam* in verse, which must be excused as a poetic licence.

BLANDITIÆ: though *blanditia* is not only in Plautus, Propertius, and in the rhetor Rutilius, but also in Cicero, *blanditia popularis*, pro Planc. *In cive excelso atque homine populari, blanditiam, ostentationem*, 4. de Rep.

CAULÆ, always plural.

CEREMONIÆ. But Cicero has *Ceremoniam polluere*, pro Sext. Rosc. and elsewhere. This word occurs also in the singular in Cæsar, Tacitus, Suetonius, and Gellius, who expressly observe that the ancients spoke in this manner.

CLITELLÆ, a pannel, or pack-saddle.

COMPEDES. Nevertheless we find *compede* in the ablative in Hor. Juven. Mart. and Colum.

COPIÆ, to signify troops or forces; though *copia* in this sense is in Plautus, Virgil, and Cæsar.

CRATES, *a hurdle, sub cratim supponi.* Plaut.

CUNÆ, always plural, a cradle; Whence also comes *Cunabula, orum.*

DAPES. But *daps, dapis, dapem,* and *dape* are in Cato. Livy has *ad ministerium dapemque adhibitis.* And Ovid.

Nunc dape, nunc posito mensæ nituere Lyæo.

DECIMÆ, where we must always understand *partes.* Though *decimam vovere* is in Cicero, and *decimam partem* in Plautus.

DELICIÆ. But the singular *delicia* and its genitive *deliciæ* are found in ancient writers. *Mea voluptas, mea delicia.* Plaut. Appul. uses also *delicies;* but it was a very common thing for the nouns in *a* to terminate also in *es: luxuria, luxuries; materia, materies,* &c. See the first list p. 131.

DIRÆ, subaud. *imprecationes* or *execrationes,* and therefore is an adjective.

DIVITIÆ, always plural.

EPULÆ. But in the singul. we say *epulum.* See p. 131.

ESQUILIÆ or EXQUILIÆ, a Roman mount so called from the word *excubiæ;* because it was the place where King Tullus ordered a guard to be kept.

EUMENIDES. But *Eumenis* is in Statius.

EXCUBIÆ. EXEQUIÆ.

EXUVIÆ, spoils taken from the enemy. It comes from *exuo,* for which reason it is taken for the cast skin of a snake.

FACETIÆ. But in Gellius we read *facetia sermonis.* And in Appul. *facetiæ habere.*

FALÆ, a high tower made of timber, to shoot or throw darts out of. They call them *falas,* because there was always a number of them. But Vossius thinks it is very likely they would have said *falam,* if there had been but one, though there is no authority for it.

FALERÆ, or PHALERÆ.

FASCES, for the bundles of rods, carried before the Roman magistrates, always plural, according to Charisius, who mentions nevertheless that Cicero hath, *fuscem unum si nactus esset.*

FAUCES. Yet in Ovid's *Ibis* we read ——*perstricta fauce Poëtæ.*

And in Phædrus, *fauce improba.*

FERIÆ, always plural, according to Charif. Diomed. and Phocas, and also according to Gellius; though in the ecclesiastic acceptation it is frequently used in the singular; which ought not however to be imitated in any other kind of writing.

FIDIBUS canere, is very usual. But in verse we meet also with the singular.

Cedit clara fides Cyllenia, Cic. in Arat.

Persius, Horace, Ovid, have used it in the same manner.

FORES. But in the singular is not only used by comic writers and other poets, but also by Cicero. *Aperuit forem scalarum,* pro Cornelio Balbo. Which is quoted even by the ancient interpreter of Horace, on the second sat. of the first book.

FORTUNÆ, to denote one's fortune or estate, is always plural according to Charisius and Diomedes: but *fortuna* in the singular signifies *chance* or *fortune.*

FRUGES, the fruits of the earth.

GENÆ, and yet we meet with the singular in several passages in Pliny.

GERRÆ, trifles or toys.

GINGIVÆ, gums. Though Catullus has,

——*defricare gingivam.*

GRATES, χάριτες*, the graces,* plural because there are many.

GROSSI, generally plural; yet the singular is in Pliny and in Macr.

HABENA, is in the same author, as also in Virgil.

——*Ille actus habena.*

IDUS, always plural, *the ides of the month.*

ILLECEBRÆ. *Illecebra* is not only in Plautus, but likewise in Cic. *Juventutis illecebra.* In 1 Catil. *Maxima est illecebra peccandi,* pro Mil.

INDUCIÆ, though the ancients according to Gellius, have sometimes used it in the singular.   IN-

INEPTIÆ, more frequently plural, but sometimes used in the singular.
Ego illius ferre possum ineptias. Ter. in Eun.
——*Video ego tuam ineptiam.* Ter. in Adelph.
Ineptia stultitiáque adeo & temeritas. Plaut. in Merc.
Prudentius has used it in the same manner.

INFERIÆ, *offerings or sacrifices to the infernal gods for the dead.* This is manifestly a noun adjective, and supposeth *res*, which they called INFERIÆ, *quia inferebantur.* Here they had also *inferium vinum,* as when they said, *macte hocce vino inferio esto;* when they offered nothing but wine, which they called also CALPAR, a word which according to Festus and Varro, properly signified the vessel, and was afterwards taken for the wine taken out of the vessel for sacrifice.

INIMICITIÆ. But we read in Cicero; *parvam inimicitiæ culpam,* pro Rege Dejotaro. *Inimicitiam hominum.* 2. Catilin. *Odium, inimicitia, discordia.* 4. Tusc. &c. Ennius and Pacuvius have used it in the same manner.

INSIDIÆ, an ambuscade.

KALENDÆ, the calends, that is the first day of the month.

LACTES is ranked among the plural and feminine nouns by Diomedes. Priscian also allows it to be of this gender, but says that the singular is *hæc lactis;* which he proves by the authority of Titinnius, who said *lactis anguina,* as he quotes from Pomponius in the plural, *per lactes tuas.* And Vossius is for having this to be always a noun feminine, contrary to the opinion of Scioppius in his annotations. For with regard to the passage which they quote out of Probus's universals, we may affirm it to be of dubious authority, because in one place he says *bi lactes,* and lower down *bæ lactes;* nor is it to be found in every edition, witness that of Ascensius; besides he produces no authority for it, and Priscian has two in his favour, to which we might join this passage of Pliny, *ab hoc ventriculo lactis per quas labitur cibus.*

LATEBRÆ. Though Cicero has, *ne quæratur latebra perjurio.*

LENDES, always masculine and plural, according to Diomed. and Charis.

LITERÆ, for an epistle or letter sent to a friend. Though we meet with it also in the singular in this sense, and particularly among the poets.
Quam legis à rapta Briseide litera venit, Ovid.

MANUBIÆ, spoils taken from the enemy: it comes from *manus,* the hand.

MINÆ, for menaces, or for battlements, is plural: but for a kind of coin called *Mina* or *Mna,* it is singular; as also for a breast or teat without milk, so called according to Festus, *quia minor facta;* or for a sheep that has no wool on its belly, according to Varro de R. R. Heretofore it was used in this number also for *menaces,* if the following passage be properly restored by Joseph Scaliger. *Minas singulariter dici pro eo quod pluraliter dicitur, Curiatius autor est. Item M. Cato in suasione Minâ cogi nullâ potuit.*

MINUTIÆ, more usual in the plural. Though we meet also with *minutia* in Seneca, and with *minutiem* in Appul.

NÆNIÆ. But Varro, Plautus, Festus, Quintilian, and others, have used it in the singular.

NARES, according to Diomedes. But the genitive singular is in Horace, *Emunctæ naris.* The ablative in Claudian.
——*tenerâ venantem nare molossi.*
We meet also with the nominative,
——*Et lati rictus & panda loquenti Naris erat,* Ovid.
But *Nar* is the name of a river and masculine in later writers.
——*Et Nar vitiatus odoro Sulfure,* Ovid.
Whereas Cic. made it a neuter. See the genders p. 14.

NONÆ, NUGÆ.

NUNDINÆ. But in the singular we say *Nundinum,* as Nonius shews.

NUPTIÆ.

OPERÆ, taken for persons. But we read it also in the singular in this signification.
——*Accedes opera agro nona Sabino* Hor. sat. 2. 7. ult.
As on the contrary we meet with it in the plural, though taken for work, *Qui operas in scriptura pro magistro dat.* Cic. One that has the business of a public place, particularly in the matter of the Customs.

OPES,

OPES, for riches: but for power, it is used in the singular. *Non opis est nostra.* Virg. it is not in our power. *Dives opis natura suæ.* Horat. Where *opis suæ* is not for *opum suarum*, as some have pretended to understand it, but rather to signify power; all that Horace meant in this verse being, that nature is rich within herself, and able to do every thing.

PALEÆ and PALEA. It is pretended that the former is said of chaff or straw, and the latter of the wattles or gills under a cock's neck. But in Colum. we find it also in this sense, *paleæ ex rutilo rubicantes*; and Horace has it in the singular in the other, *hornam paleam*, to signify this year's straw, book 1. sat. 6. Virgil has made use of the genitive.

Necquicquam pingues paleæ teret area culmos, Georg. 1.

Which Servius has presumed to censure, as being said contrary to the rules of the art; but he never considered that Cicero has indiscriminately said, *auri navem everlat an paleæ*, in Parad. and *paliarum navem evertit*, 4. de fin.

PARTES, to signify parties or factions.

PLAGÆ, for wide nets, or the arming cords of a net.

PRÆSTIGIÆ, arum; though in Quintilian we read, *hujus præstigiæ*.

PRECES, according to Charisius and Diomedes, but the ablative singular is in Plaut. Hor. Ovid, Pers. Seneca. And even in Cicero, *si prece utamur*. The dative is in Tertull. *Nibil est preci loci relictum.* The accusative in Plautus, *nunc te oro per precem.* The nominative was *precis*, or by syncope *prex*: παρακλησις, *obsecratio prex*, Gloss. Cyrill.

PRIMITIÆ, but it is an adjective and supposeth *partes*.

QUADRIGÆ, see BIGÆ, p. 157.

QUISQUILIÆ, the sweepings of an house, the chats and whitlings of wood, all things that are of no value. *Quisquilias seditionis Clodianæ*, Cicero. Nevius, in Festus, has used it in the singular.

RELIQUIÆ; but it is of its own nature an adjective.

RETES. See nouns of different termination, p. 140.

SALEBRÆ; but it has its singular, *Hæret in salebis*, Cic.

SALINÆ: but it is an adjective, and supposeth TABERNÆ, just as we understand *vas*, when we say SALINUM, a salt-cellar.

SARCINÆ. Yet Plautus has, *sarcinam imponam seni.* And Propertius, *sarcina fida*, in the same manner as Ovid, *sarcina magna.*

SCALÆ, more usual in the plural, though in the civil law we read it also in the singular.

SCOPÆ (*a broom*) is plural, because it is composed of different small pieces. Charisius however acknowledges that SCOPA is also used, though Vossius does not think it is to be found in any pure author, but pretends that the following passage of Suetonius in the life of Nero, *alterius collo & scopa deligata*, is corrupted, and that we ought to read *scopera*, as Politian had observed. Indeed the diminutive *scopula* is in Colum. and thence also comes the name of the herb called *scopa regia*, in Pliny and others.

SUPPETIÆ.

TENEBRÆ. Though Lampridius has, *repentina caligo ac tenebra in Circo Cal. Jan. oborta.* In Commodo.

TRICÆ, any let or impediment, trifles, fooleries. The same as APINÆ, small nuts, trifles, gewgaws.

Sunt apinæ, tricæque & si quid vilius istis, Mart.

But *Apina* and *Trica* in the singular, are the names of towns in Apulia.

VALVÆ, folding doors.

VIRES, always plural, according to Charisius, though there is a greater probability of its coming from the singular *vis*, which formerly made *viris* in the genitive, the same as *sus*, *suris*, whence comes *surire*; or at least that they said also *hæc virit*, whence they formed *vis*. See p. 134.

To these we may add the names of towns, as *Athenæ*, *Micenæ*, though, as Priscian observes, we find some of those in the singular. For the Latins said *Cyrenas* and *Cyrenen*; *Thebas* and *Theben*, &c. See what has been mentioned concerning these plurals when we were treating of the genders, p. 24.

NEUTERS.

ÆSTIVA. HYBERNA. STATIVA: but they are properly adjectives.

ARMA, arms.

AVIA.

NOUNS DEFECTIVE IN THE SINGULAR.

AVIA. ἄπολα. But it is an adjective the same as *invia*, *pervia*, *devia*. Hence Plautus hath also *avius locus*. Lucretius.

Avius à vera longè ratione vagaris.

And others the same.

BATUALIA. See *Palaria* lower down.

BONA, for property and wealth.

BREVIA, for fords, shelves, or shallow places.

CASTRA, *orum*, signifying a camp or a fort, is always plural according to Charisius and Phocas. And the reason hereof is, because it is called, *quasi conjunctio casarum*, so that it properly signifies multitude: though Servius quotes out of Plautus, *castrum Pœnorum*, and though the diminutive *castellum* is in use. But in the Æneid, book 6th,

Pometios castrúmque Inui.

Castrum is the name of a town, as Servius takes notice, where the god Pan was worshipped; called *Inuus*, says he, *ab ineundo.* And this town is not *Corneto*, as Erithreus imagined, this last place being on the sea coast of S. Peter's patrimony. Whereas this town was in the antient *Latium*, on the coast of the *Rutuli*, as Cluverius observes.

CETE, κήτη. We say also *cetus*, whence comes the genitive *ceti.*

COMITIA, to denote the meetings of the people. But to signify the place where they meet, we say *Comitium*. Cic. Plaut. Ascon.

COMPITA. Though the antients said likewise *compitum*, and also *compitus*, a cross-way, or street.

CREPUNDIA, children's play-things.

CUNABULA, a child's cradle, the clothes with which the child was tucked in the cradle, and metaphorically childhood.

DIARIA, according to Charisius, because they used to give the slaves several days provision or allowance, all at once. But if they wanted to express the allowance of one day, Vossius thinks they might have said for instance; *hodie servo diarium non dedit*.

DONARIA, for gifts and presents offered to the gods: but for the places where these gifts were received, we find also *donarium*, as Servius observes; and this word is taken improperly for the whole temple, according to Papias.

EXTA, the entrails.

FLABRA, to signify the winds in Virg. 2. Georg. Where Servius remarks, that it is always plural; but we meet also with *flabrum* in Papias.

FRAGA, strawberries. It is always plural, not only in Virgil and the rest of the poets, but also in Pliny. Yet as in all these passages the sense requires this number, as they are speaking then in the plural, one would think, says Vossius, that we might say in the singular, *hoc fragum majus est isto*; though there is no authority for it. But in familiar subjects, as this author observes, the want of authority is no proof that such a word cannot be said nor even be introduced into a language, because all that is allowed to be good language in familiar conversation is not always committed to writing, and those who may perhaps have wrote concerning it, are not all come down to us.

GESA or GÆSA, a kind of heavy dart or javelin, *Virg. Liv.* Yet we read *gesum* in Festus, and in Papias.

JUGA. But *jugum* we find in Cæsar, Virgil, Propertius, Ovid, Statius, and others.

JUGERA. But in Tibullus we read *jugere pascat ovem*, which should come from the nominative *juger*, or *jugus, eris*, according to Priscian, though very rare in the singular: as on the contrary *jugerum* is more rare in the plural, though we read *jugeris* in the ablative plural in Varr. See p. 132.

ILIA. But we say also ILE, the flank where the small guts are, Pliny, Servius.

JUSTA; but it is an adjective, and supposeth *funera*.

LAMENTA; though *lamentum* is used by Papias.

LAUTIA, *Liv.* the presents which the Romans sent to foreign ambassadors.

LICIA. But *licium* is made use of, were it only in the formula of finding stolen goods, *per lancem liciúmque conceptis:* when the person who had any thing stolen from him, went to look

look for it at another's house with a bason and a girdle of hemp or flax; for the theft thus discovered was called *conceptum furtum lance ac licio*. Whence also comes *actio concepti*, because an action lay good against the person in whose house they found the goods they had lost.

LUMINA. But it is taken in the singular both for the eye——*Cui lumen ademptum*, Virg. and for the day; *si te secundo lumine offendero*. Enn. the day following.

LUSTRA, in the plural signifies a bawdy house or stews, or a den whither wild beasts retire to. But *lustrum* denotes the space of five years, when the citizens were taken account of, and the city purified, whence comes *lustrare*.

MAGALIA and MAPALIA, small cottages, though the latter is in the singular in Valerius Flaccus.

——*Cœit è sparso concita mapali
Agrestium manu.*

MOENIA.

NUTRITIA, *orum*, the recompence given to a nurse. But it is evidently an adjective.

OBLIVIA, for oblivion——*Et longa oblivia potant*, Virg. Though Tacitus uses it also in the singular even in this sense; *silentio, deinde oblivio transmisit*.

OLIMPIA, PYTHIA, and the like, are real nouns adjective, where we are to understand *certamina*.

ORGIA, subaud. *festa*, the mystic rites of the Bacchanal revels.

PALARIA. The place where the soldiers were exercised, according to Scaliger, or rather the exercise itself, according to Charisius. And therefore it is an adjective, which supposeth either *loca*, or *exercitamenta*. In the same manner as BATUALIA: but with this difference, that BATUALIA (*quæ vulgo batalia*, says Adamantius in Cassiodorus) was a combat between two; and *Palaria* was the exercise of a single soldier round a pole fixed in the ground, which they called *palum*.

PARENTALIA; but it is an adjective, and supposeth *opera*, or the like. Hence S. Cyprian has used it in the singular, *parentalis labes*, in his treatise *de lapsis*. We find also *parentales umbræ*, in Ovid.

PARAPHERNA, Ulpian. All things the woman bringeth her husband, beside her dowry, παρὰ φέρνην, *præter dotem*.

PASCUA, *orum*. But we read *viride pascuum*, in Varro; *Ager sine pascuo*, in Columella. Instead of which they used also to say *pascua, æ*, in the singular, as we find it in old authors, and those of later ages, Tertullian, Minucius Felix, and others.

PRÆBIA, or PROHIBIA, Varro, a preservative against witchcraft.

PRÆCORDIA, always plural, though in the old glossaries we read, *hoc præcordium*.

RAPACIA, or RAPICIA, the tender leaves of rapes.

REPOTIA, a banquet which they used to make the day after marriage.

ROSTRA, *the place of common pleas at Rome*, always plural, because there was a pulpit set in it, trimmed with stems or forefronts of the ships taken from the *Antiates*, and therefore this word always expresses a plurality.

SERTA, *orum*, a chaplet. But this is a noun adjective, and we say not only *sertum* and *serta*, as Servius observes, but also *sertos flores, sertas coronas*.

SPECTACULA, θεωρίας : but *spectaculum* is in Pliny.

SPOLIA. And yet we read *spolium* in Virgil.

SUBSELLIA, always plural, speaking of the benches or seats in the theatre, because there were several. Yet Plautus has, *imi subsellii virum*.

TEMPORA, the temples. But the singular is in Virg.

——*it hasta Tago per tempus utrumque.*

It is also in Catullus and in Lucretius.

VADA, a ford or shallow place in a river. But *vadum* is in Sallust: *vado transire*, in Cæsar and in Livy; Terence uses also in a metaphorical sense, *res est in vado*, the business is safe, or out of danger.

VERBERA: but in the singular we meet with the genitive *verberis*, and with the ablative *verbere*. See the Genders, p. 33.

VIN-

NOUNS DEFECTIVE IN THE SINGULAR.

VINACEA, taken substantively for the kernels or husks of grapes, or for grape-stones, is always plural; taking it adjectively we say, *acinum vinaceum*, &c.

VISCERA, see p. 169.

UTENSILIA. Though Varro has *utensile*.

ZIZANIA, *orum*, but it hardly occurs any where except in the Fathers and in the sacred writings.

To these we may join the names of cities, *Susa*; of islands, *Cythera*; of countries, *Bactra*; of mountains, *Acroceraunia*, that have no singular, when they are thus used in the plural.

We may add also the names of festivals, as *Bacchanalia*, *Cerealia*, where we are to understand *festa*. Which shews that they are adjectives, and therefore may be used in the sing. as Macrob. acknowledges, by expressing the substantive, *Bacchanale festum*, &c. And these nouns were heretofore of two declensions. See p. 118.

OBSERVATIONS

On indeclinable nouns.

HAVING given a list of those nouns which grammarians reckon defective in either number, we must also take notice of those which are either indeclinable (that is, which have only the termination of the nominative) or are used only in some cases. Of the latter I shall subjoin a particular list, but first I must mention a word or two concerning the former.

INDECLINABLES are of two sorts: for there are some which without any variation are used nevertheless with one ending for every case; as *nequam, tot, totidem, quot, quotquot, aliquot, quotcunque,* which are adjectives.

As all nouns ending in I, *gummi, sinapi,* &c. which are substantives and of the neuter gender. Those in U, *veru, cornu,* &c. except that heretofore they formed the genitive in US, as we shall observe hereafter.

As all numeral nouns to an hundred, and even *mille,* which is never an adjective, as we shall shew when we come to treat of sesterces.

As the names of letters, *alpha, beta.*

As Hebrew and barbarous names, *Adam, Noë, Cham, Abraham,* &c. Though we sometimes say *Adæ, Abrahæ,* which is owing to the Latin terminations we give them, *Adas, Abrahas,* &c.

There are other indeclinables which are not used in every case, but only in some, as *fas, nefas, farra, mella, cete, mele, tempe,* which in the plural are never used but in three cases. The nom. *hoc fas est;* the voc. *ô fas et æquum:* the accusat. *per fas et nefas.*

Here we may also place *Astu,* taken for Athens itself, though Priscian ranks it among the other indeclinables like *cornu:* but Vossius says there is very little probability of its being found in the dative or in the ablative. Terence has made use of the accusative. *An in Astu venit?* that is to the city of Athens, according to Donatus.

Hereto we may join *git,* a kind of small grain; *frit,* the little grain at the top of the ear of corn; and *hir,* the hollow of the hand, though Priscian gives it *hiris.*

We may also add *expes,* which has only the nominative and the vocative.

And we might likewise add *glos* and *instar,* with some others which we refer to the following list, because heretofore the ancients declined them.

THE

THE SIXTH LIST.

Of nouns that have not all their cases.

We may consider five sorts of nouns that have not all their cases: some have but one, others two, others three, others four, and others five.

Of those that have but one case, some have only the genitive, others only the accusative, and others only the ablative. I shall reduce them all to an alphabetical order, to render them more easy to find upon occasion, and I shall mention what cases of each are in use.

AMBAGE has only the ablative singular, as we have above observed. In the plural we say, *ambages, ambagibus.* See the list of the plural feminines, p. 157.

ASTUS, *craft,* cunning, is in the nominative singular in Silius. *Non ars aut astus belli,* &c. The ablative is in Terence. *Quod si astu rem tractaverit.* That is, *astute,* according to Donatus: and this word comes from the Greek Ἄςυ, *urbs,* because, says Festus, those who live in towns, become more cunning and knavish than other people.

CHAOS hath its ablative in Virg. 4. Georg.

Atque Chao densos divûm numerabat amores.

That is, *à chaó narrabat creḃros amores deorum,* says Servius.

When it is taken for the name of a divinity, it hath *Chaon,* in the accusative, as in Ovid.

Et noctem noctisque deos, Erebúmque Chaónque.
Convocat.

CRATE, is an ablative. Nor do I think that the nominative singular is to be found in Latin authors, though it be marked in dictionaries. We must also take notice that Robert Stephen's dictionary quotes from Pliny, *dentata crates,* whereas in Pliny it is in the plural. *Cratésque dentatas supertrahunt,* lib. 18. c. 18. just as he quotes also from Juvenal *rara crates,* whereas in this poet it is in the ablative.

Sicci terga suis rarâ pendentia crate, Sat. 11.

And it is proper to observe that there are a great many such mistakes in this dictionary, a work in other respects of great merit, that may easily lead us astray, unless we are upon our guard. Which is owing without doubt either to this, that R. Stephen could not fully examine what cases were unusual in this language; or to this, that in regard to the examples he quotes, perhaps he believed that the great thesaurus, where the passages are at full length, would sufficiently shew in what manner and in what case they were applied.

The accusative *cratim* we find often in Plautus: and Charisius gives it also *cratem.* But the plural *crates,* is more common, *an hurdle, a barrow.* Thence also comes *craticula,* a grid-iron.

CUJUSMODI, EJUSMODI, HUJUSMODI, are hardly ever met with but in the genitive in the compound word. Separately we say, *quis modus, is modus, hic modus;* and the same in the other cases.

CUIMODI, is more extraordinary, and more remote from its simple than the rest. For it is a genitive; hence in Cicero there was *cuicuimodi* for *cujuscujusmodi,* or (*cujuscunquemodi*) as Priscian observes, which Vict. acknowledges he saw in all the antient manuscripts, though through the carelessness or ignorance of transcribers we find *cui modi* restored in a great many passages. They used also to say *alimodi* for *aliusmodi,* as may be seen in Festus. And this syncope has some analogy to that which we have above observed in the declensions, p. 62. of *jusjurandi,* for *jurisjurandi; alterutrius,* for *alteriusutrius,* &c.

DAMNAS, is a word syncopated for *damnatus,* and therefore hath its cases *damnati, damnato,* &c. so that it does not properly belong to this place, no more than *satias*, which we shall see presently.

DAPS is in Cato, as also *dapis, dapem, dape*. But the nominative is no longer current, no more than *ops* or *frux*, which we shall see in their proper place.

DICA is in Cic. *Scribitur Heraclio dica*. But the accusative is more usual a great deal; *dicam scribere*, Ter. *subscribere*, Plaut. *impingere*, Ter. to bring or enter an action against one, to arrest him or serve him with a process, *dicas sortiri*, Cic. &c.

DICIS, has only the genitive, *dixit aut egit hæc dicis causa*, for form or fashion's sake, in his defence, to excuse himself. It is in Cic. *Verrin*. 6. and *pro Milone*, in the life of Atticus by Cornelius Nepos, in Pliny, Ulpian, Victorius, and others.

DITIO, is unusual in the nominative, as Diomedes, Donatus, Priscian, Servius, and the moderns have observed. But we say, *Ditionis terminus, ditioni permittere, in ditionem concedere, in ditione esse*, the examples of which are common in authors.

FEMEN is obsolete; but we use the gen. *feminis*; dat. *femini*; abl. *femine*. Which Charisius and Victorius give to FEMUR. The genitive is in Cæsar, *Stipes feminis magnitudine*, of the thickness of one's thigh: in the ablative in Cic. *Signum Apollinis, cujus in femine nomen Myrenis inscriptum est*. And in Virgil, *Eripit à femine*, according to Caper, Charisius, and Servius whom I have followed, though Priscian reads *à femore*. But Vossius prefers the former reading to the latter. We find the plural in Plautus, in Pseud. *femina summa*. And in Pliny, *Femina atteri adurique equitatui notum est*.

FORS and FORTE, are both used, as *fort fortuna*, Ter. unexpected good fortune: *forte fortunâ*, by good fortune. The accusative is more scarce, though we find it in Varro, *fortem fortunam*, 4. de L. L. And the dative is also in antient inscriptions, FORTI FORTUNÆ.

FRUX. We say *frugis, frugi, frugem, fruge. Frugis bonæ*, Gell. *Frugi bonæ*, Plaut. *Ad frugem bonam se recipere*, Cic. Even *frux* is in Enn. *Si jam data sit frux*, where we see it is a fem. though it be no longer in use.

Now FRUGI may be a dative, or even an antient genitive for *frugis*, in the same manner as we have seen *cuimodi*, for *cujusmodi*, and as they used to say *fami* for *famis*, &c. And it is in this sense we ought to take *frugi*, which we frequently find by itself for *bono frugi*, and signifies the same as *homo bonæ frugis*, a good husband, a thrifty sober man.

GLOS, *the husband's sister, or brother's wife*, according to Priscian, makes *gloris* in the genitive, but without authority; so that it has hardly any more than the nominative and the vocative.

IMPETE, is an ablative which the gloss. of Philox. explain by ὁρμηδὸν : but we find also the genitive *impetis*, in Lucret. and Silius. Priscian is even of opinion that as of *indigeo* is formed *indigeis, etis*; of *tereo, teres, etis*, &c. so of *impeto* is formed *impes, impetis*, though there is no instance of this nominative. *Impetibus crebris* is in Lucretius, whether we take it from hence, or from *impetus, hujus impetûs*.

INCITAS or INCITA, are accusatives which suppose *lineas* or *loca*, an extremity or the farthest bound: *redigi ad incitas*, to be at his wit's end; a metaphor taken from the game of draughts, when one can move the men no farther. See the list of ellipses in the remarks after the syntax, But we say also *incitus, a, um*, moved, hasty, quick, violent; which is evidently quite another meaning. For these nouns being compounded of *cieo, moveo*, the particle *in* is negative in the former, while it marks only a quicker motion in the latter. *Vis incita venti*, Lucr. *Inciti delphini*, Cic. &c.

INFICIAS, occurs also in the accusative only. Philoxenus's gloss. render it by ἄρνησιν, *negationem*. So that we say, *ire inficias*, to deny; just as we say *ire exequias*, to go to a funeral; *ire suppetias*, to assist; where we always understand the preposition *ad*, by which these accusatives are governed, as shall be shewn in another place.

INGRATIIS, has only the ablative. *Vobis invitis atque amborum ingratiis*, Plaut.

Tuus pater vult tempore tuam unicam tuis ingratiis, Id.

Where the adjective *tuis* plainly shews that *ingratiis* is not an adverb, but

but a noun substantive, and proves at the same time that Giffanius had no foundation for saying that *tuis ingratiis* was not Latin, though we meet with it more than once in this author. For it is a mistake to pretend that *ingratiis* is put there to serve the measure of the verse instead of *ingratis*, as Giffan. pretends; because quite the contrary it is *ingratis* that is used for *ingratiis*, as may be seen not only in Plautus, but also in Lucret. and Terence.

INSTAR is a noun like *exemplar*: Probus himself gives it *instaris*, though Charisius condemns this genitive. Hence S. Austin in his grammar allows it to have only three cases. *Instar*, he says, *quod est similitudo, tres habet casus tantum; nominativum, accusativum, vocativum; & est numeri tantùm singularis*. The nominative is in Cic. *Plato mihi unus, instar est omnium:* in Ulpian, *Si proponatur instar quoddam operis*. And in Virgil, *Quantum instar in ipso est*, Æn. 6. where we see it is of the neuter gender. The accusative is in Cic. *Terra ad universi cœli complexum, quasi puncti instar obtinet*. And in Justin, *Vallis ad instar castrorum clauditur*. Also in Appuleius; *ad instar inclyti montis:* and in Solinus, *ad instar omnis Ægyptii*. Which shews the little foundation that Servius had for saying that *instar* was not put with a preposition. But *instar* properly denotes the representation of a thing present, whence comes *instare*, as also *instaurare*, according to Festus.

JOVIS, was heretofore used in the nominative; we have still its other cases, but in the nominative and vocative we make use of Jupiter, which is a syncopated word for *Jovis-pater*, according to Gellius, just as we still say *Marspiter*, for *Mars-pater*. See the declensions, p. 70. But *Jupiter* was also called *Diespiter*, for *Dici-pater*. See Gellius book 5. c. 12.

MANCIPI, is no more than a genitive for *mancipii*, though Priscian makes it the dative of *manceps*. *Res mancipi*; Cic. wherein a man hath the property and full possession. Just as he says *lex mancipii*, with two *ii*, the conditions in the making over any thing. For MANCIPIUM was properly a certain right, according to which none but Roman citizens had a power of contracting with one another in regard to particular lands or goods belonging to the district of Rome and the territory of Italy.

MANE, though it commonly becomes an adverb, as when Cicero says, *bene mane*, early in the morning, is nevertheless of its own nature a noun, as when Persius says, *clarum mane:* and Mart. *Sed mane totum dormies*. The ablative is in Colum. *sub obscuro mane*; and this ablative heretofore ended in *i*, *a mani usque ad vesperam*, Plaut.

NAUCI, is a genitive. *Nauci non facere*, Plaut. not to value a straw. Hence it is that Nevius in Festus has also *nauco ducere*; and Festus has made use of it in the accusative; *Naucum ait Ateius philologus poni pro nugis*.

NECESSE and NECESSUM are nouns neuter. The one comes from *necessis*, and the other from *necessus*.

NECIS, is ranked in this class without the least foundation. For we not only find *necis*, *neci*, *necem*, *nece*; but even the nominative *nex* is in Cicero and elsewhere, *Insidiatori & latroni quæ potest adferri nex injusta?* pro Milon.

NIHIL is not properly indeclinable: for being the same as NIHILUM, whence it has been formed by syncope, we may say that it makes *nihili* and *nihilo*, like the other.

OBEX, is not usual according to Phocas, but only the ablative *obice*; as if Plautus had not said, *iste obex*, in Mercat. Plin. *nullæ obices*, in Panegyr. and others in the same manner. See the genders, p. 54.

OPS, is in Charisius and in Priscian, and is taken for plenty, or for assistance. See OPES in the list of plural feminines, p. 160.

Ops was heretofore an adjective, whence comes also *inops*, that is, *omni ope destitutus*, says Festus.

PECUDIS, has at least four cases: the genitive, *impurissimæ pecudis sordes*, Cic. The dative, *pecudi dare viva marito*; Enn. where *pecudi marito* is only an apposition, so that it is in vain some have pretended to infer from hence that heretofore they said *hic pecus:* the accusative *pecudem auream cum appellaret*, Tacit. The ablative, *quâ pecude nihil genuit natura fœcundius*, Cic. speaking of swine. But

M 4 Charisius

Charisius ranks it among the nouns that have neither nominative nor vocative. This shews the impropriety of the following expressions, though they are so commonly used, *egregia pecus, morbida pecus*, &c.

With regard to the distinction given by some, that *pecus, pecudis*, signifies no more than a beast; and *pecus, pecoris*, a flock; it is certain notwithstanding that both are indifferently used for a sheep, a wether, an elephant, and for all sorts of cattle. See L. Valla, lib. 4. c. 42. *Pecudes* refers even to fishes in Virg.

Cum tacet omnis ager, pecudes, pictæque volucres,
Quæque lacus late liquidos tenent, &c. Æn. 4.

For one would think that having put *quæ* in the feminine in the second verse, there is no other word to which it can be more naturally referred than to this, which is in the first verse. But *pecus, oris*, neuter, frequently denotes a multitude in the singular.

Ignavum fucos pecus à præsepibus arcent, Virg.
Cujum pecus, Id. which cannot perhaps be said of *pecudis*, feminine.

Both of them may be applied to a stupid heavy fellow, though *pecudis* is more usual in this sense.

PLUS, has only four cases, the nominative, *plus duo millia cæsa*, Liv. the genitive, *pluris est eloquentia*, Cic. the accusative, *plus quingentos colaphos infregit mihi*, Ter. the ablative, *plure tanto altero*, Plaut. And the glossaries render *plus* by πλεῖον; so that it wants only the vocative and the dative.

PONDO, about which grammarians have made such a mighty pother, is only a real ablative, like MUNDO: this shews that heretofore they said *pondus, pondi*; and *pondus, ponderis*; so that *pondo* performs the same office as *pondere*; *corona aurea libræ pondo*; a gold crown of a pound weight. See the genders, rule 8. annot. and what shall be said hereafter, when we come to treat of the figure ellipsis.

PRECIS, is an old nominative, whence by syncope they have made *prex*. S. Cyril's gloss. περέκτοτι, *obsecratio, prex*. We find it in the dative; *nihil est preci loci relictum*, Ter. In the accusative *nunc te oro per precem*, Plaut. In the ablative *prece & obsecratione uti*, Cic. *Quintus non modò, non cum magna prece ad me, sed acerbissimè scripsit*, ad Attic.

The plural PRECES is very common.

PROCERIS, according to Charisius hath also four cases. Which seems more probable, says Vossius, than the opinion of those who will have it that there is no more than PROCEREM.

And the same ought to be said of *bilicem, triplicem, septemplicis*, and *triplicis*, though grammarians rank them also in the number of nouns that have but one case. For we find *bilex* for δίμιτος, woven with a double thread; and *trilex* for τρίμιτος, woven with three threads, as we see in the old glossary, published by H. Stephen, where one would think that we ought rather to read *bilix* and *trilix*, since they have a long increase.

Loricam consertam hamis, auróque trilicem, Virg.

PUS, neuter, besides the nom. accus. and vocat. which are usual, hath also the genitive *puris*; the dative *puri*; and the ablat. *pure*, which we read in Celsus and other writers. And therefore it is without foundation they have been ranked among the defectives.

REPETUNDÆ, is an adjective which supposeth *pecuniæ*, and therefore it may have every case. And thus we might say, for instance, *mittere legatos ad res repetundas*, and the like. But the reason of our meeting with hardly any more than the genitive *repetundarum*, and the ablative *repetundis*, is because verbs of accusing govern only these two cases.

SATIAS, is a syncope for *satietas*; and therefore its genitive must be *satietatis*. This is so much the more agreeable to truth, as we meet with this syncope likewise in the other cases, *satiate* for *satietate*, Lucr. *satiatem* for *satietatem*, &c.

SIREMPS, is an old word, which according to Festus, signifies *similis re ipsa*, all alike, of the same nature. It is used in the nominative and the vocative: and the ablative is *sirempse* according to Charisius. Cato has made use of the nominative. *Et præterea rogas, ut in quemque adver-*

fus ea, fi populus condemnarit, fi remps lex fiet, quafi adverfus legem fecifset. In diffuaf. leg. frum. We meet with it alfo in the old laws: *Qui ager ex publico in privatum commutatus fit, de eo agro firemps lex efto, quafi is ager P. Mucio, & I. Calpurnio confulibus per totam rempublicam.* Fragm. legis Agrar. That whatever lands fhall be transferred from the public into private hands, fhall enjoy the fame privileges and immunities, as thofe which the lands of the republic enjoyed all over Italy, under the confulate of Mucius and Calpurnius. And Cujas hath obferved that thus we fhould read the following paffage of Sen. ep. 92. *Omnium quæ terram premunt, firemps lex efto*: whereas the old reading was downright nonfenfe, *feré miles efto.* But in Plautus's prologue to his Amphyt. where we read

Sirempfe legem juffit effe Jupiter.

The old editions have, *fimilem rem ipfe in legem juffit effe Jupiter.* Which gives room to conjecture that the right reading is *firempfe, in lege,* &c. a conjecture favoured by Voffius.

SOLUS, fee *unus,* p. 152.

SORDIS, is in the nominative in S. Ambrofe, but this is not to be imitated. The other cafes, *hujus fordis, hanc fordem,* and *hac forde,* are ufual.

SPONTE, which Servius calls an adverb, is rather an ablative, as it appears by the Greek; *fponte,* ἀπροαιρέτως, *gloff. Philox.* ἱκουσία γνώμη, *gloff.* Syril. This appears alfo by the adjective joined to it, *fponte meâ, fuâ fponte;* &c. We read likewife *fuæ fpontis* in Colum. and in other writers. But the nominative is obfolete, though we read in Aufonius,

Sponte ablativi cafus, quis rectus erit? fpons.

SUPPETIÆ, is in Plautus. The accufative *fuppetias* is very common.

TABI and TABO, are both ufed: *Stillantis tabi faniem,* Lucan; *et terram tabo maculant,* Virg.

TANTUMDEM, is nominative and accufative. The genitive is *tantidem;* the other cafes are unufual.

TEMPE, is not declined. Wherefore it is a miftake in Ortelius, to conclude his defcription of this place by faying: *atque hæc de Tempis.* But there are a great many more fuch in his works, which fhews that he was lefs fkilled in grammar, than in geography.

VICEM and VICE, are ftill in ufe. But Phocas gives it alfo the genitive *vicis,* which Livy ufed, lib. 1. *ne facra regiæ vicis defererentur.* And the antient interpreter of S. Luke, c. 1. *In ordine vicis fuæ.* According to Charifius it hath alfo the dative *vici.* The nominative fhould therefore be *vicis,* or by fyncope *vix;* but we find no fuch word, not even among the grammarians, though it cannot be denied but the adverb *vix* is derived from thence.

VIRUS hath the genitive *viri,* and the dative *viro,* in Lucretius, though probably they are to be found in no other author.

VIS, hath four cafes in the fingular. See p. 133.

VISCUS, neuter, which Phocas will allow to have only the ablative *vifcere,* which we find in Ovid, *trahentia vifcere tela;* hath alfo *vifceris* in the genitive, according to Charifius. Moreover, the nominative *vifcus,* is in Suetonius, Lucretius, and Celfus. And the plural VISCERA, is very common.

VISCUS, mafculine; fee p. 152.

There are fome more nouns of the like fort, which may be feen in the lift of adverbs, in the remarks following the fyntax.

But there are others mentioned by the grammarians as wanting fome cafes, which it would be of no ufe to take notice of in this place, becaufe of the great number of examples to the contrary.

There are others of which they make no mention at all; thefe ought not to be ufed however without great caution, as *fpecierum,* and *fpeciebus;* Cicero rejects them in his topics, and we have taken notice of them in the declenfions, p. 125.

This

This shews that we must depend upon the reading of good books, and the established custom of authors, which shall be always marked down in this work, in every thing that relates to the principal difficulties that may occur in writing.

ANNOTATION.

Hitherto we have treated of what relates to nouns, either as to their gender, or declension. We must now proceed to verbs, and speak of their preterites and supines; reserving some observations, of a more curious and more important nature, as well concerning the nouns, and verbs, as every other part of grammar, to the end of the syntax.

BOOK IV.

OF

THE CONJUGATIONS

OF VERBS,

OR

The Rules of their Preterites and Supines.

I N verbs we ought chiefly to confider the preterite, becaufe of the tenfes depending thereon; and the fupine, becaufe of a great many nouns and participles that are formed from thence.

The PRETERITE in *I*, being conjugated by *ifti*, *it*, properly fpeaking, is no more of one conjugation than of another: or to exprefs myfelf with more propriety, it forms its particular conjugation, as I have already obferved in the rudiments, ending conftantly in I, and forming conftantly the tenfes depending thereon by the fame analogy without any exception. But this termination ftill admits of a very great diverfity, becaufe of the vowel or confonant that precedes it.

The preterite, generally fpeaking, may be formed of the fecond perfon of the prefent, by changing S into VI, as *amo, amas, amavi; fleo, es, evi; peto, is, ivi; audio, is, ivi.*

In regard to which we may alfo take notice of two general exceptions.

The firft that the V confonant being changed into U vowel, the other preceding vowel is dropped to prevent too great an hiatus, or concurrence of vowels, as *domo, as, domui,* for *domavi; moneo, es, monui,* for *monevi; arguo, is, argui; aperio, aperui,* &c.

The fecond, that fometimes a fyllable or letter is fuppreffed, either in the middle of the word, as *juvo, as, juvi,* for *juvavi: caveo, es, cavi,* for *cavevi:* or at the end, as *lego, legi,* for *legivi; folvo, folvi; venio, veni:* or in both; as, *fundo, is, fudi,* for *fundivi,* which fhould come from *fundivi.*

The SUPINES are generally formed of the preterite, by changing the two laft letters into TUM; as *amavi, amatum; juvi, jutum: flevi, etum: rapui, raptum,* &c.

Now it often happens that the fuppreffion of a fyllable or letter in the preterite is not communicated to the fupine, fo that the fupine is formed juft as if the analogy was complete: as *ruitum* from *rui,*

rui, for *ruivi*; *fugitum* from *fugi*, for *fugivi*. But it sometimes also receives a syncope particular to itself, as *ictum* for *icitum*, from *ico*, *ici*, for *icivi*: *ruptum* for *rupitum*, from *rumpo*, *rupi*, for *rupivi*. Thus *alo*, from *alui*, for *alivi*, makes *alitum*, and by syncope *altum*. And some others in the same manner.

Those in uï, generally speaking, made only ITUM or UTUM in the supine, for UÏTUM; as *monuï*, *monitum* : *arguï*, *arguitum* : *suï*, *sutum*, &c.

Further, the Latins have often imitated the Greek analogy: so that as the Greeks change the characteristics β and π into ψ in the first conjugation: γ and κ into ξ in the second: in the same manner the Latins say *scribo*, *scripsi*; *carpo*, *carpsi*; *dico*, *dixi*; *jungo*, *junxi*. Also *vincio*, *vinxi*: *sancio*, *sanxi*, and the like; the verbs in O pure often following the impure termination.

And as the Greeks change δ and τ into σ in the third, so the Latins say not only *lædo*, *læsi*, *læsum*; *sentio*, *si*, *sum*, and the like: but also *flecto*, *flexi*; *necto*, *nexi*; for *flecsi*, *necsi*, &c.; the *x*, as we shall observe in the treatise of letters, being equivalent to *cs* and *gs*.

They have also given now and then a reduplication to their verbs in imitation of the Greek augment, as *mordeo*, *memordi*, or *momordi*; *pendeo*, *pependi*; *cædo*, *cecidi*; *pello*, *pepuli*, &c.

Such is in short the general analogy of the preterites and supines, which is certainly greater than most people imagine. We may mention it here by the way, that we shall treat of it more particularly hereafter. Though in regard to beginners, it is, I think, very difficult to hit upon a shorter and easier way of learning and retaining them, than by the rules we are going to lay down.

These very often comprize in a single line the verb, its preterite, and supine, and with such a connexion, that it is hardly possible to remember one without recollecting the other at the same time. And the choice collection of Latin verbs translated into our own language, and thrown into the examples, will perhaps be of service to youth by shewing them at the same time the force and real signification of the words.

GENERAL RULES.

Rule I.
Of the compounded verbs.

1. *The simple and compounded verbs are conjugated alike.*
2. *But there are several exceptions which we shall elsewhere observe.*

Examples.

1. The compounded verbs are conjugated like their simples from whence they form their preterite and supine, as

AMO, amávi, amátum, amáre; *to love.*
Rédamo, ávi, átum, áre, *to love him that loveth us.*
SE'DEO, sedi, essum, ére, *to sit, to be set or placed, to sit still, to be idle.*
Possídeo, possédi, posséssum, possidére, *to possess.*

2. There are several that do not intirely follow their simple, which we shall take notice of in the sequel, but more particularly at the end of all the rules.

Annotation.

If you are at a loss to find out the preterite of a compounded verb, you must strive to find its simple, by dropping the compounding particle, the more easily to see its preterite; as *exaudio*, dropping the *ex* remains *audio, audivi, auditum*; and therefore *exaudio* must make *exaudivi, exauditum*.

But we are to observe that compounded verbs frequently change the first vowel of the simple into I: as *sedeo, possideo*, and not *possedeo: ago, adigo*, and not *adago*.

Sometimes they change it into E, as *carpo, discerpo*.

Sometimes other changes are made which the use of authors will point out; as from *ago* comes *cogo*, for *coago*, and *coago* for *conago*, according to Quintilian.

Rule II.
Of verbs that redouble their first syllable in the preterite.

1. *The reduplication of the first syllable of simple verbs is frequently dropped in their compounds.*

2. *Except all thofe of* difco, *and* pofco.
3. *Five of* curro. 4. *And* repúngo.

EXAMPLES.

1. There are a great many verbs, which have a reduplication in the preterite, when they are fimple, and lofe it when compounded: as

MO'RDEO, mo-mórdi, morfum, mordére: *to bite.*
Remórdeo, remórdi, remórfum, remordére; *to bite again; to chaftife again; to revenge.*
PE'NDEO, pe-péndi, penfum, pendére; *to hang up, to hang on, at, or from.*
Impéndeo, impéndi, impénfum, impendére: *to hang over one's head, to threaten, to be near at hand.*
SPO'NDEO, fpo-póndi, fponfum, fpondére; *to promife freely, to be furety for another, to betroth.*
Refpóndeo, refpóndi, refpónfum, refpondére: *to anfwer.*
TO'NDEO, to-tóndi, tonfum, tondére: *to clip, to poll, to browfe.*
Detóndeo, detóndi, detónfum, ére; *to fhear, clip, or poll, fo as to leave nothing behind.*
CADO, cé-cidi, cafum, cádere: *to fall, to flip, to fall out, to happen.*
O'ccido, óccidi, occáfum, occídere: *to fall down, to die, to be flain.*
Récido, récidi, recáfum, recídere: *to fall back, to recoil.*
CÆDO, cecídi, cæfum, cæ'dere: *to lafh, to beat, to cut, to kill.*
Occído, occídi, occífum, occídere: *to kill.*
CANO, cé-cini, cantum, cánere: *to fing.*
Cóncino, cóncini, concéntum, concínere: *to agree or accord in one fong or tune; to fing one's praife on an inftrument, to prophefy, to confent.*
PENDO, pe-péndi, penfum, péndere: *to weigh, to efteem, to pay.*
Impéndo, impéndi, impénfum, ĕre: *to fpend, to employ.*
TUNDO, tú-tudi, tunfum, túndere: *to beat or thump, to beat in a mortar, to threfh.*

Re-

OF PRETERITES AND SUPINES. 175

Retúndo, rétudi, retúfum, retúndere: *to blunt or dull, to quell.*

TANGO, té-tigi, tactum, tángere: *to touch.*

Attíngo, áttigi, attáctum, attíngere: *to touch lightly, to reach.*

TENDO, te-téndi, tenfum, téndere: *to ftretch out, to bend a bow, to endeavour.*

Osténdo, osténdi, osténfum, osténdere: *to fhew, to point at.*

2. Thefe retain the reduplication.

DISCO, dí-dici, dífcere: *to learn.*

Addífco, addídici, addífcere; *to learn more, to learn by heart.*

And in the fame manner all its other compounds.

POSCO, po-pófci, pófcere: *to afk for, to demand.*

Depófco, depopófci, depófcitum, depófcere: *to call for or demand with importunity.*

And in the fame manner all its other compounds.

3. CURRO, cucúrri, curfum, cúrrere: *to run.*

It retains its reduplication in many of its compounds, and particularly in

Præcúrro, præcu-cúrri, præcúrfum, præcúrrere; *to run or make fpeed before, to anfwer a forefeen objection.*

We find it alfo very often in *decúrro, excúrro, procúrro, percúrro,* though they are likewife ufed without a reduplication. See rule 55.

4. PUNGO, pú-pugi, punxi, punctum, púngere: *to prick.*

One of its compounds retains the reduplication.

Repúngo, repúpugi, repúnxi, repúnctum, repúngere: *To prick again, to do one fhrewd turn for another.*

ANNOTATION.

The other compounds of *curro*, not mentioned here, are very feldom found with the reduplication: but as to thofe above expreffed, Cæfar hath, *cùm regiones Galliæ percucurriffet.* Livy; *Quum plures armati excucurriffent*; and in another place, *etfi ferocius procucurriffent.* Pliny, *ad mortem decucurrit.* Q. Curtius, *ad Philotam decucurriffe:* Tertull. *Oportebat legis adimplendæ caufas præcucurriffe.* We find alfo *accucurriffe* in Cic. *ad Attic.*

Thefe reduplications are a kind of imitation of the Greek augment; whence they were all formed heretofore in E, *memordi, pepugi, fpepondi:* which Gellius fays were ufed by Cæfar and Cicero.

Juft

Just as we still say *fefelli* from *fallo*; *peperi* from *pario*; *tetigi* from *tango*; and in Pliny, *tetuli* from *tollo*; and such like.

And so we may say the same of *do*, *dedi*. But its compounds, as well as those of *sto*, *steti*, shall be sufficiently explained in their particular rules; since except the four compounds of *do* of the first conjugation which make *dedi* like itself, the others do not properly retain the reduplication of the simple, but rather assume a particular reduplication of their own.

Now it is to be observed that heretofore there was a far greater number of verbs that reduplicated, than there are at present. Hence we still find *despopondisse* and *despoponderas* in Plautus: Gellius also quotes from the same author *præmomordi*. Varro has made use of *detotonderat*, according to Priscian. *Scindo* also made *scicidi*: which Asmonius in the grammar he wrote to Constantine, thought was the only one in use.

RULE III.

Of those which having changed the A into I, take an E in the supine.

1. *If the* A *of the simple verb be changed into* I, *when that verb is compounded, its supine will assume an* E.
2. *But those in* DO *and* GO *retain the* A.

EXAMPLES.

1. Those verbs which change A into I in their compounds, assume an E in the penultimate of the supine: as,

FÁCIO, féci, factum, fácere: *to do.*
Perfício, perféci, perféctum, (*and not* perfáctum) perfícere: *to perfect, to finish.*
JÁCIO, jeci, jactum, jácere: *to throw.*
Rejício, éci, éctum, (*and not* áctum) ícere: *to cast or fling back.*

2. The compounded verbs that end in DO and in GO, follow their simple intirely, without taking an E in the supine, as

CADO, cécidi, casum, cádere: *to fall, to fall out, to happen.*
Récido, récidi, recásum, recídere: *to fall back.*
FRANGO, fregi, fractum, frángere: *to break.*
Effríngo, effrégi, effráctum, effríngere: *to break up, or open; to break in pieces.*
AGO, egi, actum, ágere: *to do any business, to treat or deal with, to act, to drive, to lead.*

A'digo,

A'digo, adégi, adáctum, adígere : *to drive, to bring to, to force.*
TANGO, tétigi, tactum, tángere : *to touch.*
Contíngo, cóntigi, contáctum, contíngere : *to touch or lay hold of, to handle.*

ANNOTATION.

This rule ought also to be understood of the preterite of the verb passive, which is constantly formed of a participle that depends on the active supine. And this is a remark that particularly regards the verbs deponent; for as from *rejicior* comes *rejectus,* so from *confiteor* comes *confessus*, though *fateor* makes *fassus* with an *a.* But properly speaking it is understood only of those verbs that have an A in the penultimate of their supine; as *rápio, rapui, raptum ; arripio, arreptum :* and not of those which have A only in the antepenultimate, as *habeo, habitum.* Hence we ought to say *adbibitum* and not *adbebitum* ; because this A is not in the termination of the supine which is ITUM.

Therefore it may be said that all the other verbs follow the rule of their simple, unless they be particularly excepted.

RULE IV.
Of those that have no preterite.

All verbs without a preterite, are likewise without a supine.

EXAMPLES.

Verbs that have no preterite have no supine, as *glisco, gliscere,* to grow or spread itself: *pólleo, pollēre* to be able, to have power: *lābo, labāre,* to totter, to be ready to drop down.

Nevertheless we may except *tundo.* See the 37th rule.

RULE V.
Of the syncope.

The syncope incident to verbs is when a syllable is cut off; as when we say amásti *instead of* amavísti.

EXAMPLES.

The syncope is a contraction or cutting off, which frequently happens in the preterite, especially of those that terminate in VI : as
PE'TII, *instead of* petívi : *I have asked.*
Amásti, *for* amavísti : *thou hast loved.*

Nosti, *for* novísti : *thou hast known.*
Norunt, *for* novérunt : *they have known.*
Revocásti, *for* revocavísti : *thou hast recalled.*
Prostrásse, *for* prostravísse : *to have overthrown, or beaten down.*
Adiíssét, *for* adivíssét : *he might have gone towards.*

ANNOTATION.

The syncope happens also sometimes to the other preterites, as
Extínxti, *Virg.* *instead of* extinxísti ; *thou hast extinguished.*
Extínxem, *Virg. for* extinxíssem ; *I might have extinguished.*
Evásti, *Hor. instead of* evasísti ; *thou hast escaped.*
Surréxe, *Hor. instead of* surrexísse ; *to have got up.*

But this manner of speaking is less to be imitated, except it be in regard to the verbs.

But if you should chuse to extend this rule to the formation of the other preterites, and also of the supines, according to the general analogy we have given of them, you may consult what has been above said at our entering upon the conjugations, p. 171.

THE FIRST CONJUGATION.
Rule VI.
General for verbs of the first conjugation.

The first conjugation makes the preterite in AVI, *as* amo, amas, amávi; *and its supine in* ATUM, *as* amo, amas, amátum.

Examples.

Verbs of the first conjugation generally make their preterite in AVI, and their supine in ATUM; as
AMO, amas, amávi, amátum, amáre : *to love one cordially, to be obliged to, or thank, to delight in.*
A'damo, ávi, átum, áre : *to love greatly, wantonly.*
Rédamo, ávi, átum, áre : *to love him that loveth us.*
A'MBULO, ávi, átum, áre : *to walk, to go a foot-pace, to glide along.*
Obámbulo, ávi, átum, áre : *to walk about, to walk by one's side.*
BEO, ávi, átum, áre : *to bless, to make one happy or glad.*
CA'LCEO, ávi, átum, áre : *to put on shoes, to shoe.*
CREO, ávi, átum, áre : *to create, to beget, to breed, to cause, to choose, to ordain.*

Récreo,

OF PRETERITES AND SUPINES 179

Récreo, ávi, átum, áre; *to bring to life again, to recover, to refresh, to comfort.*

* ENU'CLEO, eávi, eátum, eáre: *to take out the kernel, to declare or explain.*

* DELI'NEO, eávi, eátum, eáre: *to delineate, to draw the outlines, to make a rude draught.*

* ILLA'QUEO, eávi, eátum, eáre: *to intangle, to biafs.*

MEO, meávi, meátum, meáre: *to go or pafs any manner of way.*

Cómmeo, ávi, átum, áre *to go in company, to go to and fro, to come, to move.* Whence we have commeátus, *a paffport, a furlow, a place through which one paffes or repaffes, a going and coming, a carriage, a convoy of a fhip or fleet, a company of foldiers, provifion of victuals either public or private.*

Rémeo, ávi, átum, áre; *to return, or come back again.*

NA'USEO, ávi, átum; áre: *to be fea-fick, to vomit or to be ready to vomit.*

    Take particular notice of thefe verbs in *eo* of the firft conjugation, in order not to confound them with others in *eo* of the fecond.

NU'NTIO, ávi, átum, áre: *to tell or relate, to carry news, to carry orders, to fhew or advife.*

PRONU'NTIO, as, ávi, átum, áre: *to pronounce.*

    The reft in IO are generally of the third or fourth conjugation.

UNDO, ávi, átum, áre: *to rife in furges, to fpread or diffufe itfelf, to overflow.*

Exúndo, ávi, átum, áre: *to overflow, to fpread far.*

Fecúndo, ávi, átum, áre: *to make fruitful.*

Inúndo, ávi, átum, áre: *to overflow, to overwhelm, to come pouring on amain.*

Redúndo, ávi, átum, áre: *to overflow, to abound, to redound.*

    Take particular notice of thefe compounds of *undo*, in order not to confound them with thofe of *do, dedi.*

ALIE'NO, Abaliéno, ávi, átum, áre: *to alienate, to fell, to deliver up the poffeffion or right of a thing to another, to difcard or cut off, to create divifion between people, to fet them at variance.*

DICO, ávi, átum, áre: *to dedicate, to appoint or defign, to devote, to fet apart or beftow, to vow or promife.*

N 2   A'bdico,

A'bdico, ávi, átum, áre: *to difown or renounce, to abrogate or difannul, to reject or refufe, to difinherit, to abdicate or lay down.*

VOCO, ávi, átum, áre: *to name, to call, to invite.*

A'dvoco, ávi, átum, áre: *to call or fend for friends to affift us with their authority or prefence in our affairs, and to furnifh our advocate with the means of gaining our caufe, and of fupporting our right: to plead for or advife one; to fummon together; to call up or conjure.*

LéGO, ávi, átum, áre: *to fend as an ambaffador or lieutenant, to difpatch or fend away, to intruft, to bequeath.*

Allégo, ávi, átum, áre: *to fend one as a meffenger or ambaffador, to depute one for a bufinefs, to alledge by way of excufe, to fet one down in writing.*

APPE'LLO, ávi, átum, áre: *to call, to name, to intitle; to mention; to fpeak familiarly to one; to call in queftion or accufe; to call to witnefs; to call to one for help; to call upon for a thing, to dun; to appeal, to proclaim, to pronounce.*

* AUCTO'RO, ávi, átum, áre: *to bind or engage one, as by covenant or hire, for fervice; to prefs foldiers or lift them into pay.* Whence comes auctoratus miles, *an inlifted foldier.* Exauctorátus, *a cafhiered or difbanded foldier.* Auctoraméntum, *a ftipulating or contracting, whence arifeth an obligation to ferve; the hire or wages of fuch fervice; a donative or prefent.*

Rule VII.

Of the verbs *do* and *fto* with their compounds.

1. Do *makes* dĕdi, dătum.
2. *And* fto *makes* ftĕti, ftătum.
3. *Its compounds have* STĬTI, STĬTUM, *and more ufually* STĀTUM.

Examples.

1. Do, dĕdi, dătum, dăre; *to give, to beftow; to tell or fhew; to intruft.*

Cir-

Circúndo, circúndedi, circúndatum, circúndare: *to surround, to inclose.*

Peſſúndo, dĕdi, dătum, dăre: *to overthrow, to caſt under foot, to lay waſte.*

Satíſdo, ſatíſdedi, ătum, ăre: *to put in ſufficient ſureties for performance of covenants.*

Venúndo, venúndĕdi, ătum, ăre: *to ſell.*

ANNOTATION.

Only theſe four compounds of *do* are of the firſt conjugation, the reſt are of the third.

Dor the preſent of the indicative paſſive, and *der* the preſent of the ſubjunctive paſſive, are unuſual.

2. STO, ſtĕti, ſtātum, ſtāre: *to ſtand, to ſtand ſtill, to take part with or againſt, to reſt upon or agree to, to acquieſce, ſtand to, or be determined by.*

3. Its compounds make STITI and STĬTUM, and more uſually STĀTUM.

Aſto, áſtiti, áſtitum, aſtáre: *to ſtand, to ſtand by, to aſſiſt.*

Conſto, cónſtiti, cónſtitum *or* conſtátum, conſtáre: *to ſtand together; to be conſiſtent or agree with one's ſelf; to conſiſt, or be made up; to abide, continue or be; to appear, to be plain; to coſt or ſtand in.*

Exto, éxtiti, éxtitum, extáre: *to ſtand out, to ſtand or ſtick up, to be, to remain, to be ſeen above others, to ſpring out.*

Diſto, díſtiti, *very little uſed*, diſtáre: *to be different, to be diſtant.*

Inſto, ínſtiti, ínſtitum, átum, áre: *to be inſtant or earneſt with one, to preſs, to perſiſt in a thing, to purſue, to be near.*

Obſto, óbſtiti, ĭtum, átum, áre: *to reſiſt, to hinder, to hurt.*

Præſto, præſtiti, ĭtum, ătum, áre: *to ſtand before; to bring out; to give or procure; to cauſe, make, or perform; to ſhew or approve; to excel; to warrant, to anſwer; to make good or defray, to oblige one's ſelf, &c.*

Reſto, réſtiti, ĭtum, átum, áre: *to ſtay or ſtand, to remain.*

Subſto, ſúbſtiti, ĭtum, átum, áre: *to ſtand ſtill, to bear up, to ſtand his ground.*

ANNOTATION.

From the supines in *átum* are usually formed the participles in *rus, facilè se id præstaturum*, Cic. which occurs much oftener than *præstiturum. Constatura fides*, Lucan. *Extatura*, Pliny. *Quosdam obstaturos*, Quint. *Instaturos victores*, Frontin.

RULE VIII.
Of *lavo, poto*, and *juvo*.

1. Lavo *makes* lāvi, lautum, lōtum, *and* lăvātum.
2. Pōto, potávi, pōtātum, *and by syncope* pōtum.
3. Jŭvo *has hardly any supine; but* adjutum *is usual*.

EXAMPLES.

1. LĂVO, lāvi, lōtum, lautum, lăvātum, lavăre: *to wash*. Rélavo, relávi, relótum, relavăre, *to wash again*.
2. PŌTO, potávi, pōtātum *or* pōtum, potáre: *to drink*.

Compóto, ávi, átum, áre: *to drink together*.
Perpóto, ávi, átum, áre: *to drink continually, to drink off or up*.
Epóto, epotávi, epótum: *to drink up, to suck in*.

3. JŬVO, jūvi, jūtum, *seldom used*, juváre: *to help, to assist, to please*.

A'djŭvo, adjúvi, adjútum, adjuváre: *to help, to assist*.

ANNOTATION.

Lavatum indeed comes from *lavo, as*; but *lavi, lautum*, and *lotum*, seem rather to come from *lavo, is*, which we read in Horace: *Qui Xantho lavis amne crines*. And Virg. *Lavit ater corpora sanguis*, 3. Georg. For from the preterite *lavi*, is regularly formed *lavitum*, of which by syncope they have made *lautum*, and afterwards by changing *au* into *o, lotum*. From *lautum* comes *lautus*, genteel, well bred, clean, neat, noble, splendid. And *lautitiæ*, good cheer, daintiness in entertainments. From *lotum* comes *lotium*, the water you wash your mouth with; or urine because it washes the body withinside.

Potum is also a syncope for *potatum*, which is still more usual in its compounds. We say also *potus sum*, but in another sense, as we shall observe in our remarks at the end of the syntax.

Jutum, which Vossius and Alvarez thought was not to be found uncompounded, is read in Tacitus, Annal. lib. 14. c. 4. *Placuit solertia tempore etiam juta*. And in Pallad. lib. 4. tit. 10. *Stercorati & humoribus juti (rami.)* And if we give credit to Gronovius in his notes on Livy, we ought to read it in some other passages of this

this author, which seem to be corrupted. It seems that they said also *juvavi*, which we find in the poet Manilius, whom Vossius believed to have lived in the reign of Theodosius. We meet also with *adjuvatum* and *juvāturus*, as if they came from the supine *juvatum*. *Adjuvaturos nos divinam providentiam, vel periculo nostro,* Petron. Which is no more to be imitated, than that expression of those who so often make use of *adjuvarunt* for *adjuverunt*, though without any authority.

RULE IX.
Of those which make ŭi and ITUM.

1. Sŏno, cŭbo, dŏmo, tŏno, vĕto, crĕpo, *make* ŭi, ITUM.
2. *But* discrepo *oftener makes* discrepávi.
3. Mico *has* ŭi, *but no supine*.
4. Dímico *more usually hath* AVI, ATUM.

EXAMPLES.

1. SŎNO, sŏnui, sŏnitum, sonáre : *to sound*.

A'ssono, ónui, ónitum, áre : *to answer by sound like an echo*.

Cónsono, ónui, ĭtum, áre : *to ring again, to echo ; to agree or be suitable*.

Díssono, ŭi, ĭtum, áre : *to be discordant ; to disagree*.

I'nsono, ŭi, ĭtum, áre : *to sound as a trumpet, to play on*.

Pérsono, ŭi, ĭtum, áre : *to make a great noise, to resound*.

Résono, ŭi, ĭtum, áre : *to resound*.

CŬBO, cŭbui, cŭbĭtum, cubáre : *to lie down, to sit at table*.

A'ccubo, accúbui, accúbitum, accubáre : *to sit opposite, to sit at table*.

Décŭbo, decúbui, decúbitum, decubáre : *to lie down*.

E'xcŭbo, ŭi, ĭtum, áre : *to lie out, to stand centry*.

I'ncŭbo, ŭi, ĭtum, áre : *to lie or sit upon, to brood or hover over, to cover or shadow*.

O'ccŭbo, ŭi, ĭtum, áre : *to die, to fall, to lie down*.

Prócŭbo, ŭi, ĭtum, áre : *to lie over, to spread over*.

Récŭbo, ŭi, ĭtum, áre : *to lie down again; to lie along, to loll*.

Sécubo, ŭi, ĭtum, áre : *to lie apart*.

Supércubo, ŭi, ĭtum, áre : *to lie upon*.

ANNOTATION.

There are a great many other compounds of *cubo*, that are of the third conjugation, and these add an M to the present, as

Accúmbo, accúbui, accúbitum, accúmbere: *to lie down, to sit down at meat*. You will find them lower down, rule 32.

DOMO, dŏmui, dŏmitum, domáre: *to tame*.
E'domo, ŭi, ĭtum, áre: *to tame thoroughly*.
Pérdomo, ŭi, ĭtum, áre: *to tame thoroughly*.
TONO, tŏnui, tŏnitum, tonáre: *to thunder*.
I'ntono, ŭi, ĭtum, áre: *to thunder, to make a loud noise, to speak loud, in a passion*.
Cóntono, ŭi, ĭtum, áre: *to thunder all round about*.
VETO, vétui, vétitum, vetáre: *to forbid, to let or hinder: it was also the word pronounced by the tribune when he made use of his intercession or negative voice*.
CREPO, crépui, crépitum, crépare: *to make a noise, to crackle, to burst*.
Cóncrepo, ŭi, ĭtum, áre: *to make a noise, to rustle, to creak as a door in opening*.
I'ncrepo, ŭi, ĭtum, áre: *to rattle or make a noise, to strike or beat, to chide, to accuse or blame*.
Récrepo, ŭi, ĭtum, áre: *to tingle, to ring, or sound again*.

2. Díscrepo, ŭi, *but more usually* discrepávi, ĭtum, *and* átum, áre: *to give a different sound, to disagree*.

3. MICO, mícui, *hath no supine*, micáre: *to glitter or shine; to move briskly; to pant or beat as the heart or pulse; to move the finger up and down very swiftly, the number of which were guessed at for the determining things in question, as they hit or mistook the number of figures; it was used to determine the price in buying and selling*.
E'mico, ŭi, (*heretofore* ávi, Solin.) áre: *to shew forth, to leap, to shew himself, to excel*.
Intérmico, *to shine in the midst, or among*.
Prómico, *to shew out, or appear at a distance*.

4. Dímico, *sometimes* ŭi, *like its simple; but oftener* ávi, *and* átum, áre: *to fight, to give battle*.

RULE X.
Of *plico* and its compounds.

1. Plico *makes also* ŭi ITUM,

2. *And*

2. *And* AVI, ATUM, *both of which it gives to four of its compounds.*
3. *But verbs formed of a noun and* plico, *have only* AVI, ATUM.
4. *The same may be said of* réplico, *and* súpplico.

EXAMPLES.

1. PLICO *heretofore made* plícui, plícitum; *and* plicávi, plicátum, plicáre: *to fold.*

2. This verb is rarely used except in the tenses formed of the present. But it gives this double preterite and supine to four of its compounds; namely to those which are formed of *ad, con, ex, in.*

A'pplico, ávi, átum, üi, ĭtum, áre: *to apply; to set or lay one thing near another, to bring or direct, to board, to land, to determine.*

Cómplico, ávi, átum, üi, ĭtum, áre: *to fold up or wrap together.*

E'xplico, ávi, átum, üi, ĭtum, áre: *to explain, to unfold, to develop.*

I'mplico, ávi, átum, üi, ĭtum, áre: *to intangle, to twine, to fold or clasp.*

3. Those verbs which are formed of a noun and *plico,* have only AVI and ATUM, as

Dúplico, ávi, átum, áre: *to double, to fold in two.*

In the same manner *triplico*, to fold in three; *quadrúplico*, to fold in four: *multiplico*, to make many folds, to multiply. And the like.

4. The same may be said of these two:

Réplico, ávi, átum, áre: *to unfold, to display, to turn the inside outward; to reply, to repeat.*

Súpplico, ávi, átum, áre: *to intreat, to present a petition.*

ANNOTATION.

Priscian says that the four compounds here first mentioned, more rarely make *avi.* But Vossius affirms that *avi* is more usual in Cic. Which may be easily seen by any body in the Apparatus Ciceronianus. *Ad scribendam historiam se applicaverunt,* 2. de Orat. *Cogitationes meas explicavi,* ad Attic. And this verb EXPLICO generally makes *avi,* when taken in this sense, to expound or explain.

plain. But when it relates to navigation it has also *ii*. Though Cicero has made use of the latter preterite in the former signification for the sake of numbers, as Gellius observes.

We find also *circumplicasse*, and *circumplicatus*, twisted about, twined ; *displicatus*, scattered, separated ; *perplicatus*, twisted, plaited.

Rule XI.
Of those which make UI and CTUM.

1. Frico, *and* seco, *make* UI, CTUM.
2. *But* neco *prefers* AVI, ATUM.

Examples.

1. FRICO, fricŭi, frictum, fricáre : *to rub.*

A'ffrico, affricŭi, affrictum, affricáre : *to rub against or upon a thing.*
Défrico, defricŭi, ctum, áre : *to rub hard, to clean.*
I'nfrico, ŭi, ctum, áre : *to rub in, or upon.*
Réfrico, réfricŭi, ctum, áre : *to rub hard or again ; to rub, or to rehearse something unpleasing ; to torment ; to pain.*
SECO, secŭi, sectum, secáre : *to cut, to carve, to cut off, or asunder ; to rend or tear.*
Déseco, desecŭi, desectum, desecáre : *to cut off, or down.*
Dísseco, dissecŭi, dissectum, dissecáre : *to cut in pieces.*
Intérseco, intersecŭi, ctum, áre : *to cut, or chop in.*
Réseco, resecŭi, resectum, resecáre : *to pare, to clip.*

2. NECO, *makes also* necŭi, nectum, *especially in its compounds ; but for itself it chuses* necávi, necátum, necáre : *to kill.*

E'neco, enecŭi, enectum, ávi, átum, áre : *to kill, to suffocate, to poison.*
Intérneco, internecávi, internecŭi, internectum, internecáre : *to put all to the sword.*

ANNOTATION.

We meet with *necui* in Ennius : and in Phædrus we read *hemisem necuit protinus*, speaking of the adder ; unless we chuse with Vossius and some others to read *nocuit*. For *noceo* heretofore governed an accusative, as we shall shew in the syntax ; and *necui* is so very rare, that Priscian thought it was to be found only in very old authors. But the participle in US, formed of the supine in CTUM is very usual in compounds —— *Bos est enectus arando,*
Hor.

Hor. *Fame & frigore enecti*, Lucret. *Enectus siti Tantalus*, Cic. But speaking of the sword, we say rather *necatus ferro*, according to Priscian, whereas *nectus* means some other violent death.

Of the preterite in AVI.

Almost all the verbs of the first conjugation that are excepted in the preceding rules, heretofore made AVI and ATUM, according to the general rule. There are even some that retain it still; as *cubo, cubávi, cubátum, cubáre*. We find also *micaverit*; the verbal noun *micatus, ûs; emicarunt, emicaturus,* &c.

Hence in Horace we likewise find *intonata, sonaturum*. Hence also Tertullian hath; *Quod tonitrua sonaverint*. And Appul. *Classicum personavit*. Ulpian has made use of *præstavit*. There are even some that more usually have the preterite in *avi*, as we have already observed. The compounds of *frico* generally made *atum*. We find in Cic. *refricaturus:* in Sen. *emicaturus:* in Colum. *secaturus:* in Florus *domaverunt:* and others in other writers, as experience will shew.

Hence also it comes that verbal nouns in *io* taken from the supines of this conjugation, have very often an *a* in the penultimate. Which Valla believed was without exception, because we say *vetatio* and not *vetitio*; *domatio* and not *domitio*; *emicatio* and not *emicitio*; *juvatio* and not *juvitio* nor *jutio*; though we say *jutum* in the supine. Yet he was mistaken in making this so general a rule. For we find *fricatio* and *frictio*, the latter being in Pliny and Celsus; *incubatio* and *incubitio*; *accubatio* and *accubitio*, &c. *Sectio* is more usual than *secatio*. Which may help to corroborate what Priscian advances, that such verbs of this conjugation as form the preterite in *ui* were heretofore of the third.

THE SECOND CONJUGATION.
RULE XII.
General for the verbs of the second conjugation.

The second makes ŭi, ITUM.
As móneo, mónui, mónitum.

EXAMPLES.

Verbs of the second conjugation always end in EO, and usually form the preterite in ŭI, and the supine in ITUM; as

MO'NEO, mónüi, mónitum, monére: *to admonish, to warn.*

Admóneo, admónüi, admónitum, admonére: *to admonish, to put in mind, to acquaint, to demand payment.*

Com-

Commóneo, commónŭi, ĭtum, ére : *to warn, to advise.*
A'RCEO, árcui, (árcitum *seldom used*) arcére : *to keep off, to drive away.*
Coérceo, ŭi, ĭtum, ére : *to restrain, to bridle, to keep under, to hinder, to bind, to compel, to comprehend or contain.*
Exérceo, ŭi, ĭtum, ére : *to exercise, to ply, to practise, to till, to occupy, to employ, to vex, to instruct, to train up, to get or earn.*
TE'RREO, térrui, ĭtum, ére : *to affright.*
Detérreo, ŭi, ére : *to deter, to intimidate.*
Extérreo, extérrui, extérritum, exterrére : *to frighten.*
Pertérreo, ŭi, ĭtum ére : *to scare, to put in great fear.*
HABEO, hábui, hábitum, habére : *to have; to dwell or continue in a place, to esteem.*
Adhíbeo, ŭi, ĭtum, ére : *to apply, to call, or send for, to admit, to join, to approach, to place near, to add, to make use of a thing, to employ it, to give, to deliver, to treat a person well or ill, to consult, to correct*.*
Cohíbeo, ŭi, ĭtum, ére : *to keep close or hold in, to hinder, to keep under, to restrain, to stop, to check, to contain, to inclose.*
Débeo, ŭi, ĭtum, ére : *to owe, to be obliged to a person.*
Exhíbeo, ŭi, ĭtum, ére : *to shew, to exhibit.*
Inhíbeo, ŭi, ĭtum, ére : *to hold in, keep back or curb, to stay or stop, to hinder or forbid, to menace, to intimidate.*
Perhíbeo, ŭi, ĭtum, ére : *to speak, to affirm, to give, to report, to esteem or account.*
Prohíbeo, ŭi, ĭtum, ére : *to hinder, to forbid.*
Redhíbeo, ŭi, ĭtum, ére ; *to return a thing one hath bought for some fault, and turn it on his hands that sold it.*
CAREO, ŭi, ĭtum, ére : *to want, to be free from, to be deprived of.*

ANNOTATION.

Some give *cassum* to *careo :* and it is true that we meet with *cassus* in authors; as *nunc cassum lumine lugent,* Virg. they mourn for him as dead, as deprived of life : but *cassus* is a noun, the same as. *lassus* and *fessus,* which ought not to be taken for supines,

* The signification of this verb often depends on the following noun, as *adhibere auxilium, cibum, potum, consolationem, consuetudinem,* and many others.

since

since we can form no participle from them, as *caſſurus*, *feſſurus*, &c. And this is the opinion of Priſcian lib. xi. Servius neverthelefs infifts that *caſſum* is faid for *quaſſum*, as if it came from *quatio*, by changing the Q into C. But Nonius rejects this opinion, and derives it *ab araneariu.raſſibus, quòd ſint leves*, he ſays, *& nullius ponderis*. Which is alſo confirmed by Servius.

RULE XIII.
Exception for the ſupine.

1. Dóceo *makes* doctum:
2. Téneo, tentum:
3. Cénſeo, cenſum.
4. Miſceo, miſtuim, *and heretofore* mixtum.
5. Tórreo, toſtum.

EXAMPLES.

Theſe verbs follow the general rule in the preterite, which they form in üi, and are excepted only as to the ſupine.

1. DO'CEO, dócui, doctum, docére: *to teach, to prove.*

Condóceo, üi, ctum, ére: *to teach together.*
Dedóceo, üi, ctum, ére: *to unteach, or teach otherwiſe.*

2. TE'NEO, ténüi, tentum, tenére: *to keep, to hold, to know, to catch one in a fact.*

Its compounds change E into I in the preſent and preterite, but not in the ſupine.

Abſtíneo, abſtínüi, abſténtum, abſtinére: *to abſtain, to curb one's ſelf, to avoid, to cut off, to hinder, to withdraw, to leave, to quit.*

Contíneo, tínüi, téntum, ére: *to hold together, to hold in, to keep cloſe, to keep within bounds, to keep back, to bridle, to refrain.*

Detíneo, tínüi, téntum, ére: *to detain, to hinder, to retard.*

Diſtíneo, tínüi, téntum, ére: *to hinder, to keep, or hold employed.*

Obtíneo, tínüi, téntum, ére: *to obtain what one aſks, to accompliſh or effect, to poſſeſs, to have in one's power, to be maſter of a thing.*

Pertíneo, tínüi, téntum, ére: *to belong, to reach, lie, or extend from one place or perſon to another, to tend to or drive at.*

Re-

Retíneo, tínüi téntum, ére: *to hold or keep back, or in; to restrain or govern; to retain or preserve.*

Sustíneo, tínüi, téntum, ére: *to hold or stay up, to support, to bear with, to suffer or undergo, to curb or keep in, to put off, to defer.*

3. CE'NSEO, cénsui, sum, censére: *to think, to judge, to give one's opinion; to vote or give one's suffrage; to tax, levy, rate, cess or assess, as the censors did the people; to pay the rate or cess, or to inroll or set down in order to pay.*

Recénseo, üi, sum, ére: *to muster, to survey, to count, to recite.*

Succénseo, üi, sum, ére: *to be angry with one.*

4. MI'SCEO, míscui, místum: *and heretofore* mixtum, miscére: *to mingle, to disturb.*

Admísceo, üi, ístum, ére: *to mingle with, to meddle with.*

Commísceo, üi, ístum, ére: *to mingle together, to jumble.*

Immísceo, üi, immístum, immiscére: *to mingle with.*

Intermísceo, üi, ístum, ére: *to intermingle.*

Permísceo, üi, ístum, ére: *to mingle together thoroughly, to confound, to disorder.*

5. TO'RREO, tórrui, tostum, torrére: *to roast, to broil, to scorch.*

ANNOTATION.

Attineo, üi, and *pertineo, üi,* have no supine: but *atténtus* comes from *attendo*. From the supine *absténtum,* comes *abstentus,* in the civil law, kept out of possession. *Scævol. Papin. Ulpian.* And in S. Cyprian, *absténti,* those who are kept from the communion.

Censeo, was also used heretofore in an active sense, whence comes *census sum,* the preterite in Ovid. *Recenso senatu* in Suetonius. . But they likewise said *censio,* of the fourth conjugation, whence comes *censitor* in Ulpian, and the participle *recensitus,* the penultima long in Claudian from *recensire.*

Mixtum comes from *mistum,* as they heretofore said *Ulyxes* for *Ulysses.* Some reject it as a corrupt word, and Priscian writes only *mistum.* Yet it occurs sometimes among the ancients, and borders very near upon the Greek word μίξις, *mixtio.*

Careo, which is hereto added by Despauter, follows simply the general rule. See the annotation to the preceding rule.

Rule XIV.
Of the verbs neuter that have no supine.

1. *Verbs neuter that make the preterite in* üi, *have no supine.*
2. *(Nor has* tímeo *any supine, though it be a verb active.)*
3. *We are to except* váleo, pláceo, cáreo, méreo, jáceo, páreo, líceo, nóceo, dóleo, láteo, cáleo, præ'beo, óleo.

Examples.

1. A verb neuter is that which is conjugated like the active, and hath no passive. Those which make üi, follow the general rule in regard to the preterite, but have no supine, as

CLAREO, clárüi, ére: *to be clear, to be illustrious, to be manifest.*

FLOREO, flórüi, ére: *to flourish, to be in esteem.*

LI'QUEO, üi, ére: *not much used; to melt.* Delíqueo, delícui, ére: *to be dissolved, to melt.*

MI'NEO, üi, ére, Lucr. *to exist, to be above, to hang ready to fall.* It is unusual except it be compounded.

Emíneo, emínui, eminére: *to shew itself above others, to overtop, to excel, to be notorious.*

Immíneo, üi, ére, Lucr. *to hang over head, to be at hand, to be like to come to pass ere it be long, to seek after, to have a design upon.*

Præmíneo, üi. ére: *to surpass, to excel.*

Promíneo, üi, ére: *to jut or stand out, to shew itself from afar, to hang over.*

PA'LLEO, pállui, pallére: *to be pale, to grow pale.*

PA'TEO, pátui, ére: *to be open, to lie plain or spread out, to be extended in length.*

PO'LLEO, üi, *(seldom used)* pollére: *to be able, to be powerful, to excel.*

Æquipollére: *to be of the same force or value;* præpollére: *to be of great power, to excel others.*

RAU'CEO, ráucui, raucére: *to be hoarse.* We say also *ráucio* of the fourth.

SI'LEO,

SI'LEO, síluj, ére: *to hold his peace, to keep silence, to be quiet or still.* It is said of every thing that is capable of making any noise, and therefore denotes the cessation of such actions as properly belong to each thing; as *luna silet,* the moon does not shine.

SPLE'NDEO, üi, ére: *to shine out, to be bright.*

STU'DEO, üi, ére: *to study, to desire, to endeavour, to serve, to assist, to favour, to labour, to fancy, to give one's self to it, to be passionately fond of, to take care of, to provide for.*

2. TI'MEO. tímui, timére: *to fear, to be afraid of.* It is a verb active, but it follows the rule of the neuters.

3. The following are excepted, and form their supine according to the general rule, though they be verbs neuter.

VA'LEO, válüi, ĭtum, ére: *to be strong, to be of authority, force or power; to be in health, to be in force, to profit, to avail, to be of importance, to be worth.*

Conváleo, üi, ĭtum, ére: *to wax strong, to recover health, to grow, to get force.*

Inváleo, üi, ĭtum, ére: *to wax strong, to recover, to be in health, to grow in use.*

Præváleo, üi, ĭtum, ére: *to prevail, to be better or of more value, to excel, to be stronger.*

PLA'CEO, plácui, plácitum, placére: *to please.*

Compláçeo, üi, ĭtum, ére: *to please, or be well liked.*

Displíceo, displícui, displícitum, displicére: *to displease.*

CA'REO, cárui, cáritum: *to be without, to want.*

ME'REO, mérui, ĭtum, ére: *to earn or gain, to deserve either good or evil, to take pay for service in war, to purchase or to get whether by desert or otherwise, to take by way of reward.*

We say also méreor, méritus sum, meréri, *which signifieth the same thing.*

But *ma'reo* has a different meaning: see rule 77.

Eméreo, or eméreor: *to deserve, to have served one's time at war, to be discharged from further service or duty, to be no longer obliged to serve.*

Proméreo, or prom éreor: *to deserve, to render service, to do pleasure, to oblige.*

JA'-

OF PRÉTERITES AND SUPINES.

JA'CEO, ŭi. ĭtum, (*whence comes* jacitúrus) jacére: *to lie along or at length, to be fallen, to be sunk.*

PA'REO, párŭi, páritum, parére: *to appear, to be plain or manifest, to obey.*

Appáreo, ŭi, ĭtum, ére: *to appear, to be seen, to shew himself.*

Compáreo, ŭi, ĭtum, ére: *to appear, to be extant.*

LI'CEO, lícui, licitum, licére: *to be lawful, to be prized or valued, to be set at a price for what it is to be sold.* It has a passive signification, and on the contrary

LI'CEOR, licéris, lícitus sum, ére, hath an active signification: *to cheapen a thing, to bid money for it.*

NO'CEO, nócui, nócitum, nocére: *to hurt, to endamage.*

DO'LEO, ŭi, ĭtum, ére: *to be in pain, to ake, to be sorry, to be displeased, to grieve, to pity, to repine, to fret.*

Condóleo, ŭi, ére: *to ake, to be in much pain; to condole.*

Indóleo, ŭi, ĭtum, ére: *to be sorry, to feel pain.*

LA'TEO, ŭi, ĭtum, ére: *to lie hid, to be unknown.*

Delíteo, delítui, *without a supine*, tére: *the same, or to conceal one's self.*

CA'LEO, cálŭi, cálitum, calére: *to be hot, to grow warm.*

Incáleo, incálŭi, incálitum, incalére: *to be warm.*

PRÆ'BEO, præbŭi, ĭtum, ére: *to minister to, to allow, to afford, to give, to offer, to give occasion to, to cause.*

OLEO, ólŭi, ólitum, *or even* étum, ólére: *to smell, savour, or scent of, to yield a smell or savour; to stink or smell strong:* and heretofore *to grow;* also *to ruin, to destroy.*

ANNOTATION.

We might give here some more verbs neuter in *eo*: but their supines are rare or unusual, as well as a good many of these here, which have yet their participles and their verbal nouns, as *valiturus* in Ovid, *præbiturus* in Colum. *Præbitus* in Livy, and *præbitor* in Cic. *coalitus*, Tacit. *jaciturus*, Statius, *caliturus*, Ovid, *latiturus*, and even *latito*. Cic. and the like.

EMINEO, and the others which Despauter derives from *maneo*, come from the old verb *mineo*, which is still read in Lucretius.

Inclinata minent in eamdem prodita partem, de rer. nat. l. 6.
And the right etymology of these verbs is to derive them from *mina*, signifying a high place; whence comes *minæ, minarum*, battlements, or the copings of a wall; and thence also *minæ* threats.

No′ceo, of which some have doubted, is read in the supine in Cæsar: *Ipsi verò nihil nocitum iri*, 5. Bell. Gall. And thence also comes the participle *nociturus*.

On the contrary, Pateo, which Despauter joins to these, has only *patui*, without a supine: for *passum*, can come only from *pando* or from *patior. Crinibus Iliades passis*, Virg. *Passis velis provehi*, Cic. *Multa, quoque & bello passus*, Virg. &c. And we shall find that Diomedes, lib. 9. derives it also from thence.

Oleo, heretofore made also *olévi*, according to Priscian, but he gives no authority for it. The supine *oletum* seems to have been used; which some have attempted to prove by this passage of Persius,
——— *veto quisquam hic faxit oletum.*
Though *oletum* is here no more than a simple noun substantive.
The preterite *olui* is more usual.
Vina ferè dulces oluerunt mane Camœnæ.
But the supine, whether in *itum*, or in *etum*, is rarely used except in the compound verbs, for which we shall give the next rule.

Rule XV.
Of the compounds of *oleo*.

1. *The compounds of* oleo *that signify to smell, make* üi, itum.
2. *Those of another signification, more usually have* evi, etum.
3. *But* abolévi, *makes* abólitum.
4. *And* adolévi, adúltum.

Examples.

1. O′leo, *to smell, to savour*, is in the foregoing rule. In regard to its compounds, those which retain this usual signification of the simple verb, retain also most frequently its preterite üi, and form the supine in ITUM, as

Obóleo, obólui, obólitum, ére: *to smell, to yield a smell or savour*.

Peróleo, perólui, perólitum, ére: *to smell very strong, to stink*.

Redóleo, redólui, ïtum, ére: *to smell, to cast a smell or stink*.

Subóleo,

Of Preterites and Supines.

Subóleo, ŭi, ĭtum, ére: *to savour or smell a little, to suspect or mistrust.*

2. The other compounds of this verb, that have not this signification, more usually form EVI and ETUM: as

Exóleo *or* exoléfco, exolévi, étum, ére: *to wax stale; to grow out of use, to be forgotten.*

Obsóleo *or* éfco, évi, étum, ére: *to grow out of use or fashion, to decay, to lose its grace and authority.*

3. Abóleo, évi, ĭtum, ére: *to abolish, to consume, to wash away.*

We say likewise aboléfco, *in a passive signification.* Memória hujus rei propè jam aboléverat: *was almost extinct.*

4. Adóleo *or* adoléfco, adolévi, adúltum, adoléré: *to grow, to worship by burnt offerings, to burn.*

ANNOTATION.

O'LEO, as we have already observed, had heretofore three significations, *to smell or yield a smell, to grow,* and *to ruin or destroy.* In the first signification it came from ὄδωδα, the Attic præterite of the verb ὄζω, *oleo*, by changing *d* into *l*, in the same manner as of δάκρυω they have made *lacryma*, and the like. Hence, according to Festus, the antients said *odefacit*, for *olefacit*, just as we still use *odor* with a *d*.

In the second signification, *oleo* comes from *alo*, to grow, to nourish, of which was first formed *olo*, as it is still in antient writers; and thence come *proles* and *soboles*.

In the third signification it comes from ὀλίω, ἕλλυμι, *perdo*; whence also comes *aboleo*, to abolish.

Adultum is from *adoltum*, taking *u* instead of *o*; and *adoltum* is only a syncope of *adolitum*. We meet also with *adolui*; whence should come *adolitum*; which some say relates rather to the burning of incense and to sacrificing; though it is read in both senses. *Postquam adoluerit juventus,* Varro apud Prisc. Now *adolesco* is the same as *accresco*; for as of *creo* is formed *cresco*, so of *oleo*, derived from *alo*, is formed *olesco*, and thence *adolesco*, whence comes *adolescens*.

Exoleo makes *exolevi*, whence is formed *exoletus*: *Domi reliqui exoletam virginem,* Plaut, that is, *past the prime, growing stale.* The same author makes use of *obolevit*, and Lucilius of *peroleffe* for *peroleviffe*, to smell strong.

Quis totum scis corpus jam peroleffe bisulcis, lib. 30.

But neither this verb, nor *jubuleo*, nor evi, oleo or adolefco, nor *redoleo* or *redolefco*, are perhaps to be found in the preterite tense in any classic author. We must not therefore be surprised, if some insist on their forming ŭi, and others EVI, though the surest way is always to follow the distinction of the signification, according to

Verepous and Alvarez, as we have also observed in the rule. Hence *inolevit* occurs several times in Gellius. *Inoleverat illi hæc vox*, &c.

Nevertheless the fathers frequently make use of *inolitus*, as *inolitæ concupiscentiæ vitium*, &c. The corruption of an inbred concupiscence, or which hath grown up with one, or one hath been accustomed to. And this seems to be in favour of those who derive it from *soleo*.

The verbs in SCO which we have inserted here among the examples, are of the third conjugation; but the reason of our placing them is because they are formed and borrow their preterite of the verbs in EO.

Rule XVI.

Of *arceo* and *taceo* with their compounds.

1. A'rceo *makes* árcui *without a supine.*
2. *But its compounds have* üi, ITUM.
3. Táceo *hath also* üi, ITUM.
4. *But its compounds have no supine.*

Examples.

1. A'RCEO, árcui; *the supine* árcitum *is obsolete,* arcére: *to keep off, to hinder, to drive away.*

2. Yet its compounds preserve the supine.

Coérceo, coércui, coércitum, ére: *to restrain, to stop, to bridle, to keep under, to bind, to contain, to compel.*

Exérceo, üi, ĭtum, ére: *to exercise, to practise, to occupy, to vex and trouble, to find one work, to employ, to get or earn.*

3. TA'CEO, tácui, tácitum, tácere: *to hold one's peace, to say nothing, to be quiet.* It is said also of inanimate things, as *sileo* above mentioned.

4. Its compounds have no supine;

Contíceo, contícui, ére: *to hold one's peace, to keep silence, to become dumb or speechless.*

Obtíceo, üi, ére: *to be struck silent, to leave off speaking.*

Retíceo, *to hold one's peace, to conceal, to keep a thing secret, not to let one's grief or resentment appear.*

Rule XVII.

Of the verbs in VEO.

1. *Verbs active in* VEO *make* VI *and* TUM.
2. *But* Fáveo *has* fautum, *and* cáveo, cautum.

3. *Verbs*

Of Preterites and Supines. 197

3. *Verbs neuter in* VEO *have no supine.*
4. *And many of them have neither preterite nor supine.*
5. Férveo *makes* férbui.
6. Conníveo *hath* conníví *and* conníxi.

Examples.

1. Verbs active in VEO, form the preterite in VI, and the supine in TUM, as

FO'VEO, fovi, fotum, fovére : *to keep warm, to cherish, to nourish, to keep or maintain, to favour.*

MO'VEO, movi, motum, movére : *to move, to stir, or shake, to stir up or provoke, to remove, to turn out, to eject, to rescind or make void, to take away, to degrade, to depart from, to leave a place.*

Emóveo, vi, tum, ére : *to remove, to put out of its place, to make void, to banish, to transplant.*

VO'VEO, vi, tum, ére : *to vow, to promise a thing to God, to desire, to wish.*

Devóveo, vi, tum, ére : *to vow, to consecrate, to make a solemn promise to God, to make an offering; to devote to one's service, to engage.* It is also taken in a bad sense, *to accurse, or damn, to give one to the devil, and to wish that mischief may happen to him.*

2. FA'VEO, *makes* favi, fautum, (*and not* fatum,) favére : *to favour, or countenance, to be of a person's side, to wish him well, to desire.*

CA'VEO, cavi, cautum, ére : *to beware of, to take care of; to prevent; to avoid; to take security by bond or otherwise; to give security by hostages; to be bound for; to advise as a lawyer doth his client; to appoint, settle, or provide.*

3. The verbs neuter in VEO have never a supine, as

LA'NGUEO, lángui, languére : *to languish, to be sick, to droop, to fade, to grow heavy, to be cloyed and weary.*

Relángueo, relángui ; Claud. *the same thing.*

PA'VEO, pavi, pavére : *to fear, to be afraid.*

Expáveo, expávi, expavére : *to be struck with fear.*

4. Many of these neuters have neither preterite nor supine, as A'VEO,

A′VEO, avére : *to have a strong or ardent desire.*
CE′VEO, cevére Perf. *to wag or move the tail as dogs do when they fawn upon one.*
Fláveo flavére : *to be yellow, or to grow yellow.*
Líveo, livére : *to be black and blue, or pale and wan ; to be rusty and foul ; to grudge, to envy.*
  5. FE′RVEO, férbui, fervére : *to be hot, to boil, to be in a chafe or heat, to be transported by any passion.*
Desérveo, desérbui, deservére : *to grow cool, to be abated.*
  6. CONNI′VEO, conníví, *more usual,* connixi, vére : *to wink, to connive at, to dissemble a thing.*

ANNOTATION.

These supines in TUM seem to be only a syncope for ITUM. *Fovi, fotum* for *fovitum*. In like manner *fautum* for *favitum*, and *cautum* for *cavitum,* whence came *cavitio* in Festus. And as we read *cavi,* so we read also *catus,* in Hor. and in Cic. wise, circumspect ; sly, subtil ; and *catè* craftily, slily, in Plaut.

FE′RVEO should make *fervüi,* as *moneo, monüi :* but they have made it *ferbui,* by changing the *v* consonant into *b.* They say also *fervi : Sperabam jam deservisse adolescentiam,* Ter. in Adelph. which Lucilius made use of.

Fervit aqua et fervet ; fervit nunc, fervet ad annum.
But Quintilian does not approve of it.

Rule XVIII.
Of sorbeo and its compounds.

Sórbeo *makes* sórbui, sorptum ;
Sorpsi *is very rarely used.*

Examples.

SO′RBEO, sórbui, sorptum, sorbére : *to sup as one doth an egg ; to suck in, to drink up.*
Absórbeo, absórbui, -ptum : *to suck in, to absorb, to swallow, to carry away violently as with a storm, to destroy.*
Exsórbeo, exsórbui, exsorbére : *to swallow up.*
Resórbeo, üi, ére : *to swallow or sup up again.*

ANNOTATION.

Some grammarians, among others Despauter, will needs have it that *sorbeo* makes also *sorpsi.* But if heretofore they said *sorpsi,* it is because it came from *sorbo, sorpsi, ptum,* as *scribo, psi, ptum,* and

and not from *sorbeo*. Hence Probus speaking of the verbs in BEO, says that *sorpsi* is a barbarous word. And Caper also maintains that we ought not to say *sorbo*, but *sorbeo*; nor *sorpsi*, but *sorbui*; adding that we should not imitate Lucan, who has *absorpsit* for *absorbuit*.

Absorpsit penitus rupes & tecta ferarum, lib. 4.
Velius Longus also condemns *sorpsit*; *as a word very remote from the antient purity of the Latin tongue*. We find moreover that Cicero frequently makes use of *absorbuit, exsorbuit*, but never of *absorpsit* nor *exsorpsit*. Pliny has used the simple verb in the same manner; *Qui coagulum lactis sorbuerint*. The supine *sorptum* occurs likewise in this author, though it seems that heretofore they said *sorbitum*, whence also comes *sorbitio*. *Absorptus* occurs frequently in the sacred writings.

Rule XIX.

Of some other verbs that make VI and TUM.
1. Fleo, déleo, víeo, *have* EVI, ETUM.
2. *To which you may join the compounds of* pleo.
3. *As also* neo.   4. Cleo *makes* IVI, ITUM.

Examples.

1. FLEO, flevi, fletum, flere: *to weep, to cry*.
Défleo, évi, étum, ére: *to bewail, to weep for*.
E ffleo, évi, étum, ére: *to cry one's eyes out*.
DÉLEO, delévi, delétum, delére: *to blot out, to deface*.
VÍEO, viévi, viétum, viére: *to bind with twigs; to bend, to tie up*.

2. PLEO is no longer used, but only its compounds; as
Adímpleo, adimplévi, adimplétum, adimplére: *to fill*.
Cómpleo, évi, étum, ére: *to fill, to perfect, to accomplish*.
Éxpleo, évi, étum, ére: *to fill, to fill to the brim, to cloy, to satiate*.
Ímpleo, évi, étum, ére: *to fill, to accomplish, to satisfy*.
Óppleo, opplévi, opplétum, opplére: *to fill full*.
Répleo, replévi, replétum, replére: *to fill up, to replenish*.
Súppleo, évi, étum, ere: *to fill up, to supply that which is wanting, to fill the place of one that is wanting, to help one to speak where he cannot answer*.

3. NEO, nevi, netum, nere: *to spin*.
4. ClEO, cies, civi, citum, ciére: *to excite, to stir up, to call*.

ANNOTATION.

We say also *cio, cis, civi, citum, cire*, of the fourth conjugation, whence *cieo* seems to have taken its preterite: their compounds follow rather the fourth than the second.

Accio, accis, accívi, accítum, accíre: *to send for or call one.*

DELEO comes from the antient verb *leo*, which is still read in Horace, as we shall observe hereafter in the rule of *lino*.

RULE XX.
Of verbs that make DI and SUM.

1. Prándeo *and* video *make* DI, *and* SUM.
2. Sedeo *has* sedi, sessum.
3. Strideo *has* stridi, *but never a supine.*

EXAMPLES.

1. PRÁNDEO, prandi, pransum, prandére: *to dine.* We say likewise *pransus*, but in a passive sense.

VIDEO, vidi, visum, vidére: *to see, to take heed, to have an eye to, to perceive or understand, to visit and go to see, to consider, to judge, to order, to prepare, to be quick sighted.*

Invídio, invídi, invísum, ére: *to envy, to be loth or displeased to see.*

Prævídeo, prævídi, prævísum, prævidére: *to foresee.*

Provídeo, provídi, ísum, ére: *to foresee, to provide, to prevent.*

2. SÉDEO, sedi, sessum, sedére: *to sit, to be set or placed.*

Its compounds change the E of the present tense into I: as

Assídeo, assédi, asséssum, assidére: *to sit by or at, to sit close at, to attend.*

Consídeo, consédi, conséssum, ére: *to sit together.*

Desídeo, ére: *to sit still, to be idle.* } They have seldom
Dissídeo, ére: *to be at variance.* } any preterite.

Insídeo, édi, éssum, ére: *to sit or rest upon, to lie in wait, to beset.*

Obsídeo, obsédi, obséssum, ére: *to sit about, to besiege.*

Præsídeo, édi, essum, ére: *to preside, to have the management, care, or charge of.*

Resídeo, édi, éssum, ére: *to sit down, to rest or sit still, to remain or abide, to continue, to reside, to stick*

OF PRETERITES AND SUPINES.

or cleave to, to decline, to subside, to shrink or sink down, to abate.

Subsídeo, édi, éssum, ére: *to rest or settle at the bottom, to rest, stay, or remain, to lie in ambush, to wait.*

Supersédeo, édi, éssum, ére: *to sit upon, to omit to do a thing, to let pass, to supersede, to surcease, to give over, to leave off, to defer.*

3. STRI´DEO, stridi, stridére: *to crack, to make a noise.*

It has no supine: we say also *strido*. See rule 36.

ANNOTATION.

Verbs that have E in the preterite of the simple, retain it also in the preterite of the compound, though it be changed into I in the present; as we have here an instance in *sedeo*. We must except only the compounds of *teneo*, which retain the I of the present tense in their preterite. See rule 13. num. 2. in the examples.

RULE XXI.

Of other verbs which form DI, SUM, with a reduplication in the preterite.

1. Mórdeo *makes* momórdi, morsum.
2. *And* tóndeo, totóndi, tonsum.
3. *So* Péndeo *hath* pepéndi, pensum;
4. *And* spóndeo, spopóndi, sponsum.

EXAMPLES.

These verbs redouble the first syllable in the preterite; but this reduplication is lost in their compounds, according to rule 2.

1. MO´RDEO, mo-mórdi, morsum, mordére: *to bite, to detract.*

Admórdeo, admórdi, sum, ére: *to bite hard, to gnaw; to bite or cheat some one.*

Obmórdeo, órdi, sum, dére: *to bite all round, to gnaw.*

Remórdeo, remórdi, órsum, ordére: *to bite again, to chastise again, to gnaw, to grieve one, to cause remorse.*

2. TON´DEO, to-tóndi, tonsum, tondére: *to clip, to poll, to browze.*

Detóndeo, detóndi, detónsum, dére: *to shear, clip, or poll.*

3. PE´NDEO, pe-péndi, pensum, pendére: *to hang up, at, on, from, or about; to depend, rest, stay,*

stay, or rely on; to linger, to be in suspense, to be in pain for, to be unsettled through hope or fear.

Appéndeo, appéndi, appénsum, ére: *to hang by. But we say also* appéndo; appéndere aurum: *to weigh out gold.* See rule 37.

Depéndeo, depéndi, énsum, ére: *to hang down, to hang upon, to depend, to be in suspense.*

Impéndeo, di, sum, ére: *to hang over one's head, to threaten, to be near at hand.*

4. SPONDEO, spo-póndi, sum, ére: *to promise freely, to engage, to betroth.*

Despóndeo, despóndi, sum, ére: *to promise freely, to betroth, to promise in marriage, to despair of, to despond.*

Respóndeo, respóndi, responsum, ére: *to answer, to reply; to give counsel to those that ask advice; to agree, to act suitably, to correspond, to be proportioned; to succeed, to answer expectation; to stand, or be set right over against; to pay or satisfy.*

Rule XXII.
Of verbs that make SI, SUM.

Rídeo, múlceo, suádeo, múlgeo, hǽreo, árdeo, térgeo, *and* máneo, *make* SI, SUM: *But* júbeo, *hath* jussi, jussum.

Examples.

All these verbs make SI in the preterite, and SUM in the supine.

RIDEO, risi, risum, ridére: *to laugh at, to smile, to look pleasant.*

Arrídeo, arrísi, arrísum, ére: *to laugh at, to smile or look pleasant, to please or give content.*

Derídeo, si, sum, ére: *to laugh to scorn, to deride, to despise.*

Irrídeo, irrísi, irrísum, irridére: *to laugh to scorn, to scoff.*

MULCEO, mulsi, mulsum, (*and* mulctum, Prisc.) ére: *to stroke or lick, to sooth gently, to charm, to delight, to make gentle, to appease, to asswage.*

Permúlceo, si, sum, (*and also* xi, ctum) permulcére: *to stroke, to please, to asswage, to cajole, or treat gently.*

SUA-

SUA'DEO, suási, suásum, adére: *to counsel, to persuade.*

Persuádeo, si, sum, ére: *to persuade, to advise or put one upon.*

Dissuádeo, si, sum, ére: *to dissuade.*

MU'LGEO, mulsi, *and* xi; sum *and* ctum, ére: *to milk.*

Emúlgeo, emúlsi, emúlsum, emulgére: *to milk out or stroke*

HÆ'REO, hæsi, sum, ére: *to stick, to be fixed, to be close to, to doubt, to stop, to be at a stand, to demur.*

Adhæ'reo, si, sum, ére: *to stick to, to adhere.*

Cohæ'reo, cohæ'si, cohæ'sum, cohærére: *to stick or hang together, to be joined to, to be all of a piece, to agree.*

Inhæ'reo, inhæ'si, inhæ'sum, inhærére: *to cleave or stick in, to keep in, to be wholly given to, to dwell near to.*

A'RDEO, arsi, sum, ére: *to burn, to scorch, to be earnest and hot to do a thing, to love, to desire passionately.* It is taken both in an active and passive sense.

Exárdeo, exársi, exársum, exardére: *to be all in a flame, to be very vehement.*

Inárdeo, inársi, inársum, inardére: *the same.*

TE'RGEO, tersi, tersum, tergére: *to wipe, to cleanse.* We say also tergo, tersi, tersum, térgere: *the same.*

Detérgeo, detérsi, detérsum, detergére: *to wipe, brush, or cleanse; to wipe off, rub off, or cut off; to break down a parapet or battlement, to break and carry off the oars.*

MA'NEO, mansi, sum, ére: *to remain, to wait.*

Permáneo, si, sum, ére: *to continue to the end, to remain, to persist.*

JU'BEO, jussi, jussum, jubére: *to bid, order, or appoint; to decree or ordain publicly; to charge, to command; to exhort, to encourage, to wish.*

Fide-júbéo, -jússi, -jússum, -jubére: *to be surety, or undertake for.*

RULE XXIII.
Of those which make SI, TUM.

Indúlgeo *and* tórqueo *make* SI, TUM.

Examples.

These two verbs have SI in the preterite, and TUM in the supine.

INDU'LGEO, indúlfi, indúltum, indulgére: *to indulge, to be kind and civil, to excuse, to dispense with, to give one's self up to, to concede, to grant.*

TO'RQUEO, torfi, tortum, torquére: *to wreath, to twist, to whirl about, to bend, to curl, to wrack, to torture, to vex, to burl or fling, to wrest, to pervert.*

Contórqueo, fi, tum, ére: *to wind about, to twist; to turn round; to fling or burl.*

Detórqueo, fi, tum, ére: *to turn aside, to warp or draw aside, to misconstrue.*

Diftórqueo, fi, tum, ére: *to set awry, to wrest aside.*

Retórqueo, fi, tum, ére: *to writhe back, to cast back, to bandy, to untwist, to retort.*

ANNOTATION.

We meet likewise with *torfum* in antient writers. *Detórfum*, Cato; but this is not to be imitated.

Rule XXIV.
Of those which make XI, and CTUM.

Lúgeo, múlgeo, *and* áugeo, *have* XI, *and* CTUM.

Examples.

The three following verbs have XI in the preterite, and CTUM in the supine.

LU'GEO, luxi, ctum, ére: *to mourn.*

Elúgeo, xi, ére: *to leave off mourning, to mourn for one the full time, to be in affliction.*

Prolúgeo, xi, ére: *to mourn and lament beyond the usual time.*

MU'LGEO, mulxi, mulctum, mulgére: *to milk.* It forms also *mulfi, mulfum.* See the 22d rule. But the supine *mulctum* is most used.

A'UGEO, auxi, auctum, augére: *to increase.*

Adáugeo, adáuxi, adáuctum, adaugére: *the same.*

ANNOTATION.

Luxi may come from *luceo*, in the following rule. But the supine *luctum* is no where to be found, according to Priscian, though *luctus* is derived from thence.

Mulxi seems to be derived from *mulfi*, the same as *mixtus* from *miſtus*. But the supine *mulctum* is proved not only by its derivatives *mulctra* and *mulctrale*, but moreover by the compound *permulctus*; hence Salluſt, as quoted by Priſcian, hath *verbis permulcti*. This verb also forms *mulſum*, rule 22. But *mulctum* is more natural as well as more uſual; for which reaſon Voſſius affirms he would not ſay *ruſtica it mulſum*, but rather *it mulctum*.

RULE XXV.
Of thoſe which make SI or XI, without a ſupine.

1. A'lgeo, fúlgeo, túrgeo, úrgeo, *have* SI.
2. Frígeo, lúceo, *have* XI; *and all without a ſupine*.

EXAMPLES.

1. Theſe four verbs have the preterite in SI, but without a ſupine.

A'LGEO, alſi, algére: *to be grievouſly cold.*
FU'LGEO, fulſi, fulgére: *to ſhine.*
Affúlgeo, affúlſi, affulgére: *to ſhine upon.*
Effúlgeo, effúlſi, effulgére: *to ſhine forth; to ſhew itſelf; to reflect a ſhining brightneſs, to ſhine bright.*
Refúlgeo, refúlſi, refulgére: *to ſhine.*
TU'RGEO, turſi, turgere: *to ſwell.*
U'RGEO, urſi, urgére: *to preſs on, to preſs down, to urge, to be earneſt upon, to puſh on, to purſue, to conſtrain, to vex, to moleſt.*

2. The following have XI, but without a ſupine.

FRI'GEO, frixi, frigére: *to be, or grow cold.*
Perfrígeo, perfríxi, perfrigére: *to be very cold.*
Refrígeo, refríxi, refrigére: *to cool again, to wax cold.*
LU'CEO, luxi, lucére: *to give light, to ſhine; to be apparent.*
Collúceo, collúxi, collucére: *to ſhine, to give light.*
Dilúceo, xi, ére: *to ſhine; to be clear or manifeſt.*
Elúceo, xi, ére: *to ſhine forth; to be apparent and manifeſt.*
Illúceo, xi, ére: *to ſhine upon; to be day; to be conſpicuous.*
Pollúceo, xi, ctum, ére: *to make bright, to ſhine forth, to offer up viands by way of ſacrifice, to give a ſumptuous banquet, to expoſe to public view, to profane, to proſtitute.*
Sublúceo, sublúxi, sublucére: *to give a little light, to ſhine ſomewhat, to glimmer.*

ANNOTATION.

ALGEO seems heretofore to have made *alsum*, whence comes *alsius* in Cicero; *Nihil alsius, nihil amœnius*; nothing cooler, nor more pleasant. *Alsiosus* is in Pliny.

From *perfrigeo*, comes the verbal noun *perfrictio*, a vehement shivering by reason of cold.

From *refrigeo*, comes *refrictus*, cooled, appeased; which seems to shew that *frigeo* had heretofore a supine. But these nouns are rarely used, nor are they to be found in authors of pure latinity.

Polluceo seems also to have had formerly its supine, whence comes *polluctum, i,* Plin. a sumptuous banquet.

Here we may observe that all verbs of this second conjugation are in EO, and that there are very few of this termination in any of the rest. There are only *beo, calceo, creo, cuneo, enucleo, laqueo, lizeo, meo, nauseo,* and *screo,* of the first; with *eo* and *queo* of the fourth.

THE THIRD CONJUGATION.

This conjugation has no general rule either for the preterite, or for the supine; hence it will be more convenient for us to range the verbs according to the termination of the present, than of the preterites.

RULE XXVI.
Of the verbs in CIO.

1. Fácio *makes* féci, factum,
2. *And* jácio, jeci, jactum;
3. Elício, *has* UI, ITUM.
4. *But the other compounds of* lácio,
5. *As also the compounds of* specio, *make* EXI, ECTUM.

EXAMPLES.

1. FÁCIO, féci, factum, facére: *to do, to make.*

Of its compounds, some are formed of other verbs or of adverbs, and retain A, as

Arefácio, areféci, arefáctum, arefácere: *to dry, to make dry.*

Assuefácio, féci, fáctum, ěre: *to accustom, to inure.*

Benefácio, éci, fáctum, ěre: *to do good, to do one pleasure.*

Calefácio, féci, fáctum, calefácere: *to warm.*

Commonefácio, éci, áctum, ěre: *to warn, to advise.*

Labefácio, labeféci, labefáctum, ěre, *to loosen, to shake and make to totter.*

Lique-

Liquefácio, éci, áctum, ácere : *to melt, to soften.*
Satisfácio, éci, áctum, ácere : *to satisfy, to content a person, to discharge one's duty towards him, to pay or discharge a debt any way, to confess a charge and beg pardon.*
Stupefácio, féci, fáctum, ácere : *to astonish, to stun one.*
Tepefácio, éci, áctum, ácere : *to warm, or make warm.*
Terrefácio, éci, áctum, ácere : *to frighten.*

The other compounds of *fácio*, that are formed of a preposition, change A into I, and assume an E in the supine.

Affício, afféci, afféctum, afficere : *to affect, influence, or have power over; to move, with respect either to body or mind.*
Confício, éci, éctum, ĕre : *to do, to dispatch, to finish, to bring to pass, to perform, to manage a business, to make evident or to prove, to infer, to consume, to waste, to destroy, to kill, to get or procure, to gather, to obtain, to acquire, to spend.*
Defício, éci, éctum, ĕre : *to leave or fail one, to want, to decay, to revolt, to faint or be discouraged.*
Effício, éci, éctum, ĕre : *to effect, to do, to accomplish.*
Infício, éci, éctum, ĕre : *to stain, to colour ; to infect, to poison, to corrupt ; to imbrue, to instruct.*
Interfício, éci, éctum, ĕre : *to slay, to kill, to destroy, to consume, to burn.*
Offício, éci, (*without a supine*) ĕre : *to hurt, to hinder, to oppose, to resist.*
Perfício, éci, éctum, ícere : *to perfect, to finish, to complete.*
Profício, éci, éctum, ĕre : *to profit, to advantage ; to be good or serviceable ; to proceed or go forward.*
Refício, éci, éctum, ĕre : *to repair, amend or make anew; to refresh, to inspirit ; to cure or recover ; to renew, to fill up, to make.*
Suffício, éci, éctum, ĕre : *to suffice, to supply or furnish, to substitute, to stain, to infect.*

2. JACIO', jéci, jactum, jácere : *to throw.*

Its compounds change A into I, and assume E in the supine.

Abjício, abjéci, abjéctum, ĕre : *to throw or cast away;*
to

to throw or fling ; to leſſen ; to undervalue ; to ſlight or neglect ; to be diſcouraged, to leave off, to renounce, to depart from one's purpoſe, to proſtrate one's ſelf.

Adjício, éci, éctum, ĕre : *to caſt unto, to caſt upon, to add, to apply.*

Conjício, éci, éctum, ĕre : *to caſt together, to conjecture, to gueſs, to foreſee, to draw conſequences, to think, to find, to invent, to interpret as dreams.*

Dejício, éci, éctum, ĕre : *to throw or caſt down or out of the way ; to put out of office, to diſſeize ; to remove, or put away.*

Ejício, ejéci, ejéctum, ejícere : *to throw or caſt out.*

Injício, injéci, injéctum, injícere : *to caſt or throw in, to put on.*

Interjício, éci, éctum, ĕre, *to throw or place between or among.*

Objício, éci, éctum, ícere : *to throw to, to lay in the way, to object, to lay to one's charge.*

Porrício, éci, éctum, ĕre : *to reach or ſtretch out ;* it is properly a term uſed in ſacrifices, and ſignifies to lay the entrails upon the altar for the burning of them.

Projício, éci, éctum, ĕre : *to throw away, to reject.*

Subjício, éci, éctum, ícere : *to lay or put under, to make ſubject, to ſuggeſt or bring into mind ; to anſwer or reply.*

Trajício, trajéci, trajéctum, trajícere : *to paſs over, to croſs, to bore or run through, to decant, to tranſpoſe.*

3. Elício, elícui, elícitum, ĕre : *to draw out, to intice out.*

It is compoſed of LA'CIO, which is no longer in uſe. Its other compounds form EXI, ECTUM, as

4. Allicio, alléxi, éctum, ĕre : *to allure or intice, to attract, to draw on.*

Illicio, illéxi, illéctum, illícere : *to allure, to intice, to inveigle.*

Pellício, éxi, éctum, ĕre : *to inveigle, to wheedle, to cajole, to flatter.*

5. SPE'CIO, is now grown obſolete, but its compounds form alſo, EXI, ECTUM ; as

Aſpício, aſpéxi, aſpéctum, ĕre : *to ſee, to behold.*

Circunſpício, éxi, éctum, ĕre : *to look about, to conſider, to caſt one's eyes all round.*

OF PRETERITES AND SUPINES.

Despício, éxi, éctum, ícere: *to look down, to despise.*
Dispício, éxi, éctum, ére: *to look on every side, to consider, to think seriously.*
Inspício, éxi, éctum, ére: *to look upon, to pry into.*
Suspício, éxi, éctum, ére: *to look up, to admire.*

ANNOTATION.

Among antient writers we meet also with *allicui, illicui, pellicui,* but they are no longer used.

Conspicor and *suspicor* come also from *specio,* but they are deponents of the first conjugation.

RULE XXVII.
Of *fodio* and *fugio.*

1. Fódio *makes* fodi, fossum;
2. *And* fúgio, fúgi, fúgitum.

EXAMPLES.

1. FO'DIO, fodi, fossum, ére: *to dig, to mine, to prick.*
Confódio, ódi, óssum, ére: *to dig, to stab.*
Defódio, defódi, óssum, ére: *to dig down, to bury.*
Effódio, ódi, óssum, ódere: *to dig out, to dig up.*
Perfódio, ódi, óssum, ódere: *to dig through.*

2. FU'GIO, fúgi, ítum, ére: *to run away, to escape, to shun, to avoid.*
Defúgio, úgi, ítum, ére: *to avoid, to shun, to refuse to accept of, to disapprove, to invalidate.*
Diffúgio, gi, ítum, ére: *to fly or run away, to run into different places, to eschew, to refuse to do a thing.*
Effúgio, gi, ítum, ére: *to run away, to escape, to shun.*
Perfúgio, gi, ítum, ére: *to fly for succour, or shelter.*

RULE XXVIII.
Of the verbs in PIO.

1. Cápio *makes* cépi, captum;
2. *The obsolete* cœpio *has* cœpi, cœptum, *whence may come* incípio.
3. Rápio *hath* rápui, raptum.
4. *But* cúpio, *makes* IVI, ITUM.
5. *And* sápio *chuses* sápuï *without a supine.*

VOL. I. P EXAM-

Examples.

1. CA′PIO, cepi, captum, cápere : *to take, to seize or lay hold of, to elect, to call to a ministry, to consecrate, to oblige one to enter into holy orders, to please, to accept, to receive.*

Its compounds change the A into I, and assume an E in the supine.

Accípio, épi, éptum, ĕre : *to take, to receive, to hear, to learn, to consent, to approve, to interpret, to enter into possession, to be capable of something, to treat well or ill, to cry out, to reprimand.*

Concípio, épi, éptum, ĕre : *to comprehend, to conceive, to undertake, to meditate, to form, to have imprinted on one's mind, to dictate, to prescribe a form of words to which another man must swear, to draw up an oath in form; to look for stolen goods in another man's house, with a bason in one's hand, and a hemp girth about the reins, which was a pagan superstition.* See above.

Decípio, decépi, decéptum, decípere : *to deceive.*

Excípio, excépi, excéptum, excípere : *to take, to gather, to learn, to hear say, to receive, to withdraw, to extract, to write what another says, to surprize, to except, to mark, to make an exception of some principal point in a law, or contract, to succeed or follow.*

Incípio, incépi, incéptum, incípere : *to begin.*

Occípio, occépi, occéptum, occípere : *to begin.*

Præcípio, épi, éptum, ĕre : *to prevent, to take first, to foresee, to command, to teach.*

Recípio, recépi, éptum, ĕre : *to take again, to receive, to recover, to conceal or receive stolen things, to betake, to promise, to undertake, to come to one's self, to recover one's courage, to entertain or harbour, to accept, to admit of or allow, to win or make himself master of a place, to retain a cause upon a just action being brought, to reserve to himself or to his own use in bargaining, to return.*

Satisaccípio, épi, éptum, ĕre : *to take sufficient security or bail.*

Suscípio, épi, éptum, ĕre : *to undertake, to take upon one, to answer.*

2. Heretofore they said also,

COE′PIO, cœpi, cœptum: *to begin.* Alium quæstum
cœ-

cœ'piat, Plaut. *Let her take to another trade.* But this verb is no longer used except in the preterite and the tenses depending thereon; *cæpi, cæ'peram, cæpissem, cæp'ero, cæpisse.*

Its compounds retain the diphthong *æ* of the preterite; so that *incipio* and *occipio* coming from *cápio,* make *incæ'pi, incæ'ptum; occæ'pi; occæ'ptum:* and coming from *cápio; incépi, inceptum; occépi, occeptum,* according as we have above distinguished them.

3. RA'PIO, rápui, raptum, rápere: *to pull or take by violence, to plunder, to ravish.*

Its compounds change A into I, and take an E in the supine.

Abrípio, ŭi, éptum, abrípere: *to drag away by force, to carry away.*

Corrípio, ŭi, éptum, ĕre: *to catch up hastily, to seize on, to take up, to rebuke.*

Dirípio, dirípui, diréptum, dirípere: *to tear asunder, to pluck away by force, to rob, to ransack.*

Prorípio, ŭi, éptum, ĕre: *to take away by force, to slink away.*

4. CU'PIO, cupīvi, cupītum, ĕre: *to desire, to covet, to wish one well, to love him, to be glad to serve and oblige him.*

5. SA'PIO, *makes also* sapívi, *or* sápii, *but more generally* sapui, *without a supine,* sapere: *to favour, smell or taste of; to relish, to be wise.*

Its compounds change A into I.

Desĭpio, desipívi, desípui, ĕre: *to be a fool, to dote.*

Resĭpio, ívi, ŭi, ĕre: *to be wise, to come to one's wits.*

ANNOTATION.

Very likely *sapio* was heretofore of the fourth conjugation, and therefore has retained *sapivi* and *resipivi.* Which Diomedes sufficiently confirms, where he says that *resipio* is of the fourth, and makes *resipere* in the infinitive. From *resipuisse* comes *resipiisse,* and afterwards *resipisse,* which we read in Terence; as *sapisti* in Martial for *sapivisti.* But the supine of this verb is obsolete.

RULE XXIX.
Of the verbs in RIO and TIO.

1. Pário *forms* péperi, partum, *instead of* páritum.

2. Quătio

2. Quátio *heretofore made* quaſſi, quaſſum;
3. *Whence its compounds have taken* CUSSI, CUSSUM.

Examples.

1. PÁRIO, pĕpĕri, partum, *for* páritum, párere: *to bring forth young, to breed, to bear, to produce, to acquire.*

Its compounds change A into E, and are of the fourth conjugation.

Apério, apérui, apértum, íre: *to open.* See the 68th rule.

2. QUÁTIO *heretofore made* quaſſi, quaſſum, quátere: *to ſhake, to brandiſh, to ſhatter, to batter, to make one ſhiver.*

Its compounds have thence borrowed CUSSI, CUSSUM.

Concútio, concúſſi, concúſſum, concútere: *to ſhake, to brandiſh, to make tremble, to pelt.*

Decútio, decúſſi, decúſſum, decútere: *to ſhake down, to beat down.*

Diſcútio, diſcúſſi, diſcúſſum, diſcútere: *to ſhake or beat down, to put or drive away, to ſhake off, to diſcuſs, to examine.*

Excútio, excúſſi, excúſſum, excútere: *to ſhake off, to make to fall out, to ſhake out, to examine, to canvaſs.*

Incútio, incúſſi, incúſſum, incútere: *to ſmite, to ſtrike, to caſt into, to daſh upon.*

Percútio, percúſſi, percúſſum, percútere: *to ſtrike, to beat, to kill, to make an impreſſion on the mind, to delight.*

Repercútio, repercúſſi, repercúſſum, repercútere: *to beat or ſtrike back, to reflect, to dazzle.*

ANNOTATION.

Partum is a ſyncope for *paritum*, which is no longer in uſe, though from thence be formed the participle *pariturus*. *Si quintum pareret mater ejus, aſinum fuiſſe parituram*, Cic. Ennius, according to Priſcian, ſaid *parire* of the fourth; ſo that it is no wonder if the compounds have ſtill continued in this conjugation, as we ſhall obſerve in the 68th rule.

Quatio heretofore made *quaſſi, quaſſum*. But the preterite is unuſual according to Chariſius and Priſc. The ſupine *quaſſum* is in Servius. *Qaſſum*, he ſays, *eſt quaſi quaſſum & nihil continens*, in 2. Æn. Hence alſo it comes that we uſe, *quaſſæ rates*; and the frequentative verb *quaſſo*.

Rule

Of Preterites and Supines. 213

Rule XXX.
Of the verbs in UO,

1. *Verbs in* üo *make* üi, utum:
2. *But* struo *hath* struxi, structum;
3. Fluo *hath* fluxi, fluxum;
4. Pluo *has only* plui.
5. Ruo *makes* rui, rúitum;
6. *But its compounds have only* RUTUM.

Examples.

1. Verbs in üo make the preterite in üi, and the supine in utum, as

A′RGUO, árgui, argútum, arguére: *to reprove, to lay to one's charge, to accuse, to blame, to shew, to prove, to convince or convict.*

Redárguo, redárgui, redargútum, redargúere: *the same.*

A′CUO, üi, útum, ĕre: *to whet, to point, to improve, to excite, to provoke.*

Exácuo, exácui, exacútum, ĕre: *to whet, to point.*

E′XUO, éxui, exútum, exúere: *to put off cloaths, &c. to divest, to strip, to shake off, to free.*

I′NDUO, índui, indútum, indúere: *to put into, to put on, to dress, to cover over.*

I′MBUO, ímbui, imbútum, úere: *to soak or season, to entertain, to furnish, to store, to instruct, to imbrue, to wet, or dye.*

The compounds of LAVO, or of the unusual verb LUO.

A′bluo, áblui, ablútum, ablúere: *to wash away, to purify, to blot out.*

A′lluo, állui, allútum, allúere: *to flow near to, to wash.*

Díluo, dílui, dilútum, dilúere: *to temper, mix, or allay, to wash or rinse, to purge or clean, to explain, to clear up.*

E′luo, élui, elúitum, elúere: *to wash out, to rinse.*

Intérluo, intérlui, interlútum, úere: *to flow or run between.*

Pólluo, üi, útum, úere: *to spoil, to corrupt, to defile, to pollute.*

MI′NUO, üi, útum, ĕre: *to diminish, to lessen, to abate.*

Dimínuo, üi, útum, ĕre: *to diminish, to lessen, to fall from his rank, to lose his dignity, rights, and liberty, &c. to degrade.*

STA'TUO, státui, statútum, statúere: *to ordain, to establish, to build, to set or place, to pass judgment, to appoint or assign, to resolve or conclude.*

Its compounds change A into I; as

Constítuo, constítui, constitútum, constitúere: *to set, to range, to dispose; to constitute, to ordain, to regulate, to establish; to constitute or make; to appoint, to assign; to settle or determine; to purpose, design, or intend; to agree, to promise; to appoint a day and place for payment; to decide an affair upon the spot, to determine each particular affair; to settle the proceedings at law, to agree about the point in dispute, to appoint a judge, to name commissioners, to draw up a deed, to give or receive summons for appearance.*

Destítuo, destítui, útum, úere: *to forsake, to disappoint, to deceive.*

Instítuo, instítui, útum, úere: *to institute, to begin, to purpose, to deliberate, to ordain, to instruct, to teach, to prepare, to procure, to regulate.*

Prostítuo, üi, útum, úere: *to prostitute, to set open to every one that cometh.*

Restítuo, üi, útum, úere: *to set again in his first state, to restore, to re-establish, to repair, to set to rights.*

SUO, sui, sutum, súere: *to sew or stitch.*

A'ssuo, üi, útum, úere: *to sew unto, to piece.*

Cónsuo, üi, útum, úere: *to sew or stitch up, to join together.*

Díssuo, üi, útum, úere: *to unstitch, to unrip, to break off by little and little.*

Résuo, résui, resútum, resúere: *to sew again; to unstitch.*

TRI'BUO, tríbui, tribútum, tribúere: *to give, to grant; to attribute, to divide.*

Attríbuo, üi, útum, úere: *to attribute, to assign, to give, to pay, to appoint.*

Contríbuo, üi, útum, úere: *to contribute, to deliver, to divide, to separate, to attribute, to assign, to account or reckon among, to elect into a kingdom, to put one's self under protection, to join one's self to, to enter into society.*

Distríbuo, üi, útum, úere: *to distribute, to divide.*

2. STRUO, struxi, structum, strúere: *to pile up, to place, to order; to build; to contrive.* A'd-

OF PRETERITES AND SUPINES.

A'dstruo, *or* ástruo, úxi, úctum, úere: *to build near to, or join one building to another; to superadd or accumulate; to attribute; to affirm; to prove; to confirm.*

Cónstruo, úxi, úctum, úere: *to heap up, to put together; to construct, to build, to frame; to fit, to set in order, to suit.*

Déstruo, úxi, úctum, úere: *to demolish, to pull down, to destroy, to provide or prepare; to set in order; to furnish or store with things, to equip, to fit out; to give orders; to instruct.*

O'bstruo, obstrúxi, úctum, úere: *to stop up by building against, to stop the way to, to eclipse, to render less noted or admired.*

3. FLUO, fluxi, fluxum, fluére: *to flow, to melt; to flow from, to slip or pass away; to fall to ruin, to decline; to slacken, to grow remiss; to spread abroad, to abandon one's self to pleasure.*

A'ffluo, xi, xum, ĕre: *to flow upon, to abound.*

Cónfluo, xi, xum, ĕre: *to flow together, to gather from different parts, to resort, to abound.*

Défluo, xi, xum, ĕre: *to flow or swim down, to fall down, to fall off, to be at an end, to decay, to flow all out, to cease to flow.*

Díffluo, díffluxi, xum, ĕre: *to flow or run all about, to melt, to abound, to spread.*

E'ffluo, xi, xum, ĕre: *to flow or run out, to run, to slip and slide away, to decrease, to vanish away, to decay, to be quite lost, to be intirely forgot.*

Pérfluo, xi, xum, ĕre: *to run as a leaky vessel doth, to let the liquor out; to run through.*

4. PLUO, plui: *it follows the rule in regard to its preterite, but hath no supine,* plúere: *to rain.*

5. RUO, rui, rúitum, rúere: *to fall, to fall down; to rush, to run headlong; to level or pull down; to throw or tumble; to overthrow, to shock; to dig or drag out of the ground.*

6. Its compounds form the supine in UTUM, according to the general rule.

Córruo, üi, utum, úere: *to fall together, to fall or tumble down, to decay, or come to utter ruin; to fail, to miscarry, to fall into error.*

Díruo, dírui, dírutum, úere: *to break or pull down, to overthrow, to destroy.*

E'ruo, üi, utum, úere: *to pluck out, to tear up, to dig up, to overthrow, to destroy.*

I'rruo, üi, utum, úere: *to run hastily or furiously in or upon a thing; to rush upon.*

O'bruo, óbrui, óbrutum, obrúere: *to cover over, to hide in the ground, to bury, to overwhelm, to oppress.*

Próruo, prórui, utum, úere: *to cast or beat down violently, to overthrow.*

ANNOTATION.

FLUO seems heretofore to have had, not only *fluxum*, but also *fluctum*, since the verbal nouns *fluxus* and *fluctus* are both in use.

PLUO. Priscian, after observing that the verbs in UO form their preterite, by changing *o* into *i*, excepts this among the rest, allowing it only to have *pluvi*. Hence in his time they read in Livy, *lapidibus pluvisse* and *sanguine pluvit*, as it is still read in some old editions, where the most correct have *pluisse* and *pluit*. Which shews it to have been the same preterite, which changed according to the times. Yet Vossius believes that *pluvi* came from the old verb *pluveo*, and quotes from Plautus, *ut multum pluverat*, Prol. Men. But even in this passage the MSS. have *pluerat*, as is observed in the Dutch edition. Hence this preterite is looked upon as quite obsolete as well as the supine *plutum*, though we read *complutus* in Solinus, to signify *wet with rain*.

Ruo had also *rutum* in the supine, whence comes *ruta cæsa*, Cic. *moveable goods, things that may be carried away.* Yet Lucan has *ruiturus*. We find also *diruitam ædiculam* in an old inscription of S. Mark at Rome, as we say *eruiturus*, though the usual supine is *erutum*.

RULE XXXI.

Of the verbs in UO that have no supine.

1. Métuo, luo, cóngruo, réspuo, íngruo.
2. *As also the compounds of* nuo, *have no supine.*

EXAMPLES.

1. These verbs follow the general rule of those in üo, in regard to the preterite, which they form in üi, but they have no supine.

ME'TUO, métui, *(heretofore* metútum, Lucr.*)* metúere: *to fear.*

Præmętuo, üi, ére: *to fear beforehand.*

LUO, lui, lúere: *to pay, to expiate or atone, to suffer punishment.*

CO'NGRUO, cóngrui, ére: *to agree with, to suit.*

Ingruo,

I'ngruo, ingrui, ingrúere: *to assail, or set upon with violence, to be near at hand, to come, to fall suddenly upon.*

RE'SPUO, réspui, respúere: *to spit out again, to refuse, to reject, to dislike, to slight.*

It is compounded of SPUO, spui, sputum, ĕre: *to spit.*

Neither have other compounds hardly any supine.

E'xpuo, éxpui, expúere: *to spit out, to reject.*

I'nspuo, ínspui, inspúere: *to spit upon or into.*

2. NUO is used only in its compounds; as,

A'bnuo, ábnúi, abnúere: *to deny or refuse, properly by countenance or gesture.*

A'nnuo, ánnui, annúere: *to nod, to hint or intimate a thing by a nod, to assent, to grant.*

I'nnuo, ínnui, innúere: *to nod or beckon with the head, to make signs to one.*

Rénuo, rénui, úere: *to refuse or deny by a shake of the head.*

ANNOTATION.

Batuo makes also *batui*, without a supine, *batuere*, to beat.

Cluo likewise made *clui, cluére*, to shine, to be famed or esteemed, to fight, whence comes *clupeus* or *clypeus*, a buckler. Cicero has made use of the participle; *multum cluentes consilio & linguâ, plus tamen auctoritate & gratiâ sublevabant.* But the preterite of these two verbs is no longer current.

Luo heretofore made *luvit* in Lucil.

We meet also with *annuvit* in Ennius, as if it came from *annueo.* Priscian likewise takes notice of the supines *annutum* and *innutum*, but it is without authority, and only analogously to the other verbs in *üo:* yet some of these verbs seem to have had a supine, because we still say *nutus*, Cic. *renutus*, Plin. *luiturus*, Claud.

RULE XXXII.
Of the verbs in BO.

1. *The verbs in* BO, *make* BI, BITUM.
2. *But* scribo, nubo, *have* PSI, PTUM.
3. Scábo, *and* lambo *are without supines.*
4. *All the compounds of* cúbo, *have* ÚI, ITUM.

EXAMPLES.

1. The verbs in BO make BI in the preterite, and BITUM in the supine: as

BIBO, bibi, bíbitum, bíbere: *to drink,*

Cóm-

Cómbibo, cómbibi, íbitum, íbere: *to drink together.*
Ebíbo, ébibi, ebíbitum, ebíbere: *to drink up all, to suck dry.*
Imbibo, ímbibi, imbíbitum, imbíbere: *to drink in, to receive in, to imbibe.*
GLUBO, glubi, ĭtum, ĕre: *to pull off the bark of a tree, to pull off the skin, to flea, to strip.*
Deglūbo, deglúbi, deglúbitum, deglúbere: *the same.*

2. These two form the preterite in PSI, and the supine in PTUM.

SCRIBO, scripsi, scriptum, scríbere: *to write, to compose.*
Adscríbo or ascríbo, psi, ptum, ĕre: *to write unto, to write amongst, to add or join, to enroll, to enregister, to impute or attribute, to assign or annex, to subscribe or underwrite.*
Circumscríbo, psi, ptum, ĕre: *to draw a circle round, to circumscribe, to limit, to surround, to circumvent, to cheat, to abolish, to break, to cast out of office.*
Conscríbo, psi, ptum, ĕre: *to write, to compose, to enroll, to enlist soldiers, to range in a particular order.*
Descríbo, psi, ptum, ĕre: *to copy and write out, to draw out or describe, to divide or distribute, to order, make, or appoint, to define, to explain.*
Exscríbo, psi, ptum, ĕre: *to write out, to copy.*
Inscríbo, psi, ptum, ĕre: *to write in or upon, to inscribe, to intitle, to superscribe, to imprint, to ingrave, to implead.*
Perscríbo, psi, ptum, ĕre: *to write at large or throughout, to take a copy of in writing, to register, to pay a creditor by a bill, or note, to prescribe, to write, to describe.*
Præscríbo, psi, ptum, ĕre: *to write before, to prescribe, to write directions, to give a model or pattern, to command, to ordain, to regulate, to limit.*
Proscríbo, psi, ptum, ĕre: *to post up in writing, to publish any thing to be sold; to banish, to proscribe, or outlaw one, to sequester him, and seize his estate.*
Rescríbo, psi, ptum, ĕre: *to write back, to write over again in order to correct, to answer or to write against, to pay money by bill, to give orders for money upon a person, to return what one has borrowed, to assign over to somebody.*

Subscríbo, psi, ptum, bĕre: *to subscribe, to write under, to sign one's name to a thing, to agree with one, to approve, to join, or take part with another in a suit of law, to sign the charge brought against a person, to appear as his accuser and to support the charge, to judge, to condemn, to mark, to censure, to express or qualify the misdemeanour censured, to give in an account, to make a declaration of his estate before the censors.*

Transcríbo, psi, ptum, ĕre: *to transcribe, to write or copy out; to transfer, pass away, or give his right to another; to pay in discharge for another, and to write the name of the person you pay to.*

NUBO, nupsi, nuptum, núbere: *to marry, to take a husband:* but properly it signified *to cover or to be vailed.* Instead of nupsi we often find nupta

Connúbo, psi, ptum, bĕre: Apul. *to marry together.* Whence comes, connúbium, *marriage;* more commonly used than the verb,

Enúbo *and* Innúbo, úpsi, ptum, ĕre: Liv. *to be wedded to a husband.* Properly *to be married out of one's order, estate or degree.*

Obnúbo, psi, ptum, ĕre: Virg. *to vail, or cover.*

3. These two have no supine, and follow the rule in regard to the preterite.

SCABO, scabi, scábere: *to scratch, to claw.*

LAMBO, lambi, lámbere; *to lick, to lap.*

4. The compounds of CUBO, which are of the third conjugation, add an M to the present, which they drop in the preterite and supine.

Accúmbo, accúbui, accúbitum, accúmbere: *to lie down, to sit near to.*

Discúmbo, discúbui, discúbitum, discúmbere: *to be seated, to sit at table.*

Incúmbo, bui, bĭtum, bĕre: *to lean or lie upon, to apply one's self earnestly and vigorously to a thing, to incline or tend unto.*

Occúmbo, occúbui, occúbitum, occúmbere: *to die.*

Recúmbo, ŭi, ĭtum, ĕre: *to lie down, to sit at table, to lean, to rest.*

Procúmbo, ŭi, ĭtum, ĕre: *to lie down flat, to tumble or fall down, to hang or bend down towards the ground, to lean or rest himself upon.*

ANNOTATION.

Vossius makes *glubo* have *glupsi, gluptum,* and produces the authority of Plautus *deglupta mænas.*

The writers of the lower empire have also used *Lambio, ivi,* according to Adamantius in Cassiodorus, *lib. de Orthograph.* or even *lambio, lambui,* like *rapio, rapui,* according to Vossius; hence in the book of Judges, c. 7. we read also *lambuerint, lambuerant, lambuerunt,* which we find in Plantin's royal, and all the other best editions of the vulgate.

The reason why *accúmbo* and the rest have here an *m,* is because heretofore they used to say *cumbo* for *cubo,* just as we still say *jungo* for *jugo.*

RULE XXXIII.
Of the verbs in CO.

1. Dico, duco, *make* XI, CTUM :
2. Ico, vinco, *have* ICI, ICTUM.
3. Parco *hath* perpérci, párcitum, *as also* parsi, parsum.

EXAMPLES.

1. These two have XI, CTUM.

DICO, dixi, dictum, dícere : *to speak, to say, to pronounce a discourse or sentence, to harangue, to plead, to administer justice, to be of opinion, to give one's opinion, to appoint a day, to give in evidence, to promise in express terms the portion and marriage of a person, to alter the proceedings at law, to say a good thing or a bon mot, to let fall a jest or a poignant raillery, to taunt, to compliment, to ask pardon after having said something that was not agreeable.*

Abdíco, xi, ctum, ĕre : *to reprove, to disallow, to abandon, to refuse, to reject, to give the cause against one in law, to make him lose his cause, to forbid, to dissuade, to disagree, to be contrary.*

Addíco, xi, ctum, ĕre : *to deliver to the highest bidder, to sell and deliver, to set to sale, to confiscate, to give over to bondage, to sentence to bondage such as could not pay their debts, to design for some use, to favour, to authorise, to approve or ratify as used by the augurs, to devote and to apply one's self to some function or exercise, to condemn.*

Condíco, xi, ctum, ĕre : *to appoint, order, or agree upon a thing ; to undertake, to promise ; to claim in a legal way, to bring an action against a person, to fix a day.*

Edico,

Of Preterites and Supines.

Edíco, xi, ctum, ĕre: *to order, to appoint, give warning or notice; to publish by edict or proclamation; to advertise and tell before hand; to tell plainly, to declare.*

Indíco, xi, ctum, ĕre: *to denounce, bid, or proclaim; to publish, to appoint; to declare exactly the time; to ordain as a magistrate; to declare war.*

Interdíco, xi, ctum, ĕre: *to forbid straitly; to bar or hinder; to put forth an order or send out an injunction.*

Prædíco, xi, ctum, ĕre: *to foretell or tell before hand, to prophesy, to prognosticate.*

DÚCO, duxi, ductum, ĕre: *to lead, to guide, to conduct, to command, to draw, to prolong, to defer, to think, to esteem, to wheedle or cajole.*

Abdúco, xi, ctum, ĕre: *to lead away or along with one, to carry off, to take by force; to debauch, to remove from, or withdraw.*

Addúco, xi, ctum, ĕre: *to lead one to, to engage, to persuade; to bring, to straiten or draw closer, to bend, to shrivel, to shrink up.*

Condúco, xi, ctum, ĕre: *to conduct or bring along with him, to assemble, to undertake to do a thing at a price, to take a piece of work at great, to finish, to be useful or serviceable, to hire or bargain for.*

Circundúco, xi, ctum, ĕre: *to lead about; to abolish, to deface; to cheat, to impose upon.*

Dedúco, xi, ctum, ĕre: *to conduct, to reconduct, to accompany, to lead forth, to draw, to bring down, to turn out, to subtract or abate, to destroy, to diminish, to cut off, to transplant, to remove or withdraw, to introduce one person to another, to launch ships.*

Edúco, xi, ctum, ĕre: *to lead forth, to draw out, to nourish, to bring up.*

Indúco, xi, ctum, ĕre: *to introduce, lead, or bring in; to persuade; to make void, or cancel, abolish, disannul, rase, or strike out; to cover or draw over; to draw in, cajole, or deceive.*

Obdúco, xi, ctum, ĕre: *to bring, throw, lay, or put over; to lead against, to cover over, to oppose, to join the following to the preceding day.*

Perduco, xi, ctum, ĕre: *to bring through, to bring to a conclusion, to finish, to bring one to, to persuade, to carry on, on, to continue, to bring down, or lower a sum in contracts.*

Prodúco, xi, ctum, ĕre : *to stretch out, to produce or bring out, to prolong, to draw out in length, to gain time, to defer or put off, to promote, to dignify.*

Sedúco, xi, ctum, ĕre : *to draw aside, to seduce, to deceive.*

Subdúco, xi, ctum, ĕre : *to take or draw away, to remove ; to reckon, to cast an account, to deduct ; to steal, to filch ; to cheat ; to bring a vessel ashore, to draw or lift up, whence cometh* funis subductárius, *the rope of a crane.*

Tradúco, xi, ctum, ĕre : *to carry, lead, bring, or convey from one place to another ; to pass through, or to cross ; to traduce a person, to expose him to public shame; to pass muster, as when the cavalry were reviewed; to pass away, as one doth the time.*

Transdúco, xi, ctum, ĕre : *to lead over, to remove from one place to another, to transport.*

2. ICO, ici, ictum, ícere : *to strike, to touch.*

VINCO, vīci, victum, víncere : *to vanquish, to overcome, to defeat, to gain his cause.*

3. PARCO, pĕpĕrci, párcitum, *and* parsi, parsum, párcere : *to spare, to pardon, to use moderately, to abstain from, to bear with, to favour or support.*

Compárco, compársi, compársum, árcere : *to spare or husband a thing well.*

ANNOTATION.

VINCO takes the *n*, because it comes from the old verb *vico*, derived from νικῶ, whence also comes *pervicax*, one that is obstinate, and wants always to conquer or get the better.

PARCO. Corn. Fronto, an antient grammarian, and Verepeus, who wrote on Despauter, make *parsi* more scarce than *peperci*. But this distinction has no manner of foundation, no more than that of Donatus, who pretends that *parsi* is to husband or spare; and *peperci*, to pardon, which Servius absolutely denies. *Parcitum* comes from the preterite *parcui*, which was to be found in Nevius, according to the formation mentioned, p. 173. This supine we read in Pliny, book 30. chap. 4. according to some editions, *Italiæ parcitum est vetere interdicto patrum, ut diximus.* And yet it is from thence that *parcitas* comes, which we still read in Sen. 1. *de Clem.* From *parsum* cometh also *parsurus*, in Varro and in Livy, according to Priscian.

RULE XXXIV.
Of the verbs in SCO.

1. *Verbs in* SCO *change it into* VI *and* TUM,
2. *But* Pasco *hath* pavi, pastum.
3. Agnósco, *and* cognósco *make* ITUM:
4. Posco *makes* popósci, póscitum.
5. Disco *has only* dídici, *but no supine.*
6. Compésco *and* dispésco, *make* üi, *and heretofore had* ITUM.
7. *And* conquinesco *had heretofore* conquéxi *without a supine.*

EXAMPLES.

1. The verbs in SCO form the preterite by changing SCO into VI, and the supine by changing it into TUM; as

CRESCO, crevi, cretum, créscere: *to grow, to increase.*

Accrésco, accrévi, accréscere: *to grow, to increase.*

Excrésco, évi, ĕtum, ĕre: *to grow out much, or up; to increase, to rise.*

Concrésco, évi, ĕtum, ĕre: *to grow or be joined together; to congeal, to be frozen; to clot, to curdle.*

Decrésco, decrévi, decrétum, decréscere: *to decrease, to diminish.*

NOSCO, novi, notum, nóscere: *to know.*

Ignósco, ignóvi, ignótum, ignóscere: *to pardon.*

Internósco, óvi, ótum, óscere: *to know a thing among others, to discern from others.*

Prænósco, prænóvi, ótum, ĕre: *to foreknow.*

QUIE'SCO, quiévi, quiétum, quiéscere: *to rest.*

Acquiésco, acquiévi, acquiétum, acquiéscere: *to delight in, to put one's comfort or satisfaction in, to be easy; to acquiesce, to assent, or be satisfied with.*

SCISCO, scivi, scitum, scíscere: *to inquire, to ordain or decree, to give his voice or suffrage, to make a law.*

Adscísco *or* ascísco, ívi, ítum, ĕre: *to attribute to himself, to take to himself, to call for, to admit, to receive, to approve; to call in, to fetch in; to bring in use; to associate, to ally.*

Conscísco, conscívi, ítum, ĕre : *to vote by common consent, to make an order or act.*

Descísco, ívi, ítum, ĕre : *to revolt, to go over to the opposite party, to alter from himself, to quit the party he had embraced, to abandon his enterprize.*

SUE'SCO, suévi, suétum, suéscere : *to be accustomed.*

Assuésco, assuévi, assuétum, assuéscere : *to accustom himself.*

Desuésco, desuévi, desuétum, éscere : *to disuse himself.*

2. PASCO, pavi, pastum, *it resumes its S in the supine*, páscere : *to feed, to nourish, to please, to delight.*

Depásco, vi, stum, ĕre : *to feed as beasts do, to graze, to browze ; to cause his cattle to feed upon, to waste, to embezzle.*

3. AGNO'SCO, agnóvi, ágnitum, agnóscere : *to know, to find out, to acknowledge, to allow.*

Cognósco, cognóvi, cógnitum, óscere : *to know, to learn, to take cognizance of, to examine, to hear a matter debated; and as judge to determine it.*

Recognósco, óvi, ĭtum, ĕre : *to recognize or acknowledge, to review, to call or bring into remembrance, to muster over, to correct or amend, to take an inventory.*

4. POSCO, popósci, póscitum, póscere : *to ask, to demand.*

Depósco, depopósci, óscere : *to demand, to ask, to make a request.*

Expósco, expopósci, ĭtum, ĕre : *to ask earnestly.*

Repósco, repopósci, repóscere : *to ask again that is one's own.*

5. DISCO, dídici, *heretofore* díscitum, díscere : *to learn.*

Addísco, addídici, addíscere : *to learn, to learn more.*

Edísco, edídici, edíscere : *to learn, to learn by heart.*

Dedísco, dedídici, dedíscere : *to unlearn.*

Its compounds preserve the reduplication. See rule 2.

6. COMPE'SCO, compéscui, *heretofore* ĭtum, éscere : *to keep within the same pasture; to hold, bridle, or curb ; to appease, to allay, to assuage.*

DISPE'SCO, ŭi, *heretofore* ĭtum, éscere : *to drive cattle into separate pastures, to drive them home from pasture ; to separate, to divide.*

7. CON-

OF PRETERITES AND SUPINES.

7. CONQUINI'SCO, *heretofore* conquéxi, *without a supine,* conquiníscere:' *to duck the head, to bow or bend the body, to stoop.*

ANNOTATION.

From the supine of CRESCO, *cretum,* comes *cretus* for *procreatus,* as in Virg. *Sanguine Trojano cretus.* In like manner *concretus* for *coalitus.* *Concretus aër,* Cic. thick heavy air. *Concretum corpus ex elementis,* Id. compounded of elements. But we hardly ever meet with this supine in another sense. For when Virgil describing the spots of the soul, saith
—————————— *Penitúsque necesse est,*
Multa diu concreta modis inolescere miris :
He does not mean that they grew up with the soul, but they gathered and stuck to her, *conjuncta & inglutinata,* says Servius. It is true nevertheless that this same poet says in another place, *excretos à matribus agnos,* well grown ; and that Priscian produces another example of *decretus,* in this same signification, as we shall observe in the remarks after the syntax ; but this is very rare.

Agnosco and *cognosco,* come from *nosco, novi, notum,* which follows the general rule, but they assume an I in the supine, *agnitum, cognitum.* And yet heretofore they followed their simple, hence we find *agnotus* in Pacuvius, and Priscian quotes *agnoturus* from Sallust.

The preterite *novi* is often translated in the present tense : *novi hominem,* I know him : *novi,* I know it.

We meet with *noscito,* as if it had *noscitum* in the supine, whence comes *ignoscicturus* in Piso, 2. annal. But *ignoturus* is in Cic. *in Catil.* The compounds of *nosco* take a *g,* as coming from the old verb *gnosco,* taken from γινώσκω, which even Varro made use of. *Quæ stram gnoscite. Ignosco* and *cognosco* come from *in* and *con,* casting off the *n,* as *agnosco,* cometh from *ad,* casting off the *d.*

Posco hath *poscitum* in the supine, according to Priscian and several, but it is very rarely used. Yet we read *expositum caput* in Seneca. *Disco* hath no supine according to Erasmus and Melancthon ; but we find *disciturus* in Apuleius, which shews that heretofore they said *discitum.* Priscian also admits of *compescitum* and *dispescitum,* from *compesco* and *dispesco* ; in which he has been followed by Despauter. On the contrary Verepeus and Alvarez do not allow of these supines. All that can be said upon the matter is this, that heretofore they were used, though they are not so at present, there being no authority for them.

Conquinisco formerly made also *conquéxi,* according to Caper, as mentioned by Priscian, but we find no authority ; for which reason we should avoid making use of it. Now *conquiníscere* signifies properly to stoop, *in modum eorum qui alvum sunt exoneraturi,* says Vossius ; and it comes from *conquinire* for *cunire, quod est stercus facere,* says Festus, whence also comes *inquinare.*

RULE XXXV.
Of inceptive verbs.

1. *The inceptive verbs either have no preterite nor supine:*
2. *Or they borrow them from their primitives;* thus calésco *takes* cálui *from* cáleo.

EXAMPLES.

Inceptive verbs are so denominated, because they generally denote the action in its beginning.

1. These verbs have of themselves neither preterite nor supine; as

HISCO, híscere: *to gape, to open the mouth, to chark, chap, or open.*
Dehísco, *the same.*
Fatísco, fatíscere: *to chink, chop, or cleave, to split, to gape; to be weary, to tire.*
Labásco, labáscere: *to fail or decay, to be ready to fall, to give ground.*
Hebésco, hebéscere: *to grow blunt, dull, languid, feeble.*
Herbésco, herbéscere: *to wax green, to bring forth herbs or grass.*
Ingravésco, ingravéscere: *to grow more heavy or lumpish; to become worse, to increase:*
Lapidésco, lapidéscere: *to wax hard as a stone, to turn to stone.*
Mitésco, mitéscere: *to grow tame, gentle; to be appeased.*
And such like.

2. These verbs frequently borrow the preterite and supine of their primitive; as

Ardésco *borrows* arsi, arsum *of* árdeo, árdes: *to burn.*
Calésco *borrows* cálui, *of* cáleo, cales: *to be hot.*
Erubésco, erúbui, *from* rúbeo: *to be red, to blush.*
Horrésco, hórrui, *from* hórreo: *to tremble for fear.*
Refrigésco, ixi, *from* frígeo: *to grow cold, to begin to be cool, to be less vehement and earnest.*

ANNOTATION.

FATISCO cometh from *fatim* for *affatim*, and from *hisco*; just as from *fatim* cometh also *fatigo*. Priscian will have it that *fessus* comes from *fatiscor*, and *defessus* from *defetiscor*. But Diomedes apprehends them to be simple nouns, the same as *lassus*, and his opinion is the most followed. See p. 188.

SENESCO makes *senui* and *senectum*, whence cometh *senectus*, the substantive as well as the ablative, as *ætas senecta*, Plaut. *senecto corpore*, Sall. Also *senecta, æ*, old age.

RULE XXXVI.
Of the verbs in Do.

1. *The verbs in* DO *make* DI *and* SUM.
2. *But* rudo, *and* strido, *have no supines*.
3. Cómedo *sometimes hath* ESTUM.
4. Pando *hath* pansum *and* passum.

EXAMPLES.

The verbs in DO change DO into DI in the preterite, and into SUM in the supine.

1. CUDO, cudi, cusum, ĕre: *to hammer, to forge; to stamp or coin.*

Excúdo, excúdi, excúsum, excúdere: *to beat or strike out, to stamp or coin, to forge.*

Incúdo, incúdi, incúsum, incúdere: *to forge.*

Recúdo, di, sum, ĕre: *to hammer or forge anew; to stamp new.*

CANDO is not used, but only its compounds; as

Accéndo, accéndi, sum, ĕre: *to light, to burn.*

Incéndo, incéndi, incénsum, incéndere: *to set on fire, to burn, to provoke, to animate, to encourage.*

Succéndo, di, sum, ĕre: *to burn, to inflame, to set on fire.*

FENDO is likewise disused, but its compounds are current, as

Deféndo, di, sum, ĕre: *to defend, to keep, to preserve; to resist, to hinder, to keep off, to shelter, to maintain.*

Offéndo, di, sum, ĕre: *to hit or run against, to light upon or find, to offend, to displease; to mistake or take a false step, to meet with a rub, to have ill success.*

MANDO, mandi, mansum, mándere: *to chew, to eat.*

PREHENDO *or* PRENDO, di, sum, ĕre: *to take, to lay hold, to grasp, to catch.*

Apprehéndo, di, sum, ĕre: *to take hold of, to learn, to understand.*

Comprehéndo, di, sum, ĕre: *to take or lay hold of; to comprehend or contain; to comprehend or understand.*

Deprehéndo, di, sum, ĕre: *to take unawares or in the fact, to discover, to perceive.*

SCANDO, scandi, scansum, scándere: *to mount, to climb.*

Ascéndo, ascéndi, ascénsum, ascéndere: *to ascend, to climb, to advance himself to.*

Conscéndo, éndi, sum, dĕre: *to mount, to climb, to take shipping, to go on board, to imbark.*

Descendo, éndi, sum, ĕre: *to descend, to sink with too much weight, to come down to the palace or to court (because the Roman nobility heretofore resided on the hills) to set about a thing, to speak, to accuse, to fight, to take the field, to come to blows: to acquiesce, to agree, to condescend, to suit himself, to resolve upon extreme remedies, to alight, to come or to set foot on shore.*

Exscéndo, di, sum, ĕre: *to debark, to land, to alight, &c.*

EDO, edi, esum, édere, *vel* esse: *to eat, to consume.*

It follows the general rule: as also its compounds *ambédo*, to eat or gnaw round about: *exédo*, to eat up, to consume.

3. But cómedo, comédi, comésum, *sometimes takes* coméstum, comédere: *to eat, to consume.*

2. These two follow the general rule in regard to the preterite, but they have no supine, as

RUDO, rudi, rúdere: *to bray like an ass.*

STRIDO, stridi, ĕre: *to crack, to make a whizzing, to hiss.*

4. PANDO, pandi, pansum, *a regular supine, and also* passum, pándere: *to open, to spread, to unfold.*

Dispándo, dispándi, dispánsum *and* dispáſſum, dispándere: *to unfold, to stretch out, to spread about.*

Dispéndo (*Plaut.*) éndi, énsum, *and* éſſum, ĕre: *the same.*

Expándo, di, sum, *and* áſſum, ĕre: *to spread out, to display.*

Oppándo, di, sum, *and* áſſum, ĕre: *to spread out, or hang over against.*

Propándo, propándi, propánsum *and* propáſſum, propándere: *to spread abroad.*

ANNOTATION.

1. We must carefully distinguish *incusum* and *excusum*, which come from *incudo* and *excudo*, from *incuſſum* and *excuſſum* with two *ſſ*, which come from *incutio* and *excutio*, in the 29th rule. But CUDO, says Priscian, heretofore made *cuſi*, according to Diomedes,

Charisius

Charifius and Phocas; though he himfelf allows it only to have *cudi*, as it is in Virg. *Scintillam excudit Achates.*

2. Apuleius hath alfo *rudivi*, which may come from the ancient verb *rudio*, whence alfo is derived *ruditus*, like *grunnitus*.

We ufe alfo *ftrideo*, of the fecond conjugation. See the 19th rule.

3. The fupine *comeftum* may be proved by this paffage of Salluft; *comefto patrimonio*, as it is quoted by Didymus, if we believe Diomedes. But according to the fame Diomedes it is better to fay *comefum*, as we fay *ambefa*.

Ipfi tranftra novant, flammis ambefa reponunt, Virg.
Ambefas fubigat malis abfumere menfas, Virg.

4. PANDO, makes *paffum* in the fupine, becaufe, as Servius obferves, the letter *n* is frequently dropped in the verbs, whereof we fhall meet with fome examples in the 38th rule and elfewhere. Neverthelefs Charifius makes *pandor* to have *paffus fum, vel panfus*; and the latter frequently occurs in ecclefiaftic authors. Pliny likewife hath *expanfa retia*: and we read *difpanfae* in Lucretius. And indeed we often meet with manufcripts where thefe fupines have an *n*: which fhews that *panfum* cannot be condemned.

RULE XXXVII.
Of the verbs in DO that have a reduplication.

1. TENDO *makes* teténdi, tenfum, *and* tentum.
2. Pendo *hath* pepéndi, penfum.
3. Pedo *hath* pepédi, péditum.
4. Tundo, *had heretofore* tútudi, *but now only* tunfum.
5. *Its compounds have* TUDI, TUSUM.

EXAMPLES.

1. TENDO, teténdi, *(and heretofore* tendi*)* tenfum, *and* tentum, téndere: *to ftretch out, to extend, to fpread, to pitch a camp, to aim at, to tend, to make forward, to go, to advance towards, to favour.*

Its compounds lofe the reduplication.

Atténdo, atténdi, fum, tum, ěre: *to attend, to apply, to give the mind to.*

Conténdo, di, fum, tum, ěre: *to ftretch or ftrain, to labour or ftrive, to march, to be on his way, to quarrel, to debate, to be pofitive in a thing, to undertake, to make it good, to prefs or urge one with entreaties.*

Deténdo, deténdi, fum, tum, ěre: *to unftretch, to unbend; to take down a tent.*

Difténdo, di, fum, tum, ěre: *to ftretch or reach out, to fill or ftuff out.*

Inténdo,

Inténdo, di, sum, tum, ĕre: *to bend or stretch, to point at, to go along, to turn some way or other, to apply, to endeavour, to strain, to pretend, to intend, or design, to apply; to augment, to tune an instrument, to menace, to present a sword to one's breast, to commence a suit against one, to bring a charge against him, to want to declare war.*

Osténdo, di, sum, tum, ĕre: *to shew.*

Perténdo, di, sum, tum, ĕre: *to extend or stretch over, to go through with and complete.*

Porténdo, di, sum, tum, ĕre: *to signify before a thing happeneth; to portend or foretel.*

Præténdo, di, sum, tum, ĕre: *to hold or hang a thing before; to pretend, to cloak or colour.*

Proténdo, di, sum, tum, ĕre: *to stretch forth, to defer, to spread abroad.*

2. PENDO, pepéndi, sum, ĕre: *to weigh, to esteem, to rate, to pay.*

Appéndo, di, sum, ĕre: *to hang by, to weigh out or pay.*

Depéndo, di, sum, ĕre: *to weigh, to give by weight, to pay.*

Expéndo, di, sum, ĕre: *to weigh, to rate, to ponder or consider, to examine, to pay.*

Impéndo, di, sum, ĕre: *to spend, to bestow or employ.*

Perpéndo, di, sum, ĕre: *to weigh exactly, to poise thoroughly in one's mind, to try exactly.*

Repéndo, di, sum, ĕre: *to pay or weigh back in exchange, to compensate.*

Suspéndo, di, sum, ĕre: *to hang up, to delay, to keep one in suspense.*

3. PEDO, pepédi, péditum, pédere, Hor. *to fart.*

Oppédo, oppédi, oppédere, Id. *to fart against one, to affront and contradict.*

4. TUNDO, *heretofore* tútudi: *the supine* tunsum, *is regularly formed;* túndere: *to beat or smite, to beat in a mortar, to thresh, to bruise flat, to knock or drive in, to forge or hammer.*

5. From this old preterite its compounds have taken TUDI, losing the reduplication; and the supine they form in TUSUM, losing the *n.*

Contúndo, cóntudi, contúsum, contúndere: *to beat or knock,*

knock, to batter or bruise, to strike down, to repress, to tame, to humble.

Obtúndo, óbtudi, obtúsum, obtúndere: *to beat or buffet all over, to break or blunt the edge, to weaken or render less smart; to make hoarse; to make heavy or dull; to teaze, tire out, or dunny with tediousness and frequent repetitions.*

Retúndo, di, sum, ĕre: *to blunt or dull; to quell, allay, repress, or silence.*

ANNOTATION.

1. The Supine in TUM is more usual in several of the compounds of *tendo*, as *contentus*, stretched: and in like manner *distentus, obtentus, prætentus, protentus*. Yet *ostensum* is oftener used than *ostentum*, which occurs only in very old writers, from whence however cometh *ostentare*, and the dative *ostentui*, as *ostentui habere*, as well as the ablative *ostentu*, and the neuter *ostentum*, in Cic. any thing that happeneth contrary to the ordinary course of nature, and is supposed to foreshew something to come, either *good* or *bad*. Now *ostendo* is compounded of *ob* and *tendo*, just as *asporto*, from *ab* and *porto*, whether it is by a change of the *b* into *s*, or whether it has been rather owing to their having formerly made use of *obs* for *ob*, as we say *abs* instead of *ab*: whence also cometh *obscænus*, from *cænum*; *obscurus*, from *cura*, &c.

2. We likewise meet with a great many of these verbs without the reduplication, *Vectigal quod regi pendissent*, Liv. *Nostro tendisti retia lecto*, Propert. Which several not having rightly understood, have made it *nexisti*. But not to mention that Aldus and Regius's editions have *tendisti*, we meet with it also in Sen. *Et quà plena rates carbasa tenderant*. In Hercul. fur.

3. Most grammarians refuse a supine to PEDO, which Vossius does not, because, he says, we find *peditus* in Catullus, which must undoubtedly have come from *peditum*, as *crepitus* from *crepitum*

The antients used *tudo* instead of *tundo*, whence is derived the frequentative verb *tudito* in Ennius, and the noun *tudes*, an hammer, a beetle. Of this old verb they formed by reduplication the preterite *tutudi*, which Charisius and Priscian give to *tundo*. And Diomedes besides *tutudi* lets it also have *tunsi*. But neither of them are any longer to be found in authors of pure latinity. The supine *tunsum* may be authorised by the participle *tunsus*.————
Tunsis gemit area frugibus, Georg. 3.

RULE XXXVIII.
Of the compounds of *do* and *sido*.

1. *The compounds of* do *make* DIDI, DITUM.
2. *But* abscóndo *makes* abscóndi.
3. Sido *hath* sidi *without a supine*.

4. *Its compounds borrow* SEDI *and* SESSUM *of* sédeo.

EXAMPLES.

1. The verb *do, das,* is of the first conjugation; *dare,* to give. But most of its compounds are of the third, forming DIDI in the preterite, and DITUM in the supine.

Abdo, ábdidi, ábditum, ábdere: *to hide, to remove.*
Addo, áddidi, ĭtum, ĕre: *to add.*
Condo, cóndidi, cónditum, cóndere: *to build, to compose, to hide, to inclose.*
Credo, crédidi, dĭtum, dĕre: *to credit or believe, to think, to imagine, to trust, to put confidence in, to lend, to put into one's hands, to commit or intrust, whence cometh* créditum, *a debt, any thing committed to one's trust, credit, a trust.* Credo, *like* opínor, *frequently implies also a tacit irony.*
Dedo, dédidi, déditum, dédere: *to yield, to surrender, to give up, to give over, to put himself under the protection: whence cometh* dedititius.
Dido, dídidi, díditum, dídere: *to give out, to spread abroad, to distribute, to divide.*
Edo, édidi, éditum, édere: *to utter, to put forth; to set out in writing, to publish; to declare, to tell, to name; to bring forth; to produce or shew; to prescribe a form, to utter oracles.*
Indo, ĭdi, ĭtum, ĕre: *to put or set in: to put or lay upon.*
Perdo, dĭdi, dĭtum, ĕre: *to lose, to spoil, to corrupt, to kill, to destroy.*
Prodo, pródidi, próditum, pródere: *to betray, to defer, to disclose, to accuse, to divulge, to manifest, to transmit by writing.*
Trado, dĭdi, tum, ĕre: *to give from hand to hand, to deliver, to teach.*
Vendo, véndidi, vénditum, véndere: *to sell, or set to sale.*

2. Abscóndo, abscóndi, dĭtum, cóndere: *to hide.*

3. SIDO, sidi, ĕre: *to perch, to light, as birds do; to sink, or go to the bottom.*

4. Its compounds borrow their preterite and supine of SE'DEO, as

Afsido, afsédi, afséssum, afsídere: *to sit down, to sit by one.*
Con-

Consído, confédi, conféffum, considere: *to fit down, to pitch or light, as a bird doth, to settle, to sink or go to the bottom.*

Desído, édi, éffum, ĕre: *to settle, to sink or fall down, to sit down or go to stool.*

Insído, infédi, inféffum, insidere: *to light upon, to sit upon.*

Obsído, édi, éffum, ĕre: *to seat himself in, to surround, to besiege, to keep blocked up.*

Resído, refédi, reféffum, residere: *to sit down, to abide in a place.*

Subsído, édi, éffum, ĕre: *to settle, to descend to the bottom; to abide; to stop, or stay.*

ANNOTATION.

1. We read in Plautus *concredui* for *concredidi*, in Cafina. But it may be taken from *creduo*, which he himself made ufe of, *in Aulul.* For as of δόω they formed *duo*; and of δῶ, *do*; in like manner they faid *perdo* and *perduo*; *credo* and *creduo*.

2. Formerly they ufed alfo to fay, *abfcondidi*, according to Prifcian. The fupine *abfconditum* is in Cic. as well as *abfconditus* and *abfcondite*. But they faid alfo *abfconfum*, whence cometh *abfconfio* in Pliny; *abfconfor* in Julius Firm. and *abfconsè* for λάθρα in the old gloffaries.

3. Sido makes *fidi*, even according to Prifcian, though he acknowledges it was ufually avoided, becaufe it ought rather to make *fifi*. Hence he is of opinion that in this ftate of uncertainty it is far better to take the preterite of *fedeo* for the fimple, and to fay *fido, fedi*. Yet *fidi* is in Columella, *Patiemúrque picem confidere, & cum fiderit*, &c. This verb hath no fupine; but in regard to its compounds they muft certainly follow thofe of *fedeo*, as hath been already mentioned.

RULE XXXIX.
Of the verbs in NDO which lofe N.

1. Frendo *makes* frendi, freffum:
2. Fundo *hath* fudi, fufum; *fo* findo, fidi, fiffum; *and* fcindo, fcidi, fciffum.

EXAMPLES.

1. Frendo, frendi, *follows the general rule in regard to the preterite;* freffum *lofeth the* N *and doubleth the* S; fréndere: *to grind or gnafh the teeth together; to grunt, to break or bruife.*

2. FUNDO, fudi, fufum, fúndere: *to pour out; to caft metal, to yield or give in abundance; to throw into,*

into, *to pour into*; *to throw into a loosenefs*; *to diffuse*, *to scatter*; *to squander*; *to discomfit*; *to utter*; *to speak*.

Confúndo, confúdi, confúsum, confúndere: *to confound, to mix together, to throw into confusion*.

Effúndo, effúdi, effúsum, effúndere: *to pour out, to yield or give in abundance*; *to empty*; *to disembogue*; *to lavish, to waste riotously*; *to come or run forth in companies*; *to spread abroad*; *to relate*; *to discomfit*.

Infúndo, infúdi, infúsum, infúndere: *to pour into*; *to diffuse*; *to spread*.

Offúndo, údi, úsum, úndere: *to pour or sprinkle upon*; *to spread, or throw over*; *to impose upon, to deceive*; *to darken*; *to cover with clouds*.

Perfúndo, di, sum, děre: *to pour all over, to wash, to bathe*; *to bedew, to besprinkle*; *to imbrue, season, or give a tincture to*; *to fill, to replenish the soul with joy*; *to seize him all over*.

Profúndo, di, sum, děre: *to pour out*; *to pour out in great abundance, to spend extravagantly, to lavish, to squander away*; *to shoot out*; *to spread*; *to moisten*; *to shew itself to the very bottom*.

FINDO, fidi, fissum, findere: *to cleave, to slit, to divide*.

Diffindo, diffidi, diffissum, diffindere: *to cleave in two*.

SCINDO, scidi, scissum, scindere: *to cut, to pull in pieces, to tear, to break off, to divide, to break open, to refresh or renew*.

Abscindo, ábscidi, abscissum, abscindere: *to cut, to cut off, to rent off*.

Conscindo, cónscidi, conscissum, conscindere: *to cut or tear in pieces, to slash*.

Rescindo, ĭdi, íssum, ěre: *to cut off*; *to cut or break down*; *to retrench, to rip up*; *to abolish, to cancel, or repeal*.

FIDO. See the 77th rule of the verbs neuter passive.

Rule XL.
Of the verbs that make SI, SUM.

Ludo, dívido, claudo, lædo, trudo, rado, plaudo, *and* rodo, *have the preterite in* SI, *and the supine in* SUM : *the same must be said of the compounds of* vado.

EXAMPLES.

These nine verbs change DO into SI in the preterite, and into SUM in the supine.

1. LUDO, lusi, lusum, lúdere : *to play, to make pastime, to cheat, to banter, to write verses, to play at a game, to put a trick upon one.*

Ablúdo, si, sum, dĕre : *to disagree, to be unlike.*

Allúdo, si, sum, ĕre : *to play and sport with one, to play upon one or banter, to allude unto.*

Delúdo, si, sum, ĕre : *to delude, to cheat, to deceive : to frustrate or disappoint.*

Elúdo, si, sum, ĕre : *to avoid, to elude, to shift off, to parry.*

Illúdo, illúsi, illúsum, illúdere : *to play upon one, to mock, to jeer.*

2. DI'VIDO, divísi, ísum, ídere : *to divide, to distribute ; to distinguish a law or opinion, that contains several points.*

3. CLAUDO, clausi, clausum, cláudere : *to shut, to conclude, to finish.*

Its compounds come rather from CLUDO, which is even used by some authors.

Exclúdo, exclúsi, exclúsum, exclúdere : *to shut out, to put out, to hinder, to exclude, to reject, to drive out, to banish, to cast off, to hatch eggs.*

Inclúdo, inclúsi, inclúsum, inclúdere : *to include or inclose.*

Præclúdo, præclúsi, præclúsum, præclúdere : *to shut or stop up a passage, to hinder one from entering.*

Reclúdo, si, sum, reclúdere : *to open, to manifest, to reveal.*

4. LÆDO, læsi, læsum, lædere : *to hurt, to offend, to injure.*

Its compounds change Æ into I long ; as

Allído, allísi, sum, ĕre : *to dash or throw any thing against the ground, to break.*

Collído, collísi, collísum, collídere : *to beat, knock, or bruise together ; to dash one against another.*

Illído, illísi, illísum, illídere : *to dash or beat against.*
But Illæ´sum, *sound and unhurt*, is a noun, because there is no such verb as *illædo.*

5. TRUDO, trúsi, *seldom used*, trusum, trúdere : *to thrust, to push.*

Abstrúdo, abstrúsi, abstrúsum, údere : *to hide, to conceal; to cast away.*

Detrúdo, si, sum, ěre : *to drive away, to put out, to shove from, to defer.*

Extrúdo, extrúsi, extrúsum, extrúdere : *to thrust out.*

Intrúdo, intrúsi, sum, intrúdere: *to thrust in, to intrude.*

6. RADO, rasi, rasum, rádere : *to shave, to scrape, or scratch up.*

Abrádo, si, sum, ěre : *to scrape or shave off, to cut or chop off, to get from another.*

Corrádo, si, sum, ěre : *to scrape or rake together.*

Erádo, erási, erásum, erádere : *to scrape out, to put out, to blot out.*

7. PLAUDO, si, sum, ěre: *to clap hands, to applaud.*

Appláudo : compláudo *or* -ódo, si, sum, děre : *to applaud.*

Expláudo *or* -ódo, si, sum, ěre : *to drive out, to hiss, to reject, to explode, to fire off a great gun.*

8. RODO, rosi, rosum, ródere : *to gnaw, to backbite.*

Arródo, arrósi, arrósum, arródere : *to gnaw, to nibble.*

Corródo, corródi, corrósum, corródere : *to gnaw, to corrode or fret.*

9. VADO, vasi, vasum, *very little used without its compounds*, vádere : *to go.*

Evádo, si, sum, ěre : *to escape, to run away, to avoid, to pass over, to get or come to, to go or reach to, to climb, to become or grow.*

Invádo, inválsi, invásum, invádere :'*to invade, to attack, to take by storm, to fall upon.*

Pervádo, perválsi, pervásum, pervádere : *to go over or through, to pass through, to spread over all.*

ANNOTATION.

The preterite of *rado* is hardly to be met with uncompounded. Neither are the preterite and supine of *vado* more current. The preterite however is in Tertull. *Ad tum ex Libya Hammon vasit*, lib. de Pall. And in Mart. according to Aldus's edition, *et breve vasit opus.* Where others read *rasit.*

RULE

Rule XLI.

Of *cado, cædo* and *cedo,* with their compounds.

1. Cado *hath* cécidi, cafum :
2. *Its compounds, all but three, have no supine.*
3. Cædo *makes* cecîdi, cæfum ; *its compounds* cîdi, cîfum.
4. Cedo *hath* ceffi, ceffum ; *its compounds have the fame.*

Examples.

I have joined thefe three verbs together becaufe of the refemblance they bear to each other, that they may be more eafily remembered.

1. CADO, cécidi, cafum, cádere : *to fall, to flip or flide down, to tumble down, to fink or droop, to be difheartened, to be laid as the wind, to be caft in law, to fuit or agree with, to be capable, to arrive, to pafs, to fucceed, to chance or fall out, to come, to be.* From thence alfo cometh CADÚCUS, *ready to fall, unable to bear up itfelf.* Bona cadúca, *goods efcheated to the prince or lord :* fundi cadúci, *lands fubject to the right of amortization.*

2. The compounds of this verb change the A into I fhort ; but there are only three of them that have its fupine; viz. íncĭdo, occĭdo, récĭdo. The others go without.

A′ccido, áccidi, accídere : *to fall down at, or before, to fall, to happen, to come to, to be.*

Cóncido, cóncidi, concídere : *to fall all of a fudden, to die.*

E′xcido, éxcidi, excídere : *to fall out or away, to fail or forget, to fail or perifh, to be forgotten.*

I′ncido, ĭdi, incáfum, incídere : *to fall into, to fall in or upon, to meet with, to befall or happen.*

O′ccido, óccidi, occáfum, occídere : *to fall, to die.*

Récido, récidi, recáfum, recídere : *to fall back, whence comes* recafúrum *in Cic.* Id ego puto ad níhilum recafúrum.

3. CÆDO, cecîdi, cæfum, cæ′dere : *to cut, to whip, to beat, to ftrike, to kill, to diffect, to fell by auction, and by retail.*

It makes the reduplication by E fimple, changing the diphthong Æ into I long in the fecond fyllable, as well of its preterite as of the present of its compounds, which lose this reduplication, according to the second rule.

Abscído, abscídi, abscísum, ĕre: *to cut off.*
Accído, accídi, accísum, dĕre: *to cut all round, to bring to the ground, to demolish, to weaken.*
Circumcído, di, sum, ĕre: *to cut or pare about, to lop, to circumcise.*
Concído, di, sum, ĕre: *to cut in pieces, to chop, to beat, to kill.*
Decído, di, sum, ĕre: *to cut off, to decide or determine as arbitrator, by cutting off all subject of dispute, to appoint, to transact, to determine an affair, to compound, to capitulate.*
Excído, di sum, ĕre: *to cut out.*
Incído, di, sum, ĕre: *to cut, to ingrave; to etch, to grave; to pare about; to cut or make shorter.*
Occído, di, sum, ĕre: *to kill, to torment.*
Præcído, di, sum, ĕre: *to cut, pare, or chop off; to take away clean; to prevent.*
Recído, di, sum, ĕre: *to cut off, to pare.*
Succído, di, sum, ĕre: *to cut down, to fell trees; also to mow corn.*

    4. CEDO, cessi, cessum, cédere: *to give place, to give up or resign, to give ground, to retreat, to pass away, to come, to happen, to fall out, to belong and devolve to a person.* Hence cometh the word céssio, *speaking of the term or time appointed for doing any particular thing, or when the day of payment is come, and we have a right to demand our money.*

Abscédo, abscéssi, abscéssum, abscédere: *to withdraw, to depart, to leave off, to suppurate.*
Accédo, éssi, éssum, édere: *to draw near, to be added to, or increased, to govern, to engage in some employment, to submit, to agree, to suit himself, to consent, to be like, to be conformable, to be comparable, to be accessory or joined to another thing so as to increase it.* Accédit quod, &c. *There is this moreover, which is often translated by, besides, farther,* &c.
Concédo, éssi, éssum, dere: *to give place to, to grant,*

to allow, to consent or give way, to abate, to submit, to yield to, to permit, to give, to pardon, to quit, to agree, to condescend, to depart, to retire or withdraw, to go.

Decédo, decéssi, éssum, ĕre: *to yield or give place to; to pay honours to; to depart, to retire, retreat or withdraw; to quit his place, office, or government; to relinquish a thing; to be diminished or abated; to weaken or decay; to shun one's company; to die.*

Discédo, éssi, éssum, ĕre: *to depart, to go away; to put to the vote; to give his vote even without rising from his place; to be of a contrary opinion; to change sentiment; to retire when the war is at an end, and to lay down his arms; to open or gape; to come well off; to gain or lose his cause; to remain unpunished; to be changed; to except.*

Excédo, éssi, éssum, dĕre: *to be gone, to remove, to go out, to withdraw, to exceed, to surpass, to go beyond bounds and measure.*

Incédo, éssi, éssum, dĕre: *to go in state,* or simply, *to walk, to go.*

Intercédo, éssi, éssum, dĕre: *to come between, to oppose, to hinder, to intercede, to go between, to interpose. To be betwixt two things, as time, union, connection, division, enmity, friendship, &c. to happen or chance, to come in the mean time, to withstand, to engage or be surety for one's debt.*

Præcédo, éssi, éssum, dĕre: *to precede, to go before, to excel, to surpass.*

Procédo, éssi, éssum, dĕre: *to procced, to go or come forth, to march on; to walk in state, to go or come along; to advance, rise, or increase; to go forward; to go before; to prosper or succeed.*

Recédo, éssi, éssum, dĕre: *to retire or withdraw, to retreat, to give ground, to go from, to be at a distance, to return, to go back.*

Secédo, éssi, éssum, dĕre: *to go apart, to withdraw.*

Succédo, éssi, éssum, dĕre: *to come under; to come into; to approach, to come to; to succeed, or come in the place; to go well forward, to have good success.*

O B-

OBSERVATION.

On the preterites of some verbs in DO.

Here therefore we should take particular notice that *cedo* with a simple E makes *cessi, cessum, cédere:* and *cædo* with Æ, makes *cecĭdi* with a simple E in the preterite, because the *æ* of the present tense is changed here into *i* long, and the syllable CE is only an augment in imitation of the Greeks, just as in *fallo, fefelli*; in *tollo, tetuli*, and the like, but the supine *cæsum* resumes the *æ, cædere,* to cut. *Cado* makes also *cec.di*, but with the *i* short in the penultima. All these little differences occasioned this Latin verse.

Cedo facit *cessi ; cecĭdi cado; cædo cecídi.*

But we meet also in the pandects with *accedisse* for *accessisse*, and with *accederat* for *accesserat*, which seems to be too good authority to find fault with.

We must also take particular care not to be mistaken in regard to the compounds of *cado* and *cædo*. Those of *cado* change A into I short; and those of *cædo* change Æ into I long, as *occĭdo, occĭdi, occá um, occídere*, to die, to fall, from *cado:* and *occído, occídi, occísum, occídere*, to kill, from *cædo.* See the examples above given.

We should also take notice of the compounds of *Sido.* For *confido* with an S makes *confēdi, confíssum,* according to the 38th rule. And *concído* with a C, makes *concídi, concísum,* from *cædo :* or *cóncĭdi,* without a supine, from *cado.*

Notice ought also to be taken of the preterite of the compounds of *scindo :* for *cónscidi* with SC, and *conscíssum* with two *ss* at the end, come from *conscindo,* where the S is doubled merely to lengthen the quantity of the syllable CI, which from being short in the preterite, is long in the supine. And heretofore it was written also with a single S, as in Justin, *abscisis auribus,* and the like. See its other compounds in the 39th rule.

Rule XLII.
Of the verbs in GO.

1. *The Verbs in* GO *make* XI, CTUM.
2. Figo, frigo, *have also* XUM.
3. Pergo *hath* perréxi, perréctum ; *and* surgo, surréxi, surréctum.

Examples.

1. The verbs in GO make the preterite in XI, and the supine in CTUM. As

CINGO, cinxi, ctum, ĕre : *to tie about, to gird; to surround or defend ; to surround or inviron, to besiege.*

Accíngo, accínxi, accínctum, accíngere : *to gird to, to prepare for, to go about a thing briskly, to provide himself with, to arm himself.*

Præ-

Præcíngo, xi, ctum, ĕre: *to begirt, to encompass, to inclose, to get himself ready.*
JUNGO, junxi, ctum, gĕre: *to join, to put together, to associate, to yoak.*
Adjúngo, xi, ctum, gĕre: *to join to, to associate, to couple, to take in alliance, to take part with, to bring over or reconcile.*
Conjúngo, xi, ctum, conjúngere: *to join together, to ally, to unite.*
Disjúngo, xi, ctum, ĕre: *to separate, to disjoin, to divide.*
Injúngo, xi, ctum, ĕre: *to join with or upon, to injoin, to command, to inflict a punishment, to give orders, to join together, to build near, to assemble, to bring near, to bring or lay upon.*
Sejúngo, xi, ctum, ĕre: *to separate.*
Abjúngo, abjúnxi, abjúnctum, abjúngere: *to part or separate.*
MUNGO, xi, ctum, *very little used*, gĕre: *to wipe one's nose.*
Emúngo, emúnxi, emúnctum, ĕre: *to wipe or snuff the nose, to snuff a candle, to cheat one of his money.*
PLANGO, planxi, planctum, plángere: *to beat or strike against; to lament, bewail, or bemoan.*
TINGO, tinxi, tinctum, tíngere: *to dye, to colour, to paint.*
Intíngo, xi, ctum, ĕre: *to dip in, to steep in, to dye or colour.*

The compounds of FLIGO, which is grown obsolete, from whence however cometh *flictus*, Virg. *a striking or dashing against.*
Afflígo, xi, ctum, ĕre: *to afflict, to vex, to torment, to persecute, to ruin, to throw on the ground, to oppress, to trample under foot, to demolish, to weaken and bring low, to make unhappy.*
Conflígo, conflíxi, conflíctum, conflígere: *to contend, to encounter.*
Inflígo, inflíxi, ctum, ĕre: *to lay upon, to strike, to bring upon, to fling.*
REGO, rexi, réctum, régere: *to govern, to conduct.*
A'rrigo, arréxi, arréctum, arrígere: *to lift up or raise, to encourage.*

Dírigo, éxi, ctum, ĕre: *to direct, to conduct, to regulate; to level or aim; to order, to set in array; to refer one thing to another; to rule or guide, to measure or mark out.*

E'rigo, eréxi, eréctum, erígere: *to erect or make upright, to rouse or excite, to set up, to lift or hold up, to comfort or relieve.*

Pórrigo, porréxi, porréctum, ĕre: *to stretch, to extend, to reach.*

The verbs ending in GUO are also comprehended here, because we say GO, not GUO, as for example the compounds of STINGUO, unusual.

Distínguo, distínxi, distínctum, distínguere: *to divide, to separate, to distinguish, to mark, to diversify, to set or inamel.*

Extínguo, extínxi, extínctum, extínguere: *to extinguish, to quench, to appease or stint, to abolish, to destroy.*

Præstínguo, xi, ctum, ĕre: *to render obscure, to put out; to stifle, to deface, to dazzle the sight.*

UNGUO or UNGO, unxi, (*and heretofore* ungui) unctum, úngere: *to anoint, to smear, to bedawb, to perfume.*

Exúngo, exúnxi, exúnctum, exúngere: *to anoint.*

Inúngo, inúnxi, inúnctum, inúngere: *the same.*

Perúngo, perúnxi, ctum, perúngere: *to anoint all over.*

The two next have CTUM and XUM.

2. FIGO, fixi, fixum, *and sometimes* fictum, fígere: *to fix, to fasten, to run through.*

Its compounds have rarely more than the former supine.

Affígo, affíxi, affíxum, ĕre: *to fasten, to clap close, to fix upon, to attribute.*

Confígo, xi, xum, ĕre: *to fix, to run through, to fasten, to nail.*

Defígo, xi, xum, ĕre: *to fix, to fasten against a wall or any other place, to ingrave, to imprint, to place, to set, to put before one's eyes, to represent, to astonish, to surprize, to shock.*

Infígo, infíxi, infíxum, infígere: *to fix or fasten in.*

Refígo, refíxi, refíxum, refígere: *to fasten anew, to pluck down what is fastened, to cancel, to abrogate and disannul.*

FRI-

FRIGO, frixi, frixum *and* frictum, frígere: *to fry, to parch.*

3. PERGO, perréxi, perréctum, pérgere: *to go, to continue, to pursue, to persevere, to hasten, to go forward.* It is also taken for *to begin to speak or act.*

SURGO, surréxi, surréctum, surgere: *to rise.*

Assúrgo, assurréxi, assurréctum, assúrgere: *to rise up, to stand up, to rise up to one, to do him reverence.*

Consúrgo, réxi, réctum, consúrgere: *to rise up together.*

Exsúrgo, exurréxi, réctum, exúrgere: *to rise up, to spring, or issue.*

Insúrgo, insurréxi, éctum, ĕre: *to rise up against, to make head against.*

Resúrgo, éxi, éctum, ĕre: *to rise or flourish again, to rise from the dead, to recover.*

ANNOTATION.

FIGO hath also *fictum* according to Diomedes. *Sagittis confictus.* Scaur. Giffanius in his *Index* proves the same by the authority of Cic. and Varr. Scipio Gentilis has observed that Callistratus spoke in the same manner: *Si quando navis vel inficta, vel fracta,* &c.

FRIGO hath also *frictum*; *frictum cicer,* Hor. *frictæ nuces,* Plaut. *raro fricta.* Pliny.

SURGO comes from *rego,* as much as to say *surrego,* or *sursum rego me;* for which reason *surgo* and *surrigo,* have the same preterite and supine, whence cometh *surrecta cornua,* Colum. *surrecto mucrone,* Livy.

With regard to *pergo,* some derive it from *ago*; but since it does not follow the preterite of the latter, there is a greater probability of its coming from *rego.*

RULE XLIII.

Of those verbs which drop their N in the supine.

Pingo, stringo, fingo, *drop their* N *in the supine, and make* ICTUM.

EXAMPLES.

These three verbs follow the general rule, but they lose their N in the supine.

PINGO, pinxi, pictum, *(and not* pinctum*)* píngere: *to paint, to stain, to deck or set out.*

Appíngo, appínxi, appíctum, appíngere: *to join unto, to fasten, to add; to paint.*

Depíngo, depínxi, depíctum, ĕre: *to paint, to represent.*

Expíngo, xi, ctum, ĕre: *to paint, to draw.*

STRINGO, ſtrinxi, ſtrictum, (*and not* ſtrinctum,) ſtrin-
gere: *to graſp or hold faſt, to tie hard or cloſe, to curry a horſe, to gather, to lop or cut, to touch lightly upon, to make naked or bare, to draw his ſword.*

Adſtríngo, xi, ctum, ĕre: *to tie hard or cloſe, to bind, to oblige, to conſtrain.*

Conſtríngo, xi, ctum, ĕre: *to bind faſt, to tie, to conſtrain or compel, to reſtrain or bridle.*

Deſtríngo, xi, ctum, ĕre: *to cut or lop off, to gather or pull fruit, to ſcrape or raſe off, to diminiſh.*

Diſtríngo, xi, ctum, ĕre: *to bind cloſe, to buſy or take one up, to rub or cleanſe the body, to curry a horſe, to ſtrike, prick, or touch ſoftly, to chip or pare, to draw a ſword, to diſtract or put into confuſion.*

Obſtríngo, xi, ctum, ĕre: *to bind cloſe, to tie up, to oblige.*

Perſtríngo, xi, ctum, ĕre: *to wring hard, to tie up cloſe; to dazzle; to touch any thing in diſcourſe, to glance at it; to offend highly, to raze or grate; to ſay a thing in few words; to cenſure, to find fault with, to reproach; lightly to run over, to graze upon.*

FINGO, finxi, fictum, (*and not* finctum) fingere: *to make, to faſhion, or mould; to frame or build; to imagine, to invent, to contrive; to feign or counterfeit; to ſuit or accommodate.*

Affíngo, affinxi, affictum, affingere: *to form or faſhion; to deviſe or frame; to invent or add to a ſtory; to counterfeit and reſemble.*

Confíngo, xi, ctum, ĕre: *to form or make; to feign, to invent, to ſhape or faſhion.*

Effíngo, xi, ctum, ĕre: *to faſhion, to work, to ingrave; to repreſent or expreſs; to imitate.*

ANNOTATION.

Priſcian, and after him Deſpauter with ſome others, join RINGO to the abovementioned. But this verb is no longer uſed, as Verepeus hath juſtly obſerved: in lieu of which we make uſe of the deponent *ringor*. *Ille ringitur, tu rideas*, Ter. This verb has never a preterite, but very likely it had one formerly, ſince we ſtill ſay *rictus*, a grinning or ſcornful opening of the mouth. Cicero makes uſe of its compound: *Ille libenter accipiet, bi ſubringentur, ad Attic.*

RULE XLIV.
Of the verbs which make IGI or EGI, and ACTUM.

1. Tango *makes* tétigi, tactum:

2. Pango,

2. Pango, pegi, panxi, pactum.
3. *From the old verb* pago *comes* pépigi.
4. *These have* EGI, ACTUM, *viz.* frango, ago, compíngo, cogo, impíngo, suppíngo.
5. Dego, pródigo, fátago, *have* EGI *without a supine.*

EXAMPLES.

1. TANGO, tétigi, tactum, tángere : *to touch, to strike, to meddle with.*

Its compounds change A into I, but take A in the supine.

Attíngo, ĭgi, áctum, ĕre : *to touch lightly, to reach or to arrive at, to treat of, to be related to, to belong to or to concern.*

Contíngo, ĭgi, áctum, ĕre : *to touch or lay hold of, to arrive at, to hit, to reach to, to befall one, to attain to.*

Obtíngit, óbtigit, (*it has only the third person*) obtíngere : *it falleth to by lot, it happeneth.*

Pertíngo, pértigi, pertáctum, pertíngere : *to extend, or reach along.*

2. PANGO, *heretofore* pegi, *now* panxi, pactum, pángere : *to strike or drive in, to plant, to compose verses.*

In regard to its compounds, some of them retain A, and form the preterite more elegantly in ANXI ; as

Circumpángo, panxi, pactum, pángere : *to set or plant round.*

Depángo, depánxi, depáctum, pángere : *to plant, to fasten in the ground.*

Repángo, pánxi, áctum, repángere : *to set or plant, to graff.*

4. Others change A into I, and forming the preterite in EGI, they resume A in the supine ; as

Compíngo, égi, áctum, ĕre : *to compact or put together, to make or frame a thing of several pieces, to fasten, to bind close, to set in.*

Impíngo, impégi, impáctum, impíngere : *to hit, dash, or throw against, to run aground ; to stumble, to clap or fasten upon.* Plaut.

Suppíngo, égi, áctum, ĕre : *to fasten underneath, rarely used.*

3. PAGO, *is obsolete; but from thence comes* pépigi, *I have covenanted or agreed upon.*

ANNOTATION.

4. There are some who derive the latter compounds from the verb *ago*; but be that as it may, we must take care not to confound them with those of *pingo, xi*; to paint, which are in the 43d rule.

3. *Pépigi* comes from the old verb *pago*, as *cecidi* from *cado*, according to Quintilian. And this verb was borrowed from the Doric πάγω instead of πήγω. But *pegi* came from *pango*, as *fregi* from *frango*. *Tonsillam pegi lævo in littore*, Pacuv. apud Priscian. Turnebus takes notice that Cicero has made use of it in the 2. de leg. *Requiri placere terminos, quos Socrates pegerit*. Where *pegerit* is the same as *panxerit*, whereas *pepigerit* would make quite another sense, and be taken for *pactus fuerit*. For instead of *pago* we now use *paciscor*, taken from *paco, is*, for *pago*. Which does not hinder *pango* from being also formed of the latter verb, by adding *n*, in imitation of the Greeks, who frequently use this last letter in their derivatives, as of φθάω, φθάνω, *prævenio*, and a multitude of others.

On the contrary the verb following *frango* makes its preterite as if it were from *frago*, by dropping of *n*; whence also comes *fragilis*: and *frago* should come from ῥάγω for ῥήγω, *to break*; by adding the Æolic digamma, of which we shall have something to say in the treatise of letters.

All these form the preterite in EGI, and the supine in ACTUM.

FRANGO, fregi, fractum, frángere : *to break, to bruise, to weaken, to wear out, to destroy, to violate, or infringe, to vanquish.*

Confríngo, égi, áctum, confríngere : *to break open.*

Defríngo, égi, áctum, defríngere : *to break down or off.*

Effríngo, égi, áctum, ĕre : *to break in pieces, to break open.*

Infríngo, égi, áctum, ĕre : *to break, to break down, to break in pieces, to bruise.*

Perfríngo, égi, áctum, ĕre : *to break through, to break or dash in pieces.*

AGO, egi actum, ágere : *to do, to pursue, to drive, to lead, to treat or deal with, to speak, to plead, to dwell, to live, to throw, to govern, to act or personate, to esteem.*

Its compounds change A into I short, as ;

A'bigo, égi, áctum, ágere : *to drive away; to send away, to drive away cattle; also to steal cattle.*

A'digo, adégi, adáctum, adígere : *to drive, to bring to, to force.*

A'm-

A′mbigo, égi, áctum, ĕre : *to doubt, to be in suspence, to dispute or quarrel.*

E′xigo, exégi, áctum, ĕre : *to require, to demand, to pray, to end or finish, to dispatch, to examine, to spend or pass away, to drive out, to banish.*

Rédigo, égi, áctum, ĕre : *to bring back again, to constrain, to drive or force back, to gather, to heap together, to amass, to turn into money, to compel to return, to subdue, to make easy.*

Satiséxigo, égi, áctum, ĕre : *to demand security.*

Súbigo, égi, áctum, subígere : *to bring under, to subdue, to constrain, to tame, to till, to whet, to beat or stamp, to dig or cast up.*

Tránsigo, transégi, transáctum, transígere : *to pass or thrust through, to pierce, to transact business, to conclude, to make an end of a controversy.*

Pérago, (*it retains the* A) perégi, peráctum, perágere : *to finish, to accomplish, to perform, to perfect, to convict, to cause sentence of condemnation to be passed.*

5. Cogo, coégi, coáctum, cógere : *to gather, to assemble, to make thick, to curdle, to compel, to rally or bring up, to drive in, to collect taxes, to draw up or range under certain heads, to conclude and infer, to reduce to reason.*

And in like manner compíngo, impíngo, suppíngo, See p. 245.

6. These other three compounds have no supine.

Dego, degi, dégere : *to lead, to pass, to spend, to continue, to live, to dwell.*

Pródigo, égi, ĕre : *to drive forth, to lash out or lavish, to squander away,* Varr.

Sátago, satégi, satágere : *to be busy about a thing, to be in great care about it, to bustle and keep a pudder, to have enough to do, to intermeddle, to over-do, to over-act.*

RULE XLV.

Of pungo, *and of* lego *with its compounds.*

1. Pungo *makes* punxi, *or rather* púpugi, punctum.

2. Lego *hath* legi, lectum.

3. *But three of its compounds make* EXI, ECTUM.

EXAMPLES.

1. PUNGO, punxi, *very little used except when compounded,* púpugi, punctum, púngere.: *to prick or sting; to gall, to vex.*
Its compounds form their preterite different ways.
Compúngo, compúpugi, *Rob. Steph.* compúnxi, *Voss.* compúnctum, compúngere: *to prick, to sting, to vex.*
Dispúngo, dispúnxi, dispúnctum, dispúngere: *to cancel, to efface, to note, or set down, to examine or balance an account.*
Expúngo, expúnxi, expúnctum, úngere: *to put or cross out, to expunge, to put out things written by setting pricks under every letter, to pay.*
Repúngo, repúpugi, *and* repúnxi, *Steph. and Voss.* repúnctum, repúngere: *to prick or goad again; to vex again, to be revenged.*

2. LEGO, legi, lectum, légere: *to gather, to gather up, to heap up, to read, to choose, to draw, to receive, to associate, to admit, to coast by, to coast or keep to the coast, to recite, to call over the senate when the unworthy members were expelled in order to keep the others to their duty.*
Some of its compounds preserve E, as
A'llego, allégi, alléctum, allégere: *to choose one into a place, or into a society, to admit.*
Præ'lego, prælégi, præléctum, prælégere: *to read to one,* as a master to his scholars; *to expound; to pass or go by.*
Rélego, relégi, reléctum, relégere: *to read over again, to gather again, to go back.*
Others change E into I, as
Cólligo, égi, éctum, ěre: *to gather, or bring together; to tie, or truss up; to recover himself or take heart; to call to mind, to recollect; to harness, or join together; to pack up his awles; to acquire; to conclude; to infer.*
Delígo, delégi, deléctum, delígere: *to choose; to gather, to pick.*
E'ligo, elégi, eléctum, elígere: *to choose, to pick out.*
Séligo, selégi, seléctum, selígere: *to choose out, to pick and lay aside, to cull.*

3. There

Of Preterites and Supines.

3. There are three of its compounds which have EXI, in the preterite, and retain the supine of the simple in ECTUM.

Díligo, diléxi, diléctum, dilígere: *to favour or respect; to love dearly.*

Intélligo, intelléxi, intelléctum, intellígere: *to understand, to know, to comprehend, to see, to learn.*

Négligo, negléxi, negléctum, ĕre: *to neglect, to despise.*

ANNOTATION.

The two last had heretofore EGI, *intellegi*, Ulp. *neglegi*, Priscian and Diomedes.

RULE XLVI.

Of mergo spargo *and* tergo.

Mergo, spargo, *and* tergo *make* SI, *and* SUM.

EXAMPLES.

MERGO, mersi, mersum, mérgere: *to put under water, to immerse, to sink.*

Demérgo, demérsi, sum, ĕre: *to dive, to sink to the bottom, to plunge over head and ears.*

Immérgo, si, sum, ĕre: *to plunge or dip over head and ears.*

Submérgo, submérsi, sum, ĕre; *to drown, to sink under water.*

SPARGO, sparsi, sparsum, spárgere: *to strew or throw about; to sow; to sprinkle or bedew; to spread abroad, to publish.*

Its compounds change A into E; as

Aspérgo, aspérsi, aspérsum, aspérgere: *to besprinkle, to wet or moisten; to corn, to powder, to season; to asperse or bespatter; to intermix or interlace; to give a little, or a sprinkling.*

Conspérgo, si, sum, ĕre: *to besprinkle, to strew.*

Dispérgo, si, sum, gĕre: *to scatter, to disperse, to spread abroad.*

Inspérgo, si, sum, ĕre: *to sprinkle, to cast upon or among; to scatter.*

TERGO, tersi, tersum, térgere: *to wipe, to clean, to scour.*

The same as TERGEO. See the 21st rule.

Abstérgo, érsi, érsum, ĕre: *to wipe clean; to wipe off or away.*

Detérgo,

Detérgo, detérsi, érsum, ĕre: *to wipe, brush, or scour; to clear up, to uncover; to break the oars by running foul against them.*

RULE XLVII.
Of those verbs which either have no supine, or no preterite.

1. Ningo, clango, *and* ango, *have* XI, *without a supine.*
2. *But* vergo *and* ambigo *have neither preterite nor supine.*

EXAMPLES.

These three verbs form the preterite in XI, pursuant to the general rule; but they have never a supine.

NINGO, ninxi, níngere: *to snow.*
ANGO, anxi, ángere: *to strangle, throttle, choak, or strain; to teaze, to vex, or trouble one.*
CLANGO, clanxi, clángere: *to sound a trumpet.*

2. The two next have neither preterite nor supine.

VERGO, vérgere: *to decline, to bend, lie, or look toward.*
Devérgo, devérgere: *to bend, or decline downward.*
A'MBIGO, ambígere: *to doubt, to be in suspense; to dispute, or quarrel.*

ANNOTATION.

To these some join *fugo*; but the verbal noun *fuctus*, which we read in Pliny, shews plainly that the supine was heretofore usual.

ANGO hath *anctum*, according to Priscian; but we find no authority for it in Latin authors; though it is encouraged by the antient Greek glossaries; *ancti*, ἀγχόμενοι. It has *anxum* according to Diomedes, who likewise insists that *angor* hath *anxius sum*. But *anxius* is a noun and not a participle, though it is derived from hence, as well as *anxietas*. *Clango* hath *clangui* in the vulgate, *clanguerunt*, Num. 10. where Pagninus and the modern interpreters have restored *clanxerunt*.

Vergo hath *versi, versum*, according to Robert Stephen; and *verxi*, according to Diomedes. But for this we find no authority in any Latin author.

Ambigo is derived from *am*, and from *ago*, adding *b*; just as *amburo* comes from *am* and from *uro*. *Am* itself cometh from the Greek ἀμφὶ; and this particle *am* even Cato has made use of, *am terminum*, for *circum terminum*.

RULE XLVIII.
Of the verbs in HO, and of *Meio*.

Traho, *and* veho, *take* XI, CTUM:
And Meio *hath* minxi, mictum.

EXAM-

Examples.

TRAHO, traxi, tractum, tráhere: *to draw, to drag, to delay.*

A'bstraho, abstráxi, abstráctum, abstráhere: *to drag away, to draw away, to abstract, to free, to separate.*

A'ttraho, attráxi, attráctum, attráhere: *to attract, to draw to one, to entice.*

Cóntraho, contráxi, contráctum, contráhere: *to draw together, to procure or get, to shrink in, to draw in, to contract or shorten, to contract or bargain, to furl the sails.*

Détraho, detráxi, detráctum, detráhere: *to draw off; to pluck or pull away; to detract, disparage, or speak ill of; to diminish or abate.*

Dístraho, distráxi, distráctum, distráhere: *to pull or draw asunder, to part, to separate, to divide, to break off; to sell; to delay or put off a thing; to make a diversion.*

Prótraho, protráxi, áctum, ĕre: *to drag along, to draw forth, to protract or delay.*

Rétraho, xi, ctum, ĕre: *to draw or pull back, to withdraw.*

Súbtraho, subtráxi, subtráctum, subtráhere: *to take away, to subtract; to diminish; to draw out; to withdraw.*

VEHO, vexi, vectum, véhere: *to carry any manner of ways, to convey by land or water.* It is also translated by the passive verb; *vehens* (subaud. *se*) *being carried.*

A'dveho, advéxi, advéctum, advéhere: *to import, or export, to carry by sea, or land.*

Cónveho, xi, ctum, ĕre: *to carry off or convey by cart, beast, or ship.*

E'veho, evéxi, ctum, ĕre: *to carry out, to convey, to extol and lift up.*

I'nveho, xi, ctum, ĕre: *to bring in or upon; to import; to carry or bear; to inveigh or speak bitterly against.*

Pérveho, xi, ctum, ĕre: *to carry along, to convey to the place appointed.*

Próveho, provéxi, provéctum, provéhere: *to carry on, to convey, to advance, to promote, to prefer.*

Tránsveho, xi, ctum, ĕre: *to carry, convey, or pass over.*

MEIO,

MEIO, minxi, ctum, ĕre: *to piſs, to make water.*

ANNOTATION.

Heretofore they ſaid *mingo*, which we ſtill find in the ancient grammarians; and thence alſo comes *mingens* in the ſcripture. But now it is become obſolete, though *minxi* and *mictum* are derived from thence. Diomedes makes it alſo to have *meii*.

Rule XLIX.
Of the verbs in LO.

1. *Verbs in* LO *have* UI, ITUM.
2. *But* alo *hath alſo* altum; òcculo, colo, *and* cónſulo, *have* U'LTUM.
3. Volo *and its compounds have no ſupine.*
4. Excéllo *and* Præcéllo *make* UI, ELSUM; Antecéllo *makes* UI *without a ſupine.*
5. Percéllo *takes* CULI, CULSUM; *but* recéllo *has neither preterite nor ſupine.*

Examples.

1. The verbs in LO ought, generally ſpeaking, to form their preterite in ŭi, and their ſupine in ITUM, according to the analogy above obſerved, p. 171. Thus we ſay MOLO, mólŭi, mólitum, mólere: *to grind.* E'molo, emólŭi, emólitum, mólere: *to grind thoroughly; to ſpend, to conſume.*

2. But very often there is a ſyncope in the ſupine; as ALO álŭi, álitum, *and by ſyncope,* altum, *leſs uſual,* álere: *to nouriſh, to maintain, to cheriſh,* and in like manner

O'CCULO, occúlŭi, occúltum, *(for* occúlitum) occúlere: *to hide, to cover.*

COLO, cólŭi, cultum, cólere: *to till the earth, to inhabit, to honour, to reſpect, to worſhip, to practiſe or exerciſe.*

A'ccolo, accólŭi, accúltum, accólere: *to live near, to be near.*

E'xcolo, ŭi, últum, ĕre: *to till or cultivate; to garniſh, deck, or poliſh; to inſtruct; to perform or practiſe.*

I'ncolo, incólŭi, incúltum, incólere: *to inhabit.*

Récolo, recólŭi, recúltum, recólere: *to till or dreſs again; to bring into remembrance, to recollect; to furbiſh, refreſh or adorn.*

Of Preterites and Supines.

CONSULO, consúlui, consúltum, consúlere: *to consult, to consult with, to give counsel, to provide for or take care of, to consider or regard.*

3. VOLO, vis, vult; *the preterite,* vólüi: *it follows the general rule in regard to the preterite, but has no supine.* Velle; *ta be willing; to desire, to wish; to wish one well, to favour, to be willing to serve him; to pray, to encourage; to mean, to design.*

Nolo, nólüi, nolle: *to be unwilling, not to will; not to favour or be of one's side, to be against one.*

Malo, málüi, malle: *to have rather, to choose preferably.*

4. CELLO, an obsolete verb, made üi and ELSUM, whence come the following verbs.

Antecéllo, antecéllüi, *without a supine,* antecéllere: *to excel, to surpass, to surmount.*

Excéllo, excéllüi, excélsum, excéllere: *to excel, to surpass.* Whence cometh excélsus, a, um: *high, elevated.*

Præcéllo, præcéllüi, præcélsum, præcéllere: *to excel, to surpass, surmount, or be much better; to preside over.* Whence cometh præcélsus, a, um: *most high.*

5. Percéllo pérculi, percúlsum, percéllere: *to overthrow, overturn, or beat down; to astonish, amaze; to affect deeply, to strike to the heart.*

Recéllo, *hath neither preterite nor supine:* recéllere, Liv. Appul. *to thrust or push down; to bend or thrust back.*

ANNOTATION.

CELLO, came from the Greek κέλλω, *moveo.* Among its compounds *antecello* hath no supine. *Excello* and *præcello* seem to have had supines formerly, since from thence are still derived *excelsus* and *præcelsus*, which seem nevertheless to be rather nouns adjectives than supines or participles. We say also *excello: effice ut excelleas*, Cic. whence according to Priscian cometh *excellui:* whereas *excello* ought to make *exculi:* as *percello, perculi;* unless we choose to say that this is a syncope for *percellui.*

Some there are, and among the rest Alvarez, who would have us say *perculsi*, in the preterite of *percello*, which should make the supine *perculsum.* But Vossius believes that the several passages brought to confirm this reading, are corrupted: and Lambin in his commentary on Hor. lib. 1. od. 7. declares expressly that *perculsit* is not Latin, and that *percello* hath no other preterite than *perculi.* And yet Vossius says that notwithstanding all this, he himself left *perculsi* in a passage of Cicero's, which he quotes on the 2d satyre of the 3d book. *Si eorum plaga* PERCULSI *afflictos se & stratos esse fateamur*, Ex Tusc. 3. But it is evident that *perculsi* is here only a participle,

participle, and that it proves nothing in regard to the preterite of the active, which Vossius does not seem to have considered. Now *percuti* and *perculsum* are formed of *percello*, by the change of *e* into *u*, just as in *pulsum*, taken from *pello*; and in its preterite *pepuli*, for *pepeli*. They say also *procello*, *procelli*, Plin. Jun. which is the same as *percello*, but less used. From thence however cometh *procella*, *a storm*.

RULE L.

The second part of the verbs in LO.

1. Pello *makes* pépuli, pulsum;
2. Vello, *hath* velli *or* vulsi, vulsum.
3. Sallo *hath* salli, salsum:
4. Fallo, feféli, fulsum: *but* reféllo *has only* reféli.
5. Psallo *hath* psalli *without a supine.*
6. Tollo *makes* sústuli, sublátum: attóllo *hath neither preterite nor supine.*

EXAMPLES.

The verbs in this second part of the rule form their preterite and supine in a different manner.

1. PELLO, pépuli, pulsum, péllere: *to drive away.*

Appéllo, áppuli, appúlsum, appéllere: *to drive to, to bring to land, to the coast or shore, to cast anchor, to go towards, to arrive, to apply, to devote one's self to, to appear before one, to split against the rocks.*

Compéllo, cómpuli, compúlsum, compéllere: *to drive or bring together; to compel, or constrain.*

Expéllo, éxpuli, expúlsum, expéllere: *to drive out, to thrust out, to banish.*

Impéllo, ímpuli, impúlsum, impéllere: *to thrust, drive, or push forward; to push in; to constrain one to do a thing; to strike; to hit against.*

Perpéllo, puli, pulsum, lĕre: *to force or constrain one to do a thing; to persuade, or prevail with.*

Propéllo, li sum, ĕre: *to drive or put away; to push or thrust forward or back; to repulse or keep off.*

Repéllo, répuli, úlsum, éllere: *to repel, to oppose; to beat or thrust back; to turn away.*

2. VELLO, velli, *more usual;* vulsi, vulsum, véllere: *to pluck.*

Avéllo,

Avéllo, avélli, avúlfum, avéllere : *to pull or drag away; to part, or keep afunder.*
Divéllo, élli, úlfum, éllere : *to take away by force ; to loofe, hinder, or undo ; to pull afunder.*
Evéllo, evélli, fum, ĕre : *to pluck up or out ; to pull off; to root out.*
Revéllo, revélli, and ulfi, ulfum, éllere : *to pluck or tear off; to extirpate.*
3. SALLO, falli, falfum, fállere : *to falt, to pickle.*
SA´LIO, falívi, falítum, falíre: *of the fourth conjugation.*
4. FALLO, fefélli, falfum, ĕre : *to deceive, to beguile, to cheat, to difappoint, to mifs, to be miftaken, to efcape notice, to be ignorant of.*
Reféllo, refélli, without a fupine, reféllere : *to confute, to difprove.*
5. PSALLO, pfalli, pfállere : *to fing, or play on an inftrument.*
6. TOLLO *takes* fúftuli, fublátum, tóllere : *to take away, to lift up, to bring up, to educate, to have children, to kill or make away with, to abolifh, to deftroy, to take along with.*
Attóllo, *hath neither preterite nor fupine,* attóllere : *to lift or raife up, to take up, to extol or fet off, to carry away,*
Extóllo, éxtuli, elátum, extóllere : *to lift or hold up, to raife up, to praife.*
Suftóllo, fúftuli, fublátum, ĕre : *to lift up, to take away or make away with, to pick up, to educate or bring up.*

ANNOTATION.

We find *appulferit* apud. Ju. C. Ulpian in Pandect. Florentin. which Scipio Gentilis hath attempted to maintain. And thence a doubt arifes whether *pello* had not heretofore *pulfi.*

Vulfi and *vulferunt* frequently occur in Lucan: *revulfi* is in Ovid; but Cicero generally makes ufe of *velli.*

TOLLO made heretofore *tuli* or *tétuli* according to Charifius, whence its compounds take alfo their preterite by dropping the reduplication : and *tetuli* is found even in Plautus, Terence, Catullus and others, but this preterite came more likely from *tolo* for *tolero.* For *tollo* fhould make *tetulli,* as *fallo* makes *feſelli.* It feems alfo that heretofore they faid *tolli,* whence comes *tolliſſe* in Ulpian, according to Scaliger.

Attollo hath neither preterite nor fupine. becaufe *attuli* and *allatum,* which are derived from thence, have been adopted by *adfero*

and

and changed their signification. The preterite *suftuli*, properly speaking, comes from *suftollo*: but besides its having been borrowed by *tollo*, it has also been lent to *suffero*, so that this preterite serves for three verbs, just as *extuli* has been also lent to *effero*.

Rule LI.

1. *Verbs in* MO *make* UI, ITUM.
2. Sumo, como, demo, promo, *more elegantly make* SI, TUM.
   Tremo *takes* ŭi *without a supine*.
3. Emo *hath* emi, emptum.
4. *And* premo, pressi, pressum.

Examples.

1. Verbs in MO make ŭi and ITUM, as

FREMO, frémŭi, frémitum, frémere: *to make a great noise, to roar, to bluster*.

I'nfremo, infrémŭi, ĭtum, ĕre: *to make a great noise*.

GEMO, gemŭi, gémitum, gémere: *to mouth, to groan*.

I'ngemo, ŭi, ĭtum, ĕre: *to lament, to bewail*.

TREMO, trémŭi: *it follows the general rule in regard to the preterite, but has no supine*, trémere: *to tremble, to shake, to quake for fear*.

2. There are four that more elegantly make SI, TUM, though they have frequently PSI, PTUM.

COMO, comsi, comtum, cómere: *to comb or deck the hair; to trim, to attire, to make gay, or trick up*.

DEMO, demsi, demtum, ĕre: *to take away from a whole, to abate, to diminish, to cut off, to except*.

PROMO, promsi, promtum, prómere: *to draw out, to bring forth, to draw as wine out of a vessel, to utter, to disclose, to lay open*.

PROMTUS also signifieth *ready, prompt, easy, quick, bold*.

Depromo, si, tum, ĕre: *to draw or fetch out*.

Exprómo, si, tum, ĕre: *to draw out, to shew forth, to produce or bring, to tell plainly*.

SUMO, sumsi, sumtum, súmere: *to take, to receive; to pretend, to assume or arrogate; to lay out, to bestow; to employ; to advance a proposition or postulate, to take for granted*.

Assúmo, úmsi, úmtum, úmere: *to take and draw to himself; to take as granted; to take upon him, or assume too much; to regain or recover.*   Ab-

Of Preterites and Supines.

Absúmo, absúmsi, absúmtum, absúmere: *to consume, to waste.*

Consúmo, súmsi, súmtum, mĕre: *to spend lavishly, to waste, to consume or destroy, to lay out.*

Desúmo, úmsi, úmtum, desúmere: *to pick out or choose.*

Insúmo, úmsi, úmtum, úmere: *to employ, to spend.*

Præsúmo, præsúmsi, præsúmtum, præsúmere: *to take first or before; to presume; to guess, to presuppose.*

Resúmo, resúmsi, resúmtum, resúmere: *to take up again, to resume.*

3. EMO, emi, emtum, émere: *to buy.*

Its compounds change E into I short, and resume the E in the preterite and supine.

A'dimo, adémi, adémtum, adímere: *to take away, to free from, to keep from.*

Dírimo, dirémi, dirémtum, dirímere: *to break off, to separate; to interrupt business; to delay; to determine or make an end of.*

E'ximo, exémi, tum, ĕre: *to take out, to take away; to set aside; to free, to deliver, to preserve; to gain time; to waste, to spend; to acquit; to exempt.*

Intérimo, interémi, interémtum, interímere: *to kill.*

Périmo, émi, émtum, ímere: *to kill, to destroy or deface, to abolish, to suppress.*

Rédimo, émi, émtum, ímere: *to redeem or ransom; to buy off; to recompense or make amends for; to take a farm upon a rent; to take a thing in bargain or by the great; to take a lease; to become the party to whom the thing is delivered by judgment; to undertake to furnish victims, ammunition, provisions, &c.*

ANNOTATION.

I have removed the P from the termination of the preterite and supine of all these verbs, by the authority of Terentius Scaurus in his orthography, of Victorinus who was cotemporary with Donatus, as also of S. Jerome, of Lambinus, of Sanctius and of Vossius, who tell us plainly that it is repugnant to the analogy of the language. And indeed the termination *psi* ought to be kept for the verbs in *po*, just as π is changed into ψ among the Greeks. I am not ignorant that Priscian writes *sumpsi, compsi,* &c. and that the same writing is remarked in most of the antient manuscripts. But as Sanctius observes it is a corruption which crept in when the purity of the language was lost; a corruption so manifest, that on a thousand other occasions they inserted the *p*, saying *dampnatio* for *damnatio* and the like.

Hence also it comes that in French there are several who write *dompter*, which is evidently an error, for not only the pronunciation of the language opposes it, this *p* not being founded; but even those who write *demo, dempsi,* do not so much as pretend that it was ever customary to say *domo, dompsi,* but only *domo, domui,* as it is in the 9th rule p. 183.

4. PREMO, pressi, pressum, prémere : *to press; to squeeze, to strain; to straighten; to oppress; to trample upon; to crush; to pursue; to persecute.*

Its compounds change E into I short in the present, and resume E in the preterite and supine.

Cómprimo, comprèssi, compréssum, comprímere : *to press together; to hold in or keep close; to force, to shut, to trample upon, to hide; to lay up, to keep; to hoard up all sorts of provisions; to appease, to stop, stay, or repress; to ravish or deflower.*

Déprimo, éssi, éssum, ímere : *to thrust, press, or weigh down; to sink; to make one stoop; to humble.*

E'xprimo, éssi, éssum, mére : *to press, wring, or strain out; to extort; to constrain; to copy out or imitate; to express, to pourtray, to draw out; to declare and make apparent.*

I'mprimo, éssi, éssum, ére : *to imprint, to ingrave, to set a mark.*

O'pprimo, éssi, éssum, ímere: *to oppress, to stifle, to fall heavy upon, to inslave, to overpower, to surprize or take unprovided.*

Réprimo, éssi, éssum, ímere: *to keep within bounds; to contain, to hinder or hold in; to restrain or repress; to check; to appease.*

Rule LII.
Of the verbs in NO.

1. Cano *makes* cécini, cantum.
2. *Its compounds have* üi, ENTUM.
3. Pono *hath* pósüi, pósitum.
4. Gigno, génüi, génitum :
5. Temno *hath* temsi, temtum ; *the preterite is seldom used except in the compound* contémno.

OF PRETERITES AND SUPINES.

EXAMPLES.

The verbs in NO form their preterite and supine differently.

1. CANO, cécini, cantum, cánere : *to sing, to publish, to celebrate, to sing in concert, to sound, to write verses, to praise one highly, to sound an alarm; to report or proclaim aloud; to foretel, to prophesy; to play upon an instrument ; to speak to his own advantage, to seek his private interest.*

2. Its compounds change A into I short, and form ÜI, ENTUM; as

Cóncino, concínüi, concéntum, concínere : *to agree or accord in one song ; to sing ; to sound or play as instruments do ; to agree or consent.*

I'ncino, incínüi, incéntum, incínere : *to sing; to play upon instruments.*

O'ccino, occínüi, *and sometimes* occánüi, occéntum, ĕre : *to chirp, to sing inauspiciously as birds do.*

Præ'cino, præcínüi, præcéntum, præcínere : *to sing before, to lead the chorus, to mumble a charm, to prophesy.*

Récino, recínüi, recéntum, recínere : *to sound or ring again, to repeat.*

3. PONO, pósüi, pósitum, pónere : *to put, to place, to set ; to plant ; to reckon ; to put the case, to suppose; to propose, or propound; to consider; to esteem; to blame; to do good; to attribute;. to give ; to trust.*

Appóno, appósüi, appósitum, appónere : *to put or set to ; to join, to add; to lay upon or nigh to ; to mix or put in ; to suborn or procure.*

Compóno, üi, ĭtum, ónere : *to put or lay together; to set or place; to set in order; to join close together ; to appease, compose or settle ; to compose or write ; to adjust or take an order about ; to dispose or methodize ; to finish or make an end of; to reconcile ; to regulate ; to put to bed ; to bury.*

Depóno, üi, ĭtum, ĕre : *to lay or put down ; to put off, to lay aside ; to resign, or give up ; to leave off ; to deposit ; to stake down, to wager.*

Dispóno, üi, ĭtum, ĕre : *to dispose, to range, to put in order.*

Expóno, üi, ĭtum, ĕ : *to put out, or set on shore ; to set forth;*

forth; *to lay abroad in view*; *to leave to the wide world*; *to expose or subject*; *to teach or expound*; *to shew, declare, or give an account of, to explain, to represent.*

Impóno, üi, ĭtum, ĕre: *to put in, or upon; to impose upon, to deceive; to impose, to enjoin; to subject, to overpower; to set over; to imbark.*

Interpóno, üi, ĭtum, ĕre: *to put in, or mix; to put between, interpose or meddle.*

Oppóno, üi, ĭtum, ĕre: *to put before or against, to oppose, to offer against as an argument, to pretend for an excuse or defence.*

Poſtpóno,: *to set behind, to esteem less, to leave or lay aside.*

Præpóno, üi, ĭtum, ĕre: *to put before; to prefer, to set more by; to give one the charge or command; to make one ruler or chief.*

Propóno, üi, ĭtum, ĕre: *to propose, to set before one, to offer, to resolve.*

Repóno, repósüi, repóſitum, repónere: *to put or set again; to reserve, to keep close; to reply, to retort; to be even with; to render like for like; to repair or set up.*

Sepóno, sepósüi, sepóſitum, sepónere: *to lay apart, to reserve.*

Tranſpóno, tranſpósüi, tranſpóſitum, tranſpónere: *to transpose, or remove from one place to another.*

4. GIGNO, génüi, génitum, gígnere: *to beget, to bring forth.*

Progígno, progénüi, progénitum, progígnere: *to engender, to beget.*

5. TEMNO, temſi, temtum, témnere: *to despise.*

Its preterite is used only in the compound verb.

Contémno, contémſi, contémtum, contémnere: *to undervalue, to despise, to make no account of.*

ANNOTATION.

Heretofore the compounds did not change the vowel of the simple. For which reason they said, *occano, occanere cornua*, Tacit. The preterite also followed the nature of the present; hence they said, *canui, concanui, cornicines occanuerunt*, Sal. apud Priſc. &c. They said also *conſiſti* for *conſtiti*; *premi* for *preſſi*; and in like manner the rest.

Poro, formerly made *poſivi*, Plaut. *depoſivi*, Catul.

Gigno,

OF PRETERITES AND SUPINES.

Gigno, takes its preterite from the old verb, *geno*, *ui*, which we read in Cato, Varro, and others.

Though *tentum* is not used, yet we find the verbal noun *temtor*, in Seneca in Agam.

RULE LIII.
The second part of the verbs in NO.

1. Sterno *hath* stravi, stratum;
2. *So* sperno, *hath* sprevi, spretum,
3. Cerno, crevi, cretum;
4. Sino, *takes* sivi, situm.
5. *And* lino *hath* levi, litum; *as also* lini *and* levi.

EXAMPLES.

All the verbs comprized in this second rule in NO, form their supine by changing VI into TUM, pursuant to the analogy abovementioned, p. 171. as

1. STERNO, stravi, stratum, stérnere: *to spread or cover, to strow; to lay down; to prostrate; to throw or strike down, to lay flat along; to pave; to spread or cover the couches, or the table, to harness or accoutre a horse.*

Constérno, constrávi, constrátum, constérnere: *to shew, or cover all over; to pave or floor.*

Destérno, destrávi, destrátum, destérnere: *to uncover.*

Prostérno, prostrávi, prostrátum, prostérnere: *to overthrow or beat down; to lay flat, to prostrate.*

Substérno, substrávi, substrátum, substérnere: *to strew, or put under, to subject, to bring under.*

2. SPERNO, sprevi, spretum, spérnere: *to despise, to neglect, to reject.*

Despérno, desprévi, desprétum, despérnere: *to slight, to despise much.*

3. CERNO, crevi, cretum, cérnere: *to judge, to see; to discern; to determine; to sift; to separate, to distinguish; to dispute about an affair; to engage with, to fight; to enter upon an estate. From thence comes* crétio, *the act whereby a person declares himself heir to the deceased within a limited time; the clause of the testator. See the following annotation.*

Dercérno, decrévi, decrétum, decérnere: *to appoint, to order, to decree, to judge; to give sentence, to conclude, to decide, to fight or combat, to determine a dispute by the sword, to design or purpose, to charge each other with crimes.*

Discérno, discrévi, discrétum, discérnere: *to discern, to distinguish, to separate; to judge or determine.*

Secérno, secrévi, secrétum, secérnere: *to put asunder, to separate one from another, to distinguish.*

4. SINO, sivi, situm, sínere: *to suffer, to permit.*

Désino, desívi, *or* désii, désitum, desinere: *to leave or desist; to omit for a time; to give quite over; to terminate or end.*

5. LINO, lini, livi, *or* levi, litum, linere: *to anoint; to daub or paint; to besmear.*

Allino, allíni, allívi, allévi, állitum, allínere: *to anoint, to rub softly.*

Délino, delíni, delívi, delévi, délitum, delínere: *to blot, to deface.*

Illino, illíni, ívi, évi, ítum, ĕre: *to anoint; to daub; to lay over or colour.*

O'blino: *the same.*

Rélino, relíni, relívi, relévi, rélitum, relínere: *to open that which is stopped, to set abroach, to tap.*

ANNOTATION.

CONSTERNO is both of the first and third conjugation: of the first when it implies any great trouble and disquietude of mind: *Consternata multitudo,* Liv. seized with dread and fear: of the third when it relates to corporeal things: *Humi constrata corpora.*

CERNO has seldom a preterite but when it signifies *to determine* or *to declare himself heir.* For when it signifies simply *to see,* it hardly ever has any preterite, as Vossius after Verepeus observeth. We must own that there is the authority of Titinnius for it in Priscian; but in regard to the other which he brings from Plautus, in Cistel. *Et mihi amicam esse crevi,* we had better abide by Varro's explication of it, *constitui:* for in the very same comedy, there is also the following passage, *Satin' tibi istud in corde cretum est?* as Joseph Scaliger reads it. True it is that the others read *certum,* but Vossius attributes this to a comment.

The verbal noun *cretia* is generally used by the civilians. *Libera cretio,* when the heir has no charge upon his estate; *simplex cretio,* the right of accepting of the succession, which right not being common to all heirs was an advantage. This shews that we ought not absolutely to reject the supine of the simple in this signification, though it be certainly less usual than that of the compounds.

Now *cerno,* according to Sanctius and Joseph Scaliger, comes from κρίνω, *judico,* for which reason it is applied to every thing where judgment, and discernment or distinction and choice are requisite. Hence it is not only taken for *to sift,* and *to range flour,* but likewise for *to inherit,* and *to share the estate,* and also *to fight;* because heretofore

OF PRETERITES AND SUPINES.

tofore difputes about inheritances were decided by the fword, as Stobeus, and even as Ennius in Cicero obferveth,

Ferro, non auro, vitam cernamus utrique.

From thence alfo comes *crimen*, that is, *id de quo cernitur aut judicatur*; as likewife *crines*, the hairs of one's head, *quia difcernuntur*, fays Sanctius.

SINO, makes fometimes *fini*, retaining the confonant of the prefent, according to what we have faid concerning it in the annotation of the preceding rule.

LINO makes *litum* in the fupine. *Et paribus lita corpora guttis*, Virg. But its preterite varies: we find *levi* in Colum. *lini* in Quint. *Mariti tui cruore parietem linifti*, in Declam. *linti*, in Varr. *Cum oblinierit vafa.* Yet the moft ufual now is *levi*, from whence they derive *relevi*, in Terence. *Relevi dolia omnia*, Heaut. act. 3. fc. 1. I have broached all my wine. But there is a greater probability of its coming from *releo, evi*, of the fame original as *deleo, evi*, whofe fimple we read ftill in Horace.

——— *Græcâ quod ego ipfe teftâ*
Conditum levi ———

that is, *fignavi*: whence alfo comes *letum*, death, according to Prifcian, *quia delet omnia*. And this feems fo much the more probable, as the fignification of this verb hath a greater relation to the paffage of Terence, than that of *lino*: and as according to Diomedes himfelf, *deleor* hath *delitus* and *deletus*. So that according to him, Varro faid, *delitæ litteræ*; juft as Cicero faid, *ceris deletis*. As to *linivi* or *linii*, and *linitum*, they properly come from *linio*, which is of the fourth conjugation.

RULE LIV.
Of the verbs in PO and QUO.

1. *Verbs in* PO, *require*, PSI, TUM.
2. *But* rumpo *hath* rupi, ruptum.
3. Strepo, *hath* ftrépüi, ftrépitum.
4. Coquo, *makes* coxi, coctum.
5. Linquo *hath* liqui *without a fupine*.
6. *But its compounds take* LICTUM.

EXAMPLES.

Verbs terminating in PO, make PSI, PTUM; as CARPO, carpfi, carptum, cárpere: *to gather, to take, to carp or find fault with.*

Its compounds change A into E; as

Decérpo, érpfi, érptum, ére: *to gather, to pull or pluck off, to leffen.*

Difcérpo, érpfi, érptum, ére: *to pluck or tear in pieces.*

Excérpo, érpfi, érptum, ére: *to pick out or choofe.*

CLEPO, clepfi, (*heretofore* clepi,) cleptum, clépere: Cic. *to fteal or pilfer.*

REPO, repfi, reptum, répere: *to creep, to crawl; to go softly; to spread abroad as vines do.*
Irrépo, irrépfi, irréptum, irrépere: *to creep in by stealth; to steal into, or get in by little and little.*
Obrépo, obrépfi, obréptum, obrépere: *to creep in privately; to steal by degrees, to surprize; to come beyond, to over-reach craftily.*
Subrépo, subrépfi, subréptum, subrépere: *to creep along; to creep from under; to steal softly, or by little and little.*
SERPO, ferpfi, ferptum, férpere: *to creep, to slide on the belly as serpents do; to proceed by little and little; to spread itself; to augment or increase.*
Inférpo, inférpfi, inférptum, inférpere: *to creep in, to enter softly.*
SCALPO, fcalpfi, fcalptum, fcálpere: *to scratch, to scrape, to claw, to rake; to ingrave, to carve.*
Excálpo, excálpfi, excálptum, excálpere: *to pierce or drill out; to scratch out, to erase.*
SCULPO, fculpfi, fculptum, ěre: *to carve in stone; to grave in metal.*
Excúlpo *and* infcúlpo, pfi, ptum, ěre: *to carve, to ingrave.*

2. RUMPO, rupi, ruptum, rúmpere: *to break, to burst; to marr, or spoil.*
Abrúmpo, abrúpi, abrúptum, abrúmpere: *to break or throw off; to cut asunder; to break off, or leave.*
Corrúmpo, corrúpi, corrúptum, pěre: *to corrupt, to spoil.*
Dirúmpo *or* Disrúmpo, rúpi, tum, ěre: *to break, to break in pieces; to burst.*
Erúmpo, erúpi, erúptum, erúmpere: *to break or burst out; to issue or sally out, to attack, or set violently upon; to vent or discharge.*
Irrúmpo, irrúpi, irrúptum, irrúmpere: *to break in violently, to enter, or rush by force; to attack or set upon.*

3. STREPO, ftrépui, ftrépitum, pěre: *to make a noise.*
Cónstrepo, constrépui, constrépitum, constrépere: *to make a great noise or din; to quarrel.*
O'bstrepo, obstrépui, obstrépitum, obstrépere: *to make a noise against, or before; to interrupt by noise; to disturb or interrupt.*

Of Preterites and Supines.

Pérstrepo, perstrépui, épitum, ĕre: *to make a great noise or din.*

Examples of verbs in QUO.

4. COQUO, coxi, coctum, cóquere: *to boil, to digest.*
Cóncoquo, concóxi, concóctum, concóquere: *to boil, to digest, to ripen.*
Décoquo, decóxi, decóctum, decóquere: *to boil or seethe, to boil away; to consume or waste, to spend all; to bankrupt, or break one.*
E'xcoquo, excóxi, excóctum, excóquere: *to boil thoroughly; to boil away.*

5. LINQUO, liqui, línquere: *to leave, to abandon; to discard.*

It has never a supine, but its compounds have: as
Delínquo, delíqui, íctum, ĕre: *to omit, to fail in his duty; to offend, to do wrong.*
Relínquo, relíqui, relíctum, relínquere: *to leave; to forsake; to relinquish.*
Derelínquo, derelíqui, derelíctum, derelínquere: *to leave, to forsake utterly.*

Rule LV.
Of the verbs in RO.

1. Tero *hath* trivi, tritum.
2. Quæro, quæsívi, quæsítum.
3. Fero *takes* tuli, latum:
4. Gero, *hath* gessi, gestum:
5. Curro, cucúrri, cursum:
6. Verro, verri, versum.
7. Uro, ussi, ustum.
8. *But* furo *hath neither preterite nor supine.*

Examples.

The verbs in RO form their preterite and supine different ways.

1. TERO, trivi, tritum, térere: *to rub or break, to bruise, to wear, to waste, to use often.* Tritus, *worn, thread-bare, frequented.*

A'ttero, attrívi, attrítum, attérere: *to rub against or upon; to wear out; to bruise, to waste; to lessen or detract from.*

Cóntero,

Cóntero, contrívi, contrítum, contérere: *to break or bruise small; to waste; to spend; to wear out with using.*

Détero, detrívi, detrítum, detérere: *to bruise or beat out; to rub one against another; to diminish; to wear out; to make worse.*

E'xtero, ívi, ítum, ĕre: *to wear out; to beat out; to grind; to thresh; to rub out.*

I'ntero, intrívi, intrítum, intérere: *to crumb, or grate bread* or the like *into a thing.*

O'btero, obtrívi, obtrítum, obtérere: *to crush, to bruise, to trample upon, to overrun, to destroy.*

Prótero, protrívi, prótritum, protérere: *to trample, to crush to pieces.*

ANNOTATION.

Tero heretofore made *terüi* (just as *sero serüi* in the next rule) hence according to Priscian we should read *priusquam teruerunt* in Plautus, Pseud. act. 3. sc. 2. as we find it in the old editions; as well as in those of Tibullus and Tacitus, supported by excellent manuscripts, where this preterite is to be found. Lipsius also observes that the Tacitus of the Vatican library hath *Mox atteritis opibus*, lib. 1. hist. But this is now become obsolete.

2. QUÆRO, quæsívi, quæsítum, quæ'rere: *to seek, to acquire or get, to purchase; to ask, to inquire; to make inquisition, to rack; to dispute; to go about, to assay or endeavour.*

Its compounds change Æ into I long; as

Acquíro, sívi, sítum, ĕre: *to acquire, to get, to purchase, to obtain; to add.*

Anquíro, sívi, ítum, ĕre: *to enquire or make diligent search; to acquire or join to; to make inquisition; to sit upon examination and trial of offenders.*

Conquíro, conquisívi, ítum ĕre: *to search for diligently; to get together.*

Disquíro, sívi, sítum, disquírere: *to search diligently, or on every side.*

Exquíro, sívi, ítum, ĕre: *to inquire diligently, to examine or search out; to pray for, or ask.*

Inquíro, inquisívi, inquisítum, inquírere: *to inquire, to ask, to examine or search; to take an information in order to a prosecution at law.*

Perquíro, sívi, ítum, ĕre: *to make diligent or narrow search into; to ask or demand.* Re-

Requíro, requisívi, requisítum, requírere: *to seek again, to look for; to inquire; to ask; to seek in vain; to stand in need of.*

3. FERO, tuli, latum, ferre: *to carry; to bear; to suffer, to bring; to get; to have; to propose; to bring in a bill in order to be made a law; to set it down as laid out or received; to give his vote; to have another person's vote; to judge; to make a law; to proffer or give, to carry off the booty, to plunder.*

A'ffero, *or* ádfero, áttuli, allátum, afférre: *to bring; to report, or bring word; to alledge, to plead, or bring for excuse.*

Aúfero, ábstuli, ablátum, auférre: *to take away, to carry away; to take; to get, to obtain; to hinder or deprive; to carry off, to plunder or rob.*

Díffero, dístuli, dilátum, differre; *to scatter abroad; to carry up and down; to tear in pieces; to transport; to put off or delay; to differ, to be unlike; to vary or not agree; to distract, or tease.*

E'ffero, éxtuli, elátum, efférre: *to carry forth or out; to transport; to carry off; to divulge; to bring forth; to carry forth to burial; to convey; to praise, magnify, or set off; to honour; to carry himself beyond bounds; to be vain glorious; to utter or pronounce.*

O'ffero, óbtuli, oblátum, offérre: *to bring to or before, to offer, to present, to expose to.*

Súffero, sústuli, sublátum, sufférre: *to carry away, to take away, to demolish.*

But when it signifieth, *to bear* or *suffer*, it has neither preterite nor supine; because as it borrows these only from *tollo* or rather from *justóllo*, they constantly preserve their first signification.

The other compounds of this verb make no change in the preposition of which they are compounded, except it be in the supine, as

Cónfero, cóntuli, collátum, conférre: *to bring or put together; to give, to contribute; to confer, discourse, or talk together; to join; to put; to apply; to compare; to defer or put off; to advantage or avail; to impute, attribute, or cast upon; to lay out, to employ, or give his time and care to a thing; to fight, to engage in battle; to go, to betake himself to.*

Dé-

Défero, tŭli, látum, férre: *to carry or bring, to bring or carry word; to offer, to present; to implead one, or complain of him; to refer to another's decision.*

I'nfero, íntuli, illátum, férre: *to bring in or into; to bury; to lay to, to apply; to bring upon, to be the cause; to set a foot in, to come in; to wage war against; to attack, to use violence; to introduce a discourse; to conclude from premises, to infer, to compute an expence; to set it to his account.*

Pérfero, tŭli, látum, férre: *to carry, bear, or convey through, or unto the designed person or place; to bear patiently, to endure; to obtain what one asks.*

Póstfero, tŭli, látum, férre: *to put after or behind; to set less by, to esteem less; to place or set behind, to antedate.*

Præ'fero, tŭli, látum, férre: *to bear or carry before; to prefer, to esteem more; to choose rather; to make a shew of, to pretend; to anticipate, to be before hand in an undertaking, to antedate.*

Prófero, tŭli, látum, férre: *to set forward, to thrust, or hold out; to produce or bring in; to shew or manifest; to tell, publish, or make known; to defer, or prolong; to alledge; to advance; to utter or pronounce; to put a later date; to enlarge or extend.*

Réfero, tŭli, látum, férre: *to bring or carry back; to ask one's opinion, to refer to one's consideration, to move as in council, senate, &c. to report, or relate; to propose or move; to give an account of; to reckon; to set to his account; to transfer to another, to impute; to requite or be even with; to be like, to resemble; to recall; to draw back; to attribute.*

4. GERO, gessi, gestum, gérere: *to bear, or carry; to wear; to have or shew; to manage; conduct, carry on, to do, execute or atchieve; to act for another, to represent him.*

A'ggero, aggéssi, aggéstum, aggérere: *to heap, to lay on heaps; to exaggerate.*

Cóngero, congéssi, congéstum, congérere: *to heap or pile up; to amass; to build nests.*

Dígero, digéssi, digéstum, digérere: *to divide or distribute; to dispose or set in order; to digest or concoct; to to diffolve, difcufs, or diffipate ; to loofen, enfeeble, or wafte ; to accomplifh, or execute ; to obey punctually.*

E'gero, égeſſi, egéſtum, egérere : *to empty, to carry out.*

I'ngero, éſſi, éſtum, érere: *to throw, pour, caſt in, or upon ; to heap upon ; to meddle with an affair.*

Régero, regéſſi, regéſtum, regérere : *to caſt up again ; to fling back ; to retort ; to ſet down, or put in writing that which one hath read, or heard.*

Súggero, ſuggéſſi, ſuggéſtum, ſuggérere : *to allow or afford ; to ſuggeſt, to put in mind.*

5. CURRO, cucúrri, curſum, cúrrere : *to run.*
Its compounds loſe the reduplication, five excepted.

Accúrro, accúrri, *and* accucúrri, accúrſum, accúrrere : *to run to.*

Circumcúrro, cúrri, ſum, ĕre : *to run about.*

Concúrro, concucúrri *ſeldom uſed ; and* concúrri, úrſum, úrrere : *to run with others, to run together ; to gather, or flow together ; to run againſt one another, to fall foul on one another as ſhips do ; to grapple or ſtrive with, to come to blows ; to give the ſhock or charge ; to concur, to meet or join together.*

Decúrro, decucúrri *and* decúrri, decúrſum, decúrrere : *to run down or along ; to run haſtily ; to run a-tilt ; to run over or go through with ; to paſs over.*

Diſcúrro, diſcúrri, diſcúrſum, diſcúrrere : *to run hither and thither.*

Excúrro, excúcurri *and* excúrri, excúrſum, excúrrere : *to make a little journey or excurſion ; to ruſh haſtily ; to ſhoot out in length or breadth ; to run out into other matters ; to exceed ; to ſally out ; to make an inroad.*

Incúrro, ri, ſum, ĕre : *to run in, upon, or againſt ; to incur ; to make an incurſion ; to light on ; to fall into.*

Occúrro, occúrri, occúrſum, occúrrere : *to run to ; to come together ; to haſten to ; to meet ; to appear before ; to prevent, to anticipate ; to occur, or come readily into one's mind ; to anſwer by way of prevention ; to meet with an objection foreſeen.*

Percúrro, percúrri, *and ſometimes* percucúrri, percúrſum, percúrrere : *to run in great haſte ; to run with ſpeed over, or through ; to make its way over, or through.*

Præcúrro, præcucúrri, præcúrſum, præcúrrere : *to run before ;*

before; *to out run*; *to fore run or happen before*; *to answer a foreseen objection*; *to excel.*

Procúrro, procucúrri *and* procúrri, procúrsum, procúrrere: *to run forth or abroad; to run or lie out in length.*

Recúrro, recúrri, recúrsum, recúrrere: *to run back, or make speed again.*

Succúrro, ri, sum, ĕre: *to help, to relieve: to come into one's mind or remembrance.*

ANNOTATION.

Here we see what compounds of *curro* preserve or drop the reduplication, pursuant to what hath been observed in the 2d rule, p. 175. We meet also with *accucúrri* in Cic. *Sed tamen opinor propter prædes suos accucurrisse*, ad Attic. But it is likewise observable that even *curro* itself sometimes loseth its reduplication. *Pedibus stetisti, curristi nummis*, Tertull. *lib. de fuga.* Which happeneth also to some of the rest that are reduplicated.

6. VERRO, verri, versum, vérrere: *to brush, to scour; to draw along, to rake.*

7. URO, ussi, ustum, ĕre: *to burn, to light up; to gall; to vex.*

Adúro, adússi, adústum, adúrere: *to burn, to scorch; to chafe or gall.*

Combúro, ússi, ústum, ĕre: *to burn or consume with fire; to scorch, or dry up.*

Exúro, ússi, ústum, úrere: *to burn out.*

Inúro, inússi, inústum, inúrere: *to mark with an hot iron; to write; to enamel; to put, or print in; to brand or fix upon; to set off or adorn.*

8. FURO. This verb wants the first person: we say only

FURIS, furit, fúrere: *to be mad;* without preterite or supine.

ANNOTATION.

VERRO according to Servius makes *versi*, and according to Charis. *verri: quod et usus comprobat*, adds Prisc. and this is what we have followed. The supine *versum* is in Cic. *Quod fanum denique, quod non eversum atque extersum reliqueris*, in Ver. And in Cato, *conversa villa:* as also Seneca in his Dial. according to Diomedes, *versa templa.* Hence in this passage of Virgil,

Et versá pulvis inscribitur hastá.

We ought, according to this author, to take *versá* rather for *drawn or dragged along*, than for *turned or inverted*. But *verro* seems heretofore to have had also *verritum*, whence Apul. took *converritorem*, in Apol.

Varro,

Varro, in Prisc. infists upon our saying, *furo, furis, furit*. Servius makes it have also *furui*; and in Sedulius we read, *furuerunt jussu tyranni*. In some other writers of more modern date we meet likewise with *furuisse*; but none of this is to be imitated.

RULE LVI.

Of sero and its compounds.

1. Sero, *signifying to plant, makes* sevi, satum.
2. *Its compounds take* sevi, situm.
3. *But in any other signification they make* UI, ERTUM.

EXAMPLES.

1. SERO, sevi, satum, sérere: *to sow, to plant.*
2. Those compounds which retain the same signification as the simple, retain also its preterite, and change A into I short in the supine, making SEVI, SITUM.

A'ssero, assévi, ássitum, ĕre: *to plant, sow, or set by, or near to.*

Cónsero, consévi, sĭtum, érere: *to sow, set, or plant; to join, or put together.*

Díssero, dissévi, dissitum, érere: *to sow or plant here and there.*

I'nsero, insévi, insitum, insérere: *to sow in, or among; to implant, to ingraff; to imprint, to ingrave.*

Intérsero, intersévi, intérsitum, intersérere: *to sow, set, or plant between.*

O'bsero, obsévi, óbsitum, ĕre: *to plant, or sow round about.*

3. Those which have a different signification from the simple, make ŭi and ERTUM; as

A'ssero, assĕrŭi, assértum, assérere: *to avouch or assert; to claim, challenge, or usurp; to pronounce free by law; to free or rescue:* whence cometh assertor, *a deliverer;* and assértio, *a claim of one's liberty, or a trial at law for it.*

Cónsero, erŭi, értum, érere: *to join, put, or lay together; to interlace, to interweave; to fight hand to hand, to come to handy strokes, to pretend to fight in order to keep possession of his estate or property, of which the plaintiff having been disappointed, he petitioned the prætor to put him again in possession of it. And this was called also* interdictum de vi (subaud. illata.) *The prætor's sentence.*

Désero, deférüi, defértum, deférere : *to forsake.*
Díssero, differüi, disfértum, differere : *to discourse or reason, to declare.*
E'xero, exérüi, exértum, exérere : *to thrust out or put forth; to discover, to shew.*
I'nsero, üi, értum, ěre : *to put or thrust in; to insert, to intermix.*
Intérsero, interférüi, interfértum, interferere : *to put between, to intermingle.*

ANNOTATION.

It is very probable, says Vossius, that heretofore there were two or three *sero*'s; one derived from ἵρω, *necto, ordino*; and the other from ἴρω, *dico*; the third taken from the future σπερῶ, by dropping the π, and making it *sero*, to sow. Hence in the first signification, which almost includes the second, it made *serüi, sertum;* whence also cometh *serta*, garlands of flowers, chaplets; *series*, an order or concatenation: and in the third it had *sevi, satum*. For *consevi* and *insevi*, relate to planting or sowing; and *conserüi, inserüi*, to the order and disposition of things. This distinction however was confounded, especially upon the decline of the Latin tongue, when they said *serüi* instead of *sevi*, which they extended also to its compounds. And the reason of this perhaps might be, because σπείρω, fut. σπερῶ, was taken heretofore also for *necto*, as Vossius in his Etym. observeth. Thus one might say, that *sero* had always the same original; since *differere*, to discourse, for instance, signifies nothing more than to form a series and as it were a concatenation of words.

Rule LVII.
Of the verbs in SO.

1. *Verbs in* SO *make* IVI, ITUM.
2. *But* incésso *hath only* incéssi.
3. Pinso *hath* SI, SUI, ITUM, *as also* pinsum *and* pistum:
4. Viso *hath* visi, *but never a supine*.
5. *And* depso *hath only* dépsüi.

Examples.

1. Verbs in SO make IVI, and ITUM; but their preterite frequently admits of a syncope.
ARCE'SSO, arcessívi *or* arcéssii, essítum, arcéssere: *to go to call, to call; to send for; to fetch, or trace; to procure; to accuse, to impeach.*
Lacésso, lacessívi *or* lacéssii *or* lacéssi, lacessítum, lacéssere:
to

to put, or drive forward; to importune, to disturb, to provoke, to tease.

Facéſſo, facefsívi, facéſſii *or* facéſſi, facefsítum, facéſſere: *to do, to go about to do; to get one gone, to go away, to ſend packing; to leave; to give trouble.*

Capéſſo, capefsívi, capéſſii *or* capéſſi, sítum, capéſſere: *to take, to go about to take, to take in hand, to take the charge or government of, to undertake the management of ſtate affairs.*

This ſyncopated preterite is the only one left in the following.

2. INCE'SSO, incéſſi, *without a ſupine,* incéſſere: *to go or come, to approach or be at hand; to aſſault, to attack or ſet upon; to provoke, to affront, to anger or vex; to ſeize the mind, and poſſeſs it with ſome particular movement.*

3. PINSO, pinſi, *and* pinſui, pinſitum, pinſum *and* piſtum: *to bruiſe or pound; to knead.* The antients ſaid alſo *piſo.*

4. VISO, viſi, viſere: *to go to ſee, to come to ſee; to viſit.*

Inviſo, invíſi, invíſum, invíſere: *to go to ſee, to viſit.*

Reviſo, revíſi, revíſum, revíſere: *to return or come again to ſee.*

5. DEPSO, dépſui, (*heretofore* depſi, *Varr.*) sĕre: *to knead or mould, to work dough till it be ſoft; to tan, or curry leather; to ſeeth or boil:* Non.

Condépſo, condépſui, condépſere: *to knead together, to mingle.*

Perdépſo, perdépſui, perdépſere, Catul. *to knead, to wet or ſoften thoroughly.*

ANNOTATION.

Accerſo is frequently uſed inſtead of *arceſſo*; Voſſius ſays it is a corrupt word, though eſtabliſhed now by uſe, inſtead of which we ought to ſay *arceſſo.* And thus Priſcian writes it, let P. Monet ſay what he will in his *Del. Lat.* The reaſon is becauſe *arceſſo* cometh from *arcio,* taken from *ad* and *cio*; juſt as *laceſſo* from *lacio*; *faceſſo* from *facio*; and *capeſſo* from *capio.* See the orthographical liſt at the end of the treatiſe of letters.

Theſe four verbs in *ſo* were heretofore of the fourth conjugation, for which reaſon we meet with *arceſsíri* in Livy, *laceſſíri* in Colum. and the like. And perhaps it is owing to this that their ſupine in *itum* has the penultimate long.

Viso makes only *visi* without a supine; but *visum* comes from *video*. For *viso* alone signifies all in one word, *eo visum:* though we read in Terence, *voltis-ne eamus visere,* Phor. act. 1. sc. 2. But *viso* is the frequentative formed of this supine *visum*, just as *pulso* comes from the supine *pulsum*, taken from *pello*. But no verb can be formed of a supine derived from itself, since on the contrary it is the verb that forms the supine.

Rule LVIII.
Of verbs in TO.

1. Flecto, pecto, necto, plecto, *make* XI, *and* XUM.
2. *But the three last make also* XUI.
3. Meto *hath* méssui, messum.
4. Mitto *hath* misi, missum;
5. *And* peto, petívi, petítum.

Examples.

The verbs in TO form their preterite and supine variously.

1. FLECTO, flexi, flexum, fléctere: *to bend, to bow, to crooken, or turn.*

Circumflécto, circumfléxi, circumfléxum, circumfléctere: *to bend about, to fetch a compass.*

Deflécto, defléxi, defléxum, defléctere: *to bend or bow down; to turn aside; to digress from a purpose.*

Inflécto, infléxi, infléxum, infléctere: *to bow or bend, to crooken.*

Reflécto, refléxi, refléxum, refléctere: *to turn back, to bend or bow back; to stay one from doing a thing; to cause to reflect, or consider.*

2. There are three that have a double preterite.

PECTO, pexi, *less usual,* péxui, péxum, péctere: *to comb, to card.*

Depécto, depéxi, depéxui, depéxum, depéctere: *to comb down or off.*

NECTO, nexi, néxui, nexum, néctere: *to knit, tie, join, or fasten together; to hang one thing upon another, to link; to be bound to serve one's creditor for default of payment: for which reason those people were called* nexi.

Annécto, annéxi, annéxui, annéxum, annéctere: *to knit, join, or tie unto, to annex.*

OF PRETERITES AND SUPINES. 275

Connécto, connéxi, connéxui, connéxum, connéctere: *to connect, knit, tie, or link together; to join or add to.*
Innécto, xi, xui, xum, innéctere: *to knit, tie, or bind about.*
PLECTO, plexi *less usual*, pléxui, plexum, pléctere: *to punish, to beat, to strike; to twist or twine.*
Implécto, xi, xui, xum, impléctere: *to fold, to interweave, or twine about.*

3. METO, méssui, messum, métere: *to reap, to mow; to crop or gather.*
Démeto, deméssui, deméssum, ĕre: *to reap or mow; to crop; to chop or cut off.*

4. MITTO, misi, missum, míttere: *to send; to send an account, to certify, to write; to cast or throw; to let alone, to supersede, to cease, to forbear; to let out, to bleed; to let go, to dismiss, to send away; to disband troops.*
Admítto, admísi, admíssum, admíttere: *to admit, to receive; to gallop, to push on; to let go; to put the male to the female; to commit; to approve, to favour.*
Commítto, commísi, commíssum, commíttere: *to suffer, to put in; to receive, to introduce, to settle people together by the ears; to offend, to commit a crime; to begin; to be due; to devolve; to be mortgaged; to deserve; to seize upon, to confiscate; to give cause or occasion; to join or close together.*
Demítto, demísi, demíssum, demíttere: *to set down; to thrust down; to let fall; to humble, to submit.*
Dimítto, dimísi, dimíssum, dimíttere: *to dismiss, to disband, to send away; to let fall or drop; to leave; to let go.*
Emítto, emísi, emíssum, emíttere: *to send forth or out; to let go or escape; to throw or fling; to publish; to utter; to set one free.*
Immítto, immísi, immíssum, immíttere: *to place or put in; to send forth; to cast or throw; to send with an evil purpose; to admit or suffer to enter; to let grow in length.*
Intermítto, intermísi, intermíssum, intermíttere: *to intermit, to leave or put off for a time, to discontinue, to cease.*
Manumítto, si, ssum, ĕre: *to manumise, or make a bondman free.*

Omítto,

Omítto, omíſi, omíſſum, ĕre: *to lay aſide; to throw away; to leave off; to leave out, to neglect; to paſs by, or not to mention, to omit.*

Permítto, permíſi, permíſſum, permíttere: *to permit, to give leave, to deliver up, to allow, to ſuffer.*

Præmítto, præmíſi, præmíſſum, íttere: *to ſend before.*

Promítto, promíſi, promíſſum, promíttere: *to promiſe, to proteſt, to engage; to fling or dart; to let grow in length.*

Adpromítto, ſi, ſſum, ĕre: *to engage or become ſurety for another: whence cometh* adpromíſſor, *a pledge or ſurety.*

Compromítto, ſi, ſſum, ĕre: *to put to arbitration; to give bond to ſtand to an award; to conſent to a reference. From thence cometh* compromíſſum, *a bond or engagement wherein two parties oblige themſelves to ſtand to the arbitration or award of the umpire; or a depoſit of money made for that purpoſe.*

Expromítto, ſi, ſſum, ĕre: *to promiſe and undertake for another, to be ſecurity.*

Repromítto, ſi, ſſum, ĕre: *to bind himſelf by promiſe or covenant, to engage.*

Remítto, remíſi, remíſſum, remíttere: *to ſend back; to throw back; to pardon, to forgive; to leave; to leave off; to let ſlip; to ſuffer or permit; to make an abatement; to ſlack, to untie; to aſſwage; to diſſolve or melt; to be leſs forward; to leſſen; to diſpenſe with; to refund or give back; to pay.*

Submítto, íſi, íſſum, íttere: *to lower or make leſs; to put in place of another; to ſend underhand; to humble, to ſubmit; to ſend to one's aſſiſtante.*

5. PETO, petívi, petítum, pétere: *to intreat humbly, to requeſt, to aſk or crave, to demand or require; to ſeek after, to court; to go to a place, or make to it; to aim at; to ſet upon, to aſſail; to pelt.*

A'ppeto, appetívi, appetítum, appétere: *to deſire or covet earneſtly; to catch at; to aſſault or ſet upon; to aſpire to, to attempt; to approach or draw near.*

Cómpeto, competívi, competítum, compétere: *to aſk or ſue for the ſame thing that another doth, to ſtand for the ſame place; to agree, to be proper or convenient.*

I'mpeto, impetívi, impetítum, impétere: *to set upon, to attack.*
O'ppeto, oppetívi, oppetítum, oppétere: *to die.*
Répeto, repetívi, ítum, étere: *to ask or demand again; to repeat, to rehearse; to go over again; to return to, or make towards; to fetch back; to call for, to demand; to seek or recover* as by law.
Súppeto, fuppetívi, fuppetítum, fuppétere: *to ask privily and craftily,* Ulpian. Thence also cometh
Súppetit, in the third perfon: *it is ready, it is at hand, it is sufficient.* As also,
Suppétere, Cic. *to have enough, to have plenty.*

ANNOTATION.

PECTO seemeth formerly to have had also *pectitum* in the supine; whence *pectitæ lanæ*, Colum. wool well combed and carded. *Pectita tellus*, Id. Land that has been well ploughed and harrowed. And hence perhaps it is that Asper, as we find in Priscian, thought there was also *pectivi*, but this preterite is now become obsolete.

Amplector is formed of *plector*, for which reason we say *amplexus sum* from the supine *plexum*. It is the same in regard to *complector*; and one would imagine that heretofore they said also *complecto*, because we find *complexus* in a passive sense in Plautus and Lucretius. But there are other examples of the same kind, to be seen in the list of the verbs passive, and in that of the participles among the remarks which come after the syntax.

There are some who make this distinction between the preterites *plexui*, and *plexi*; that the former signifies to twist or twine, and the latter to punish: but this difference is not at all observed. What we ought rather to take notice of, is that *plexui* is much more usual than *plexi*.

RULE LIX.
The second part of the verbs in TO.

1. Verto *makes* verti, verfum;
2. Sterto *hath* ftértüi *without a supine.*
3. Sifto, *if neuter, borrows* fteti *from* fto.
4. *If active, it makes* ftiti, ftatum.

EXAMPLES.

1. VERTO, verti, verfum, vértere: *to turn; to turn upside down; to ruin, to destroy; to cast down; to dig or cast up, to plough; to happen, fall out, or prove; to translate; to quit his country, to go into voluntary exile; to be changed or altered; to depend;*

depend; to consist; to be employed or conversant.

Advérto, advérti, advérsum, advértere: *to turn to; to advert, turn, or apply one's thoughts to any thing, to observe, to perceive.*

Animadvérto, animadvérti, animadvérsum, animadvértere: *to mind or observe, to perceive: to regard; to consider or animadvert; to punish.*

Avérto, avérti, avérsum, avértere: *to turn away; to turn or drive away; to beat back or put to flight; to pervert or misemploy; to convert to another use; to keep at a distance; to preserve from some evil or mischief.*

Convérto, convérti, convérsum, convértere, *to turn about or whirl; to turn towards; to transform; to translate; to change; to apply one's mind to a thing.*

Evérto, evérti, sum, ĕre: *to turn topsy turvy; to overthrow, to destroy, to beat down; to subvert.*

Invérto, invérti, invérsum, invértere: *to turn in; to turn upside down; to turn the inside out; to invert, to change.*

Obvérto, obvérti, obvérsum, obvértere: *to turn towards or against.*

Pervérto, pervérti, pervérsum, pervértere: *to turn upside down; to pervert, to bring over to a party or opinion; to ruin, to spoil or corrupt; to batter or throw down.*

Prævérto, prævérti, sum, ĕre: *to get before or overrun; to be beforehand with; to prepossess or preoccupy; to prevent; to prefer or set before.*

Revérto, *unusual in the present*, revérti, revérsum, Cic. *to turn back as it were against his will, whether he is called back upon the road, or forced and driven back. On the contrary* redíre *signifies to come back or return merely of one's self.*

Subvérto, subvérti, subvérsum, subvértere: *to turn upside down; to undo, to subvert.*

2. STERTO, stértui, stértere, *to snore, to sleep.*

Destérto, destértui, destértere: *to awake.*

3. SISTO, a verb neuter: *to be, to stand still,* borrows its preterite of *sto, steti.*

Its compounds also follow those of *sto.*

Assísto,

OF PRETERITES AND SUPINES.

Afsísto, ástiti, afsístere: *to be near; to stand up; to stand still; to assist.*

Absísto, ábstiti, absístere: *to depart from any place or thing; to cease.*

Consísto, ĭti, ĭtum, ĕre: *to stand upright; to be settled; to abide in one place; to make an halt; to be at a stay; to consist or depend upon.*

Desísto, déstiti, déstitum, ĕre: *to desist, to cease, to stop.*

Exísto, éxtiti, éxtitum, exístere: *to rise, spring, or come off; to appear, to be seen; to be; to exist.*

Insísto, ínstiti, ĭtum, ĕre: *to stand upon; to urge, to insist upon or be instant in; to fix upon; to rest or lean upon; to proceed and hold on.*

Obsísto, ĭti, ĭtum, ĕre: *to stand or post one's self in the way; to stop; to resist, to contradict.*

Pèrsísto, pérstiti, pérstitum, persístere: *to persist, to continue to the end, to persevere.*

Resísto, réstiti, réstitum, resístere: *to stand up; to stand still, to halt; to stop; to withstand, to resist, to hold against one.*

Subsísto, súbstiti, súbstitum, subsístere: *to stand still; to stay; to stop; to resist.*

4. SISTO, *a verb active makes* stiti, statum, sístere: *to place, to set up; to have one forth coming; to appear to his recognizance.*

ANNOTATION.

From VERTO come *diverto* and *divertor* which have only one and the same preterite, namely *diverti*; as *perverto* and *pervertor* have only *perverti*. But *reverto* is not usual, though *revertor* borrows from thence the preterite *reverti,* which Cicero makes use of, and of the other tenses depending thereon. *Si ille non revertisset,* &c. Offic. 3. If he had not returned. *Reverti Formias,* ad Attic. *Legati Ameriam reverterunt,* pro Rosc. Amer. And all the antients express themselves in the same manner. Though later authors chuse rather to make use of *reversus sum.*

STERTO, according to some, makes also *sterti*, retaining the consonant of the verb, according to what we have already observed concerning the other verbs.

SISTO, in the active voice, makes *stiti* in the preterite: but *sisto* neuter borrows *steti* of *sto*: for example in the active sense I'll say, *Antea illum istic stiti, nunc hic eum sisto:* I summoned him thither the time before, and now I summon him hither. But taking it in the neuter and absolute sense, I must say, *Antea illic stetit, nunc hic sistit;* he had appeared to his recognizance there before, and

and now he appears here. The supine *statum* is used by civilians; *Si statum non esset*, Ulpian. If they had not appeared to their recognizance. And thence come *stati dies, stata sacrificia*; for *status*, says Vossius, is taken there for τεταγμένος, *ordered, fixed*. From the supine *statum* proceeds also *stator*, he who stoppeth; *Jupiter stator*, who at the prayer of Romulus, stopped the Romans, that were ignominiously fleeing from before the Sabines. But the supines of the compounds of *sisto* are perhaps unusual, though we meet with some participles formed from thence, as *exstiturus* in Ulpian.

RULE LX.
Of the verbs in VO.

1. *From* vivo, *comes* vixi, victum;
2. *From* solvo, solvi, solútum;
3. Volvo *makes* volvi, volútum;
4. Calvo *hath* calvi, *without a supine*.

EXAMPLES.

The verbs in VO form their preterite and supine variously.

1. VIVO, vixi, victum, vívere: *to live; to live merrily, and pleasantly.*

Convívo, convíxi, convíctum, convívere: *to live together; to eat and drink together.*

Revívo, revíxi, revíxum, revívere: *to recover life; to revive again.*

2. SOLVO, solvi, solútum, sólvere: *to loose, or unloose, to unty; to release, to discharge, to set at liberty; to pay either in person or by deputy, either for one's self or for another; to open; to weigh anchor, to put to sea; to resolve, explain, or answer; to dispense with the laws.*

Absólvo, absólvi, absolútum, absólvere: *to absolve; to justify; to finish, to complete, to put the last hand to; to pay, to satisfy a person's demand.*

Dissólvo, dissólvi, dissolútum, dissólvere: *to loose and dissolve; to unbind, to disengage; to disannul; to pay debts; to break or melt.*

Persólvo, persólvi, persolútum, persólvere: *to pay thoroughly, to satisfy, to make good his promise, to finish, to accomplish.*

Resólvo, resólvi, resolútum, resólvere: *to unloose, to untie; to open, or undo; to reduce, to resolve; to separate;*

OF PRETERITES AND SUPINES.

parate; *to pay back*; *to dissolve or melt*; *to make void*; *to discover*; *to abolish.*

3. VOLVO, volvi, volútum, vólvere: *to roll; to hurl; to toss; to consider, or weigh, to ruminate.*

Advólvo, advólvi, advolútum, advólvere: *to roll to, or before.*

Convólvo, convólvi, convolútum, convólvere: *to wrap or wind about; to tumble or roll together; to envelop, to encompass.*

Devólvo, vi, tum, ĕre: *to tumble or roll down; to wind off; to pour out hastily; to reduce.*

Evólvo, evólvi, evolútum, evólvere: *to roll away, or over; to pull out; to unfold, to expound; to turn over a book.*

Invólvo, invólvi, involútum, invólvere: *to wrap or fold in; to cover or hide; to tumble or roll upon; to entangle, to invelop.*

Obvólvo, obvólvi, obvolútum, obvólvere: *to muffle; to disguise, to conceal.*

Provólvo, provólvi, útum, ĕre: *to roll or tumble before one's self.*

Revólvo, revólvi, revolútum, revólvere: *to roll or tumble over, to turn over; to go over again; to peruse again; to revolve, to reflect upon, to tell, to reveal.*

4. CALVO, calvi, cálvere: *to cheat, to deceive.*

ANNOTATION.

Calvo makes *calvi*, without a supine according to Priscian. But *calvor* is preferable. *Sopor manus calvitur*, Plaut. i. e. *decipit.* And even in this passive signification, *Ille calvi ratus*, Sal. thinking he was deceived.

RULE LXI.
Of the verbs in XO.

1. Nexo *makes* néxŭi, nexum,
2. *And* texo, téxŭi, texum.

EXAMPLES.

There are only two verbs in XO, *nexo*, and *texo.*

1. NEXO, nexis, néxŭi, nexum, néxere: or Nexo, as, *the frequentative of* necto: *to tie, to link, to fasten together, to connect.*

2. TEXO, téxŭi, textum, téxere: *to weave; to knit; to make, to build; to write or compose.*

Attéxo,

Attéxo, attéxüi, attéxtum, attéxere: *to knit or weave unto, or with; to add, or join unto.*

Contéxo, contéxüi, contéxtum, ĕre: *to weave or join to; to tie together; to join or twist together; to forge or devise.*

Detéxo, detéxüi, detéxtum, detéxere: Cic. Virg. *to weave or plait; to work it off.*

Intéxo, intéxüi, intéxtum, intéxere: *to weave, knit, or imbroider, to wind or wrap in; to interlace, or mingle.*

Prætéxo, prætéxüi, prætéxtum, prætéxere: *to border, edge, or fringe; to colour, to cloke, or excuse; to cover, to encompass, to hide; to set in order, or compose.*

Retéxo, xüi, xtum, xĕre: *to unweave or untwist; to do or begin a thing over again; to bring to mind again; to break off an affair, to do and undo.*

THE FOURTH CONJUGATION.

Rule LXII.

General for the verbs of the fourth conjugation.

The fourth conjugation makes the præterite in IVI, *and the supine in* ITUM, *as* Audívi, audítum.

Examples.

The verbs of the fourth conjugation form the preterite in IVI, and the supine in ITUM. As

AUDIO, audívi, audítum, audíre: *to hear, to hearken; to mind, to attend; to hear say; to agree to, to give credit to, to be one's auditor or scholar.* It is often rendered by the passive verb; *to be spoken of, to be praised or censured.*

Exáudio, exaudívi, exaudítum, íre: *to hear perfectly; to hear; to regard; to grant what is asked.*

Ináudio, inaudívi, inaudítum, inaudíre: *to hear by report, to overhear.*

LI'NIO, linívi, linítum, liníre: *to anoint or besmear; to rub softly; to chafe gently.*

Illínio, illinívi, illinítum, illinere: *the same.*

Sublínio, ívi, ítum, íre: *to anoint or besmear a little, to grease; to lay a ground colour.* And metaphorically,

to

OF PRETERITES AND SUPINES. 283

to deceive and mock one, taken from a kind of play in which they daubed the faces of those who were asleep with soot.

MU'NIO, ivi, itum, ire: *to fortify, to strengthen or secure; to provide with necessaries; to make good and strong, to repair and pave an high way or passage; to make or prepare a passage.*

Præmúnio, ivi, itum, ire: *to fortify a place beforehand; make sure of, to secure.*

FI'NIO, ivi, itum, ire: *to finish or end; to define; to determine, appoint, prescribe, assign or limit.*

Præfinio, ivi, itum, ire: *to determine, set, or pitch upon beforehand; to prescribe or limit.*

SCIO, scivi, scitum, scire: *to know, to understand, to comprehend; to be skilful in; to see, to be certain of; to give his vote and opinion; to ordain, decree, or appoint.*

Cónscio, conscívi, conscítum, conscíre: *to know, to be privy to.*

Néscio, nescívi, nescítum, nescíre: *not to know, to be ignorant.*

Réscio, rescívi, rescítum, rescíre: *to hear and understand of a matter, to come to the knowledge of.*

CO'NDIO, condívi, condítum, condíre: *to season; to pickle, to preserve; to embalm; to sweeten, to relish.*

SE'RVIO, ivi, itum, ire: *to be a slave, to serve, to do service, to obey; to be subservient to, to attend upon; to apply himself to; to be held in base tenure not as freehold.*

Desérvio, servívi, servítum, servíre: *to serve, to do service to; to wait upon.*

EO, ivi, itum, ire: *to go, to walk, to come towards one, to come back; to put to the vote, to give one's vote, to subscribe to one's opinion, to be of a contrary opinion; to pass by one without speaking; to pay double, to go double; to take such a turn or change.*

It forms the future in IBO, as well as its compounds.

A'beo, abívi, ábitum, abíre: *to depart, to go away; to go or come; to retire; to cease to be, to be lost, to disappear, to vanish; to finish his office; to remove to some distance; to be changed into; to go off, or escape.*

A'deo, adívi, áditum, adíre: *to go to, to come to, to go to find; to address; to visit; to appear in court; to go go upon or undertake, to apply; to succeed to and take possession of an estate.*

A′mbio, ambívi, ambítum, ambíre: *to go about, to encompass; to seek for preferment, to stand for, or make an interest for any thing, or place.*

Cóeo, ívi, ĭtum, íre: *to come together, to assemble, to meet, to convene; to swarm together; to close or shut itself up close again; to shrink, to wax thick, to curdle; to couple together in generation; to join battle; to join one's self* as in alliances, confederacies, conspiracies, plots, &c.

E′xeo, ívi, ĭtum, íre: *to go out, or come out; to be gone; to quit his post; to be discovered, to be divulged; to put forth or publish; to exceed; to be out of himself, or transported beyond measure; to fall or run* as rivers do, *to end.*

I′neo, ívi, ĭtum, íre: *to go or enter into; to enter upon an employment or office, to commence; to consult, to deliberate, to consider, to think of ways and means; to concert, to form a design or plan; to gain or obtain favour; to enter into society.* Hence cometh íniens, *entering in, beginning;* as íniens mensis, íniens annus.

O′beo, ívi, ĭtum, íre: *to go up and down, or to and fro; to go round, to encompass; to go through, or all over; to go to, to come by; to look over or view; to undertake the discharge or performance; to go through with, to discharge; to be present in order to perform a thing; to die; to finish; to inherit, to take possession of an inheritance.*

Péreo, ívi, ĭtum, íre: *to perish, to be lost and spoilt, to die.*

Præ′eo, ívi, ĭtum, íre: *to go before, to lead the way; to precede; to excel; to speak, or read before; to prescribe the form of words at public ceremonies.*

Prætéreo, ívi, ĭtum, íre: *to go or pass by, or over; to go beyond; to neglect; to let pass, to pass over, to make no mention of, to leave out.*

Pródeo, ívi, ĭtum, íre: *to go or come forth, to go out of doors, to come abroad; to go before, to appear in public, to march forth, to appear extravagant in his expence.*

Rédeo, ívi, ĭtum, íre: *to return, to begin again, to grow or spring up again.*

Súbeo, ívi, ĭtum, íre: *to go under, or into; to spring or*

or grow up; *to come in place of*, *to succeed*; *to undergo*; *to endure*, *to undertake*; *to mount or climb*; *to act a part*.

Tránseo, ívi, ĭtum, íre: *to pass over or beyond*; *to pass over to the other side*; *to put to the vote*; *to give his vote*; *to go over to the party whose opinion we embrace*; *to pierce, or run through one*.

RULE LXIII.
Of those verbs that have no supine.

Géstio, inéptio, *and* cæcútio, *make* IVI *without a supine*.

EXAMPLES.

The following verbs conform to the general rule in regard to the preterite; but they have no supine.

GE'STIO, gestívi, gestíre: *to shew joy or desire by gesture of body, to leap or skip for joy*; *to long*; *to delight in a thing*.

INE'PTIO, ineptívi, íre: *to trifle, to talk, or act foolishly*.

CÆCU'TIO, cæcutívi, íre: *to be blind*.

ANNOTATION.

Obédio, which some grammarians have doubted of, makes *obedívi*, *obedítum*. *Utrinque obedítum dictatori est*, Liv. *Ramo oleæ quam maximè obedituro*, Plin.

Púnio makes *punívi* and *punítus sum*. *Cujus tu inimicissimum multo crudelius punitus es*, Cic. See the remarks after the syntax.

RULE LXIV.
Of *singúltio*, *sepelio*, *véneo* and *vénio*.

1. Singúltio *and* sepélio *make* IVI, ULTUM.
2. *From* véneo *comes* vénii *without a supine*.
3. *But from* vénio *comes* veni, ventum.

EXAMPLES.

The two first verbs conform also to the general rule in regard to the preterite, and form the supine in ULTUM.

1. SINGU'LTIO, singultívi, singúltum, singultíre: *to sob, to hickup*. Whence cometh *singúltus*.

SEPE'LIO, sepelívi, sepúltum, sepelíre: *to bury*.

The following make their preterite and supine in a different manner.

2. VE'NEO, vēnii, *without a supine*, veníre: *to be sold*.

3. VE'-

3. VÉNIO, vēni, ventum, íre : *to come, to arrive; to go.*

Advénio, advéni, advéntum, advéníre : *to arrive; to come to.*

Circumvénio, circumvéni, circumvéntum, circumveníre : *to come about or besiege ; to surround or encompass ; to deceive, to over-reach, to circumvent.*

Convénio, véni, véntum, íre : *to come together, to convene or meet ; to come or go to a place ; to agree or accord together, to be of the same opinion ; to suit, to fit ; to be fit, to beseem ; not to be contrary or repugnant ; to meet with, to come and talk with one ; to sue one in law, and to convene him before a judge ; to come into the husband's power by mutual agreement.*

Devénio, devéni, devéntum, deveníre : *to come or go down to, to go, to come ; to happen.*

Evénio, evéni, evéntum, eveníre : *to chance, to happen.*

Invénio, invéni, invéntum, inveníre : *to find ; to invent, to devise ; to get, to obtain ; to discover.*

Pervénio, pervéni, pervéntum, perveníre : *to come to, to arrive at.*

Prævénio, prævéni, præventum, præveníre : *to come before ; to prevent.*

Provénio, provéni, provéntum, proveníre : *to come forth, to increase ; to proceed, to come into the world ; to grow, to happen or chance.*

Revénio, revéni, revéntum, reveníre : *to come again, to return.*

ANNOTATION.

It is a question among the grammarians, whether from *singulti vi* the supine ought to be *singultum* or *singultitum*. Whence it appears how little either of them is used. We have preferred *singultum*, because from thence comes *singultus*. Yet *singultum* is only a sincope for *singultitum* : as *sepultum* is for *sepelitum*, which was heretofore current according to Priscian.

VENEO comes from *venum* and EO. It has neither participle, gerund, nor supine ; and it is an error to think that *venum* may be its supine, since on the contrary it is composed of *venum* ; as likewise *venundo* ; just as from *pessum* comes *pessundo* ; and from *satis*, *satisdo*. Now the supines are derived from the verbs, and not the verbs from the supines. For which reason when we say, *venum ire*, *pessum ire*, or *pessundare*, *venundare*, it implies, *ad venum* and *ad pessum*, &c. which are real nouns : hence Tacitus says in the dative, *Posita veno irritamenta*

OF PRETERITES AND SUPINES. 287

menta gulæ; and in the ablative, *nisi in iis quæ veno exercerent*, &c. We find likewise in Apul. *Me venui subjiciunt*, they expose me to sale.

In regard to *pessum*, it is plain that it is a noun. For as from *pando* comes *passus* for *pansus*, so from *pendo* comes *pessus* for *pensus*, that is, *ponderosus*. *Utraque conditio est pensior, virginem an viduam habere?* Plaut. So that *pessum ire*, is properly, *to descend and go to the bottom*, as heavy things do; hence in Plaut. we find *pessum premere*; and in Cic. *verbis aliquem pessum dare*, that is, *to revile, disparage, and to use ill,* according to Quintilian.

RULE LXV.
Of *sancio, vincio,* and *amicio.*

1. Sáncio *hath* sanxi (*heretofore* sancívi) sanctum, *and* sancítum.
2. Víncio *hath* vinxi, vinctum.
3. Amício *makes* ămĭcŭi, *and* amixi, amictum.

EXAMPLES.

1. SA'NCIO, sanxi, sanctum, *and* sancítum; *heretofore* sancívi, *or* sancii, sancíre: *to order, to establish; to enact; to confirm by penalty, to punish; to regulate; to forbid by ordinance or law, to resolve, to condemn.* From whence comes sanctio, ónis, *a confirmation, a decree, a penal statute.*

2. VI'NCIO, vinxi, vinctum, vincíre: *to bind or tie up; to hoop, to connect.*
Devíncio, devínxi, devínctum, devincíre: *to bind fast; to tie up, to oblige, to engage, to endear.*
Revíncio, revínxi, revínctum, revincíre: *to tie or bind, to gird, to tie behind.*

3. AMI'CIO, ămĭcŭi *and* amíxi, *seldom used* (*heretofore also* amicívi) amictum, amicíre: *to put on a garment; to cover; to wrap up; to veil.*

RULE LXVI.
Of the verbs which make SI, SUM; and of those which make SI, TUM.

1. Séntio *and* ráucio *take* SI, SUM:
2. *But* Fúlcio, sárcio, *and* fárcio *make* SI, TUM.

EXAMPLES.

1. There are two verbs that make the preterite in SI, and the supine in Sum.
SE'NTIO, sensi, sensum, sentíre: *to discern by the senses, to be sensible of, to perceive, to doubt, to understand,*

derſtand, to find out; to think, to be of an opinion.

Aſſéntio, aſſénſi, aſſénſum, aſſentíre; *and* aſſéntior, aſſénſus ſum, aſſentíri: *to aſſent or agree to; to be of one's mind or opinion.*

Conſéntio, conſénſi, **conſénſum**, conſentíre: *to conſent, to agree, to be of the ſame opinion; to be agreeable to.*

Diſſéntio, diſſénſi, ſum, íre: *to diſſent, to be of a different opinion.*

Præſéntio, præſénſi, præſénſum, præſentíre: *to perceive or underſtand beforehand, to foreſee, to preconceive.*

RA'CIO, rauſi, rauſum, raucíre: *to be hoarſe.*

Irráucio, irrauſi, irráuſum, irraucíre: *the ſame.*

2. There are three which have SI, TUM.

FU'LCIO, fulſi, fultum, fulcíre: *to prop, to ſupport.*

Suffúlcio, ſi, tum, íre: *to hold or bear up, to underprop; to ſtrengthen.*

SA'RCIO, ſarſi, ſartum, ſarcíre: *to botch, to mend, to patch; to repair, to make good; to make amends, to recompenſe.*

Reſárcio, reſárſi, reſártum, reſarcíre: *to patch, to mend; to recompenſe or make amends for.*

FA'RCIO, ſarſi, ſartum, ſarcire: *to ſtuff, to farce, to frank, or feed, to fat, to cram.*

Its compounds ſometimes change A into E, as

Conſércio, conſérſi, conſértum, íre: *to ſtuff or fill, to ram or cram in; to drive thick and cloſe.*

Différcio, diffěrſi, différtum, íre: *to ſtuff.*

Reſércio, reſérſi, tum, íre: *to fill, to ſtuff, to cram.*

Infárcio *retains the* A, infárſi, tum, íre: *to ſtuff or cram.*

ANNOTATION.

1. We ſay alſo *rauceo, es, ŭi*, from whence comes *raucesco*, to grow hoarſe. Even Cicero, according to the moſt approved editions ſays; *Si paullum irraucuerit*, de Orat. taking it perhaps from *rauceo*, though Priſcian reads *irrauſerit*. But *irrauſit* is from Lucilius, as well as *rauſurus*, taken from the ſupine *rauſum*.

2. Theſe ſupines in *tum* are only ſyncopated from thoſe in *itum*; as *ſartum* for *ſarcitum*: and from the latter are ſtill remaining *ſarcimen* and the participle *ſarcitus*, which we read in Cicero, *Pulvinus Melitenſi roſâ ſarcitus*, in Verr. where we ſee that they retained the conſonant of the preſent, namely the C.

RULE LXVII.
Of haúrio, ſepio *and* ſalio.

1. Haúrio *makes* hauſi, hauſtum; 2. Sé-

OF PRETERITES AND SUPINES.

  2. Sēpio, sepívi, *or* sepsi, septum:
  3. Sálio *hath* sálii *or* sálüi, saltum.
  4. *But its compounds form the supine in* ULTUM.

EXAMPLES.

1. HAU′RIO, hausi, haustum, haurire : *to draw, to fetch up; to drink or swallow up.*

Exháurio, exháusi, exháustum, exhaurire: *to draw out, to empty, to exhaust, to consume or waste.*

  2. SE′PIO, sepívi, *less usual*, sepsi, septum, sepíre: *to inclose, to hedge in, to fence.*

Consépio, consépsi, conséptum, consepíre: *to hedge in, to inclose.*

Circumsépio, circumsépsi, circumséptum, circumsepíre: *to inclose or hedge in.*

Dissépio, dissépsi, disséptum, íre: *to break down an hedge or inclosure, to dispark.*

SA′LIO *or* SA′LLIO, *to season with salt, follows the general rule*; salívi, salítum: *but*

  3. SA′LIO, sálii, *or* sálüi, saltum, salíre: *to leap; to dance; to skip; to rebound; to spring or shoot out.*

  4. The compounds of this verb follow its preterite, but make ULTUM in the supine; as

Assílio, assílüi, assúltum, assilíre: *to leap at, upon, or against; to assail.*

Desílio, desílui *or* desílii, desúltum, desilíre: *to leap down, to alight, to vault.*

Exílio, exílüi *or* exílii, exúltum, exilíre: *to leap out, to go out hastily; to skip; to leap for joy.*

Insílio, insílüi *or* insílii, insúltum, insilíre: *to leap in or upon.*

Resílio, resílüi *or* resílii, resúltum, resilíre: *to leap or start back; to rebound; to recoil; to shrink in; to unsay; to go from his bargain.*

ANNOTATION.

HAURIO heretofore made *haurii*, Varr. apud Prisc. Hence it is that Apul. frequently uses *hauritum* instead of *haustum*; hence also cometh *hauriturus*, in Juvenal. Virgil has *hausurus*, Æn. 4. as coming from the supine *hausum*. And indeed the reason of its having taken the *t*, according to Priscian, was no other than to distinguish it from *ausum*, or *ausus sum*, formed of *audeo*. Which shews that they did not prefix the aspiration *h* to it in his time, because that would have been a sufficient distinction. But the antient

VOL. I.   U   usage

usage in regard to this aspiration seems to have varied in many other words; concerning which we refer the reader to our treatise of letters at the end of this work.

Sĕ′pio, heretofore made *sepivi*, whence cometh *sepivissent* in Livy, and *sepivit* in S. Jerome; which agrees with the general analogy above observed, p. 171.

Să′lio, makes *salŭi* or *salii*, which were formed from the regular, though now unusual, preterite *salivi*. Hence there were formerly some who read *saluere per utres*, in Virg. 2. Georg. and others *saliere*, as may be seen in Diomedes and in Prisc. Thus they said *exilii* or *exilui*, *defilii* or *defilui*. *Exilui gaudio*, Cic. *Defilui de rheda*, Id.

Priscian, after Charisius, gives us also *cambio*, *campsi*, which he derives from κάμπτω, ψω, ἔκαμψα. This verb signified also *to fight, to begin, to turn*; from whence cometh *campso, as*, in Ennius, *to bend his course towards a place*. It was also taken for *to change, to sell, to recompense; to put money out at interest*, according to Cujas. But it is now become obsolete.

Rule LXVIII.
Of the compounds of Pă′rio.

1. *The compounds of* părio *make* ŭi, ERTUM.
2. *But* compĕrio *and* repĕrio *make* ERI, ERTUM.

Examples.

Pă′rio *is of the third conjugation*: părere: *to bring forth young, to be brought to bed.*

Its compounds change the *a* into *e*, and are of the fourth conjugation, making ŭi, and ERTUM; as

Apĕrio, apĕrui, apĕrtum, aperire: *to open; to declare; to explain; to discover, to disclose, to manifest, to shew.*

Adapĕrio, adapĕrui, adapĕrtum, adaperire: *to lay open; to disclose; to uncover.*

Opĕrio, opĕrui, opĕrtum, operire: *to cover; to shut up or close; to hide.*

In like manner oppĕrior, oppĕrtus sum: *to wait;* seems to take its preterite from hence. See the 75th rule.

2. These two make ERI and ERTUM.

Compĕrio, cómpĕri, compĕrtum, comperire: *to find out a thing, to know for certain and by trial.*

Repĕrio, rĕpĕri, repĕrtum, reperire: *to find; to find out or discover.*

ANNO-

OF PRETERITES AND SUPINES.

ANNOTATION.

We say also *comperior*, a deponent; but it has no other preterite than *comperi*. For *compertus* is passive; as in Livy, *Compertus stupri*; in Tacit. *Compertus flagitii*, convicted. But instead of *comperi*, they said also, *Compertum est mihi*, Catul. *Compertum habeo*, Cic. *I know for certain*.

RULE LXIX.

Of the verbs of desire, called DESIDERATIVES.

When a verb signifies a longing or desire, it has no preterite, (the same may be said of ferio *and* aïo.*)*
Except partúrio, esúrio, *and* nuptúrio.

EXAMPLES.

Verbs signifying a desire of action, are called DESIDERATIVES, and are formed from the supine of their primitive. These verbs have neither preterite nor supine; as

COENATU'RIO *from* coenátum, coenaturíre: *to desire to sup.*
Dormitúrio, dormituríre: *to desire to sleep.*
Emtúrio, emturíre: *to desire to buy.*
Mictúrio, micturíre: *to desire to make water.*

Some of them have a preterite but never a supine, as

Partúrio, parturívi, íre: *to be in labour, to be brought to bed, to bring forth* as any female.
Esúrio, esurívi, esuríre: *to be hungry, to have a desire to eat:* yet we find esuritúrus *in* Ter.
Nuptúrio, nupturívi, nupturíre: *to have a desire to marry.*

These two are also without a preterite, though they are not desideratives.

FE'RIO, feris, feríre: *to strike, to hit; to push; to conclude an agreement or alliance, to ratify; to affront with words.*
Aïo, aïs: *I say.* A defective verb.

ANNOTATION.

FERIO, according to Diomedes and Priscian, hath no preterite; nor will Varro let it have any other than *percussi*; and this is also the opinion of Charisius, where he speaks of verbs that change in their preterite. Yet in the title *de defectivis*, where he conjugates this verb at length, he gives it *ferii, ferieram, feriissem*, &c.

For which reason many learned moderns, as Mantuanus, Turnebus, Aurelius, have not scrupled to make use of these tenses; but this does not often happen.

The supine *feritum*, is still less usual, though Charisius puts in the infinitive, *feritum ire:* but in the passive he gives it only *ictus sum*, taken from *ico*. Hence Petrarch is censured for having said 8. *Africæ*.

Pax populis ducibúsque placet fœdúsque feritum.

We meet nevertheless with *feriturum* in Servius *in* 7. and upon the decline of the Latin tongue they went so far as to say *ferita, æ,* for *plaga*, Paul Diac. from whence the Italians have still retained *una ferita, a blow*.

Aio hath no preterite in the first person, according to Priscian; but in the second we say *aisti*, in the plural *aistis*, and even *aierunt*, in Tertull. See the remarks after the syntax.

OF THE VERBS DEPONENTS.

RULE LXX.
What a verb deponent is.

A verb deponent is that which hath always an active signification and a passive conjugation.

EXAMPLES.

Verbs deponents are such as have the passive termination in OR, but with an active signification; as
POLLI'CEOR: *I promise.*
VE'REOR: *I fear.*
LA'RGIOR: *I bestow.*
BLA'NDIOR: *I flatter.*

RULE LXXI.
General for the preterite of the deponents.

The preterite of the deponent is formed from a feigned active: For as amátus *comes from* amo, *so* lætátus *comes from* læto.

EXAMPLES.

As the preterite of the passive is formed from the supine of the active; so to find the preterite of the deponent we must feign or suppose an active by dropping the R, and see what preterite and supine this active would have according to the general rules above given, and from thence form the preterite of the deponent. Hence.

1. In the first conjugation all these verbs have the preterite in ATUS.

LÆTOR, lætátus sum lætári: *to rejoice. Just as if we used an active* læto, ávi, átum. *And the rest in the same manner.*

AUCTIO'NOR, átus sum, ári: *to make an open sale; to make an out-cry of goods, slaves, &c.*

ANNOTATION.

This verb is derived from *augeo, xi, ctum,* whence cometh *auctio,* a setting things to open sale: *auctor,* an owner, or seller of a thing upon warranty. *Secundus auctor,* he was surety to the purchaser, in case he was evicted, and obliged to resign what he had purchased, to another; *auctoritas,* surety, warranty: *auctionarius* as *auctionariæ tabellæ,* inventories wherein goods to be sold were written; bills of sale: *auctoratus,* hired or lent out for money; a slave or gladiator that had been sold by auction, &c. See *auctoratus* above, p. 180.

AU'CUPOR, átus sum, ári: *to go a fowling, hawking, or bird catching; to seek or get by cunning; to watch, to lie at catch for; to hunt after, to strive to obtain.*

CAU'SOR, átus sum, ári: *to pretend or plead in way of excuse, to alledge as an excuse.* Whence cometh causárius, *a military term signifying a soldier, who has a right to demand his discharge for some cause or other, as being sick or maimed.*

CONTE'STOR, átus sum, ári: *to call to witness, to make protestation of a thing, to declare openly: to put in the plaintiff's declaration, and the defendant's answer.* Whence cometh contestáta lis, contestátum judícium, *a rule given by a judge upon a cause before final sentence.*

DEBA'CCOR, átus sum, ári: *to rage, or roar like a drunken man; to give abusive language.*

DE'PRECOR, átus sum, ári: *to beseech, desire, or pray earnestly; to beg, or petition; to beg pardon; to pray or wish against a thing; to avert, or turn away.*

DO'MINOR, átus sum, ári: *to be lord and master; to domineer.*

GRA'TULOR, átus sum, ári: *to congratulate, to rejoice or be glad; to bid welcome, to wish one joy.*

INSE'CTOR *(unusual in the first person of the present tense)* átus sum, ári: *to pursue, to run after; to inveigh against, to speak ill of, to rail at one.*

INTE'RFOR, átus sum, ári: *to speak while another is speaking, to interrupt him.*

ME'DITOR, átus sum, ári: *to meditate, muse, or think upon; to exercise or practise, to study; to plot or design; to apply one's self with great care and diligence.*

MO'-

MO'DEROR, átus fum, ári: *to moderate, to refrain; to govern, to manage, to guide.*

MOROR, átus fum, ári: *to ſtay, to delay; to make one wait; to wait; to dwell; to ſtop at ſomething.*

MU'TUOR, átus fum, ári: *to borrow.*

OBTE'STOR, átus fum, ári: *to conjure or beſeech; to implore or call upon one for ſuccour; to proteſt; to call to witneſs.*

O'PEROR, átus fum, ári: *to operate, or work; to be employed; to ſacrifice, to be taken up with ſacrificing, or performing any holy rites.*

PERI'CLITOR, átus fum, ári: *to be in danger; to endanger, to expoſe; to try or prove, to make experiment.*

PE'RVAGOR, átus fum, ári: *to wander or travel over, to go and come over, to rove about; to ſpread abroad, to become public or commonly known.*

STI'PULOR, átus fum, ári: *to ſtipulate, to make a bargain; to aſk and demand ſuch and ſuch terms for a thing to be given, or done by the ordinary words of the law; to be required or aſked by another to make a contract with him.* For it is active and paſſive as we ſhall ſhew in the remarks.

Reſtípulor, átus fum, ári: *to take counter-ſecurity; to make anſwer in the law, to lay in a pledge, to anſwer to an action.*

STO'MACHOR, átus fum, ári: *to be angry, vexed, or diſpleaſed; to be in a bad humour, to be in a great fume, to fret, vex, or chafe.*

VADOR, átus fum, ári: *to put in ſureties for appearance, to give bail; to oblige one to put in ſureties; to ſtand to or defend a ſuit.*

2. In the ſecond conjugation they have the preterite in ITUS.

VE'REOR, véritus fum, veréri: *to fear.* As if it came from Véreo, üi, ĭtum.

POLLI'CEOR, pollícitus fum, pollicéri: *to promiſe.* As if it came from pollíceo.

3. In the third it is formed variouſly according to the ſupine of the active, which you are to ſuppoſe, following the rules of the termination; as

AM-

AMPLECTOR, ampléxus sum, amplécti: *(as if it came from* amplécto) *to surround or incircle; to embrace, to fold in one's arms; to comprehend; to make much of, or to address; to lay hold of, or possess one's self of; to love, to be fond of, to favour, to espouse, to receive.*

Compléctor, compléxus sum, complécti: *to embrace; to comprize or contain; to love, to be fond of, to cherish, to protect, to support.*

FUNGOR, functus sum, fungi: *to discharge an office or duty; to execute, to be in an office; to pay taxes; to enjoy; to use.*

Defúngor, functus sum, defúngi: *to be rid of a business, to go through with it; to discharge or perform his duty.*

Perfúngor, functus sum, perfúngi: *to discharge completely; to be delivered from by having undergone; to be free from.*

IRASCOR, irátus sum, irásci: *to be angry: to be sorry for.*

NASCOR, natus sum, nasci: *to be born, to be framed by nature; to spring or grow; to begin, to rise* as stars.

4. In the fourth the preterite is formed in ITUS.

BLANDIOR, blandítus sum, blandíri: *to flatter, to wheedle, to speak fair, to compliment.*

EMENTIOR, ementítus sum, ementíri: *to lye down-right, to counterfeit, to feign, to disguise, to forge or pretend, to take upon him.*

SORTIOR, sortítus sum, sortíri: *to cast or draw lots; to have any thing given by lots; to chance to get or obtain.*

EXCEPTIONS.

There are several verbs to be excepted, which we shall comprize in the five following rules.

Rule LXXII.
Of the verbs in EOR.

1. Reor *makes* ratus; *and* miséreor, misértus.
2. Fateor *hath* fassus; *but its compounds* FESSUS.

OF PRETERITES AND SUPINES.

EXAMPLES.

1. REOR, ratus sum, reri: *to suppose, to judge, deem or think.*

MISE'REOR, misértus sum, miseréri: *to take pity of one, to have mercy on him, to be sorry for him, to assist him in his misery.*

2. FA'TEOR, fassus sum, fatéri: *to confess, to own, to grant; to discover.*

Its compounds change A into I, and assume an E in the preterite according to the 2d rule, as

Confíteor conféssus sum, confitéri: *to confess.*

Diffíteor, diffitéri: *to deny;* it has never a preterite.

Profíteor, proféssus sum, profitéri: *to declare openly, to own; to profess, to shew openly; to profess, to be a professor, to give public lectures; to give in an account of lands or goods, so as to have them recorded or registered.* Whence cometh proféssio.

ANNOTATION.

Misereor had also *miseritus,* according to Robert Stephen. But we say likewise *miseror, aris,* which has the same sense, though it takes another regimen, as we shall observe in the syntax. The antients used also *misereo,* and *misero.*

Tueor regularly makes *tuitus,* as *moneor, monitus;* but *tutus* comes from *tuor,* as *argutus* from *arguor.* We find it likewise in Plautus, as well as its compounds, *contuor, intuor, obtuor.* So that there is no need of a particular rule for these verbs. We have only to observe that *tueor* is far more usual than *tuor.* And yet from *tutus* is also formed *tutari,* which is pretty common.

RULE LXXIII.
Of the verbs in OR.

Loquor, *and* sequor *take* UTUS;
And queror, questus.
Nitor *hath* nisus, nixus;
Fruor, frúitus, *and* fructus.
Labor *makes* lapsus, *and* utor, usus.

EXAMPLES.

LOQUOR, locútus sum, loqui: *to speak, to tell.*

A'lloquor, allocútus sum, álloqui: *to speak to one; to address himself to one; to speak in public.*

Cólloquor, collocútus sum, cólloqui: *to speak together, to parley, to talk with one, to discourse, to confer.*

E'loquor, elocútus fum, éloqui: *to speak eloquently; to speak out or plainly, to declare.*

Próloquor, prolocútus fum, próloqui: *to speak freely what one thinketh; to speak out or at length; to preface that which one is about to say.*

SEQUOR, fequútus fum, fequi: *to follow; to go after, to seek for.*

A'ffequor, affequútus fum, áffequi: *to overtake; to reach, equal, or match; to understand, or find out; to get, or obtain.*

Cónfequor, confequútus fum, confequi: *to follow; to follow close; to overtake; to get or obtain his wish.*

E'xequor, útus fum, ĕqui: *to do, to execute; to punish; to prosecute; to persist; to accomplish; to obtain his wish.*

I'nfequor, infequútus fum, ínfequi: *to follow after, to pursue; to persecute, to rail at one.*

O'bfequor, obfequútus fum, óbfequi: *to humour or comply with; to humour or please; to flatter or cringe to; to submit to, to obey.*

Pérfequor, útus fum, ĕqui: *to pursue, to trace, to follow on, to go through with; to sue for in a court of justice, and the process is called* perfecutio.

Prófequor, útus fum, ĕqui: *to follow after, to pursue, to prosecute; to accompany, to wait upon, to attend; to love one, to do him a kindness; to rate or chide; to describe, treat, or discourse of.*

Súbfequor, fubfequútus fum, fúbfequi: *to follow forthwith, or hard by, to come after.*

QUEROR, queftus fum, queri: *to complain, to lament; to find fault with.*

Cónqueror, conquéftus fum, ĕri: *to complain of; to complain together.*

NITOR, nifus or nixus fum, niti: *to endeavour, labour, or strive; to tend towards vigorously; to lean or rest upon; to depend, to confide in.*

Adnítor, adnífus or adníxus fum, adníti: *to endeavour; to shove or push; to lean upon.*

Enítor, enífus or eníxus fum, eníti: *to climb up with pain; to strain hard, to endeavour; to tug or pull; to travel with child; to bring forth young.*

Of Preterites and Supines.

Innítor, innífus *or* inníxus fum, inníti: *to lean or ſtay upon; to depend upon.*

FRUOR, frúitus *or* fructus fum, frui: *to enjoy; to take the profit of, to make uſe of; to take delight in, and reap the fruits of.*

Pérfruor, perfrúitus fum, pérfrui: *to enjoy fully.*

UTOR, ufus fum, uti: *to uſe, to have the uſe or benefit of; to have, to enjoy.*

Abútor, abúfus fum, abúti: *to uſe contrary to the nature or firſt intention of a thing; to apply to a wrong end, to abuſe, to ſpoil; or even to uſe freely.*

LABOR, lapfus fum, labi: *to ſlide or glide; to ſlip or fall; to fall to decay; to trip, or miſtake.*

Delábor, delápfus fum, delábi: *to deſcend as in ſpeaking or writing; to ſlip or fall down; to fall to decay; to withdraw by degrees; to vaniſh or diſappear.*

Dilábor, dilápfus fum, dilábi: *to ſlip aſide, to ſteal away; to waſte, or come to nothing.*

Elábor, elápfus fum, elábi: *to ſlide or ſlip away, to eſcape.*

Illábor, illápfus fum, illábi: *to ſlide or glide in; to fall down, or upon; to enter.*

Sublábor, sublápfus fum, sublábi: *to ſlip away privily; to fall or ſlide under; to decay by little and little.*

ANNOTATION.

Connitor, obnitor, pernitor, renitor, ſubnitor, form rather *nixus* than *niſus,* whence cometh *connixus, obnixus,* and thence *obnixè:* juſt as from *pernixus* cometh *pernix,* patient of labour, ſwift, nimble, quick. Diomedes thinks that *enixa* is more properly ſaid of a woman who has been brought to bed; and *eniſa* of any other ſtruggle or endeavour. And this difference is common enough; yet he owns himſelf that it is not always obſerved; and we find that Tacitus has put the one for the other.

FRUOR more frequently makes *fruitus* than *fructus,* which we find notwithſtanding in Lucretius and other writers. From thence comes the noun *fructus,* and the participle *perfructus,* in the ſame author, and in Cic. *in Hort.* from whence Priſcian quoteth *Summâ amœnitate perfructus eſt.* We meet alſo with *fructurus* in Apuleius. Perot will have it that this verb makes likewiſe *fretus* and *frutus,* from whence, he ſays, cometh *defrutum,* a mixture made of new wine, whereof the one half, or third part is boiled away. *Fructus* is not a Latin word, and *defructum* is put for *defruitum,* becauſe they drew all the fruit out of it, that is, all the beſt part of the wine. For as Feſtus ſays, *Defrui dicebant antiqui, ut deamare, deperire; ſignificantes omnem fructum percipere.* As to *fretus,* relying upon, and confiding in, every body muſt plainly ſee even by the ſignification

signification itself, that it is very wide from *fruor*, and is rather a noun than a participle.

RULE LXXIV.
Of the verbs in SCOR.

Apíscor *takes* aptus; ulcíscor, ultus.
Nancíscor *hath* nactus, *and* pacíscor, pactus.
Proficíscor *requires* proféctus;
As expergíscor, experréctus.
Oblivíscor *forms* oblítus;
And comminíscor, comméntus.

EXAMPLES.

API'SCOR, aptus sum, apisci, Tacit. *to find out, to obtain.* Its compound is more usual.

Adipíscor, adéptus sum, adipísci, *to acquire, to obtain, to get to, to arrive at.*

Indipíscor, indéptus sum, indipísci: *to get, to obtain.*

ULCI'SCOR, ultus sum, ulcísci: *to take revenge on; to take revenge for.*

NANCI'SCOR, nactus sum, nancísci: *to light upon, to find; to attain, to get.*

PACI'SCOR, pactus sum, pacísci: *to covenant, or bargain, to agree, to come to terms.*

PROFICI'SCOR, proféctus sum, proficísci: *to go, to be gone, to come.*

EXPERGI'SCOR, experréctus sum, expergísci: *to awake; or to be awakened.*

OBLIVI'SCOR, oblítus sum, oblivísci: *to forget; to omit.*

COMMINI'SCOR, comméntus sum, comminísci: *to invent, to devise, or imagine; to feign or forge; to recollect or call to mind, to think, to dispute, to compose, to treat or discourse of a thing.*

ANNOTATION.

Adipíscor cometh from *apíscor*, which we read in Tacitus, Lucretius and Nonius, and which makes *aptus:* from thence also is derived *indipíscor, indeptus.*

Comminíscor, comes also from *miníscor*, or *meníscor*, which made *mentus*, from whence is formed *mentio.* And this verb *meníscor* seems to be derived from the same root as *memini*, and as *manco* for *meneo*; namely from μένω, from whence cometh *mens*: just as

from

from γίνω is formed *gens*, and from μόρω, *mors*. *Expergiscor* makes likewise *expergitus*, which we find in Lucilius and Apuleius. But Diomedes insists that *expergitus* implieth one that awakes of himself; and *experrectus* one that is awakened by somebody else. *Defetiscor* hath no preterite; for *defessus* is a noun, as well as *fessus* and *lassus*. See above, p. 188.

RULE LXXV.
Of the verbs in ior.

1. Grádior *makes* greſſus; *and* pátior, paſſus: expérior *hath* expértus, *as* oppérior, oppértus. O'rdior *taketh* orſus, *and* métior, menſus.
2. Mórior *makes* mórtuus, *and* órior, ortus; *but thence alſo come the participles*, moritúrus, oritúrus; *as from* naſcor *comes* naſcitúrus.

EXAMPLES.

1. GRA'DIOR, greſſus ſum, gradi: *to go or walk, to march along.*
Aggrédior, aggréſſus ſum, ággredi: *to go unto; to accoſt; to ſet upon, to encounter, or aſſault a perſon; to enterprize, attempt, or begin.*
Congrédior, congréſſus ſum, cóngredi: *to meet or go together; to accoſt one; to join battle, to rencounter; to engage in diſpute; to go and talk with one; to converſe with.*
Digrédior, digréſſus ſum, dígredi: *to go, or turn aſide; to depart, digreſs, to go from the purpoſe.*
Egrédior, egréſſus ſum, égredi: *to go out.*
Ingrédior, ingréſſus ſum, íngredi: *to enter into, to walk or go.*
Progrédior, progréſſus ſum, progrédi: *to come or go forth; to advance, to proceed.*
Regrédior, regréſſus ſum, régredi: *to return, to go back.*
Tranſgrédior, tranſgréſſus ſum, tránſgredi: *to paſs or go over; to tranſgreſs a law; to go by ſea; to paſs, ſurmount, or exceed.*
PA'TIOR, paſſus ſum, pati: *to endure, to ſuffer, to let.*
Perpétior, perpéſſus ſum, pérpeti: *the ſame.*
EXPE'RIOR, expértus ſum, experíri: *to attempt or try; to eſſay, or prove; to find; to try his right by law, war, &c.*
OPPE'RIOR, oppértus ſum, opperíri: *to wait.*
O'RDIOR, orſus ſum, ordíre: *to begin,* properly *to ſpin*

spin or weave; to begin, or enter upon; to write or speak of.

Exórdior, exórsus sum, exordíri: *to begin.*

ME'TIOR, mensus sum, metí.i: *to measure; to pass or go over; to bound or limit.*

Dimétior, diménsus sum, dimetíri: *to measure; to account.*

Remétior, reménsus sum, remetíri: *to measure over again; to go over again.*

2. MO'RIOR, mórtuus sum, mori: *to die.* It has the participle in rus, moritúrus, Virg. *about to die,* as if it had the supine móritum.

Commórior, commórtuus sum, cómmori: *to die together.*

Emórior, emórtuus sum, émori: *to die.*

Immórior, immórtuus sum, ímmori: *to die in, or upon; to be continually upon a thing.*

O'RIOR, óreris, *of the third conjugation*; or órior, oríris, *of the fourth,* ortus sum, oríri: *to rise or get up; to rise as the sun; to rise, or spring; to rise, or begin; to appear; to be born.* It has the participle in rus, oritúrus, Hor. *about to rise;* as if it had the supine óritum.

Abórior, abórtus sum, íri: *to miscarry; to be born before the time.*

Adórior, adórtus sum, íri: *to assault.*

Exórior, exórtus sum, exoríri: *to rise as the stars; to spring up; to be born.*

Obórior, obórtus sum, oboríri: *to arise, to spring up, to draw on; to shine forth.*

Subórior, subórtus sum, suboríri: *to rise or grow up.*

NASCOR, natus sum, *follows the rule of the verbs in* SCO. *But it has the participle in* rus, nascitúrus, *about to come to life; as if it came from* náscitum *in the supine.*

ANNOTATION.

We meet with *opperitus* in Plautus for *oppertus*. *Id sum opperitus,* in Mostel. *Orditus,* is in Diomedes, as if it came from *ordior,* in the preface to his book: *Lectio probabiliter ordita;* though he himself mentions no other participle belonging to this verb than *orsus.* But in Isaiah, chap. 25. we find *Et telam quam orditus est.* Baptista Mantuanus and Julius Scaliger have also made use of it; but in this they are not to be imitated.

Several

Several learned men have wrote *metitus*, for *mensus*; and among the rest Julius Scaliger, and Xylander: but Vossius affirms that the passages which they quote from Cic. in defence of their opinion, *Atque dimetita signa sunt: dimetiti cursus* (2. *de Nat. Deor.*) are corrupted; and that the best editions, and even the most antient of all, have *demetata*, and *dimetati*. And thus we find that Lambinus, Gruterus, Elzevir, and Robert Stephen read it. The other passage which they bring from Q. Curtius, lib. 3. *Stipendium metitum est*, cannot be found in this author, no more than *stipendium metiri*, which R. Stephen quotes out of him in his thesaurus, as likewise in his dictionary.

There are some who insist upon its being good Latin to say, *aborsus*, and *adorsus*, for *abortus*, and *adortus*, taken from *orior*; as *nullum majus adorsa nefas*, Ovid. *Adorsi erant tyrannum*, Gell. But we should read *adorta* and *adorti*; for *orsus* comes only from *ordior* and not from *orior*.

True it is that they produce from Paul the civilian, the expression, *aborsus venter*, *a belly that has discharged its burden by abortion*; but we ought to read *abortus*. And as to the distinction given by Nonius, between *abortus* a substantive, and *aborsus*; namely that the former is said of an infant just conceived, and the latter of one that had been conceived some time ago; it is destitute of foundation.

Rule LXXVI.
Of deponents that have no preterite.

Vescor, liquor, médeor, reminíscor, divértor, prævértor, ringor, diffíteor, *have no preterite*.

Examples.
These have no preterite.

Vescor, vesci: *to live upon; to eat.*
Liquor, liqui, Virg. *to be dissolved, or melted; to run or glide along* as rivers; *to drop.*
Médeor, medéri: *to heal, cure, or remedy; to attend a patient; to dress a wound; to administer comfort to a person in trouble.*
Reminíscor, reminísci: *to remember; to call to mind or remembrance.*
Divértor, divérti: *to lodge, to inn; to turn out of the road.*
Prævértor, prævérti: *to outrun or outstrip; to do a thing before another; to anticipate.*
Ringor, ringi: *to grin or shew the teeth*, as a dog doth; *to wry the mouth; to fret or chafe; to make faces.*
Diffíteor, diffitéri: *to deny, to say to the contrary.*

ANNO-

ANNOTATION.

These verbs borrow the preterite from somewhere else, when there happens to be any necessity of expressing the time past. Thus *vescor* takes it from *edo, edi*. *Liquor* from *liquefacio*, or rather from *liquefio, liquefactus*. *Medeor* takes it from *medicor, medicatus*. *Reminiscor*, from *recordor, recordatus*. ' *Reminiscor* is derived from the same root as *comminiscor*, of which we have already taken notice in the 74th rule.

Divertor and *prævertor* borrow it of *diverto* and *præverto*, rule 59. *Ringor* borrows *indignatus* of *indigner*; *diffiteor*, *inficiatus*, of *infitior*.

Rule LXXVII.
Of the verbs called neuter passive.

1. Sóleo *hath for its preterite* sólitus sum; fio *hath* factus sum; fido, fisus sum; mœ´reo, mœstus sum; áudeo, ausus sum; *and* gáudeo, gavísus sum.

2. *Several have a double preterite, as* juro, confído, *and* odi.

Examples.

1. The verbs called neuter-passives, are those which have a termination in O like the active, and the preterite in US, like the passive.

SO´LEO, sólitus sum, (*heretofore* sólüi,) solére: *to be accustomed.*

FIO, factus sum, fíeri: *to be made, to consist; to be done; to become.*

FIDO, fisus sum, fídere: *to confide in.*

Diffído, diffísus sum, ĕre: *to distrust.*

AU´DEO, ausus sum, audére: *to dare; not to be afraid.*

MOE´REO, mœstus sum, mœrére: *to grieve, to mourn, to be concerned.*

GAU´DEO, gavísus sum, gaudére: *to rejoice, to be glad, to be pleased with.*

ANNOTATION.

You are therefore to observe that these verbs are conjugated like the passive in the tenses formed of the preterite; and like the active in the tenses that depend upon the present.

2. A great many of them have a double preterite; as JURO, jurávi *and* jurátus sum, juráre: *to swear, to make oath.*

Confído, confídi *and* confísus fum, (*it comes from* fído *abovementioned*) confídere: *to trust, to confide, to rely or depend upon; to be confident, or well assured; to expect or hope.*

Odi *and* ofus fum, (*it has never a present*) odíffe: *to hate.*

ANNOTATION.

We find *folüi* in Sal. *Neque fubfidiis uti folüerat compofitis,* lib. 2. hift. Varro in the 8th *de L. L.* quotes it likewife from Ennius and Cato, and thinks it is wrong to follow the example of thofe who faid *folitus fum.* Yet the contrary cuftom has prevailed, and it would be wrong now in any body to fay otherwife. Charifius obferves that this verb hath no future, becaufe cuftom or habit never regards the time to come.

In like manner Robert Stephen gives *mærui* to *mæreo*, but without any authority. Prifcian fays it hath never a preterite; for, according to him, *mæftus* is properly no more than a noun. And it is an error which grammarians are often guilty of, thus to take the nouns for participles; as we have already fhewn in regard to *caffus, feffus, fretus,* and others.

We meet with *juratus* in Cic. in Plautus, and other writers. *Non fum jurata,* Turpil. apud Diom. *Confidi* is in Livy. *Ofus* is in Gellius, l. 4. c. 8. In Plautus, *Inimicos ofa fum femper obtuerier,* Amphitr. act. 3. fc. *Durare.* From thence comes the participle *vfurus,* Cic. More examples of this fort may be feen in the lifts annexed to the remarks on the verbs, at the end of the fyntax.

RULE LXXVIII.
Of neuters which feem to have a paffive fignification.

Líceo, vápulo, fio, *and* véneo, *are rendered by a verb paffive.*

EXAMPLES.

Thefe verbs are conjugated like the active, and yet are ufually rendered by the verb paffive.

LI'CEO, lícui: *It borrows its fupine of the verb imperfonal,* lícet, lícitum eft, lícére: *to be prized or valued; to be fet at a price for what it is to be fold.* On the contrary,

LI'CEOR, lícitus fum, *is rendered by the active;* licér.: *to cheapen a thing, to offer the price.*

VA'PULO, ávi, átum, áre: *to be beaten, or whipped; to cry bitterly.*

FIO, factus fum, fíeri: *to be made, to confift, to be done, to become.*

VE'NEO, vénii, veníre: *to be fold.*

ANNOTATION.

EXULO and NUBO, which are generally ranked in this class, have rather an active signification. For EXULO, as Sanctius observeth, is the same as *extra solum eo*. Now *eo*, seems to be active when we say *ire viam*, and the like; for which reason it has also its passive *iri*.

NUBO is the same as *obnubo*. *Mulier nubit*, says Caper, *quia pallio obnubit caput suum genásque*, lib. de orthograph.

In regard to the rest we may observe also, that

LICEO, properly signifies, *I permit*: and it may be derived from λίζω ἰάω, *permitto*, in Hesychius. Hence we say of things exposed to sale, *licent*; subaud. *se*; they expose and resign themselves to every body; and we say likewise, *per me licet*, subaud. *hoc* or *illud*, it is in your power, I permit you to do it: for *licet* the conjunction is properly no more than the third person of this verb, as we shall shew in the remarks. And *liceor*, in the passive originally implies, *I am permitted*. Thus *liceri*, to expose to sale, is the same as, *to be admitted and suffered to expose to sale*.

VAPULO, comes from ἀπόλλω for ἀπολλύω, or ἀπόλλυμαι, *pereo* or *peribo*. For the Æolians added their digamma, and said Fαπόλω, whence the Latins, says Sanctius, have taken *vapulo*; so that this verb, properly speaking, signifieth, *male plore* or *doleo*. Thus in comic writers *vapula* or *peri*, are taken for the same thing. Thus in Terence and Plautus we find that slaves when called by their masters, make answer *vapula*, by way of contempt, as much as to say, call as long as you please, or go and hang yourself. Whence also cometh the proverb *vapula Papyria*, which according to Festus, was said against those whose threats were despised; because Papyria a Roman Lady, having enfranchised a she slave of her's, this slave instead of expressing her gratitude to her benefactress, returned her this answer. For which reason, according to the same Festus, Elius says, that *vapula* is put there for *dole*, and Varro for *peri*. And he is for taking in this very sense the passage of Terence's Phormio, which Sanctius and the old editions read thus, ANT. *Non tu manes?* GE. *Vapula.* ANT. *Id tibi quidem jam fiet*, act. 5. sc. 6. And this of Plautus: *Reddin, an non mulierem, priusquam te huic meæ machæræ objicio, mastigia? S. Vapulare ego te vehementer jubeo, ne me territes*, &c. Whereto we may add that the Greeks use their ὀιμώζειν, *plorare*, *ejulare*, in the same sense, as ἐγὼ μὲν ὀιμώζειν λέγω σοι; Arist. *Imprecor tibi ut vapules*: ὀιμώξῖλαι γας προ τῶν ἄλλων, Lucian. *Nam primus omnium vapulabit*. In which signification they likewise use κλάω, *ploro*; κλάιειν λέγω σοι, Aristoph. *Lacrymas tibi denuncio, I'll give thee a good drubbing*; διυρ ἰλθ' ἵνα κλάιης, come hither that I may trim thee: διὰ τί δὴ κλαύσομαι; *why should you beat me?* Idem. And Sanctius concludes that since this verb has not a passive signification, it is false Latin to say, as the grammarians direct us, *Vapulant pueri à præceptore*. But this phrase shall be examined in the syntax, when we come to the rule of passive verbs.

FIO is neither active nor passive in its proper signification, for it is a substantive verb the same as *sum*, and comes from φύω, of which,

which, as Scaliger obferveth, 5. *de Cauf. cap.* 3. they firft made *fuo*, and afterwards *fio*; from whence are ftill left the preterite *fui*, and the infinitive *fore*. This verb had heretofore its paffive alfo according to Prifcian, as *Græco ritu fiebantur Saturnalia*, whence likewife comes the infinitive *fieri*. The preterite *factus fum*, is alfo paffive, and properly comes from *facior*, which was in ufe among the antients, and whence we have ftill remaining *afficior* and *perficior*. But *fio fenex* in the prefent, is the fame thing, according to Sanctius, as *fum fenex*,

VE'NEO, as hath been already obferved, p. 286. comes from *vénum* and *eo*; and confequently is no more a paffive than *eo*, which we have above demonftrated to be really a verb active.

RULE LXXIX.
Of imperfonals.

1. Míferet *takes* mifértum eft; *but heretofore it had* miféritum eft.
2. Tædet *makes* tæ'duit, pertæ'fum.
3. Placet, libet, piget, licet, pudet, *have* UIT, *and* ITUM eft.
4. *But* Liquet *has no preterite*.

EXAMPLES.

We have elfewhere taken notice that they give the name of verbs imperfonal to thofe which are conjugated only in the third perfon; as *opórtet, decet*, &c. And therefore their preterite is alfo formed by the third perfon of their conjugation: *opórtuit, décuit*, &c. Neverthelefs we are to except a few, namely

1. MI'SERET, mifértum eft; *it pitieth me.* And heretofore, *miféritum*, Plaut.
2. TÆDET, tæ'duit, tæfum eft; *or rather* pertæ'fum eft *from* pertæ'det: *it irketh, it wearieth.*
3. The following make UIT, and ITUM EST.

PLACET, plácuit *and* plácitum eft, Cic. *it feemeth good, or is the mind or opinion of.*

LIBET *or* LUBET, líbuit *and* líbitum eft: *it liketh, or contenteth.*

PIGET, píguit, *and* pígitum eft, Gell. *it irketh, grieveth, or repenteth.*

LICET, lícuit *and* lícitum eft: *it is lawful; it is free, or poffible.*

PUDET, púduit *and* púditum eft, Cic. *to be afhamed.*

4. LIQUET, Cic. *it appeareth, it is clear and manifest.* Without a preterite.

ANNOTATION.

The imperfonals have no imperatives; but inftead of thefe they make ufe of the prefent of the fubjunctive, *pœniteat, pugnetur,* &c.

It frequently happens that they have neither fupine nor gerund; yet we read in Cic. *pœnitendi caufa; pœnitendi vis. Nihilo magis liciturum effe plebeio, quàm Patriciis effet licitum. Non pudendo, fed non faciendo quod non decet, nomen impudentiæ effugere debemus.* In Sal. *Non eft pœnitendum*; and even *pœniturus*, which is now grown obfolete.

RULE LXXX.
Of the imperatives of dico, duco, facio *and* fero.

Dico *makes* dic; duco, duc;
Fácio, fac; *and* fero, fer.

EXAMPLES.

Thefe imperatives fhould naturally terminate in E, like *lege;* but they have dropped their final E, for which reafon we fay

Dic, *inftead of* dice : *fay thou.*
Duc, *inftead of* duce : *lead thou.*
Fac, *inftead of* face : *do thou.*
Fer, *inftead of* fere : *bear thou.*

ANNOTATION.

The compounds of *facio* with a prepofition form their imperative in E, as ufual; thus

Perficio, *imperat.* perfice ; *finifh thou.* Sufficio, *imperat.* fuffice ; *furnifh thou.*

Heretofore they faid alfo *face; orandi jam finem face*, Ter. In the fame manner *dice*, and the reft.

OBSERVATIONS
On the different Conjugations,
and on the derivative and compounded verbs.

I.

A great many verbs of one termination only, are of different conjugations, under different significations.

Appéllo,	as; *to call.*	Appéllo,	is; *to bring to land.*
Fundo,	as; *to found.*	Fundo,	is; *to shed.*
Mando,	as; *to bid.*	Mando,	is; *to eat.*
Obsero,	as; *to shut.*	Obsero,	is; *to sow.*
Pando,	as; *to bend in.*	Pando,	is; *to stretch.*
Constérnor, áris; *to be astonished,*		Constérnor, ĕris; *to be strewed,*	
or *covered all over.* See Priscian.			

Some of them differ in quantity.

Côlo,	as; *to strain.*	Cŏlo,	is; *to till.*
Dîco,	as; *to dedicate.*	Dîco,	is; *to say.*

In like manner their compounds, *abdíco,* and *abdĭco: indíco,* and *indĭco: prædíco,* and *prædĭco,* &c.

Lêgo,	as; *to delegate,*	Lĕgo	is; *to read.*

The same in regard to their compounds, *allégo,* and *allĕgo: relégo,* and *relĕgo,* &c.

Several are also of different conjugations, though in the same signification.

* Cíeo,	es.	Cio,	is, ire,	*to call.*
* Denso,	as.	Dénseo,	es,	*to thicken.*
Excélleo,	es.	* Excello,	is,	*to excell.*
* Férveo,	es.	Fervo,	is,	*to boil.*
* Fódio,	is, ĕre.	Fódio,	is, îre,	*to dig.*
* Fúlgeo,	es, ĕre.	Fulgo,	is, ĕre,	*to glitter.*
* Lavo,	as.	Lavo,	is,	*to wash.*
* Lino,	is, ĕre.	Línio,	is, îre,	*to anoint.*
Nexo,	as.	Nexo,	is,	*to twine.*
* Oleo,	es.	Olo,	is, obsol.	*to smell.*
* Sallo,	is, ĕre.	Sállio,	is, îre,	*to salt.*
* Strídeo,	es, ĕre.	Strido,	is, ĕre,	*to make a noise.*
Térgeo,	es.	Tergo,	is,	*to wipe.*
* Mórior,	ĕris.	Mórior,	îris, obsol.	*to die.*
O'rior,	ĕris.	O'rior,	îris,	*to rise.*
Pótior,	ĕris.	* Pótior,	îris,	*to enjoy.*
* Sono,	as.	Sono,	is, obsol.	*to sound.*
* Túeor,	êris.	Tuor,	ĕris,	*to preserve.*

In the same manner its compounds *intúeor, íntuor; contúeor, cóntuor; obtúeor, óbtuor,* &c.

NEW METHOD. Book IV.

ANNOTATION.

Where we have put the asterisks, it is to shew that these verbs are more usual than those of the corresponding conjugation in the same line. But where we have made no mark at all, it is to be understood that they are both used alike.

ORIOR and POTIOR are more usual in the infinitive of the fourth conjugation; but in the indicative *orior* is only of the third: and *potior* is used in both by the poets, though they more commonly make *potitur* short, that is of the third conjugation.

——— *Polydorum obtruncat, & auro*
Vi potitur, Virg.

Sometimes the same preterite comes from different verbs.
As the preterite of the compounds of sto *and* sisto.

Cónstiti	*from*	Consto	*or from*	Consísto;	*to stop.*
Extiti	*from*	Exsto	*or*	Exísto;	*to be.*
Ínstiti	*from*	Insto	*or*	Insísto;	*to pursue.*

As also the following, which change their signification.

Acui	*from*	Aceo,	*to be sour;*	*or* Acuo,	*to whet.*
Crevi	*from*	Cresco,	*to grow;*	*or* Cerno,	*to judge.*
Frixi	*from*	Frigeo,	*to be cold;*	*or* Frigo,	*to fry.*
Luxi	*from*	Luceo,	*to shine;*	*or* Lugeo,	*to mourn.*
Mulsi	*from*	Mulceo,	*to asswage;*	*or* Mulgeo,	*to milk.*
Pavi	*from*	Paveo,	*to be afraid;*	*or* Pasco,	*to fear.*
Fulsi	*from*	Fulgeo,	*to shine;*	*or* Fulcio.	*to prop.*

Some have likewise the same supine.

Cretum	*from*	Cresco,	*to grow;*	*or* Cerno,	*to see.*
Mansum	*from*	Maneo,	*to stay;*	*or* Mando, is,	*to eat.*
Passum	*from*	Pando, is,	*to open;*	*or* Pátior,	*to suffer.*
Succénsum	*from*	Succénseo,	*to be angry with one;*	*or* Succéndo,	*to burn.*
Tentum	*from*	Teneo,	*to keep;*	*or* Tendo,	*to stretch.*
Victum	*from*	Vinco,	*to overcome;*	*or* Vivo,	*to live.*

Of the gerunds of the two last conjugations.

The gerunds of the fourth, and those of the verbs in IO of the third, frequently take an *u* instead of an *e*; as *faciúndi, úndo, úndum*, from *facio. Experiúndi, úndo, úndum*; from *expérior*. And the like.

Iens, and its compounds also take an *u* in the genitive: *eúntis, pereúntis, exeúntis:* there is only *ámbiens*, that makes *ambiéntis*, surrounding; seeking for preferment: but *abiens*, makes *abeúntis*, going away.

II.

ON THE DERIVATIVE VERBS.

Derivative verbs are generally taken either from nouns or from verbs.

From nouns there are two sorts, verbs of imitation, and denominatives.

The verbs of imitation terminate either in *isso* or in *or*, as *Patrisso*, *Atticisso*, *Græcor*, *Vulpinor*. But the termination *isso* partakes a good deal of the Greek language, in which these verbs are terminated in ίζω. For which reason the Latins prefer the termination in *or*; so that we say rather *Græcor*, than *Græcisso*, Voss.

The denominatives are generally all verbs derived from a noun, as *lignor* from *lignum*; *frumentor* from *frumentum*; *rusticor* from *rus*, or from *rusticus*; and the like.

Of those which are derived from other verbs.

There are four sorts derived from other verbs. These are inceptives, frequentatives, desideratives, and diminutives.

1. INCEPTIVES end in *sco*, and generally signify that a thing is begun; as *ardesco*, I begin to burn: *maturesco*, I begin to ripen: *vesperascit*, it draweth towards evening.

They likewise imply now and then the continuation or increase of the action; as *expleri mentem nequit ardescitque tuendo*, Virg. and her flame increases by looking at him. *Exuperat magis, ægrescitque medendo*, Virg. increases and grows worse by medicine. See L. Valla, book 1.

Hereby we see that inceptives are verbs neuter, and therefore that those of an active signification do not belong to this class, notwithstanding they may have the termination; as *disco*, to learn; *pasco*, to feed.

The inceptives are formed of the second person of the present, as from *labo*, *as*; *labasco*; from *caleo*, *es*; *calesco*: though from *puteo*, *es*, we say *putisco*, changing the *e* into *i*: But of *tremo*, *is*, we regularly form *tremisco*; of *dormio*, *is*, *dormisco*.

It is the same in regard to the deponents, which are formed by feigning the active of the primitive. For *fruiscor* comes as it were from *fruo*, *is*. The impersonals also follow this analogy: *miserescit*, from *misereo*, *is*, &c.

Sometimes there is a syncope in the formation, as *hisco* for *biasco*, from the old verb *bio*, *as*.

Some of them are even supposed to come from nouns, as *ægresco* from *æger*; *repuerasco* from *puer*: though they may be said to come from the verbs *ægreo*, *repuero*, and the like, which are no longer in use: just as *calvesco*, which they generally derive from *calvus*; and *senesco* from *senex*, come from *calveo*, which we find in Pliny, and from *seneo*, in Catullus.

These verbs have neither preterite nor supine, but they borrow them of their primitives, as *incalesco*, *incalui*, from *caleo*. See the 35th rule. Though it is better to say they have none at all, because this preterite never implies an inceptive signification.

These verbs are always of the third conjugation.

2. The FREQUENTATIVES generally end in *to*, *so*, *xo*, or *co*; as *clamito*, *pulso*, *nexo*, *fodico*.

They are so called because they generally signify frequency of action, *quid clamitas*, what do you bawl so often for? But this is not general: for *viso* simply implies to go to see; *albico* and *candico*, signify no more than a whiteness just beginning or coming on, and there-

therefore are rather diminutives; in the same manner *dormito*, to be sleepy, to begin to fall asleep.

They are formed of the second supine, by changing *u* into *o*, or into *ito*; into O, as from *tractum, tractu, tracto*: from *versu, verso*: from *natu, nato*: but some change the *a* into *i*, *clamatu, clamito*.

Those in *or* are formed in the same manner, as from *amplexu, amplexor*. In ITO, as from *actum, actito*; from *hæsum, hæsito*.

Some are formed two ways, as from *dictu* comes *dicto*, and *dictito*; from *jactu, jacto*, and *jactito*.

Some are formed from the second person, as from *ago, agis, agito*; from *fugis, fugito*; from *quæris, quærito*.

The frequentatives are of the first conjugation, except *viso* which is of the third.

3. The DESIDERATIVES or verbs of desire generally end in *rio*, as *esurio*, I am hungry or have a desire to eat; *parturio*, to be in travail with, to be ready to bring forth young.

They are formed from the last supine by adding *rio*; as from *esu*, is formed *esurio*; from *cænatu, cænaturio*; and are of the fourth conjugation.

In imitation of these there have been some formed even from nouns, as *syllaturio*, in Cic.

But every verb in *rio* is not a desiderative, witness *ligurio, scaturio*, which form no supine, and have *u* long, contrary to the analogy of the rest. Neither is every desiderative terminated in *rio*, witness *capto*; *captare benevolentiam alicujus*.

4. The DIMINUTIVES end in *llo*, as *cantillo, sorbillo*, and are of the first conjugation.

ANNOTATION.

But here we are to observe that the derivatives are frequently taken in the same signification as the primitives, *hisco* for *hio*: *conticesco* for *conticeo*: *ventito* for *venio*; and the like.

III.

ON COMPOUND VERBS.

Compound verbs are formed either of nouns, as *belligero*, from *bellum* and *gero*: or of verbs, as *calefacio*, of *caleo* and *facio*: or of adverbs, as *benefacio*: or of prepositions, as *advenio*.

Sometimes the compounds change either the species, or conjugation of the simple: the species, as *sacro, execror*; *sentio, assentior*: the conjugation, as *dare, reddere*: *cubare, incumbere*.

Sometimes they change both: as *spernere, aspernari*; and the like.

But very frequently the simple is not used, when the compound is; as *leo*, whence cometh *deleo*, according to Priscian: *pedio*, whence *impedio, expedio, præpedio, compedio*: *liviscor*, whence *obliviscor*, according to Cesellius in Gass. Unless we chuse to derive it from *oblino*, heretofore *oblivi*, whence we have also *oblivio* and *oblivium*, and even the adjective *oblivius*. For the antients used in the same sense *leo* and *lino*; so that it is not at all surprising that

we

we should say *oblevi*, as coming from *leo*; just as they said *oblivi* from *lino*. Hereto we may also refer *fendo, specio, pleo, lacio, fligo*, and others, of which we have made mention in their proper place in the rules.

Some have even a simple used only in Greek, as Δύω, whence *induo, exuo*: Κίλλω, whence *antecello*, and the rest: Πειράω, whence *comperior, experior*, &c.

It often happens that the preterite of the simple is not usual, when that of the compound is; thus we say rather, *Mercurius contudit sosiam*, than *tutudit*, which is not perhaps to be found in any Latin author, though Charisius and Priscian give it to *tundo*. Thus we meet in Latin authors with *applicuit, evasit, detrusit, emunxit, delicuit*, though we do not easily find *plicuit, vasit, trusit, munxit*, nor *licuit* from *liqueo*. Thus we find the supine *retentum, contentum, enectus, internectus*, though we cannot find *tentum*, nor the simple *nectus*.

On the contrary the simple is sometimes used, when the compound is not. For we meet with *fidi* from *fido*; with *tacitum* and *taciturus* from *taceo*; but it is not so easy to find *confidi* from *confido*; nor do we find *reticitum*, or *reticiturus* from *reticeo*.

Hence we see that in all these matters custom is the chief thing to be regarded; so that we should use ourselves betimes to the reading of the purest authors, and never to employ any word whatsoever without good authority.

A METHOD

OF FINDING OUT THE PRESENT BY THE PRETERITE.

*A*S it has been the opinion of some, that it would be of service to those who enter late upon the study of the Latin tongue, to have a method of ascending to the present of the verb by means of the preterite, in such a manner that whenever they meet with a preterite, they may be able to tell from what verb it comes, without being obliged to learn the rules: I have therefore thought proper to delineate here the following scheme, to the end they may not be disappointed of the benefit they expect from it. At least there will be this other advantage arising from this essay, that it will contribute to shew the analogy of the Latin tongue in its preterites, as I have already shewn it in the difference of its genitives in regard to the declensions. Besides, these reflections may be considered, if you will, as a specimen of the utility derivable from the treatise of letters which we intend to give towards the close of this work.

Art. I.

The most natural analogy of forming the preterite.

I.

All preterites are in *i*, and conjugated by *isti, it: imus, istis, erunt* or *ere*.

The most natural analogy of forming them, is, as already we have observed, p. 171. to take them from the second person present, changing *s* into *vi*;

From whence is formed *avi*, in the first conjugation: *evi*, in the second, and *ivi* in the third and fourth. Thus TER-

OF FINDING THE PRESENT.

TERMINATIONS.				EXAMPLES.		
avi	o,	as.	1.	Amávi	Amo,	as.
evi	eo,	es.	2.	Flevi	Fleo,	es.
ivi	{ o, { io,	{ is. { ĭs. { īs.	} 3. 4.	{ Petívi { Cupívi Audívi	Peto, Cùpio, Aúdio,	} ĭs. īs.

Quæsivi comes from *quæro*, by changing *r* into *s*, to soften the sound: or rather because heretofore they said *quæso* for *quæro*, as Festus hath observed; whence we have still left *quæso*, in the sense of praying, which comes very near to that of asking.

II.

These preterites, and the tenses that depend on them, oftentimes admit of a syncope either of the *v* only, or of the *v* and the vowel that follows it.

Those in *avi* and *evi*, do not admit of this syncope either in the first or third person singular, or in the first person plural; but they suffer a syncope of an intire syllable in the other persons and tenses depending on the preterite, as

Amásti, for *amavisti*.
Amárunt, for *amavérunt*. *Flerunt*, for *flevérunt*.
Amássem, for *amavissem*.

Those in *ivi* will admit of it throughout, but the *v* is never cut off, when it is not followed by *is*:
Petii, for *petivi*.
Petiérunt, for *petivérunt*.
Petiéram, for *petiveram*.

But if the *v* be followed by *is*, then we use which syncope we please.
Petüsti, petisti, for *petivisti*.
Petüssem, petissem, for *petivissem*.

Art. II.

Four general irregularities and three particular changes in some verbs.

But though this analogy be the most natural, yet it is not the most received, except in the first and fourth conjugation; for a great many irregularities have crept into the second and third, as well as into some verbs of the other two conjugations.

These irregularities may be conveniently reduced to four general, of which the first two preserve *vi* or *ii* with some syncope, and the other two take other terminations.

The first is of the preterites which preserve *vi* with a syncope of the syllable, which according to the natural analogy ought to precede it, as *novi* from *nosco, cis*, instead of *noscivi*.

The

The 2d is of such as have ui by a syncope, which only by dropping the vowel that ought to have preceded *vi*, changes the *v* consonant into *u* vowel, as *monui* from *moneo*, *es*, instead of *monevi*.

The 3d is of those which terminate in *si*, or *ssi*, or *xi*, taking an *s*, and sometimes two, whether it be instead of the last consonant of the present, as *jussi* from *jubeo* ; *tersi* from *tergo* (which is evidently instead of *terxi* ; for this being too rough because of the *r*, they struck the *e* out of the double letter *x*) or after this consonant ; as *carpsi* from *carpo* ; *dixi* from *dico* ; *unxi* from *ungo* ; the X being equivalent to CS, or to GS.

The 4th is of those which end in *bi*, *ci*, *di*, &c. according to the last consonant of the present ; as *bibi* from *bibo* ; *legi* from *lego* : which may be owing to the syncope of the usual termination of the preterite, *legi* for *legivi*.

But beside these four general irregularities, there are other changes incident to some verbs, of which the three most usual are :

1. The change of the A (and of the *i* in compounds) into E, as *feci* from *facio* : *perfeci* from *perficio*, and sometimes into I, especially in such preterites as have a reduplication ; as *cecini* from *cano*.

2. The syncope of the *n* (and sometimes of the *m*) which precedes the last consonant of the present, as *scidi* from *scindo* : *accubui* from *accumbo* : *rupi* from *rumpo*.

3. The reduplication of the first consonant of the present, either with an E, after the example of the Greeks, as *cecidi* from *cado* : or even with the vowel of the present ; as *momordi* from *mordeo* : *pupugi* from *pungo*.

These three sorts of changes seldom happen but in the two last irregularities ; and especially the last, namely the reduplication, occurs only in the fourth irregularity. But they may sometimes happen to meet all together ; as *tetigi* from *tango*, where we see the *a* changed into *i*, the *n* taken away, and the reduplication added.

Article III.
Of the 1st general irregularity.

Preterites in vi *with a syncope that cuts off the syllable, which according to the natural analogy ought to have preceded it.*

I.

These preterites are derived from two sorts of verbs.
1. From those which end in *vo* and *veo* ; as *juvi* from *juvo*, for *juvávi* : *movi* from *moveo*, for *movévi* : and these are very easy to find ; because you have only to change the *i* into *o* or *eo*.
2. From others which have different terminations, and are more difficult.

We shall give a separate view of the one and the other. And when there happens to be any difficulty worth remarking, we shall take care to mention it after the following lists, by means of small notes to which the asterisks shall refer.

II. List

II.

List of preterites that come from verbs in *vo*, or *veo*.

    Verbs in *veo*.

* Cavi	*from* Caveo,	es, ēre: *to beware of; to take care of.*
Connivi	Conniveo,	es, ēre: *to wink, to dissemble.*
* Favi	Faveo,	es, ēre: *to favour.*
Fovi	Foveo,	es, ēre: *to cherish.*
Langui	Langueo,	es, ēre: *to languish.*
Movi	Moveo,	es, ēre: *to move.*
* Pavi	Paveo,	es, ēre: *to be afraid.*

    Verbs in *vo*.

Calvi	*from* Calvo,	is, ĕre: *to deceive.*
Juvi	Juvo,	as, āre: *to help.*
Solvi	Solvo,	is, ĕre: *to loose, to deliver.*
Volvi	Volvo,	is, ĕre: *to roll.*

* In order to distinguish these preterites in *avi*, and some others which are marked lower down with an asterisk, from those of the first conjugation; we are to observe that the first conjugation has never a dissyllable preterite in *avi*.

III.

Of preterites which come from verbs of other terminations, and are more irregular.

And in the first place,

Of those in SCO, *which generally take this termination in the preterite; as*

Agnovi	*from* Agnosco,	is, ĕre: *to know, to find out.*
Crevi	Cresco,	is, ĕre: *to grow.*
Novi	Nosco,	is, ĕre: *to know.*
* Pavi	Pasco,	is, ĕre: *to feed.*
Quievi	Quiesco,	is, ĕre: *to rest.*
Scivi	Scisco,	is, ĕre: *to ordain.*
Suevi	Suesco,	is, ĕre: *to be accustomed.*

Of some other particular preterites.

Sivi	*from* Sino,	is, ĕre: *to permit.*
1. Sprevi	Sperno,	is, ĕre: *to despise.*
* 2. Stravi	Sterno,	is, ĕre: *to strew.*
3. Sevi	Sero,	is, ĕre: *to sow.*
4. Assevi	Assero,	is, ĕre: *to plant near.*
5. Trivi	Tero,	is, ĕre: *to wear.*

1. *Spernivi, spervi,* and by transposition to soften the sound : *sprevi*.
2. The like in *stravi*, where moreover the *e* of the present is changed into *a*.
3. *Serivi, servi,* and by a syncope of the *r*, which is too rough when joined with the *v* consonant, *sevi*.
4. In like manner all the compounds of *sero*, which retain the signification of sowing, as *consevi, dissevi, insevi, intersevi, obsevi*.
5. By a syncope of the *e* instead of *terivi*.

Article

Article IV.

Of the 2d general irregularity.

Preterites in üi, *the vowel which naturally ought to have preceded it, being cut off.*

I.

When the syncope is not of an entire syllable, as in the preceding irregularity, but only of a letter, as of the *a* in *avi*; of the *e* in *evi*; and of the *i* in *ivi*: then the *v* consonant is changed into *u* vowel, to soften the pronunciation. For if from *cubavi*, which according to the most natural analogy ought to be the preterite of *cubo, as,* you take away the *a,* there remains *cubvi,* which being too harsh, they made it *cubüi*: in the same manner of *monevi,* they first made *monvi,* and afterwards *monüi.*

This irregularity is so common in the second conjugation, that it is become the general rule thereof; so that when a preterite is in *üi,* we must first of all see whether it be not derived from a verb in *eo.*

üi, eo, es; *as* florüi, floreo, es.

II.

We have therefore no necessity of remarking in particular any other preterites in *üi,* than those of the other three conjugations, which we shall do according to their alphabetical order.

1.	Accubui, *from*	Accumbo,	is, ĕre.	*To sit down at meat.*
	Alüi,	Alo,	is, ĕre.	*To nourish.*
	Amicüi,	Amicio,	is, īre.	*To cover, to put a garment.*
2 {	Aperüi,	Aperio, }	is, īre.	*To open.*
	Operüi,	Operio, }	is, īre.	*To cover.*
	Asserüi,	Assero,	is, ĕre.	*To assert.*
	Colüi,	Colo,	is, ĕre.	*To till, to honour.*
3.	Compescüi,	Compesco,	is, ĕre.	*To check, to curb.*
4.	Concinüi,	Concino,	is, ĕre.	*To accord in one song.*
	Crepüi,	Crepo,	as, āre.	*To make a noise.*
	Cubüi,	Cubo,	as, āre.	*To lie down.*
	Domüi,	Domo,	as, āre.	*To tame.*
	Elicüi,	Elicio,	is, ĕre.	*To draw out.*
5.	Excellüi,	Excello,	is, ĕre.	*To excell.*
	Fricüi,	Frico,	as, āre.	*To rub.*

1. In like manner the other compounds of *cubo,* which are of the third conjugation, as *concumbo, decumbo, recumbo,* which take an *m* in their present tense (or rather which retain it from the ancient verb *cumbo, is,*) which they reject in their preterite and supine.

2. These two compounds of *pario,* which are of the fourth conjugation, make *rū*; but *comperio* and *reperio* make *ri.*

3. In like manner *depesco, depescui; impesco, impescui,* compounded of the old verb *pesco.*

4. In the same manner the other compounds of *cano,* to sing, as *accino, accinui, recino, recinui.*

5. Also *antecellui,* from *antecello; precellui* from *precello,* compounded of the old verb *cello.*

6. Ge-

6.	Genüi,	Gigno,	is, ĕre.	To beget.
	Messüi,	Meto,	is, ĕre.	To mow.
	Micüi,	Mico,	as, āre.	To shine.
	Monüi,	Moneo,	es, ēre.	To advise.
	Necüi,	Neco,	as, āre.	To kill.
	Nexüi,	Nexo,	as, or is	To twist.
	Pinsüi,	Pinso,	is, ĕre.	To knead.
	Plicüi,	Plico,	as, āre.	To fold.
	Posüi,	Pono,	is, ĕre.	To put.
	Rapüi,	Rapio,	is, ĕre.	To plunder.
	Salüi,	Salio,	is, īre.	To leap.
	Sapüi,	Sapio,	is, ĕre.	To favour, to be wise.
	Stertüi,	Sterto,	is, ĕre.	To snore.
	Strepüi,	Strepo,	is, ĕre.	To make a noise.
	Texüi,	Texo,	is, ĕre.	To weave.
	Tonüi,	Tono,	as, āre.	To thunder.
	Vetüi,	Veto,	as, āre.	To forbid.
	Vomüi,	Vomo,	is, ĕre.	To vomit.

6. From the old verb *geno*, of which they made *gigno*; as from γίνω, in Greek, comes γίγνω, or γίγνομαι.

Article V.
Of the 3d general irregularity.
The preterite in si, *or* ssi, *or* xi, *by adding the* s, *or changing some letter into* s.

I.

This irregularity seems to proceed from the imitation of two things, which the Greeks practise in the formation of their future, whence is formed the 1st Aorist, which is often taken in the same signification as the Latin preterite.

The 1st is that as the Greeks change β (*b*) and π (*p*) into ψ (*ps*): and γ (*g*) and κ (*c*) into ξ (*x*); the Latins in like manner have changed the characteristic *b* and *p* into *ps*: *scribo, scripsi, carpo, carpsi*: and *c* and *g* into *x*, which is equivalent to *cs* or *gs*: *dixi* from *dico*: *junxi* from *jungo*: as likewise *vinxi* from *vincio*; because the *o* pure, that is, the *o* preceded by a vowel, frequently follows the *o* impure, that is, the *o* preceded by a consonant.

There are also other verbs that have different characteristics from the four abovementioned, and insert an *s* in their preterite after their characteristic; namely *m* and *n*.

Here we have marked them all down with an example to each, and with a figure expressing the number that commonly occur of each sort.

S after	{ c. cs. } x g. gs. } m. ms. n. ns. p. } ps. b. }		9. 22. 4. 1. 7. 2.	dixi *from* junxi comsi mansi carpsi nupsi	dico, jungo, como, maneo, carpo, nubo,	is, ĕre: *to say.* is, ĕre: *to join.* is, ĕre: *to attire.* es, ēre: *to remain.* is, ĕre: *to pluck.* is, ĕre: *to marry.*

II. *List*

II.

List of the preterites in si *or* xi, *by the addition of an* s *after the characteristic of the present; where we are to observe, that the* x *is equivalent to* cs *or* gs.

Allexi *from*	Allicio	is, ĕre.	⎫
Illexi	Illicio	is, ĕre.	⎬ *to inveigle, to intice.*
Pellexi	Pellicio	is, ĕre.	⎭
Aspexi	Aspicio	is, ĕre.	*to behold.*
Conspexi	Conspicio	is, ĕre.	*to consider.*
Inspexi	Inspicio	is, ĕre.	*to pry into.*
Auxi	Augeo	es, ēre.	*to increase.*
1. Carpsi	Carpo	is, ĕre.	*to pluck.*
2. Cinxi	Cingo	is, ĕre.	*to gird.*
Comsi	Como	is, ĕre.	*to attire.*
Demsi	Demo	is, ĕre.	*to abate.*
Dilexi	Diligo	is, ĕre.	*to love.*
Intellexi	Intelligo	is, ĕre.	*to understand.*
Neglexi	Negligo	is, ĕre.	*to neglect.*
Dixi	Dico	is, ĕre.	*to say.*
Duxi	Duco	is, ĕre.	*to lead.*
Frixi	Frigeo	es, ēre.	*to be cold.*
Luxi	Luceo	es, ēre.	*to shine.*
Polluxi	Polluceo	es, ēre.	*to flourish.*
Luxi	Lugeo	es, ēre.	*to mourn.*
Mansi	Maneo	es, ēre.	*to stay.*
Minxi	Mingo	is, ĕre.	*instead of which we say* meio.
Mulxi	Mulgeo	es, ēre.	*to milk.* (*to piss.*
Nupsi	Nubo	is, ĕre.	*to marry*
3. Perrexi	Pergo	is, ĕre.	*to go forward.*
Promsi	Promo	is, ĕre.	*to draw out.*
Sanxi	Sancio	is, īre.	*to enact.*
Scripsi	Scribo	is, ĕre.	*to write.*
Sumsi	Sumo	is, ĕre.	*to take.*
3. Surrexi	Surgo	is, ĕre.	*to arise.*

1. In like manner a great many others in *po.*
2. Likewise a great many more in *go.*
3. *Pergo* and *surgo* ought to make *perxi* and *surxi:* but as this pronunciation would be too harsh, an *e* has been added to the penultima: and to the end that the first syllable might not lose any part of its quantity, the *r* has been doubled: *perrexi, surrexi.*

III.

The second thing in which the Latins seem to have imitated the Greeks, is that as the latter frequently change δ (*d*) and τ (*t*) into σ (*s*): so the former also frequently change *d* and *t* into *s, lædo, læsi; sentio, sensi.*

Whence

Whence also they have *nexi* from *necto*; *flexi* from *flecto*, because *xi*, as we have already observed, is equivalent to *csi*, so that only the *t* is changed into *s*.

But this change into *s* cometh also from other consonants; and therefore it will be proper to set them all down with examples, before we give the list.

Si coming from	c	5.	Farsi	Farcio,	is, īre.	*to stuff, to fill.*
	d	12.	Arsi	1. Ardeo,	es, ēre.	*to burn.*
	g	10.	Alsi	2. Algeo,	es, ēre.	*to be very cold.*
	l	1.	Vulsi	Vello,	is, ĕre.	*to pull.*
	n	1.	Temsi	Temno,	is, ĕre.	*to despise.*
	qu	1.	Torsi	3. Torqueo,	es, ēre.	*to twist.*
	r	1.	Hæsi	4. Hæreo,	es, ēre.	*to stick.*
	t	1.	Flexi	Flecto,	is, ĕre.	*to bend.*
	tt	5.	Misi	5. Mitto,	is, ĕre.	*to send.*
Ssi coming from	b	1.	Jussi	Jubeo,	es, ēre.	*to command.*
	d	1.	Cessi	Cedo,	is, ĕre.	*to give place.*
	m	1.	Pressi	Premo,	is, ĕre.	*to press.*
	r	2.	Gessi	Gero,	is, ĕre.	*to carry.*
			Ussi	Uro,	is, ĕre.	*to burn.*
	t	1.	Quassi	6. Quatio,	is, ĕre.	*to shake.*

1. *Ardeo*, as if it were *ardo*, *o* pure for *o* impure.
2. *Algeo*, as if it were *a'go*, and *alsi* for *alxi*, by taking away the *c* out of the double letter, the same as in *arsi*.
3. *Torqueo*, as if it were *torquo*, or *torco*, the *q* being equivalent to *c*; and *torsi* for *torxi*.
4. *Hæreo*, *hæsi*, as if *hæri*, the *s* passing for *r*.
5. *Mitto*, *misi*, as if *mitsi*, whence also comes *missum*, by changing the two *tt* of *mitto* into two *ss*; but it loseth an *s* in the preterite.
6. *Quatio*, *quassi* for *quasi*, from *quato*, by changing *t* into *s*. But it doubles the *ss* to distinguish it from *quasi* an adverb.

IV.

List of the preterites in *si*, or *ssi*.

By a change of the characteristic into one or two s.

SI.

Alsi	from Algeo	es, ēre,	*to be very cold.*
Arsi	Ardeo	es, ēre,	*to burn.*
Clausi	Claudo	is, ĕre,	*to shut.*
Divisi	Divido	is, ĕre,	*to divide.*
Farsi	Farcio	is, īre,	*to stuff, to fill.*
Flexi	Flecto	is, ĕre,	*to bend.*
Fulsi	Fulcio	is, īre,	*to prop.*
Hæsi	Hæreo	es, ēre,	*to stick.*
Indulsi	Indulgeo	es, ēre,	*to indulge.*
Mersi	Mergo	is, ĕre,	*to sink.*
Mulsi	Mulgeo	es, ēre,	*to milk.*
Læsi	Lædo	is, ĕre,	*to hurt.*
Lusi	Ludo	is, ĕre,	*to play.*

Nexi *from*	Necto,	is,	ĕre, *to twist.*
Parsi	Parco	is,	ĕre, *to spare.*
Pexi	Pecto	is,	ĕre, *to comb, to card.*
Plexi	Plecto	is,	ĕre, *to beat.*
Plausi	Plaudo	is,	ĕre, *to clap hands.*
Rasi	Rado	is,	ĕre, *to shave, to scrape.*
Rausi	Raucio	is,	īre, *to be hoarse.*
Risi	Rideo	es,	ēre, *to laugh.*
Rosi	Rodo	is,	ĕre, *to gnaw.*
Sarsi	Sarcio	is,	īre, *to patch.*
Sensi	Sentio	is,	īre, *to feel; to think.*
Sparsi	Spargo	is,	ĕre, *to sprinkle.*
Suasi	Suadeo	es,	ēre, *to advise.*
Tersi	Tergeo, *or* go	es, *or* is ēre, *to wipe.*	
Torsi	Torqueo	es,	ēre, *to twist.*
Trusi	Trudo	is,	ĕre, *to thrust.*
Tursi	Turgeo	es,	ēre, *to swell.*
Vasi	Vado	is,	ĕre, *to go.*
Ursi	Urgeo	es,	ēre, *to press on.*
Vulsi	Vello	is,	ĕre, *to pull.*

SSI.

Cessi *from*	Cedo	is,	ĕre, *to give place.*
Gessi	Gero	is,	ĕre, *to carry.*
Jussi	Jubeo	es,	ēre, *to command.*
Pressi	Premo	is,	ĕre, *to press.*
Quassi	Quatio	is,	ĕre, *to shake.*

V.

Some preterites in xi *that are still more irregular, having neither* c *nor* g *in the present.*

The letter *x*, as we have already observed, generally cometh from *c* or *g*, being no more than *cs* or *gs*. And yet the following six verbs make *xi*, in an unaccountable manner.

1. Coxi *from*	Coquo	is, ĕre, *to boil.*
Fluxi	Fluo	is, ĕre, *to flow.*
Struxi	Struo	is, ĕre, *to build.*
2. Traxi	Traho	is, ĕre, *to draw.*
2. Vexi	Veho	is, ĕre, *to carry.*
Vixi	Vivo	is, ĕre, *to live.*

1. *Coxi* however is not so irregular as the rest, for *coquo* is as if it were *coco* which should make *cocsi, coxi.*

2. It may even be said, that in *traho* and *veho,* the *h* being an aspiration, is changed into *c* before *s* in the preterite *tracsi, traxi; vecsi, vexi:* because the letter *c* serves for an aspiration in many languages, and is softer, than to say *trahsi* and *vehsi.*

Article

Article VI.
Of the fourth general irregularity.

I.
Of verbs that retain in the preterite the characteristic of the present.

All preterites that do not end in *vi, üi, si,* or *xi,* take the termination *bi, ci, di,* &c. from the characteristic of their present. Wherefore having got the preterite, to find the present you have only to change *i* into *o,* or *eo,* or *io,* as *bibi, bibo: vidi, video: fodi, fodio,* &c.

There are even some preterites ending in *üi* and *si,* which derive this termination from their present, as *lüi* from *luo* ; *visi* from *viso.* And this seems to be owing entirely to a syncope, the last syllable of these preterites having been cut off: *bibi* for *bibivi,* &c.

But if in this respect it is easier to find the present of these preterites; on the other hand there are particular difficulties, because it is chiefly in these preterites that one or more of those three changes happen of which we made mention in the 2d art. namely the change of the *a* (and in a compound verb of the *i*) into *e :* the syncope of the *m* or *n :* and the reduplication of the first syllable.

For which reason we shall first of all give here a list of the different terminations of these preterites and of the presents, from whence they come, and the number of the verbs, with an example; and in the list we shall insert only such preterites as are most difficult; namely those which undergo some changes.

II.

Terminations.		Number.		Example.		
Bi	bo	4.	bibi *from*	Bibo,	is, ĕre.	*to drink.*
Ci	{ co	2.	ici	Ico,	is, ĕre.	*to strike.*
	{ cio	2.	feci	Facio,	is, ĕre.	*to do.*
Di	{ do *a great quan-*		ascendi	Ascendo,	is, ĕre.	*to ascend.*
	{ deo *(tity.*	8.	sedi	Sedeo,	es, ēre.	*to sit.*
	{ dio	1.	fodi	Fodio,	is, ĕre.	*to dig.*
Gi	{ go	4.	egi	Ago,	is, ĕre.	*to act.*
	{ gio	1.	fugi	Fugio,	is, ĕre.	*to run away.*
	{ guo	1.	langui	Langueo,	es, ēre.	*to languish.*
Li	lo	6.	psalli	Psallo,	is, ĕre.	*to sing.*
Mi	mo	1.	emi	Emo,	is, ĕre.	*to buy.*
Ni	no	2.	cecini	Cano,	is, ĕre.	*to sing.*
Pi	{ po	1.	rupi	Rumpo,	is, ĕre.	*to break.*
	{ pio	1.	cepi	Capio,	is, ĕre.	*to take.*
Qui	{ quo	1.	liqui	Linquo,	is, ĕre.	*to leave.*
	{ queo	1.	liqui	Liqueo,	es, ēre.	*to melt.*
Ri	{ ro	2.	cucurri	Curro,	is, ĕre.	*to run.*
	{ rio	1.	peperi	Pario,	is, ĕre.	*to bring forth (a child.*

324 NEW METHOD. Book IV.

Si ſo   1. viń *from* Viſo, is, ĕre, *to go to ſee.*
Ti to   2. verti   Verto, is, ĕre. *to turn.*
Ui ŭo *almoſt all.* argüi Argŭo, is, ĕre. *to reprove.*
Vi vo   3. ſolvi   Solvo, is, ĕre. *to pay.*

III.

Liſt of the preterites which retain the characteriſtic of the preſent.

1. Argui *from* Arguo,   is, ĕre. *to reprove.*
2. Aſcendi   Aſcendo,   is, ĕre. *to aſcend.*
   Bibi   Bibo,   is, ĕre. *to drink.*
   Calvi   Calvo,   is, ĕre. *to cheat.*
   Cecini   Cano,   is, ĕre. *to ſing.*
   Cepi   Capio,   is, ĕre. *to take.*
   Cucurri   Curro,   is, ĕre. *to run.*
   Egi   Ago,   is, ĕre. *to act.*
      Degi   Dego,   is, ĕre. *to dwell.*
      Prodegi Prodigo,   is, ĕre. *to laviſh.*
      Sategi Satago,   is, ĕre. *to be buſy.*
   Emi   Emo,   is, ĕre. *to buy.*
      Ademi   Adimo,   is, ĕre. *to take away.*
   Feci·   Facio,   is, ĕre. *to do.*
   Fefelli   Fallo,   is, ĕre. *to deceive.*
      Refelli Refello,   is, ĕre. *to refute.*
   Fodi   Fodio,   is, ĕre. *to dig.*
   Fugi   Fugio,   is, ĕre. *to run away.*
   Glubi   Glubo,   is, ĕre. *to flea.*
   Ici   Ico,   is, ĕre. *to ſtrike.*
   Jeci   Jacio,   is, ĕre. *to throw.*
   Lambi   Lambo,   is, ĕre. *to lick.*
   Legi   Lego,   is, ĕre. *to read, to gather.*
   Lini   Lino,   is, ĕre. *to anoint.*
   Liqui   Linquo,   is, ĕre. *to leave.*
   Momordi   Mordeo,   es, ĕre. *to bite.*
   Pegi   Pango,   is, ĕre. *to ſtrike or drive in.*
      Compegi Compingo,   is, ĕre. *to put together.*
      Impegi Impingo,   is, ĕre. *to hit againſt.*
   Pependi   Pendeo,   es, ēre. *to hang.*
   Peperi   Pario,   is, ĕre. *to bring forth a child.*
   Pepuli   Pello,   is, ĕre. *to drive away.*
   Prandi   Prandeo,   es, ĕre. *to dine.*
   Pſalli   Pſallo,   is, ĕre. *to ſing.*
   Pupugi   Pungo,   is, ĕre. *to prick.*
   Rupi   Rumpo,   is, ĕre. *to break.*
   Salli   Sallo,   is, ĕre. *to ſeaſon with ſalt.*
   Scabi   Scabo,   is, ĕre. *to ſcratch.*
   Sedi   Sedeo,   es, ĕre. *to ſit.*
   Solvi   Solvo,   is, ĕre. *to untie.*

Spo-

Spopondi	Spondeo,	es, ēre.	*to engage, to promise.*
Stiti	Sisto,	is, ĕre.	*to stop, to set up.*
Stridi	Strideo,	es, ēre.	*to crack.*
Totondi	Tondeo,	es, ēre.	*to clip.*
Tuli	Fero,	ers, rre.	*to carry.*
Extuli	Extollo,	is, ĕre.	*to lift up.*
Sustuli	Sustollo,	is, ĕre.	*to take away.*
Verri	Verro,	is, ĕre.	*to sweep.*
Verti	Verto,	is, ĕre.	*to turn.*
Vidi	Video,	es, ēre.	*to see.*
Visi	Viso,	is, ĕre.	*to go to see.*
Volvi	Volvo,	is, ĕre.	*to roll.*

1. All verbs in *uo*.
2. All verbs in *do*, except the 9 which make *si*, comprized above, in the fifth article, n. 4.

✳✳✳✳✳✳✳✳✳✳✳✳✳✳✳✳✳✳✳✳✳✳✳✳✳✳✳✳✳✳✳✳✳✳✳✳✳

ADVERTISEMENT.

CONCERNING THE METHOD OF FINDING out the present by means of the supine.

And the chief advantage that may be derived from the above lists of preterites.

SOME *perhaps may wish we had drawn up proper tables for ascending from the supine to the present, as we have done in regard to the preterite. But upon examination these tables have been judged unnecessary. For the analogy of ascending from the supine to the preterite is so natural, that the three or four lines which we have given at our entering upon the conjugations, p.* 171. *may suffice. And indeed we hardly ever find any difficulty in ascending to the preterite, when we meet with its supine. Now as soon as we have found the preterite, we may ascend to the present by the rules just now given, which are not so difficult as one may be apt at first sight to imagine; because as they are all founded in analogy and reason, to make a proper use of them it is almost sufficient that they be thoroughly understood. A little practice added to these reflections will render things as easy as they are natural; and every body will be capable of*

judging

judging by themselves of the utility that may be derived from them.

I shall only observe that these lists are extremely proper for exercising the capacities of children, to make them find out from what verb a preterite is derived, by running them over, each in its alphabetical order, and obliging them to tell the verb as soon as they hear the preterite mentioned. Adult persons, who study without a master, may likewise enter into the same sort of exercise, leaving the preterites of these lists uncovered, and hiding the remainder with a bit of paper, in order to try their memories, and to see whether they are thorough masters of these preterites: this they will compass in a very short time, provided they have some idea only of their analogy, which will almost instantly lead them to the knowledge of the present. And herein lies almost the whole use of the Latin grammar, to qualify us as quick as possible for the reading of authors. For it is to be observed, as we have already mentioned in the preface and in the advertisement to the reader, that this is the point we ought always to have in view, because it is only by practice and the use of authors that we are enabled to make any real progress in a language, and to be acquainted with its full purity. This we hope we shall prove more at large by the NEW DICTIONARY, which some time or other we purpose to lay before the public, and which may perhaps be of service to those who have made a progress, as well as to those who have but just entered upon the language, and may facilitate the understanding of ecclesiastic and profane authors.

OBSERVATIONS
On the Figure of Metaplasm,
As far as it relates to Etymology or Analogy.

HAVING finished whatever relates to the analogy of nouns and verbs, we must now, before we proceed to syntax, touch lightly upon the changes incident to words, which grammarians distinguish by the common and general name of ΜΕΤΑ´ΠΛΑΣΜΟΣ, that is, *transmutation, transformation*.

This METAPLASM or transmutation is made by adding, taking away, or changing, either a letter or a syllable.

I.
By adding.

This addition is of four sorts, which are,

1. PROTHESIS or addition, when something is put to the beginning of a word; as *gnavus* for *navus*.

2. EPENTHESIS, or interposition, when something is inserted it the middle, either a vowel, as in Virgil, *trabea* for *trabe*, a kind of cart; or a consonant, *relligio* for *religio*: *repperit, rettulit*, instead of *reperit, retulit*, &c.

3. PARAGOGE, or lengthening, when something is put at the end of the word; as *dicier* for *dici*.

4. DIERESIS, when a vowel is divided into two; *aulaï* trissyllable, for *aulai* dissyllable, *aulæ*.

II.
By taking away.

The taking away or cutting off happens four ways, according to which it hath four different denominations.

1. APHERESIS, when something is taken away or cut off from the beginning of a word; as *conia* instead of *ciconia*, Plautus.

2. SYNCOPE, when something is taken away from the middle; as *caldum* for *calidum*; *dixti* for *dixisti*, which is common: *puertia* for *pueritia*, which is more poetic. And the like.

3. APOCOPE, when something is cut off from the end; as *tun*, for *tune*: *inger mi calices amariores*, for *ingere mihi*, Catul. &c.

4. CRASIS or synerefis, when two syllables are joined in one, as *Thesei*, dissyllable, for *Theseï*, trissyllable; *vemens*, for *vehemens*, &c.

III.
By changing.

The changing is effected two ways, which are called

1. METATHESIS, or transposition, when one letter is put in the place of another, as *pistris* instead of *pristis*.

2. AN-

2. ANTITHESIS, or opposition, when one letter is intirely changed for another, as *olli* for *illi*.

So much may suffice for a general idea of these figures; for it is oftentimes both tiresome and useless, to masters as well as scholars, to overload the memory with a multitude of words and figures, which are generally more difficult to retain than the things themselves.

There are still some more figures to observe, both as to syntax and to versification; but of these we shall take proper notice when we come to treat of quantity.

The End of the First Volume.

www.ingramcontent.com/pod-product-compliance
Lightning Source LLC
Chambersburg PA
CBHW032027220426
43664CB00006B/386